A Special Issue of
Memory

Theories of Organic Amnesia

Edited by

Andrew R. Mayes
University of Sheffield, UK

John Joseph Downes
University of Liverpool, UK

Psychology Press
An imprint of Erlbaum (UK) Taylor & Francis

Psychology Press
27 Church Road
Hove
East Sussex, BN3 2FA
UK

British Library Cataloguing in Publication Data

A catalogue record for this book is available from the British Library

ISBN 0-86377-952-2
ISSN: 0965-8211

Typeset by DP Photosetting, Aylesbury
Printed and bound in the United Kingdom by Henry Ling Ltd, Dorchester

Contents

MEMORY, 1997, 5 (1/2), 1–2

Editorial

Over four years ago, when we first thought of putting this special issue on theories of organic amnesia together, we were motivated by two main feelings. The first feeling was that the explosion of research into the syndrome during the past 20 years has led to the growth of an impressive body of data that provides reasonable constraints on any theoretical account of the functional deficit or deficits underlying the condition. In other words, it is now sensible to advance well-formulated theories because they can be more than just a hand-waving exercise. Although there is still a place for pure empirical investigations, the field has reached the stage where progress will be much faster if it is more theoretically driven. Many of the articles in this Special Issue give examples of this theoretically driven approach in action and provide the best support for the above claim. Our second feeling was that many workers still seem to throw out brief theoretical interpretations in the Discussions of their papers, which take into account their results, but not other findings with which they are incompatible. In other words, an atmosphere does not yet exist in the amnesia research community in which workers feel obliged to explain all the evidence that appears relevant to their views. If their theory does not predict some previously reported data, any theoretician should be obligated to explain those data in some other way: either by arguing that they are in some way invalid; that although they are valid they can be explained in another way that indicates that they are irrelevant to the theory; or that they lie beyond the domain of the theory. Readers should bear these points in mind when they examine the articles in this Special Issue. In this, they should be helped by the target article which outlines the kind of data with which theories have to be shown to be consistent.

Three related theoretical questions need to be answered about the amnesic syndrome. First, does it comprise one or several functional deficits? Second, how exactly should these functional deficits be characterised? Third, exactly which lesions are responsible for the deficits? Once we have a reasonable degree of confidence in what the characterisation of the deficits should be and which lesions cause them, then it will become easier to determine how the lesioned brain regions normally underlie the disrupted functions and how lesions undermine the performance of these functions. Even before this stage is reached, development of theories that specify the exact characteristics of the functional deficits can benefit from the increased specification found in computer-based simulations and models. For example, a very influential view is that complex associations are initially stored in the hippocampus so that their retrieval for some time involves hippocampal activity, but eventually, perhaps through processes like retrieval and rehearsal, the memory ceases to depend on the hippocampus, but instead is stored in the neocortex. What prediction does this view make about the effect of damage to the neocortical sites where the memories for the complex associations are eventually transferred? Obviously, if damage was total the storage sites for very long-term associative memories would have been destroyed—so all such memories that were old should be lost and all new memories should eventually fade away. But what would happen to hippocampally-dependent younger associative memories and to what extent would the answer depend on the degree of damage to the cortical long-term storage sites? To stand a chance of answering questions like this, one needs to have computer-based models like that of Murre in this issue.

The articles in this issue indicate that there is some degree of convergence in thinking about the functional deficit that underlies anterograde amnesia—at least, that which follows from hippocampal damage. Several contributors advance views, which, although different in detail, all suggest that hippocampal damage disrupts memory for associative information, perhaps particularly where the components are represented in different neocortical regions. These views are compatible with the hippocampus playing a role in the consolidation and initial retrieval of such information. Even this view is not universally held as Laird Cermak holds an opposing position in which amnesia is believed to result from a specific kind of failure to process (encode and retrieve) some kinds of semantic information. There is also still disagreement about the empirical base that can be used to discriminate between different theoretical accounts. For example, John Aggleton and his colleagues have argued that selective hippocampal lesions disrupt free recall about as much as is found with other global amnesics, but that the selective lesion has a minimal effect on recognition memory—at least as it is tapped by the Warrington Recognition Memory Test. This empirical claim is disputed by Rempel-Clower et al. (1996), who report a study of three patients with post-mortem analysis in whom there is evidence of recognition impairments more or less as severe as free recall impairments despite the fact that no clear evidence was found of damage spreading bilaterally beyond the hippocampus and entorhinal cortex. The issue is a complex one that is critically relevant to any theory of the mnemonic role of the medial temporal lobes. Even with post-mortem analyses, it is of course possible that the damage responsible for recognition memory deficits lies beyond the hippocampus, but that it does not involve neuronal loss. Rather it may involve subtle disturbances related to neurotransmitters, neuronal processes such as dendrites, or aspects of neuronal metabolism. It may be that the best way to test the view that the hippocampus is important for item recall, but not for at least some forms of item recognition is through the use of neuroimaging procedures with good spatial resolution such as functional magnetic resonance imaging.

Since the target article was completed half way through 1994, challenge studies with neuroimaging have had a rapidly increasing impact on thinking about amnesia as well as about memory in general. In the future, researchers should always seek to find convergence between the findings with lesion studies of memory, and the findings with neuroimaging studies of normal and brain damaged people. Neuroimaging may also help resolve the questions about which there is still not a great deal of agreement between investigators: how many functional deficits the syndrome comprises and the precise anatomy that underlies the syndrome. For example, if the retrieval of remote memories is disrupted by different lesions from those which impair the acquisition of new memories, then different brain regions should be activated in normal people when remote memories are retrieved than when new memories are acquired and retrieved. In our view, the combined use of lesion and neuroimaging studies will lead to a much faster rate of development in the understanding of memory for facts and episodes over the next decade than has occurred in the previous 20 years.

ANDREW MAYES AND JOHN DOWNES

REFERENCE

Rempel-Clower, N.L., Zola-Morgan, S., Squire, L.R. and Amaral, D.G. (1996). Three cases of enduring memory impairment after bilateral damage limited to the hippocampal formation. *Journal of Neuroscience, 16*, 5233–5255.

MEMORY, 1997, 5 (1/2), 3–36

What Do Theories of the Functional Deficit(s) Underlying Amnesia Have to Explain?

Andrew R. Mayes

University of Sheffield, UK

John Joseph Downes

University of Liverpool, UK

INTRODUCTION

Definitions and Preamble

Organic amnesia is a syndrome with four defining features about which there is good general agreement. First, amnesics show anterograde amnesia (AA) which comprises impaired recall and recognition of facts and personal episodes encountered after the occurrence of the brain damage that triggered the syndrome. The memory deficit is usually referred to as being of explicit or declarative memory because rememberers must indicate explicitly or declare that the fact or episode is one that they have experienced at some point in their personal past. Second, amnesics show retrograde amnesia (RA) which comprises impaired recall and recognition of memories of facts and personal episodes that were acquired before the occurrence of the brain damage that triggered the amnesia. Both these kinds of memory impairment vary widely in severity in different amnesic patients. In the case of RA, this means that some patients only show impairment of explicit memories acquired months before the onset of their disorder, whereas other patients show impairment of explicit memories that were acquired up to decades before the onset of their disorder. Third, amnesics show *preservation* of immediate short-term or working memory as indicated by performance on tasks such as the digit span or Corsi blocks test (see Cave & Squire, 1992, for evidence that patients with selective amnesia perform normally on both verbal and nonverbal tests of immediate memory). Fourth, amnesics

---

Requests for reprints should be sent to Andrew R. Mayes, Department of Clinical Neurology, University of Sheffield, Royal Hallamshire Hospital, Sheffield S10 2JF, UK.

show *preservation* of intelligence as assessed by instruments such as the Wechsler Adult Intelligence Scale. One aspect of their preserved intelligence is the preservation of amnesics' ability to remember semantic information that was overlearned in the years prior to the development of their condition.

This syndrome is caused by lesions that may occur in any one of a number of distinct, if possibly interconnected, brain regions that lie close to the midline. Thus, amnesia can be caused by lesions of: (a) the midline structures of the medial temporal lobe, (b) structures in the midline diencephalon, or (c) structures in the basal forebrain. It remains a possibility that lesions in the ventromedial frontal cortex can also cause amnesia (Bachevalier & Mishkin, 1986) although the evidence for this in humans is currently minimal. As will be discussed, there is still lack of complete agreement about which structures need to be damaged within each of the aforementioned three brain regions if amnesia is to result. It also remains unresolved whether the structures involved form one neural network such that damage to any part causes the same symptoms of amnesia even though different parts may be engaged in different forms of processing. This lack of resolution is central to this paper, as it is concerned with the functional deficit or deficits which underlie amnesia. It is clearly of critical importance to determine whether one deficit underlies the syndrome or whether there are several. If there are several, this may mean that most amnesics have more than one kind of deficit and also that in amnesics with differently located lesions the underlying deficit or deficits are distinct, leading to slightly different patterns of deficit in such patients.

In fact, most hypotheses about the functional deficits in amnesia have tended to assume that the syndrome is unitary and has a single underlying functional deficit. These hypotheses can be classified in several ways. First, they differ according to whether they postulate a deficit of encoding, storage, retrieval, or some combination of these deficits. Second, they differ in relation to the kind of information to which they propose these deficits apply (e.g. all fact and episodic information, contextual associations, configural associations, complex associations etc.). There is a third way in which hypotheses might differ from each other, which is orthogonal to the first two. Hypotheses might differ from each other with respect to level, by which we mean the degree to which neural mechanisms and systems are specified. By this classification, *level one* hypotheses explain amnesia by recourse to psychological concepts, and relate the postulated deficit in a direct and simple way to a specific lesion or lesions. For example, such a hypothesis might propose that the functional impairment underlying amnesia involves a breakdown in the ability to store complex associations (see later for a discussion of what we mean by "complex"), and that lesions of the hippocampal system disrupt this ability. In contrast, *level two* hypotheses attempt to explain amnesia by recourse to the neural mechanisms that could produce the proposed psychological deficit(s). In developing the level one hypothesis that amnesia occurs when hippocampal lesions impair the ability to store complex associations, a level two hypothesis might propose that the mechanism disrupted as a result of damage to the hippocampal system is long-term potentiation, and this leads to a specific difficulty in the storage of complex associations. Such level two hypotheses should give detailed mechanisms for the operation of the postulated neural systems and explain how the psychological features of amnesia can emerge from a dysfunctional system. This may involve the development of computer models of the psychological processes, the details of which will be constrained by what is known of the architecture of the structures that are believed to underlie memory performance. At present, most hypotheses are level one in the above sense, but if they are correct, they should provide the basis for developing effective level two hypotheses.

Hypotheses of the functional deficit underlying amnesia must be able to account for the kinds of phenomena that have been reported in the literature concerning the syndrome. This is a complex issue because theorists may: (a) simply explain a kind of effect shown by amnesics in terms of their hypotheses; (b) argue that the claimed effect does not have adequate empirical support, and therefore does not require explanation; or (c) accept that it exists and, although apparently in conflict with their hypothesis, show it to be compatible by a justifiable reinterpretation of the literature concerning memory processes. One other kind of argument has played a prominent part in discussion of the functional deficits that underlie the amnesia syndrome. It is often argued that effects associated with amnesia are incidental to the syndrome because they are caused by adventitious brain damage to structures that have nothing to do with the syndrome. For example, it has often been claimed that some of the features of Korsakoff's syndrome do not result from amnesia, but rather from damage to the frontal lobes that causes memory and cognitive deficits that are unrelated to amnesia (Mayes, 1988; Squire, 1982). Such arguments presuppose a clear agreement about what amnesia is and/or which lesions cause it, which not everyone may accept.

As hypotheses about the functional deficit(s) underlying amnesia still differ from each other in radical ways, it is desirable to use the best means to discriminate between them. This can be achieved by examining the ways in which competing hypotheses make different predictions about how amnesics should perform on selected tasks. In our view, the key areas in which differential predictions can be made involve: (1) amnesics' encoding abilities, (2) the kinds of memory at which amnesics show no impairment, and, in particular, whether these include implicit memory for the kinds of individual item for which patients' explicit memory is impaired, (3) the detailed features of the explicit memory impairment of AA, and, in particular, whether some kinds of explicit memory are more impaired than others and whether patients show accelerated forgetting for any kinds of explicit memory, and (4) the detailed features of RA and, in particular, the relationship between RA and AA. Finally, all these predictions need to be related to anatomy for two reasons. The first reason is that there is a need to resolve whether amnesia is a unitary or multifaceted syndrome, which requires that the pattern of memory performance shown by patients be related to the causal lesions. The second reason is that the anatomical information is important if the theorist wishes to move from level one to level two hypotheses as is desirable.

SOME HYPOTHESES IN BRIEF

(i) Encoding/Retrieval Deficit Hypotheses

Most current hypotheses about the functional breakdown in amnesia propose that there is a kind of storage deficit which affects some or all forms of fact and episode information. Nevertheless, prominent hypotheses have been advanced that propose deficits specific to encoding or retrieval (e.g. Butters & Cermak, 1975; Warrington & Weiskrantz, 1982). The term "encoding" is sometimes used to include the consolidation of information into long-term memory, but here it is used to refer to the processes necessary for making a representation of incoming information, and relating this to what is already in memory. In other words, encoding leads to the formation of representations that may or may not be stored in memory.

Two general points can be made about stage-specific deficit hypotheses of amnesia. The first point, which applies selectively to encoding and retrieval deficit views, is that encoding and retrieval share many processes. Thus, encoding that involves meaningfully interpreting an input must involve the retrieval of semantic (and possibly episodic) memories. Conversely, when information is retrieved, a representation similar to that established during encoding must be formed. This is not, of course, to say that there is complete overlap between encoding and retrieval processes, but any deficit hypothesis that is specific to one process needs to specify exactly what subprocesses are involved.

The second point relates to a widely held dogma which is that information is stored (that is, as an episodic memory representation) in the same brain regions in which it is represented. In its extreme form this would suggest that lesions that disrupt storage will also disrupt encoding and, possibly, retrieval. This does not seem to happen in amnesia because it can be shown that patients show poor memory for information that they have encoded normally. Even so, hypotheses about the causes of amnesia should consider the relationship between the brain structures involved in the encoding, storage, and retrieval of fact and episode information.

Encoding deficit views particularly need to take account of the first of these points. For example, both Butters and Cermak (1975) and Blaxton (1992) have argued that amnesics are impaired at encoding semantic or conceptual information. As semantic encoding typically involves retrieval, it seems likely that encoding and retrieval deficits will occur together, although the retrieval deficits may be mainly of relevance in explaining RA. Warrington and

Weiskrantz (1982) argued that amnesia results either from a failure to store or to retrieve the kind of information that needs effortful elaboration by the frontal lobes. The retrieval variant, which they appeared to favour, would have to mean that the intact frontal lobes of amnesics are sufficient for elaborative encoding, but not elaborative retrieval. This position, which posits normal semantic and other kinds of elaborative encoding, needs buttressing if it is to be plausible.

All of these hypotheses postulate encoding or retrieval deficits for a specific component of the information that constitutes facts and events. Processing deficit hypotheses can also be nonspecific with respect to the type of information involved. For example, Schacter (1990) has proposed that amnesics encode and store all aspects of fact and episode information normally, but are unable to achieve explicit memory for this information because an intact memory system for facts and events has been disconnected from a system that generates aware memory. This could be construed as a kind of retrieval deficit, the nature of which has not been precisely specified.

(ii) Storage Deficit Hypotheses

Storage deficit accounts of amnesia have been dominant in recent years (e.g. see Squire, Knowlton, & Musen, 1992) and vary in two main respects. First, the nature of the postulated storage problem may vary. A widely held view is that initial storage takes place in structures damaged in amnesics, but that these structures interact with neocortical association areas which eventually act as the storage sites for fact and episode information (Squire et al., 1992; and see Nadel, 1992). A less popular alternative account is that the structures affected in amnesia normally modulate the storage sites that lie in association neocortex, so that lesions greatly reduce the efficiency of this storage (see Mayes, 1992). Both these views postulate that encoding is normal, but that the initial stages of storage into long-term memory are disrupted. A third possibility that has not been explicitly developed is that initial storage is normal, but that longer-term retention is disrupted. This kind of view might be able to account for features of RA, but would also predict an AA in which explicit memory was initially normal, as has sometimes been reported with temporal lobe epileptics with hippocampal sclerosis (see Miller, Munoz, & Finmore, 1993).

The second way in which storage deficit hypotheses vary is with respect to the kind of information for which they postulate impaired storage. Although it might seem that most hypotheses would postulate that amnesics suffer from the same kind of storage failure for all aspects of fact and episode information, it is far from clear that this is the case. It is difficult to determine in some cases whether the hypothesis is postulating a general storage deficit or a storage deficit that is specific to some component of fact/episode information. Other hypotheses clearly indicate that only some aspects of fact/episode information are not stored properly (e.g. the storage variant of the context-memory deficit hypotheses, CMDH—Mayes, Meudell, & Pickering, 1985). Storage deficit hypotheses, therefore, need to specify explicitly what information is not stored effectively, as well as the reasons for this failure. They should also indicate whether the type of information for which a storage deficit is proposed will lead to an additional *retrieval* deficit for information that is assumed to be stored adequately. For example, the storage version of the CMDH proposes that contextual associations are not stored normally by amnesics, but that although single items are stored normally, amnesics are unable to retrieve them explicitly because of their failure to store contextual associations (Mayes et al., 1985; see also Schacter, 1990).

SOME DIFFERENTIAL PREDICTIONS OF THE HYPOTHESES

All the aforementioned hypotheses need to specify exactly what lesions cause the deficits that they postulate. If several deficits underlie the amnesic syndrome, then more than one of these hypotheses could be correct provided that the postulated deficits are related to lesions in neural systems that are not serially connected. It is our contention that hypotheses about the functional deficit or deficits that underlie amnesia are underspecified because concepts like encoding, storage, and retrieval are pretheoretical. Specification can be achieved by identifying the predictions that can be made from each kind of hypothesis, particularly those predictions that distinguish between the different kinds of hypothesis. In this section, we will briefly discuss what these predictions might be. The headings refer to the primary hypotheses from which the predictions are derived.

(i) Encoding

If amnesics have an explicit encoding deficit, so that they fail to represent certain kinds of information, then they should not be able to answer questions about those kinds of information normally, even when those questions are asked immediately so as to minimise any memory contribution. If their problem is one of long-term storage or of the retrieval of normally stored information, the ability to answer such (immediate) questions should be completely normal in amnesics. Impairments in the ability to answer questions about presented items after an intervening delay (that is, not immediately after presentation of the items, as in the preceding case) cannot, of course, discriminate between encoding, storage, and retrieval problems.

(ii) Storage

(A) Implicit Memory.   Discriminative predictions derived from storage deficit hypotheses are harder to derive because very little is known still about storage processes. We will consider two predictions that apply to AA. The first prediction concerns implicit memory for the same information for which

amnesics show impaired explicit memory. Subjects show item-specific implicit memory (ISIM) by some change in the way that they behave or process (item) information when they are not aware that they are remembering. ISIM is supposed to be tapped by indirect memory tasks in which no reference is made to "memory" or the learning experience, and subjects' memories are revealed by how they process repeated items or components/associates of repeated items. In contrast, explicit memory is supposed to be tapped by direct memory tasks in which reference is made to the learning experience and subjects are asked overtly to remember information encoded during that experience. If amnesics do not store information normally, then their explicit memory for that information will be impaired, but this would also be expected if they have a retrieval deficit. If their implicit memory for that information is also impaired, we would argue that they are much more likely to have a storage, as opposed to a retrieval or other deficit, because it is probable that a common memory representation underlies performance on both explicit and implicit memory tests. It follows that if amnesics' have intact storage for items then, according to this view, their implicit memory for those items should be preserved.

There are several objections to this proposal. The first objection is the most fundamental. It is that the same information may be represented in two different memory storage systems, one for explicit and one for implicit memory. According to this, no sensible predictions concerning implicit memory performance and storage mechanisms in amnesia can be made. We think that this view is highly implausible. One variant of this view would require that the same information is held in independent stores, in which case one would expect to see double dissociations between explicit and implicit memory for the same information. Although Keane et al. (1995) have reported a patient with reasonably intact recognition, but impaired implicit memory for visually presented words, it is likely that the explicit and implicit memory involve retrieval respectively of different semantic and perceptual information assocaited with the words. Another variant of this view would be that the implicit memory representation is a necessary condition for creating the explicit memory representation of the same information. The problem with this variant lies in explaining why the mechanism is necessary, especially as there is evidence that implicit memory for specific items can last as long as explicit memory for those items. The assumption of two memory systems for the same information is redundant, and theorists wishing to retain it need to provide a strong argument to explain the redundancy.

The second objection applies to the assumption that underlies the prediction that intact storage mechanisms mean preserved implicit memory. The objection is that although implicit and explicit memory may be for the same items, they relate to *different informational features* of those items. To give an example, implicit memory for words might simply tap that part of the underlying memory representation that corresponds to the words themselves, whereas explicit memory might actually tap memory for associations between the words and other stored features of information. Storage may be intact for the words themselves but impaired for the associations, in which case amnesics' implicit memory for the words themselves will be intact. But in order to conclude that storage is completely normal, it needs to be shown that amnesics' implicit memory for *word + associated information*, like their implicit memory for the words themselves, is also intact. This may be particularly important because some theories allow that amnesics store "simple" information normally, but not more complex, "associative" information. It follows that if theorists wish to adopt the predictions linking implicit memory performance and storage mechanisms, then they need to specify precisely the information tapped by the implicit and explicit memory tests they use.

The third objection is that measures of implicit memory that are currently in use are not "pure", in that normal subjects may be adjusting their performance by using explicit memory. This is similar to the second objection in the sense that both take the form of arguing that particular experimental tests of the predictions which link implicit memory performance with storage mechanisms in amnesia fail to meet the conditions that they need to satisfy. In the former case, this is because it may be wrong to assume that indirect and direct memory tests are tapping the same informational features of the underlying memory representation, and in the latter case because it may be wrong to assume that performance on indirect memory tasks reflects the use of identical memory processes in amnesics and normal subjects. Jacoby and Kelley (1992) and others have argued that performance on both direct and indirect memory tasks may often (if not always) be mediated by both explicit and implicit memory to varying degrees, so that explicit memory could be used either to enhance or to inhibit performance on indirect memory tasks. Clearly, if this kind of criticism is taken seriously, it would be hard to interpret either intact or impaired amnesic performance on indirect memory tests.

Although, as indicated, in specific instances it may be very hard to know whether or not the predictions have been fairly tested, we believe, nevertheless, that a comparison of implicit and explicit memory provides a good means of discriminating between storage and retrieval deficit hypotheses. The study of implicit memory should also be able to discriminate between nonspecific storage deficit hypotheses and those that postulate storage deficits for various kinds of specific information. For example, the storage variant of the context-memory deficit hypothesis would predict that amnesics should show impaired implicit memory for novel contextual associations whereas a nonspecific storage deficit hypothesis should predict impaired implicit memory for all kinds of novel fact and event information.

(ii) (B) Rate of Forgetting.   The second prediction that may be derived from storage deficit hypotheses is that amnesics should show accelerated loss of explicit memory. Storage deficit accounts suggest that patients are impaired at

creating long-term memory representations of some or all aspects of fact and episode information. It is very widely accepted that these representations are not formed instantaneously but take some time to consolidate (although there is no consensus about the exact time-course of this consolidation process). If amnesics fail to show normal consolidation, then, as normal subjects' memory becomes increasingly dependent on their long-term memory representations, the patients will show a greater and greater deficit. In other words, they will show accelerated forgetting.

If amnesics encode information normally, then the only way other than through a storage deficit that amnesics can lose their explicit long-term memory pathologically quickly is through showing excessive sensitivity to interference. Such a pathological sensitivity to interference could arise directly from a retrieval deficit, but it could also arise from a primary storage problem which causes a specific retrieval difficulty. For example, impaired storage of contextual associations could impair retrieval by disrupting the ability to discriminate between intra-list (target) and extra-list (nontarget) items.

A full test of the view that amnesics have a storage deficit that accelerates rate of loss of explicit long-term memory therefore needs to eliminate two alternative explanations. First, it needs to be shown that amnesics encode normally. Second, it needs to be shown that they are not abnormally sensitive to interference. There is also a third alternative explanation of accelerated forgetting which only applies if the shortest retention interval used lies within the temporal boundaries of STM, and is therefore relatively easy to guard against. The shortest retention interval should come at a time when STM is no longer contributing to memory performance. Otherwise, if STM contributes to performance at short, but not long delays, one would predict accelerated forgetting even if amnesics consolidated LTM normally.

Little is known about the time-course of the consolidation processes that are necessary for the creation of a long-term memory, so it is difficult for storage deficit hypotheses to indicate over what delay accelerated forgetting is likely to continue. There may even be a different time-course for different kinds of information. However, although consolidation may continue for an unknown time, it is likely to begin when information is initially encoded. Accelerated forgetting should, therefore, be found from shortly after encoding if initial consolidation processes are disrupted. After the completion of consolidation, further accelerated forgetting would only be expected if amnesics have a deficit in the *maintenance* of long-term memory representations. This might occur if patients are unable to achieve some kind of dynamic transfer of long-term memory from the structures affected by amnesia to other cortical structures. This maintenance consolidation seems to be an implication of the work of Zola-Morgan and Squire (1990). If amnesics not only fail to create normal long-term memories for facts and episodes, but also to maintain such long-term memories as they succeed in creating, then they would be expected to show accelerated forgetting over delays of months or longer. One might also expect to see patients with damage to the cortical structures to which the long-term memories are transferred to show normal memory for facts and episodes at shorter delays, but impaired memory at longer delays of weeks or months. In fact, a deficit like this has been reported by De Renzi and Lucchelli (1993).

(ii) (C) Types of Information. If storage is only disrupted for a subcomponent of fact and episode information, then forgetting rate should only be accelerated when memory depends on retrieving that kind of information. For example, complex associations are associations that minimally relate three or more components, one of which is probably the background context in which studied components appeared. If only storage of such complex associations is disrupted, then forgetting rate for memories of simple associations (involving only two components) should be normal. This kind of prediction suggests that hypotheses that postulate that the functional deficit is specific to a subclass of fact and episode information should all predict that explicit memory for certain kinds of information should be more impaired than it is for other kinds of information. This should apply whether the hypotheses postulate encoding, storage, or retrieval deficits. For example, hypotheses that postulate that amnesics do not encode semantic information normally predict that they should be more impaired at explicit memory for such information than they will be for explicit memory of more perceptual information. Whether there is *any* impairment in explicit memory for the other category of information will depend on detailed features of the hypothesis and on assumptions about how normal explicit memory works. For example, there is a widely held view that recognition depends on two independent processes; recollection and familiarity (Mandler, 1980). Recollection involves retrieving associations between an item and features of the context defining the episode in which it was encountered, whereas familiarity involves the automatic attribution of previous experience based on more fluent processing of the remembered item. It seems likely that free recall just depends on a recollective process. If amnesics suffer from a selective deficit in recollection (as would be implied by a storage or a retrieval variant of the context-memory deficit hypothesis), then they should be more impaired at item free recall than at item recognition.

(ii) (D) Retrograde Amnesia. All the preceding predictions concern the form taken by AA as a means of discriminating between encoding, storage, and retrieval deficit hypotheses, and between hypotheses postulating deficits in memory for all or only some aspects of fact and episode information. But the form taken by RA also provides a means of discriminating between the hypotheses. If AA and RA are caused by a common deficit, then encoding deficit hypotheses cannot give a complete account of amnesia. The reason is obvious. RA is a deficit in explicit memory for memories that, in some cases, have been established for years. Hypotheses that postulate a similar encoding

and retrieval deficit (i.e. a processing deficit) or selective retrieval deficit hypotheses, however, may be able to give complete accounts of amnesia. Like encoding deficit hypotheses, storage deficit hypotheses also have difficulty in accounting for RA if it has the same cause as AA. However, there are two kinds of storage deficit account that can overcome this difficulty. One, mentioned earlier, proposes that in normal people an initial consolidation process establishes LTM representations in a temporary resting place, which comprises the structures damaged in amnesia, but that these representations are later transferred to more permanent sites in association neocortex (e.g. Squire et al., 1992). The time-course of this transfer needs to be specified much more precisely in humans. Although this type of process may well help to explain the differential loss of information over periods of weeks and months, it seems highly unlikely that it can explain temporal gradients of RA that extend over several decades. The second kind of account would propose that amnesics fail to consolidate information into long-term storage normally, and also that the same lesion that causes the consolidation failure to new information disrupts already consolidated long-term memories. This would require the assumption that the sites damaged in amnesics form part of the long-term storage system for fact and episode memories.

If AA and RA have a common explanation, then storage deficit hypotheses should also predict that implicit memory for some or all fact and episode memories acquired before brain damage occurred should be disturbed to broadly the same degree as explicit memory. In other words, where explicit memory is disturbed for pre-morbidly encountered facts and episodes, so also should be implicit memory. Retrieval deficit accounts should predict that such implicit memories should be normal.

Underlying what has been said about RA is the generally held view that it shows a temporal gradient in which older pre-morbid memories, sometimes acquired up to decades before the onset of the condition, are less disrupted than more recent ones. If RA and AA have a common explanation, then any hypothesis concerning the syndrome must also be able to explain this temporal gradient. This is likely to present a difficulty for any available hypothesis about amnesia, partly because the explanation must involve claims about the way in which memories change qualitatively over a period of years. There is currently no evidence independent of amnesia about such changes. As memories age they may change so as to become less dependent on the retrieval of contextual associations. If amnesia involves a deficit in the storage or retrieval of such associations, this would explain the relative preservation of older explicit memories. There needs, however, to be other evidence to support the claim that fact-episode memories become decontextualised or semanticised in the required way with the passage of time, and the temporal parameters of this change would have to be independently derived to be convincing.

In most cases of amnesia, the severity of the memory deficit remains stable over a period of years, but there are conditions such as transient global amnesia

(TGA) where recovery occurs. It might be expected that the phenomena of TGA might only be predictable by a narrow range of hypotheses about the deficit that causes amnesia. For example, when patients recover from TGA not only are they once again able to acquire new memories relatively normally, but they also show recovery from RA (except possibly for memories acquired in the days immediately preceding the attack) although memories for the episode itself are permanently lost (see Kritchevsky, 1992). As will be argued in the experimental section on RA, this pattern of impairment can be explained either in terms of recovery from a retrieval deficit or of recovery from a storage deficit. Discrimination between these two kinds of explanation would only be possible if further information were available.

So far, it has been assumed that AA and RA are caused by the same single underlying deficit. But the significance of the aforementioned predictions would be changed if it could be shown that the AA and RA found in the amnesia syndrome are separable disorders. If AA and RA are separable disorders, then one should expect to be able to find patients with selective AA and selective RA with lesions affecting structures believed to cause amnesia, but perhaps somewhat smaller in scale than those found with global amnesics. Severity of AA and RA as assessed by explicit memory tests for the same kinds of information should also correlate poorly with each other. Similar kinds of prediction should be made for any other postulated divisions of the amnesic syndrome. In each case, one would expect to see evidence of functional dissociation tied closely to evidence of anatomical dissociation. If amnesia is shown by this kind of evidence to be multifaceted, then theorists will have to show how several postulated deficits explain all the features of the syndrome in a way that takes the separate patterns of impairment into account. For example, if RA dissociates from AA and AA typically comprises dissociable deficits in memory for complex associations and memory for simpler associations and single item information, then theorists would need to postulate three kinds of deficit, indicate their underlying anatomy, and show how they combine to cause the amnesic syndrome.

The rest of this paper will very briefly outline the evidence about amnesia with which any theoretical account of the syndrome will have to deal. This evidence is sometimes conflicting, so a theorist may dispute the interpretation that we give, but, in our view, what is more important is for theorists to indicate clearly what their theory predicts that is distinctive from the predictions of other theories, and how it may best be ascertained whether or not these predictions are met.

EVIDENCE RELATING TO NEUROANATOMY

The anatomy of amnesia has been explored by trying to find amnesics who have selective and localised brain damage and also by investigating the effects of specific brain lesions in monkeys (and sometimes rats) mainly on tests of recognition. Most of the work has focused on the effects of medial temporal lobe lesions. Research with monkey models of amnesia has a complex history, but there is some degree of consensus on several issues. First, amygdala lesions do not seem to cause or exacerbate impairments in recognition memory for objects (Zola-Morgan, Squire, & Amaral, 1989). Second, lesions of the parahippocampal and perirhinal cortices produce severe impairments in object recognition memory (Zola-Morgan, Squire, Amaral, & Suzuki, 1989). Third, hippocampal lesions do not cause severe impairments in object recognition memory, but may cause mild impairments (see Zola-Morgan & Squire, 1993). This last conclusion is controversial because it has recently been claimed that selective excitotoxic lesions of the hippocampus do not affect object recognition memory over delays of between a half and three and a half minutes (Murray & Mishkin, 1993).

The evidence from humans is much scantier because of the rarity of selective lesions, but it is known that Herpes simplex encephalitis typically destroys the perirhinal and parahippocampal cortices and causes a very severe amnesia, whereas the amnesia caused by more selective hippocampal lesions, such as that reported in the patient RB seems to be much milder (Zola-Morgan, Squire, & Amaral, 1986). Very few patients with selective amygdala lesions have been studied, but the few cases available do suggest that bilateral amygdala damage may disrupt recall and recognition of nonverbal materials (for example, see Tranel & Hyman, 1990). If this were true, then amnesics with symmetrical medial temporal lobe lesions including the amygdala should show more severe explicit memory deficits for nonverbal materials. The studies have been criticised on the grounds that patients with amygdala damage often have epilepsy, which causes functional abnormality of the hippocampus, or that they may have subtle structural damage extending into the hippocampus. Even so, it is difficult to see how these criticisms can explain the pattern of results produced by the patients, but more work is clearly needed to resolve disagreements.

Knowledge about the precise location of lesions in the midline diencephalon and basal forebrain is currently less good, partly because the structures involved are small and close together. Despite this, there is growing evidence that anterior thalamic lesions cause an amnesia-like deficit in humans (Daum & Ackerman, 1994; Mark, Barry, McLardy, & Ervin, 1970), and also in other mammals (Aggleton, Keith, & Sahgal, 1991), and the lesions to other midline thalamic nuclei, particularly those that receive connections from the internal medullary lamina, may also contribute to amnesia (Graff-Radford, Tramel, Van Hoesen, & Brandt, 1990). Contrary to what was believed at the time of Victor, Adams, and Collins' (1977) monograph, there is now considerable evidence that lesions to the dorsomedial thalamus do not contribute to amnesia (for example, see Kritchevsky, Graff-Radford & Damasio, 1987). It remains unclear to what extent mammillary body lesions disrupt explicit memory, although a recent case study suggests that free recall may be impaired, but not recognition (Dusoir et al., 1990). This is compatible with evidence from rats that anterior thalamic, but not mammillary body lesions disrupt delayed nonmatching-to-position performance, a form of spatial recognition memory (Aggleton et al., 1991).

Most lesions that affect the basal forebrain tend to be large. For example, lesions of the basal forebrain caused by rupture and repair of aneurysms of the anterior communicating artery often affect orbitofrontal and medial frontal cortices, and basal ganglia as well. Nevertheless, significant amnesia has been reported in a patient with this aetiology, who was shown at post-mortem to have suffered a lesion that damaged the septum, the diagonal band of Broca, and the nucleus accumbens, but not the nucleus basalis of Meynert (Phillips, Sangalang, & Sterns, 1992). Berti, Arienta, and Papagno (1990) have described a patient with a moderate degree of amnesia, who suffered damage to the upper part of the septum, but probably not to the diagonal band of Broca. It has been argued by von Cramon and Schuri (1992) that damage to the pathways between the septum and hippocampus also causes an amnesia-like memory disorder. In so far as these lesions damage the cholinergic basal forebrain systems that interact with the hippocampus and other medial temporal lobe structures, they are likely to disrupt the cholinergic modulation of these structures and impair their functioning. There is evidence that this kind of modulatory disruption can impair function as much as structural damage to the primary processing structures in the medial temporal lobes (Robbins, personal communication).

There is also evidence that lesions to the structures that interconnect the medial temporal lobe and midline diencephalic structures implicated in amnesia can cause amnesia-like symptoms. Although the association of fornix lesions with amnesia has had a polemical history, there is strong evidence that in animals fornix lesions disrupt recognition memory for spatial kinds of information (Aggleton et al., 1991; Gaffan, 1992). In human patients with fornix damage resulting from the removal of colloid cysts, there is evidence that a mild amnesia results (Gaffan & Gaffan, 1991; Hodges & Carpenter, 1991). There is also evidence in humans that lesions of the retrosplenial cortex (which reciprocally links anterior thalamus and hippocampus) causes mild amnesia. Which pathways from the anterior thalamus to the medial temporal lobe region may be implicated in amnesia is a topic of active research, because if there are several, this might provide evidence that amnesia is heterogeneous. A possibly equivalent situation may apply to the fornical connections between hippocampus and anterior thalamus because there are two pathways, one direct and one of which goes through the mammillary bodies. It could be that damage to the two pathways has different effects.

One issue that is still unresolved is whether the different lesions discussed here all cause the same kind of memory deficit, and, if so, whether its severity is similar after the different lesions. For example, in relation to AA, it may be that lesions of the hippocampus, fornix, and anterior thalamus have similar effects (see Aggleton et al., 1991) on recognition and recall, but that mamillary body lesions only affect free recall (Dusoir et al., 1990). In contrast, lesions that damage parahippocampal and perirhinal cortex seem to cause a more severe explicit memory impairment than any of these lesions. With respect to RA, there is considerable variation across patients even with lesions in similar sites such as the midline thalamus. In recent years, a number of patients have been reported with RA that is not accompanied by a typical AA (see Kapur, 1993 for a review). There is some evidence that structures in the anterior and inferior temporal neocortex are damaged in patients with this kind of disorder, although more posterior temporal neocortex lesions have been reported to cause a similar deficit (De Renzi & Lucchelli, 1993). De Renzi and Lucchelli's patient not only showed RA, but also showed an impaired ability to retain new memories over a period of weeks despite normal performance on standard tests sensitive to AA, which are given at relatively short delays. The existence of this atypical kind of AA needs to be confirmed, as does its relationship with RA, and the implications that this form of memory deficit have for our understanding of the amnesic syndrome need to be worked out.

The current picture of the neuroanatomy of amnesia remains incomplete. There is evidence that memory is disrupted by damage to the hippocampus, fornix, anterior thalamus, and possibly to the mammillary bodies as well as the retrosplenial cortex. These structures are serially linked, so it is possible that damage anywhere in the circuit will produce a similar effect although where two parallel links are involved (as with the fornical projection) more than one deficit may be found. This issue needs to be properly explored. However, as the hippocampus receives two thirds of its cortical input from parahippocampal and perirhinal cortices, it is hard to explain why damage to these cortical structures should produce a much more severe memory disturbance than damage to the later parts of the hippocampal circuit. Either damage to these cortical structures has a much more severe effect on their back projections to other neocortical association areas than do downstream hippocampal circuit lesions or these cortices project to midline thalamic structures that are not tightly linked to the hippocampal circuit. Our current knowledge of the anatomy of amnesia, therefore, leaves open the possibility that amnesia involves several different functional deficits. One or more of these deficits could be associated with the traditional hippocampal circuit of Papez. One could involve a circuit involving the parahippocampal and perirhinal cortices and non-hippocampal midline thalamic structures, and might even involve the tighter circuit involving the hippocampus and the underlying parahippocampal and perirhinal cortices. Proof of the possibility of heterogeneity will require that selective damage to these systems or other similar ones causes different memory deficits, which cannot be explained as resulting from incidental disruption of structures not involved in amnesia, such as the frontal association cortex.

NEUROPSYCHOLOGICAL EVIDENCE

(i) Encoding

If the amnesic deficits in explicit memory that AA comprises result from a failure to encode semantic information normally, then patients should show a certain pattern of performance on explicit memory tests. This pattern has been investigated most systematically in patients with Korsakoff's syndrome (see Bauer, Tobias, & Valenstein, 1993 for a recent review). The first expectation of what should be found in patients with semantic encoding deficits concerns the effect of a semantic orienting task on explicit memory relative to performance following spontaneous encoding of the same kind of information—i.e. an adaptation of Craik and Lockhart's (1972) levels of processing task. According to Butters and Cermak (1975), amnesics have an habitual tendency not to encode semantic features despite the ability to do so, which leads to the prediction that their explicit memory should benefit to a greater extent than that of normal subjects when given a semantic orienting task to perform. Tests of these predictions with Korsakoff patients have not given completely consistent results. For example, Biber, Butters, Rosen, and Gerstman (1981) found that Korsakoff patients did improve differentially, relative to controls, in face recognition memory following a semantic orienting task compared with spontaneous learning. In contrast, in a series of experiments from Manchester (e.g. Mayes, Meudell, & Neary, 1980; Meudell, Mayes & Neary, 1980), using a wide variety of stimuli, the standard levels of processing effect was replicated, but the pattern of performance was identical in Korsakoff patients and their controls. (It remains a possibility that the differences between studies may well be related to differences between the Manchester and Boston amnesics.)

A second paradigm that has been used extensively in tests of the semantic deficit hypothesis is Wickens' release from proactive interference (PI) task (Wickens, 1970). The expectation here is that amnesics should not display release from PI following a shift of semantic category, although they may well do so following shifts involving nonsemantic information. Exactly this pattern of results has been reported by Cermak, Butters, and Moreines (1974) for Korsakoff patients. However, Kopelman (1991) has failed to replicate this finding in another group of Korsakoff patients, and it has been argued that when the effect occurs it is a result of incidental frontal lobe damage in patients (see Mayes, 1988 for a review). Furthermore, other work has shown that Korsakoff patients may show a *delayed* release from PI (Winocur, Kinsbourne, & Moscovitch, 1981) or show a normal release when cued at retrieval (Kinsbourne & Wood, 1975). It is also not clear whether failure to show release might not result sometimes from a storage deficit, as release probably depends on remembering that previously shown items belonged to a different semantic category.

One problem with these two paradigms is that conclusions about the relative efficiency of encoding operations in amnesia are inferred from a performance measure that itself is dependent on other necessary processing stages. But encoding ability can also be measured using a more direct procedure. As noted in an earlier section, if semantic information is not encoded normally by amnesics, then they should be unable to answer questions about the semantic content of briefly presented stimuli when the questions are asked immediately after presentation. We have performed an experiment to test this prediction which involved presenting 60 complex visual stimuli for six seconds each and immediately after each presentation asking subjects one question that tapped their knowledge of the spatial, colour, size, or semantic features of each stimulus (Mayes et el., 1993). Although normal subjects performed well below ceiling levels, amnesics were able to answer all categories of question just as well. Furthermore, this normality was found in the Korsakoff patients as well as in amnesics of other aetiologies.

Two points should be considered in assessing the evidence concerning whether or not some or all amnesics are impaired at encoding aspects of semantic information. First, it may be that amnesics, and particularly Korsakoff patients, have an encoding deficit with more complex aspects of semantic processing than have yet been examined. This remains possible, but might be hard to test because it will be difficult to determine whether the deficit causes amnesia or is a consequence of it, which, in turn, exacerbates the syndrome. Second, if the hypothesis is specifically aimed at Korsakoff patients, the possibility that any encoding deficits are caused by incidental frontal lobe damage needs to be seriously addressed.

A deficit in encoding semantic information would be incompatible with a finding of normal semantic learning in amnesia. Tulving, Hayman, and MacDonald (1991) have reported results with one patient whom they claim shows normal acquisition of semantic memory provided this does not involve high levels of interference. However, there are a number of problems with this finding. First, the pattern of his memory deficit does not seem to be typical of amnesia, so the precise implications of this case for the functional deficit(s) underlying the amnesic syndrome might be regarded as unclear. Furthermore, this applies particularly as the patient has damage outside traditional regions. A contrasting finding is that of Gabrieli, Cohen, and Corkin (1988) who have shown that the famous patient HM, with damage to medial temporal lobe structures, had a severe deficit for semantic information acquired after (but not before) the onset of his amnesia. Finally, if some patients do indeed show an intact ability for semantic learning then one needs to consider the possibility that the expression of such knowledge might be mediated by implicit memory processes.

(ii) Item-specific Implicit Memory

Although amnesics show preservation of motoric forms of classical conditioning and several kinds of skill learning and memory (see Mayes, 1988; and Squire et al., 1992 for reviews), it seems likely that these kinds of memory are primarily mediated by the basal ganglia and cerebellum. Motoric classical conditioning and skill memory are, therefore, likely to depend on very different kinds of memory representation, as the cerebellum and basal ganglia are organised very differently from the neocortex where most aspects of explicit memories are likely to be stored. It follows that preservation of these types of "memory" in amnesics is unlikely to have any strong implications for the functional deficits that underlie the syndrome. As already discussed, ISIM for the kinds of information for which amnesics show impaired recall and recognition may have much more theoretical relevance because it is likely that implicit and explicit memory in this case depends on the *same* memory representations.

There is still widespread disagreement about the processes and internal representations that underlie ISIM. Some take the view that implicit memory for items that were familiar prior to training does not require the creation of a new memory but instead depends on contact with pre-existing (semantic) memory representations. Although this view may be wrong—and, indeed, Jacoby and Kelley (1992) have argued that all ISIM is based on the same episodic traces that underlie explicit memory—it is safer to test predictions by examining amnesic ISIM for information that was novel prior to training. This should apply to items such as unknown faces, nonwords, and unknown visual patterns as well as associations between previously unrelated items. The added value of this approach, as indicated earlier, is that it allows one to test differential predictions relating to specific and nonspecific variants of storage deficit hypotheses.

The pattern of results shown by amnesics on indirect memory tests can be summarised quickly. Patients of various aetiologies have fairly consistently shown normal performance on indirect memory tests where verbal or nonverbal items were familiar prior to the training experience, and would, therefore, already have had a representation in memory (see Mayes, 1988; Squire et al., 1992; and Graf & Masson, 1993 passim, for reviews). It needs to be decided whether this indicates that amnesics have preserved ISIM for information that was familiar prior to training, and, if so, how this should be interpreted.

How amnesics perform on indirect memory tests that tap memory for information that was novel prior to training is far less clear. Performance appears to be normal on some indirect memory tests for certain kinds of novel information, although some workers now believe that amnesics show impaired indirect memory performance for novel associations, particularly if these are semantic in nature (see Mayes, 1988; Squire et al., 1992; and Graf & Masson, 1993 passim, for reviews). For example, we (Mayes & Gooding, 1989) and others (e.g. Shimamura & Squire, 1989) have failed to find any, let alone normal, enhanced word-stem completion priming for novel word associations in amnesics. Performance on this indirect memory task probably depends on memory for semantic associations between previously unassociated or weakly associated words. It could also be that performance on this particular task is especially susceptible to contamination by explicit memory processes, as suggested by the work of Bowers and Schacter (1990), which could explain the failure of amnesics to show the effect.

More work needs to be done before it is known with confidence whether or not amnesic ISIM is preserved for some or all kinds of novel information. It also needs to be determined whether the pattern of ISIM shown by amnesics is similar for pre- and post-morbidly acquired information. For example, if amnesics show impaired ISIM for semantic associations experienced for the first time post-morbidly, will they also show impaired ISIM for similar associations encountered pre-morbidly, and for which their explicit memory is impaired? This might be tested by examining autonomic responses to correct and incorrect pairings of famous faces and occupations when the famous people would have been encountered either pre- or post-morbidly. If the pattern were shown to be different, this would be evidence that AA and RA arise from different kinds of functional deficit.

In our view a convincing delineation of amnesics' pattern of ISIM will require a convergent operations approach in which several procedures of measuring ISIM are used that depend on different assumptions in the hope that they will produce similar and, therefore, believable results. The procedures could include: (a) tasks in which ISIM is indicated by a reduction in reaction time to repeated items so as to reduce the chances of explicit memory contributing to performance, (b) tasks where implicit memory is indicated by autonomic responses to repeated items, (c) the use of divided attention at test to eliminate explicit memory on the assumption that ISIM depends on automatic processes at retrieval, (d) the use of a modification of Jacoby's process dissociation procedure (see Jacoby & Kelley, 1992) that uses signal detection theory. At present, theorists need to interpret a somewhat uncertain pattern of evidence, but they need to be clear about what their hypotheses predict in relation to amnesics' ISIM performance, and what would constitute an appropriate test of such predictions.

(iii) Differential Explicit Memory Deficits in AA

(A) Recall and Recognition Memory.   If amnesia involves a disturbance of explicit memory for only some aspects of fact and episodic information, then one would expect patients at least to show more severe explicit memory deficits for those kinds of information, and possibly for them not to show any explicit memory deficit at all for the unaffected kinds of information. Blaxton (1992) has reported a finding that fits the latter possibility, in a study that contrasted memory associated with data-driven processing and memory for conceptually driven processing. Whereas patients with left lateralised temporal lobe epilepsy showed impaired implicit as well as explicit memory on conceptually driven tasks, they showed normal explicit as well as implicit memory for data-driven

tasks. However, we have found that amnesics are impaired at tasks in which subjects were encouraged to engage in low-level processing (see Mayes, 1988 for a review), and a recent study by Schwartz, Rosse, and Deutsch (1993) with memory-impaired schizophrenic patients has also failed to replicate this pattern.

The evidence about whether amnesics are more impaired at some kinds of explicit memory than they are at others can be quickly summarised. The evidence is conflicting. It has been reported by Hirst and his colleagues (Hirst et al., 1986; Hirst, Johnson, Phelps, & Volpe, 1988) that amnesics are more impaired at free recall of word lists than they are at recognition of word lists. Haist, Shimamura, and Squire (1991) have claimed, however, that amnesics have a comparably severe impairment in the free recall and recognition of lists of unrelated words. One possible explanation of the conflicting results, suggested by Squire et al. (1992), is that the patients of Hirst and his colleagues were more likely to have suffered frontal lobe damage. As frontal lobe damage is typically believed to affect free recall, but not recognition (e.g. Jetter, Poser, Freeman, & Markowitsch, 1986), this would explain the disproportionate deficit in free recall in amnesics with additional frontal lobe damage even when the amnesia itself would have an equal effect on recall and recognition. There is another possible reason for discrepant results in this area which we will discuss again shortly in relation to forgetting rates. This is that amnesics may be more impaired at free recall than recognition for some kinds of material, but not others. Specifically, their recall may be more impaired than their recognition for materials that are semantically organised at encoding, but not for materials that tend not to be so organised.

Like most studies comparing the severity of the amnesic deficit for two forms of explicit memory, Hirst and his colleagues employed a matching procedure. This involves matching amnesic and control performance under one of the memory conditions, usually the one that is suspected to be less affected in amnesia, and comparing performance on the second measure to determine if, as predicted, there is evidence for a differential impairment for amnesics. Matching is done to avoid floor, ceiling, and scaling effects which are otherwise unavoidable; unless one of the kinds of memory tested is completely preserved, interpretation is impossible unless such a procedure is adopted. Unfortunately, matching itself can produce artefactual results because the procedure, which usually involves testing controls at longer delays than amnesics, or giving them less learning opportunity, may affect one of the two kinds of explicit memory being compared more than the other. For various reasons, one of which relates to scaling effects, it is extremely hard to know whether this is occurring.

(iii) (B) Memory for Items and Associated Contextual Information.   The problem associated with the matching procedure also relates to the other main kind of information for which differential deficits in explicit memory have been claimed: context. Many workers have difficulty with the meaning of this

concept, but it is perhaps best viewed as those kinds of information that do not receive focal attention in any learning situation, but which help define the situation in which the learning occurred. As such, they include spatiotemporal and other background features of information. There is some evidence that amnesics are more impaired at explicit memory for aspects of spatial information, temporal information, and information about the form in which attended items were presented than they are at recognition for the attended items themselves (see Mayes, 1988 for a review). The evidence is, however, complicated. For example, with respect to temporal order memory, there is evidence suggesting that some amnesics at least show disproportionate impairments for which of two sequentially presented lists recognised items were presented in (Squire, 1982). But there is also evidence that the medial temporal lobe amnesic HM is not impaired at within-list temporal order memory judgements (Sagar, Gabrieli, Sullivan, & Corkin, 1990) and, in unpublished work, we have shown that with a mixed group of amnesics that included Korsakoff patients there was no evidence that this form of memory was more impaired than item recognition. These results suggest that temporal order memory may comprise a complex and diverse set of processes.

There are also conflicting results that relate to spatial memory deficits. Shoqeirat and Mayes (1991) found that a large group of amnesics, of mixed aetiology, who were matched on item recognition to control group performance, were disproportionately impaired on three measures of spatial memory. However, two subsequent studies have reported a different outcome. Cave and Squire (1991) have found that Korsakoff patients and amnesics with relatively selective hippocampal damage were equally impaired at item recognition and explicit memory of the items' locations. MacAndrew and Jones (1993) also found that spatial memory was not significantly more impaired that either free recall or recognition. However, in their study there was a strong trend for spatial memory to be more impaired that item recognition, and, in fact, the size of the effect was as great as in the study of Shoqeirat and Mayes (1991) and it is probable that if they had used as many amnesic subjects as Shoqeirat and Mayes, they would have also found that their amnesics were significantly more impaired at explicit memory for spatial location.

There could be several plausible interpretations of the conflicting results. First, all amnesics may be more impaired at explicit memory for spatial location than they are at recognition of target items, and when evidence for this is not found this is because the matching manipulation has a greater effect on spatial memory and so hides a genuinely greater deficit in this form of memory in amnesics. Second, all amnesics may be equally impaired at explicit memory for spatial location and item recognition, and evidence to the contrary arises because the matching manipulation has a greater effect on item recognition and so creates the illusion of there being a greater deficit in spatial memory. Third, some lesions that cause amnesia disrupt spatial memory more than item recognition whereas others do not, or some amnesic patients may have additional frontal lobe damage which selectively disrupts spatial memory.

Even if some or all selectively lesioned amnesics turn out to be more impaired at spatial memory than they are at item recognition, it would still need to be determined what are the exact characteristics of the information for which they show more severe explicit memory impairments. Although it may not be currently possible to resolve the disagreements concerning the relative extent of spatial (and other kinds of contextual or relational information) memory and item recognition deficits in human amnesics, there is also some evidence that animals with medial temporal or fornix lesions may be relatively more impaired at spatial memory (Gaffan, 1992; Parkinson, Murray, & Mishkin, 1988). Squire et al. (1992) argued that the monkeys in the experiment by Parkinson and his colleagues had lesions to parahippocampal gyrus and posterior entorhinal cortex as well as hippocampus, and these cortical structures receive a major input from parietal cortex, which is concerned with spatial information processing. In contrast, the more anterior perirhinal cortex receives a major input from inferotemporal cortex that carries visual pattern information relevant to visual object memory. One might, therefore, expect to get greater or lesser degrees of spatial and object memory disturbance depending on how posterior or anterior cortical lesions were in the medial temporal lobes. Such effects should not be found after hippocampal lesions, as the cortical information is supposedly integrated in this structure. This kind of argument, however, is unable to explain Gaffan's observations that fornix-lesioned monkeys are not impaired at delayed nonmatching-to-sample tasks (which tap item recognition) except when performance depends on retention through the use of spatial memory.

It is commonly assumed that, whether or not it is disproportionately severe, the spatiotemporal context memory deficit is similar in amnesics with different aetiologies and lesion locations. Data obtained by Parkin and Hunkin and their colleagues (see Parkin, 1992), however, suggest that the temporal memory (and also possibly the spatial memory) deficit may be of a different kind in amnesics with medial temporal lobe and midline diencephalic lesions. These workers found that Korsakoff patients performed worse than post-encephalitic patients with equivalently severe amnesia on a recognition task, performance on which relied on the ability to discriminate the temporal position of tested items (see Parkin, 1992). Consistent with this finding, Korsakoff patients were also found to be more impaired at list discrimination than were post-encephalitic amnesics, who were matched to them on recognition of list items (Hunkin, Parkin, & Longmore, 1994). It is unlikely that the Korsakoff patients' temporal memory deficit was a simple result of incidental frontal lobe damage, because another patient with a focal left anteromedial thalamic infarct was found to be impaired at list discrimination not only for verbal items, but also for abstract designs for which his recognition memory was good (Parkin, Rees, Hunkin, & Rose, 1994). This patient did not have similar problems with spatial memory. However, in further work with two kinds of list discrimination tasks, one dependent on temporal discrimination and one on spatial discrimination, it was found that there was a correlation between the two kinds of discrimination performance and target item recognition in post-encephalitic amnesics, but not in Korsakoff patients (see Parkin, 1992). These results suggest that medial temporal lobe and midline diencephalic lesions may impact on spatiotemporal contextual associative memory in different ways.

(iii) (C) Rate of Forgetting for Different Types of Information.   One difficulty with attempts to determine whether or not amnesics show differential impairment for different kinds of explicit memory is that there is no agreed upon method for making the determination. This might not matter if there was no disagreement, but unfortunately there is. Nevertheless, unless a hypothesis postulates that all aspects of fact and episode memory are equally and similarly affected, some degree of differential impairment should be predicted. One way to reduce the problem might be to examine the rate at which amnesics forget information of different kinds. Rate of forgetting experiments with amnesics have also used a matching procedure in which patients and controls are equated on memory performance at the shortest delay used by allowing patients longer learning exposures before examining performance at the longer delays. In nearly all studies, the shortest delay has been 10 minutes and the longest delay has been a week or more. Subjects have almost invariably been tested on recognition of complex visual scenes or sentences. Results have been inconsistent, so that it would be unsafe to conclude that any group of amnesics reliably shows evidence of forgetting pathologically quickly at delays beyond 10 minutes (see Mayes, 1988 for a review). For example, in a recent study, McKee and Squire (1992) found that Korsakoff patients, patients with medial temporal lobe lesions, and their normal control subjects lost the ability to recognise pictures at the same rate at delays between 10 minutes and 30–32 hours.

Three points should be made about these studies. First, nearly all the experiments have examined forgetting from delays of 10 minutes or more. Second, they have nearly all examined rate of loss of recognition. Third, they are all subject to an artefact which might result in amnesics' rate of forgetting being systematically underestimated. This artefact is simple to explain. Following the matching procedure originally described by Huppert and Piercy (1978), amnesics are given longer exposures than their controls to each item in a long list and delay is measured from the end of the list. This means that the average item presentation to test delay for the patients is much longer than it is for the controls. The result of this is that rate of forgetting for the amnesic group will be underestimated. This follows because the mathematical function describing forgetting is an exponentially decreasing one, and the matching procedure ensures that performance at the first delay is measured at a point on the amnesic forgetting curve where the rate parameter is relatively shallow and compared to an earlier point on the normal forgetting curve where the rate parameter is relatively steep. The effect may not be large, and, indeed, may even be negligible in a particular experiment. Nevertheless, the risk of underestimating amnesics' forgetting rate is present in all experiments in the published literature that have adopted Huppert and Piercy's matching procedure.

For a long time it has been widely believed that amnesics showed accelerated loss of the ability to free recall stories. In unpublished work, Isaac and Mayes (submitted) have compared the rate of loss of free recall and recognition of stories over delays up to 10 minutes. We matched amnesic and control recognition and free recall of different stories after filled delays of 15 and 20 seconds in two separate experiments. This was achieved by giving the amnesics more presentations of the stories.[1] We found that after a filled delay of 10 minutes, the patients showed accelerated loss of free recall, but not of recognition. Additional experiments were performed to show that the effect was not caused by (a) the controls surreptitiously rehearsing more than the patients, (b) residual short-term memory contributing to performance at the shortest delay, but not after a 10-minute delay (we showed this by testing severely amnesic patients with normal short-term memory, who scored nothing or almost nothing at the 15-second delay), (c) an artefact of the matching procedure. The effect was found in Korsakoff patients and in amnesics with medial temporal lobe damage. Most importantly, we also examined the amnesics' relative susceptibility to interference in the task by exposing all subjects to three stories similar to the target story that they were required to remember. Although the interfering stories were very similar to the target story, we found only a small interference effect with both free recall and recognition, which, importantly, was equivalent in the amnesics and their control subjects.

In order to determine whether this pattern of results generalised to other kinds of material we examined rate of loss of free recall, cued recall, and/or recognition of three kinds of word list in the same patients and control subjects. The first kind of list comprised semantically unrelated words. The second kind of list comprised semantically related words that were randomly ordered, and the third kind of list comprised semantically related words that were

---

[1] Given our critique of the Huppert and Piercy matching procedure in the last paragraph, an obvious objection is that the same problem must also apply to these experiments. In fact, the matching procedures are different because repeated presentations, as opposed to longer exposures distributed across a single presentation, ensure that the last experience with the to-be-remembered material, before the delay begins, is identical for both groups. If it is assumed that forgetting can only be measured from the last complete presentation of the material, then longer exposures distributed across a single presentation will give different mean-item-to-test delays for amnesic and control groups, whereas identical exposures with repeated presentations of the complete list will produce matched mean-item-to-test delays for the two groups. Even if this assumption does not apply, the prolonged presentation procedure would bias against amnesics showing faster forgetting, but this is exactly what the experiments found. The finding can, therefore, be trusted.

meaningfully arranged. The patients showed accelerated loss of free recall, but not of cued recall, for the two kinds of list that comprised meaningfully related words. However, they showed a normal rate of loss for the free recall, cued recall, and recognition of the unrelated word lists. Although there was the possibility that this last effect could have been caused by a floor effect, it accords with the results of Haist et al. (1992) which also showed that amnesics lost the free recall and recognition of unrelated word lists at a normal rate.

Our results, therefore, suggest that amnesics with lesions in several distinct sites show accelerated loss of the free recall of semantically organisable materials at delays of up to 10 minutes. They also suggest that amnesics' free recall of such materials may be more impaired than their recognition, but only after delays of a few minutes as opposed to delays of 15 or 20 seconds. They may not show disproportionate free recall deficits for unrelated lists of words or other kinds of material that are difficult to relate semantically. It is important to stress that the patients appear to have encoded the material in the same way as their control subjects, to judge by how and what they recalled at the shortest delays used, so their accelerated rate of loss of the semantically organisable materials was subsequent to what seemed to be relatively normal encoding (although they did receive more presentations of the material than their control subjects).

One feature of these results is that the free recall tests for the semantically organisable material must have depended on subjects' ability to retrieve associations between items, whereas the cued recall and recognition tests, because they were based on single items, would have done so to a markedly smaller degree. This suggests that amnesics may also lose the ability to recognise complex semantic *associations* between items in the first 10 minutes or so after learning, although their rate of loss of recognition for single items over the same time period will be relatively normal.

Whatever the pattern of accelerated amnesic forgetting is eventually shown to be, hypotheses about the functional deficit(s) underlying the syndrome will also have to explain why amnesic free recall and recognition are already impaired after a filled delay of only 15 seconds for probably all kinds of fact and episode information. A possible explanation is that the amnesics in our study had at least two deficits associated with damage to relatively independent systems. Some evidence for this might be found from studies with patients who have lateralised hippocampal sclerosis associated with temporal lobe epilepsy. There have been a number of reports that such patients with right-sided lesions show normal explicit memory for spatial information at delays of less than one minute, but are impaired at longer delays (e.g. see Pigott & Milner, 1993). Is it possible that damage to the hippocampal system disrupts the storage of complex information of the kind that underlies spatial memory in the first few minutes after learning, but that it leaves the encoding and initial maintenance of such information intact? If this were so, then damage to some other system would have to cause the more general impairment that manifests in its complete form after a filled delay of around 15 seconds.

(iii) (D) Retrograde Amnesia.   It is well known that the features of RA differ markedly across different amnesic patients. Most commonly, patients are described as showing RA with a temporal gradient in which memories are disrupted to a lesser degree roughly in proportion to how long before the onset of amnesia they were acquired. The notion that the extent of the temporal gradient in years may be a function of the severity of the underlying deficit has been criticised by Squire et al. (1992) on the grounds that severity of RA (particularly for remoter events) does not correlate well with the severity of AA (Kopelman, 1989; Shimamura & Squire, 1986). These workers argue that temporally graded RA is associated with selective damage to structures such as those in the medial temporal lobes and midline diencephalon where lesions may cause RAs with comparable gradients of several decades (Squire, Haist, & Shimamura, 1989), but that extended ungraded loss occurs after damage to regions not usually associated with amnesia, such as the frontal lobes (see Kopelman, 1989).

The conclusion of this argument may be correct, but it rests on an assumption that may be false, viz., that graded RA and AA are caused by a common underlying functional deficit and by damage to a single neural system. In this connection, it is interesting to note that RB, who had bilateral damage that appeared at post-mortem to be confined to the CA1 field of the hippocampus, was not shown to have an RA in life (although this may have been because the tests used did not tap memories from the immediately pre-morbid period) (Zola-Morgan et al., 1986). A similar absence of a significant RA was noted in the patient of Dusoir et al. (1990), who had suffered a relatively selective lesion of the mammillary bodies. In monkeys, Zola-Morgan and Squire (1990) have reported that animals with lesions of the hippocampus and parahippocampal cortex showed an RA that was significant for information that was learned up to four weeks before surgery, but not earlier, and similar results have been reported with rats (see Squire et al., 1992). An important feature of these experiments is that they can control for the degree of learning and rehearsal of the pre-morbidly acquired information, although future work needs to focus more on two further features: the effects of different lesion locations and the effect of tapping memory for different kinds of information.

Like AA, RA typically involves disruption of recall and recognition of both factual information (as tapped by tests based on various forms of public information taken from the recent past) and autobiographical information. Dissociations between autobiographical and factual memories have been reported in which autobiographical memories are usually more severely disrupted than are factual memories (e.g. Markowitsch et al., 1993), but the opposite pattern of impaired factual memory and relatively preserved autobiographical memory has also been reported (De Renzi, Liotti, & Nichelli,

1987; Grossi, Trojano, Grasso, & Orsini, 1988; Kapur, Young, Bateman, & Kennedy, 1989). Other more specific dissociations have been reported as well. For example, Warrington and McCarthy (1988) reported that a post-encephalitic patient who had a severe RA using standard measures was able to make recognition discriminations between famous and nonfamous faces and names at a normal level although he could say little about the faces and names. This effect requires replication, however, because it has not been found in other amnesic patients (see Mayes et al., 1994; Squire et al., 1992). Mayes et al. (1994) also found that amnesics were more impaired at their ability to give the temporal location of famous events and people than they were at answering other kinds of explicit memory questions about events and people. Indeed, one patient with a medial temporal lobe lesion and a very severe anterograde amnesia was only impaired at giving the dates of famous events and famous people, and showed normal ability to remember other aspects of information about the famous events and people. It seems likely that dating events and the periods of peak fame for famous people is a complex process that depends on retrieving many associations between stored pieces of information (Friedman, 1993). It needs to be confirmed to what extent disorders of autobiographical and factual memory dissociate from each other, whether other more specific dissociations occur, and precisely what relationship these dissociations have to the amnesic syndrome. One thing that is required is a more rigorous attempt to correlate anatomical lesions with the pattern and severity of RA.

Whether or not RA fractionates into explicit memory deficits for different kinds of disorders, the cause of the memory deficits that occur needs to be resolved. This question might be addressed in several distinct ways. First, it might be asked whether amnesics show preservation of ISIM for the same kinds of items for which they show explicit memory deficits. Preservation of ISIM might be an indication that RA arises from a retrieval deficit for memories that are still present in storage to a normal degree. To our knowledge this possibility has not been examined, although Squire, Cohen, and Zouzounis (1984) have provided evidence that at least patients who have become mildly amnesic after electroconvulsive shock therapy retain the skill of reading mirror-reversed words, acquired pre-treatment, despite impaired explicit memory for the training sessions themselves. There have also been claims that name cues (for example, ''John K?'') may particularly help amnesics' memory for the names of faces that were famous from the pre-morbid period (see McCarthy & Warrington, 1990), but it is unclear to what extent these cues involve implicit memory and whether they differentially help amnesics, let alone render their memory performance normal.

Second, the question might be addressed by examining the consistency of explicit memory for specific information on different occasions and whether repeated retrieval attempts improve memory. It has been argued by Shallice (1988) that consistency in responding across retrieval occasions in memory impaired patients is one criterion by which a deficit can be judged to be of the storage type, although it has been suggested that the assumptions underlying this and other criteria may be faulty (e.g. see Mayes, 1988). Whichever side of the argument is correct, both Korsakoff patients and patients with medial temporal lobe damage have been reported as showing consistency of explicit memory retrieval on RA tests given on different occasions (Squire et al., 1989). The same patients also failed to improve with repeated attempts to retrieve the same material. However, consistency has not been reported with all patients. Thus, Cermak and O'Connor (1983) found that a post-encephalitic amnesic with a severe RA was very inconsistent on different retrieval attempts, although his performance was always very impaired. These results suggest that the causes of explicit memory deficits for pre-morbid information may not be identical in all patients.

Third, recovery from RA has periodically been reported in amnesic patients and has usually been taken as a sign that they have been suffering from a retrieval deficit (see Mayes, 1988). In TGA, where the memory disorder begins to recover within a few hours, patients typically show very little explicit memory for the amnesic episode itself, but a more or less full recovery of memories from before the episode, except perhaps for events up to several days prior to its onset (Kritchevsky, 1992). This suggests that the patients' AA and RA require at least slightly different explanations. For example, it might be argued that AA is caused by a failure to consolidate memories into long-term storage, so the memories will not return when the ability to consolidate does. In contrast, memories from the pre-morbid period return when there is recovery from the processing deficit(s) and many people believe that this must be because a retrieval deficit recovers. It is not clear that this conclusion is obligatory. It is clear that should structural damage occur at the site of storage of memory representations, there can be no recovery of affected memories. However, in the case of TGA, the disorder might (temporarily) distort the neural system responsible for storage so that the existing memory representations cannot be reactivated by normal retrieval mechanisms (and new memory representations cannot be stored normally). Recovery may involve the return of the neural system to an undistorted state such that memories are once again retrievable (and new memories can be added to the system).

A number of patients have now been described who show selective or relatively selective RA (see Kapur, 1993 for a review). Although it is difficult to identify when focal RA is psychogenic in origin, most of the reported cases have been shown to have suffered a brain injury. As already indicated, focal RA may be associated with damage to the anterior temporal lobe, possibly the posterior temporal lobe, or to the frontal lobes (see Kapur, 1993; Kopelman, 1989). These are not regions that have traditionally been associated with the amnesic syndrome, although they may have direct connections with the regions that have been so associated. Patients with focal RA show variability with respect to temporal gradient, with some showing flat gradients back to childhood whereas others show temporal gradients similar to those found in patients with the full amnesia syndrome (see Kapur, 1993). Also, as noted earlier, the patients have been found to differ with respect to whether the deficit predominantly affects autobiographical or factual memory (see Kapur, 1993). Cases of focal RA need to be carefully investigated for the presence of a mild AA or an atypical AA such as that reported by De Renzi and Lucchelli (1993). It is also clearly important to discover whether these cases ever arise from a small lesion to structures associated with the global amnesia syndrome, as such cases would carry a different significance for hypotheses about the functional deficits underlying amnesia.

Although cases with relatively severe AA and at most a mild RA have sometimes been reported (e.g. Zola-Morgan et al., 1986), there is a need to examine whether such cases either show RA with a very short duration prior to the occurrence of brain injury or whether they show an RA only for selective classes of information. The evidence is certainly strong enough to suggest that substantial components of AA and RA dissociate from one another, but it is still far from conclusively favouring either dissociation or its opposite.

Whether or not RA ever dissociates from AA, it remains unclear how similar the two forms of memory disturbance are to each other. Thus, similarities or differences in ISIM have not been systematically investigated. Also, there is little evidence that explicit memory disturbances for factual and autobiographical information ever dissociate in AA, whereas this has been reported with RA. There is, however, some evidence that temporal order memory is more disturbed than recognition of item information in both AA (Squire, 1982) and RA (Mayes et al., 1994), although the effect in AA may at least sometimes result from incidental frontal lobe damage (see Squire, 1982). The relative degree of impairment of free recall and recognition in RA has not been investigated, although from the study of Kopelman (1989) with Korsakoff patients, and that of Kritchevsky (1992) with patients with TGA, there is some evidence that free recall may be more impaired. These comparisons are important because if AA and RA have a common origin it would seem probable that they will show very similar characteristics.

One of the most puzzling features of RA is its often reported temporal gradient. This varies markedly across patients and it has to be admitted that its anatomical and functional determinants are still not well understood. Given that most amnesics remember overlearned semantic information normally, one might suppose that immunity to amnesia depends on the passage of time because this provides more opportunity to rehearse and hence reorganise memories. However, Mayes et al. (1994) tried to test for this possibility by comparing recall and recognition of easy and difficult items (which should differ in the extent to which they have been rehearsed), but found that the size of their amnesic patients' RA deficit was not influenced by this variable. The properties of RA need much more investigation, because most extant theories have great difficulty in explaining its apparent features.

CONCLUDING COMMENTS

One interesting feature about the now extensive literature concerning the amnesia syndrome is that very few detailed claims about the pattern of cognitive and memory deficit shown by patients or the lesions that cause their condition, are universally accepted. There is lack of universal agreement (and sometimes lack of any agreement at all!) in several theoretically important areas that include: (a) whether the syndrome is unitary or heterogeneous, (b) the exact location of the lesions that cause it, (c) the extent to which ISIM is preserved in amnesics, (d) whether there are any forms of explicit memory that are more impaired than item recognition in AA and RA, (e) whether some or all amnesics show subtle encoding deficits, (f) whether amnesics show accelerated forgetting and, if so, what the circumstances are under which they do so. Hypotheses about the functional deficits that underlie the amnesia syndrome are valuable in so far as they help focus our attention on those aspects of memory that are critical in discriminating between different accounts, and also because they suggest improved methodologies for measuring aspects of performance critical for the different hypotheses. Although defenders of the hypotheses that are currently available can choose to ignore, or reinterpret, certain pieces of evidence, we believe that it is essential that the following rough guidelines be followed. First, researchers need to make clear what the discriminative predictions are that follow from their own hypothesis; second, they need to indicate clearly the *empirical boundaries* for their hypothesis, that is, which of the many areas covered here are within their remit, and for those outside, possible ways in which the theory could be expanded to include them. Finally, they should indicate how all the various predictions that follow from their hypothesis can be adequately tested. Future research should be able to resolve disagreements by applying improved methodologies to all the key aspects of memory described here.

REFERENCES

Aggleton, J.P., Keith, A.B., & Sahgal, A. (1991). Both fornix and anterior thalamic, but not mammillary, lesions disrupt delayed non-matching-to-position memory in rats. *Behavioral Brain Research, 44*, 151–161.

Bachevalier, J., & Mishkin, M. (1986). Visual recognition impairment follows ventromedial but not dorsolateral prefrontal lesions in monkeys. *Behavioral Brain Research, 20*, 249–261.

Bauer, R.M., Tobias, B., & Valenstein, E. (1993). Amnesic disorders. In K.M. Heilman & E. Valenstein (Eds.), *Clinical neuropsychology* (3rd edn.) New York: Oxford University Press.

Berti, A., Arienta, C., & Papagno, C. (1990). A case of amnesia after excision of the septum pellucidum. *Journal of Neurology, Neurosurgery and Psychiatry, 53*, 922–924.

Biber, C., Butters, N., Rosen, J., & Gerstman, L. (1981). Encoding strategies and recognition of faces by alcoholic Korsakoffs and other brain damaged patients. *Journal of Clinical Neuropsychology, 3*, 315–330.

Blaxton, T.A. (1992). Dissociations among memory measures in memory-impaired subjects: Evidence for a processing account of memory. *Memory and Cognition, 20*, 549–562.

Bowers, J.S., & Schacter, D.L. (1990). Implicit memory and test awareness. *Journal of Experimental Psychology: Learning, Memory, and Cognition, 16*, 404–416.

Butters, N., & Cermak, L.S. (1975). Some analyses of amnesic syndromes in brain damaged patients. In R.L. Isaacson & K.H. Pribram (Eds.), *The hippocampus* (Vol. 2). New York: Plenum Press.

Cave, C.B., & Squire, L.R. (1991). Equivalent impairment of spatial and nonspatial memory following damage to the human hippocampus. *Hippocampus, 1*, 329–340.

Cave, C.B., & Square, L.R. (1992). Intact verbal and nonverbal short-term memory following damage to the human hippocampus. *Hippocampus, 2*, 151–164.

Cermak, L.S., Butters, N., & Moreines, J. (1974). Some analyses of the verbal encoding deficit of alcoholic Korsakoff patients. *Brain and Language, 1*, 141–150.

Cermak, L.S., & O'Connor, M. (1983). The anterograde and retrograde retrieval ability of a patient with amnesia due to encephalitis. *Neuropsychologia, 21*, 213–233.

Craik, F.I.M., & Lockhart, R.S. (1972). Levels of processing: A framework for memory research. *Journal of Verbal Learning and Verbal Behavior, 11*, 671–684.

Daum, I., & Ackerman, H. (1994). Frontal-type memory impairment associated with thalamic damage. *International Journal of Neuroscience, 77*, 187–198.

De Renzi, E., Liotti, M., & Nichelli, P. (1987). Semantic amnesia with preservation of autobiographical memory. A case report. *Cortex, 23*, 575–597.

De Renzi, E., & Lucchelli, F. (1993). Dense retrograde amnesia, intact learning capability and abnormal forgetting rate: A consolidation deficit? *Cortex, 29*, 449–466.

Dusoir, H., Kapur, N., Byrnes, D.P., McKinstry, S., & Hoare, R.D. (1990). The role of diencephalic pathology in human memory disorder: Evidence from a penetrating paranasal brain injury. *Brain, 113*, 1695–1706.

Friedman, W.J. (1993). Memory for the time of past events. *Psychological Bulletin, 113*, 44–66.

Gabrieli, J.D.E., Cohen, N.J., & Corkin, S. (1988). The impaired learning of semantic knowledge following bilateral medial temporal-lobe resection. *Brain and Cognition, 7*, 157–177.

Gaffan, D. (1992). The role of the hippocampus–fornix–mammillary system in episodic memory. In L.R. Squire & N. Butters (Eds.), *Neuropsychology of memory.* (2nd edn.) New York: Guilford Press.

Gaffan, D., & Gaffan, E.A. (1991). Amnesia in man following transection of the fornix: A review. *Brain, 114*, 2611–2618.

Graf, P., & Masson, M.E.J. (Eds.) (1993). *Implicit memory: New directions in cognition, development, and neuropsychology.* Hillsdale, NJ: Lawrence Erlbaum Associates Inc.

Graff-Radford, N.R., Tramel, N., Van Hoesen, G.W., & Brandt, J.P. (1990). Diencephalic amnesia. *Brain, 113*, 1–25.

Grossi, D., Trojano, L., Grasso, A., & Orsini, A. (1988). Selective "semantic amnesia" after closed head injury. A case report. *Cortex, 24*, 457–464.

Haist, F., Shimamura, A.P., & Squire, L.R. (1992). On the relationship between recall and recognition memory. *Journal of Experimental Psychology: Learning, Memory and Cognition, 18*, 691–702.

Hirst, W., Johnson, M.K., Phelps, E.A., Risse, G., & Volpe, B.T. (1986). Recognition and recall in amnesics. *Journal of Experimental Psychology: Learning, Memory and Cognition, 12*, 445–451.

Hirst, W., Johnson, M.K., Phelps, E.A., & Volpe, B.T. (1988). More on recognition and recall in amnesics. *Journal of Experimental Psychology: Learning, Memory and Cognition, 14*, 758–762.

Hodges, J.R., & Carpenter, K. (1991). Anterograde amnesia with fornix damage following removal of 111rd ventricle colloid cyst. *Journal of Neurology, Neurosurgery and Psychiatry, 54*, 633–638.

Hunkin, N.M., Parkin, A.J., & Longmore, B.E. (1994). Aetiological variation in the amnesic syndrome: Comparisons using the list discrimination task. *Neuropsychologia, 32*, 819–826.

Huppert, F.A., & Piercy, M. (1978). Dissociation between learning and remembering in organic amnesia. *Nature, 275*, 317–318.

Isaac, C., Mayes, A.R. (submitted). Rate of forgetting of prose material in amnesics of several aetiologies.

Jacoby, L.L., & Kelley, C. (1992). Unconscious influences of memory: Dissociations and automaticity. In A.D. Milner & M.D. Rugg (Eds.), *The neuropsychology of consciousness.* London: Academic Press.

Jetter, W., Poser, U., Freeman, R.B. Jr., & Markowitsch, J.H. (1986). A verbal long-term memory deficit in frontal lobe damaged patients. *Cortex 22*, 229–242.

Kapur, N. (1993). Focal retrograde amnesia in neurological disease: A critical review. *Cortex, 29*, 217–234.

Kapur, N., Young, A., Bateman, D., & Kennedy, P. (1989). Focal retrograde amnesia: A long-term clinical and neuropsychological follow-up. *Cortex, 25*, 387–402.

Keane, M.M., Gabrieli, J.D.E., Mapstone, H.C., Johnson, K.A., & Corkin, S. (1995). Double dissociation of memory capacities after bilateral occipital-lobe or medial temporal-lobe lesions. *Brain, 118*, 1129–1148.

Kinsbourne, M., & Wood, F. (1975). Short-term memory processes and the amnesic syndrome. In D. Deutsch & J.A. Deutsch (Eds.), *Short-term memory.* New York: Academic Press.

Kopelman, M.D. (1989). Remote and autobiographical memory, temporary context memory and frontal atrophy in Korsakoff and Alzheimer patients. *Neuropsychologia, 27*, 437–460.

Kopelman, M.D. (1991). Frontal dysfunction and memory deficits in the alcoholic Korsakoff syndrome and Alzheimer-type dementia. *Brain, 114*, 117–137.

Kritchevsky, M. (1992). Transient global amnesia. In L.R. Squire & N. Butters (Eds.), *Neuropsychology of memory.* (2nd edn.) New York: Guilford Press.

Kritchevsky, M., Graff-Radford, N.R., & Damasio, A.R. (1987). Normal memory after damage to medical thalamus. *Archives of Neurology, 44*, 959–962.

MacAndrew, S.B.G., & Jones, G.V. (1993). Spatial memory in amnesia: Evidence from Korsakoff patients. *Cortex, 29*, 235–249.

Mandler, G. (1980). Recognizing: The judgement of previous occurrence. *Psychological Review, 87*, 252–271.

Mark, V.H., Barry, H., McLardy, T., & Ervin, F.R. (1970). The destruction of both anterior thalamic nuclei in a patient with intractable agitated depression. *Journal of Nervous and Mental Disease, 150*, 266–272.

Markowitsch, H.J., Calabrese, P., Liess, J., Haupts, M., Durwen, H.F., & Gehlen, W. (1993). Retrograde amnesia after traumatic injury of the fronto-temporal cortex. *Journal of Neurology, Neurosurgery and Psychiatry, 56*, 988–992.

Mayes, A.R. (1988). *Human organic memory disorders.* Cambridge: Cambridge University Press.

Mayes, A.R. (1992). What functional deficits underlie amnesia? In L.R. Squire & N. Butters (Eds.), *Neuropsychology of memory.* (2nd edn.) New York: Guilford Press.

Mayes, A.R., Downes, J.J., MacDonald, C., Poole, V., Rooke, S., Sagar, H.J., & Meudell, P.R. (1994). Two tests for assessing remote public knowledge: A tool for assessing retrograde amnesia. *Memory, 2*, 183–210.

Mayes, A.R., Downes, J.J., Shoqeirat, M., Hall, C., & Sagar, H.J. (1993). Encoding ability is preserved in amnesics: Evidence from a direct test of encoding. *Neuropsychologia, 31*, 745–759.

Mayes, A.R., & Gooding, P. (1989). Enhancement of word completion priming in amnesics by cueing with previously novel associates. *Neuropsychologia, 27*, 1057–1072.

Mayes, A.R., Meudell, P., & Neary, D. (1980). Do amnesics adopt inefficient encoding strategies with faces and random shapes? *Neuropsychologia, 18*, 527–541.

Mayes, A.R., Meudell, P.R., & Pickering, A.D. (1985). Is organic amnesia caused by a selective deficit in remembering contextual information? *Cortex, 21*, 167–204.

McCarthy, R., & Warrington, E.K. (1990). *Cognitive neuropsychology: A clinical introduction.* San Diego, CA: Academic Press.

McKee, R.D., & Squire, L.R. (1992). Equivalent forgetting rates in long-term memory for diencephalic and medial temporal lobe amnesia. *Journal of Neuroscience, 12*, 3765–3772.

Meudell, P., Mayes, A.R., & Neary, D. (1980). Orienting task effects on the recognition of humorous pictures by amnesics and normal subjects. *Journal of Clinical Neuropsychology, 2*, 75–88.

Miller, L.A., Munoz, D.G., & Finmore, M. (1993). Hippocampal sclerosis and human memory. *Archives of Neurology, 50*, 391–394.

Murray, E.A., & Mishkin, M. (1993). Effects of excitotoxic amygdalo-hippocampal lesions on visual recognition in rhesus monkeys. *Society for Neuroscience Abstracts, 19*, 438.

Nadel, L. (1992). Multiple memory systems: What and why. *Journal of Cognitive Neuroscience, 4*, 179–188.

Parkin, A.J. (1992). Functional significance of etiological factors in human amnesia. In L.R. Squire & N. Butters (Eds.), *Neuropsychology of memory.* New York: Guilford Press.

Parkin, A.J., Rees, J.E., Hunkin, N.M., & Rose, P.E. (1994). Impairment of memory following discrete thalamic infarction. *Neuropsychologia, 32*, 39–52.

Parkinson, J.K., Murray, E., & Mishkin, M. (1988). A selective mnemonic role for the hippocampus in monkeys: Memory for the location of objects. *Journal of Neuroscience, 8*, 4159–4167.

Phillips, S., Sangalang, V., & Sterns, G. (1992). Basal forebrain infarction. *Archives of Neurology, 44*, 1134–1138.

Pigott, S., & Milner, B. (1993). Memory for complex aspects of complex visual scenes after unilateral temporal- or frontal-lobe resection. *Neuropsychologia, 31*, 1–15.

Sagar, H.J., Gabrieli, J.D.E., Sullivan, E.V., & Corkin, S. (1990). Recency and frequency discrimination in the amnesic patient HM. *Brain, 113*, 581–602.

Schacter, D.L. (1990). Toward a cognitive neuropsychology of awareness: Implicit knowledge and anosognosia. *Journal of Clinical and Experimental Neuropsychology, 12*, 155–178.

Schwartz, B.L., Rosse, R.B., & Deutsch, S.I. (1993). Limits of the processing view in accounting for dissociations among memory measures in a clinical population. *Memory and Cognition, 21*, 63–72.

Shallice, R. (1988). *From neuropsychology to mental structure.* Cambridge: Cambridge University Press.

Shimamura, A.P., & Squire, L.R. (1986). Korsakoff's syndrome: A study of the relation between anterograde amnesia and remote memory impairment. *Behavioural Neuroscience, 100*, 165–170.

Shimamura, A.P., & Squire, L.R. (1989). Impaired learning of new associations in amnesia. *Journal of Experimental Psychology: Learning, Memory, and Cognition, 14*, 763–769.

Shoqeirat, M., & Mayes, A.R. (1991). Disproportionate spatial memory and recall deficits in amnesia. *Neuropsychologia, 29*, 749–769.

Squire, L.R. (1982). Comparisons between two forms of amnesia: Some deficits are unique to Korsakoff's syndrome. *Journal of Experimental Psychology: Learning, Memory and Cognition, 8*, 560–571.

Squire, L.R., Cohen, N.J., & Zouzounis, J.A. (1984). Preserved memory in retrograde amnesia: Sparing of a recently acquired skill. *Neuropsychologia, 22*, 145–152.

Squire, L.R., Haist, F., & Shimamura, A.P. (1989). The neurology of memory: Quantitative assessment of retrograde amnesia in two groups of amnesic patients. *Journal of Neuroscience, 9*, 828–839.

Squire, L.R., Knowlton, B., & Musen, G. (1992). The structure and organization of memory. *Annual Review of Psychology, 44*, 453–495.

Tranel, D., & Hyman, B.T. (1990). Neuropsychological correlates of bilateral amygdala damage. *Archives of Neurology, 47*, 349–355.

Tulving, E., Hayman, C.A.G., & Macdonald, C. (1991). Long-lasting perceptual priming and semantic learning in amnesia: A case experiment. *Journal of Experimental Psychology: Learning, Memory and Cognition, 17,* 595-617.

Victor, M., Adams, R.D., & Collins, G.H. (1977). *The Wernicke-Korsakoff syndrome: A clinical and pathological study of 345 patients, 82 with post-mortem examinations.* Oxford: Blackwell.

von Cramon, D.Y., & Schuri, U. (1992). The septo-hippocampal pathways and their relevance to human memory: A case report. *Cortex, 28,* 411-422.

Warrington, E.K., & McCarthy, R. (1988). The fractionation of retrograde amnesia. *Brain and Cognition, 7,* 184-200.

Warrington, E.K., & Weiskrantz, L. (1982). Amnesia: A disconnection syndrome? *Neuropsychologia, 20,* 233-248.

Wickens, D.D. (1970). Encoding strategies of words: An empirical approach to meaning. *Psychological Review, 77,* 1-15.

Winocur, G., Kinsbourne, M., & Moscovitch, M. (1981). The effect of cueing on release from proactive interference in Korsakoff amnesic patients. *Journal of Experimental Psychology: Human Learning and Memory, 7,* 56-65.

Zola-Morgan, S., & Squire, L.R. (1990). The primate hippocampal formation: Evidence for a time-limited role of memory storage. *Science, 250,* 288-290.

Zola-Morgan, S., & Squire, L.R. (1993). The neuroanatomy of memory. *Annual Review of Neuroscience, 16,* 547-563.

Zola-Morgan, S., Squire, L.R., & Amaral, D.G. (1986). Human amnesia and the medial temporal region: Enduring memory impairment following a bilateral lesion limited to field CA1 of the hippocampus. *Journal of Neuroscience, 10,* 2950-2967.

Zola-Morgan, S., Squire, L.R., & Amaral, D.G. (1989). Lesions of the amygdala that spare adjacent cortical regions do not impair memory or exacerbate the impairment following lesions of the hippocampus. *Journal of Neuroscience, 9,* 1922-1936.

Zola-Morgan, S., Squire, L.R., Amaral, D.G., & Suzuki, W. (1989). Lesions of the peripheral and parahippocampal cortex that spare the amygdala and hippocampal formation produce severe memory impairment. *Journal of Neuroscience, 9,* 4355-4370.

MEMORY, 1997, 5 (1/2), 37–47

Implicit Memory:
What Must Theories of Amnesia Explain?

Tim Curran

Case Western Reserve University, Cleveland, USA

Daniel L. Schacter

Harvard University, USA

In their target article on explaining functional deficits in amnesia, Mayes and Downes (this issue) discuss the relevance of implicit memory. Our commentary considers a number of implicit memory phenomena that may be especially pertinent to understanding the functional deficits of amnesia. Recent evidence suggests that amnesic patients do not benefit normally from an exact perceptual match of stimuli between study and text. We propose that this impairment may reflect one manifestation of a more general deficit in associative binding of information across different brain subsystems. This idea helps to clarify the distinction between implicit and explicit memory, and suggests that studies of implicit memory can help to elucidate the functional deficits in amnesia.

INTRODUCTION

Mayes and Downes (this issue) make several points about the relevance of implicit memory to understanding the nature of functional deficits in amnesia. We believe that one issue that they raise—the distinction between implicit memory for "old" and "new" information—is particularly important theoretically. Mayes and Downes point out that amnesic patients have consistently shown normal implicit memory for old (i.e. previously familiar) stimuli that are represented in memory prior to an experiment. However, Mayes and Downes note that amnesic patients may not show normal implicit memory for novel information that does not have a pre-existing representation in memory.

In this commentary, we consider recent evidence that bears on the question of whether amnesic patients can exhibit implicit memory for novel information by

---

Requests for reprints should be sent to Daniel L. Schacter, Department of Psychology, Harvard University, 33 Kirkland St., Cambridge, MA 02138, USA.

Preparation of this commentary was supported by grant R01 NH45398-01 A3 from the National Institute of Mental Health to D.L. Schacter and by NINDS program project grant NS26985 to Boston University.

focusing on studies of repetition priming. We note several experiments in which amnesics have shown priming deficits and attempt to characterise the processes responsible for those deficits. Some have gone so far as to argue that priming is generally impaired in amnesic patients and that the medial temporal lobe/diencephalic system that is damaged in amnesia plays a critical role in both implicit and explicit memory (Ostergaard & Jernigan, 1993). By contrast, we will argue that the medial temporal lobe/diencephalic system may play a limited role in priming that can help to clarify, rather than undermine, the distinction between implicit and explicit memory. Furthermore, we think that the characterisation of priming impairments can help to elucidate the nature of functional deficits in amnesic patients.

PRIMING OF FAMILIAR AND NOVEL INFORMATION

Mayes and Downes (this issue) conclude that priming of previously familiar stimuli is spared in amnesia, whereas priming of novel information may be impaired. As noted by Mayes and Downes, evidence for impaired priming of novel information has been best documented in experiments testing memory for novel associations between pre-experimentally unrelated words (e.g. Schacter & Graf, 1986; Shimamura & Squire, 1989; for review, see Bowers & Schacter, 1993). However, comparing priming of novel associations with single-word priming confounds two factors: novelty and association. That is, amnesics may show impaired priming of novel associations because they are unable to acquire any novel information or because they are unable to form the requisite inter-word associations. Other evidence suggests that amnesics can show implicit memory for novel information when there is no associative requirements, as with stimuli such as pseudowords (Haist, Musen, & Squire, 1992; Musen & Squire, 1991), novel objects (Schacter, Cooper, Tharan, & Rubens, 1991; Schacter, Cooper, & Treadwell, 1993), and novel visual patterns (Gabrieli, Milberg, Keane, & Corkin, 1990; Musen & Squire, 1992). Of course, it can be argued that priming of these novel stimuli takes place at a sub-stimulus level that taps pre-experimentally familiar features (e.g. letters composing pseudowords or geons composing novel objects; Bowers & Schacter, 1993). Nevertheless, it seems clear that the best documented impairments of priming for novel stimuli all include an associative component. Therefore, priming deficits in amnesic patients seem more likely to be related to associative factors rather than to novelty *per se.*

This associative priming deficit may reflect amnesics' inability to form what Mayes and Downes refer to as "complex associations". A number of researchers have emphasised that a major function of the medial temporal lobe/diencephalic system is related to the formation of complex associations between multiple stimuli (see the chapters in Schacter & Tulving, 1994). Here we discuss some specific ideas about what might constitute "complex associations", but first we will mention two recently documented priming impairments in amnesic patients that may also reflect an associative deficit in amnesia—even though the paradigms that were used are not typically thought of as involving associative factors. These experiments suggest that amnesics do not benefit normally from an exact perceptual match of target materials between study and test.

In one experiment, study–test typography was manipulated in a word fragment completion paradigm (Kinoshita & Wayland, 1993). Control subjects, but not Korsakoff amnesics, showed significantly greater priming when typography was the same at study and test than when it was different. It is possible that Kinoshita and Wayland's control subjects showed a typography effect because they made use of intentional retrieval processes that are not available to Korsakoff patients. This possibility cannot be ruled out, because Kinoshita and Wayland did not test explicit memory.

A similar result has recently been obtained in a study of auditory priming that examined whether amnesic patients exhibit voice-specific priming—more priming when speaker's voice is the same at study and test than when it is different. Schacter, Church, and Bolton (1995) examined auditory priming with a low-pass filter identification test, which had previously yielded evidence of voice-specific priming in college students under conditions in which intentional retrieval can be ruled out as the source of the effect (Church & Schacter, 1994). In Schacter et al.'s experiment, amnesic patients of mixed etiologies and control subjects heard words spoken in one of six different voices. At test, the words were degraded by low-pass filtering. Half of the words were presented in the same voice as during study, and half were repaired with a different voice from the study list. Schacter et al. found that control subjects, but not amnesic patients, showed more priming in the same-voice condition than in the repaired-voice condition (Table 1A). These observations, like Kinoshita and Wayland's failure to observe font-specific visual priming in Korsakoff patients, raise the possibility that some perceptual specificity effects in priming depend on brain systems that normally subserve explicit memory. Although modality specificity has been previously observed in amnesics (Carlesimo, 1994; Graf, Shimamura, & Squire, 1985), the apparent lack of within-modality specificity may reflect a medial temporal lobe/diencephalic contribution to font- and voice-specific effects under the experimental conditions used by Kinoshita and Wayland and by Schacter et al.

A more recent study provides suggestive evidence that amnesic patients can exhibit voice-specific priming under different experimental conditions than those employed by Schacter et al. In two experiments by Schacter and Church (1995), words were spoken by one of two voices during the study task. On a subsequent low-pass filter identification test, studied words were spoken either by the same voice used at study or by an entirely novel, unfamiliar voice. Thus,

TABLE 1
Proportion Correct in Auditory Filter Identification Experiments

A: Schacter, Church, & Bolton (1995)	Studied Words		Nonstudied Words
	Same Voice	Repaired Voice	
Amnesic Patients	0.35	0.43	0.30
	(0.05)	(0.13)	
Control Subjects	0.56	0.40	0.36
	(0.20)	(0.04)	

B: Schacter & Church (1995), Experiment 1	Studied Words		Nonstudied Words
	Same Voice	Unfamiliar Voice	
Amnesic Patients	0.49	0.44	0.34
	(0.16)	(0.11)	
Control Subjects	0.61	0.54	0.44
	(0.17)	(0.10)	

C: Schacter & Church (1995), Experiment 2	Studied Words		Nonstudied Words
	Same Voice	Unfamiliar Voice	
Amnesic Patients	0.76	0.69	0.57
	(0.19)	(0.12)	
Control Subjects	0.73	0.65	0.51
	(0.22)	(0.15)	

Values in parentheses are priming scores obtained by subtracting the nonstudied identification rate from each studied condition.

rather than repairing familiar voices from study to test, as was done in the Schacter et al. experiment, all words were tested in either the same voice or in a new voice. In this new-voice design, control subjects and a mixed-etiology group of amnesic patients showed very similar patterns of priming (Table 1B & C). Although the voice effect was nonsignificant in Experiment 1 and marginally significant in Experiment 2, the pattern and magnitude of priming effects in amnesics and controls were nearly identical (difference between Experiments 1 and 2 are reconsidered later in this paper).

To understand the difference between the repaired-voice design and the new-voice design, we have found it useful to reconceptualise such within-modality perceptual specificity effects in terms of associative binding between perceptual cues and abstract word forms. That is, the particular perceptual features of the word during the study episode (e.g. font, voice) are linked together with either an orthographic word form or a phonological word form; perceptual specificity effects on a subsequent implicit test reflect this binding. Thus, amnesics may be able to show perceptual specificity effects when studied words are unambiguously associated with familiar perceptual formats (Schacter & Church, 1995). When words and voices are repaired from study to test, amnesics do not appear to benefit from the same-voice compared to the repaired-voice conditions (Schacter et al., 1995). Therefore, when familiar voices cue both studied and nonstudied words, amnesics may lack the necessary ability to bind voices with specific studied words.

Viewed from this associative binding perspective, the repaired-voice experiment is much like experiments investigating priming of novel inter-word associations. In the novel association paradigm, subjects who exhibit an associative priming effect benefit from specific associations between a cue word and a target word. In the repaired-voice paradigm, subjects who exhibit voice-specific priming benefit from specific associations between a voice and a target word. Experiments testing novel-association priming are more analogous to the repaired- than the new-voice design, because cues and targets are repaired between study and test in associative priming experiments. In the new-voice design, the associative binding requirements may be less complex or absent. Unfortunately, nothing akin to the new-voice design has been used to study novel word associations in amnesics. Further evidence from experiments using designs analogous to the new-voice design in auditory priming are needed before we can offer confident conclusions concerning the conditions under which amnesic patients do and do not exhibit specificity effects in priming. Moreover, even with normal subjects, perceptual specificity studies have yielded notoriously inconsistent results (for review, see Roediger & McDermott, 1993).

MECHANISMS OF PRIMING IN AMNESIA

Although existing data must be interpreted cautiously, we believe that some theoretical speculation is warranted and may help to stimulate future investigation concerning the mechanisms involved in priming of novel and familiar information in amnesic patients. For instance, Ratcliff and McKoon (1988) have presented a compound-cue theory of priming that might usefully explain the difference between the new- and repaired-voice designs that we considered in the preceding section. Assume that priming is a function of the match between information in memory and the available retrieval cues. In a hypothetical repaired-voice design, the subject studies two words in two different voices (v1-A, v2-B), and then degraded versions of the words (a, b) are tested in either the same voice (v1-a) or the different voice (v2-a). If priming is a linear function of the match between individual words and individual voices— that is, cues are used additively—v2-a and v1-a would be equally primed. In both cases, the test stimulus consists of a primed word and a familiar voice, so the overall amount of additive activation is identical in the two scenarios. Consider, however, an alternative scenario in which voices and words are interactively (or nonlinearly) combined—during study, test, or both. Now, the combination of v1-a would give much stronger priming than v2-a, and a voice-specific priming effect would be observed. Thus, amnesics may lack the normal ability to use cues interactively (see also Humphreys, Bain, & Pike, 1989). In a new-voice design (study: v1-A, v1-B; test: v1-a vs. v2-a) additive cue use would give stronger priming of v1-a than v2-a, so amnesics may show some benefit.

As previously noted, associative priming deficits are generally consistent with the notion that amnesics are unable to encode, store, or retrieve complex associations. From a cognitive neuroscience perspective, this deficit may reflect an inability to bind or integrate information from different information-processing systems. For example, various priming effects appear to depend on perceptual brain mechanisms that process specific types of information (Schacter, 1990a, 1994; Tulving & Schacter, 1990). In the visual domain, priming might be subserved by both a right-hemisphere subsystem that processes low-level visual attributes and by a left-hemisphere subsystem that processes visual word forms at a more abstract level (Marsolek, Kosslyn, & Squire, 1992). Visual-specificity effects might reflect the interactive activation of these mechanisms. In auditory word priming, an abstract auditory word form subsystem interacts with an acoustic subsystem that handles prosodic information (e.g. fundamental frequency and other spectral information about a voice, Church & Schacter, 1994). If these mechanisms additively contribute to priming, their combined influence may only be observable under restricted situations (e.g. new-voice design). However, the interactive combination of voice and abstract word form information can produce voice-specificity effects in normal subjects.

Our proposal is much like other recent theories of the medial temporal lobe contribution to explicit memory (Cohen & Eichenbaum, 1993; Cohen, Poldrack, & Eichenbaum, this issue; Johnson & Chalfonte, 1994; McClelland, McNaughton, & O'Reilly, 1995; Moscovitch, 1994; O'Reilly & McClelland, 1994; Squire, 1994). According to such theories, the medial temporal lobe is critically involved with binding or integrating information that may be stored in separate cortical modules. Extensive integration is required for the construction of explicit memory episodes. Priming may be attributable to the activity of a subset of the cortical mechanisms that collectively contribute to explicit memory. Under conditions in which these subsystems singly or additively influence performance, amnesics show normal implicit memory. When information from these subsystems is interactively combined by normal subjects, amnesics are impaired. The extent of this interaction may vary continuously—from the limited interaction of perceptual mechanisms that produces perceptual specificity effects to the massive interaction of multiple brain mechanisms from which explicit memory emerges.

Our view may appear to be contradicted by the well documented finding of normal priming in amnesic patients when the perceptual format of study and test items remains constant in all conditions. If amnesics do not show normal perceptual specificity effects, it may seem reasonable to expect that control subjects would always show an advantage when study–test format is constant. However, it is possible that most priming experiments are more analogous to the new-voice than the repaired-voice design discussed earlier. Perceptual specificity effects may normally depend on some variation or recombination of perceptual formats. With no such manipulations, the bulk of the evidence suggests that amnesic patients show normal priming.

IS PRIMING GENERALLY IMPAIRED IN AMNESIA?

In contrast to our suggestion that only a specific kind of priming is impaired in amnesic patients, Ostergaard and Jernigan (1993; Ostergaard, 1994) have recently argued that priming is generally impaired in amnesia. They note a number of published reports in which priming in amnesic patients is below that of control subjects. In other cases, it is argued that the experiments often lack the statistical power to detect differences between amnesics and controls if such differences were truly to exist. Ostergaard and Jernigan conclude that implicit and explicit memory are mediated by the same brain mechanisms, especially the medial temporal lobe. By their view, the distinction between implicit and explicit memory need not reflect the contribution of distinct brain systems.

Ostergaard and Jernigan suggest that previously published reports of normal priming in amnesic patients may be an artifact of priming scores being inflated by baseline information-processing impairments. This suggestion has been addressed by testing perceptual identification performance across a wide range of conditions in a mixed group of patients with amnesia (Hamann, Squire, & Schacter, 1995). Non-Korsakoff patients showed baseline performance that was consistently similar to control subjects. Korsakoff patients showed normal baseline performance except when words were extremely small. A final experiment compared the groups on priming at four different baseline levels by manipulating the exposure duration of the words. At each level of exposure duration, Korsakoff and non-Korsakoff amnesics showed both baselines and priming that were not significantly different from controls. Hamann et al. also reviewed a number of other published reports of normal baseline performance and normal priming by amnesic subjects.

Schacter and Church (1995, see Table 1B & C) have reported analogous data in two experiments that used the new-voice design discussed earlier. In Experiment 1, target words were spoken by either a male or female speaker during the study task, and test words were spoken by the same speaker or a new speaker. In this experiment, Korsakoff amnesics showed substantially impaired baseline performance compared to control subjects, together with a trend for greater overall priming. Non-Korsakoff amnesics showed slightly lower baselines than did control subjects and slightly lower levels of priming. Internal analyses suggested that the low levels of baseline performance were attributable to the fact that some patients had difficulty discriminating words spoken by the female voice. In Experiment 2, which used only male voices (one at study and two at test), both Korsakoff and non-Korsakoff amnesic patients showed entirely normal baseline levels of performance together with normal priming. In view of these results and those of Hamann et al., we agree with Ostergaard and Jernigan that baseline performance must be considered when interpreting priming results in amnesics, and that baseline differences can pose interpretive problems (however, we disagree with their claim that lower baselines inevitably inflate priming scores, for reasons discussed at length by Chapman, Chapman, Curran, & Miller, 1994; see also, Schacter & Church, 1995). Nevertheless, such baseline differences are not always present and normal priming has been observed in the absence of baseline differences. Therefore, it seems clear to us that the medial temporal lobe/diencephalic system is not ubiquitously or inevitably involved in priming, as Ostergaard and Jernigan have contended.

CONCLUDING COMMENTS

We have argued that priming may be impaired in amnesic patients under circumstances where normal subjects bind information across multiple brain mechanisms. Mayes and Downes suggest that the comparison of implicit and explicit tasks allows for the separation of storage deficits and retrieval deficits. We agree with some, but not all, aspects of their logic. We think that they are correct that the same cortical storage mechanisms are likely to be involved in both implicit and explicit memory. For example, voice-specificity effects in priming probably depend on much of the same stored voice information that makes a contribution to explicit voice recognition. We also agree that the application of this logic depends on equating the ''informational features'' that are tapped by the implicit and explicit tasks (see Schacter, 1990b). However, if amnesics lack the ability to bind information across multiple brain systems, Mayes and Downes' approach of comparing implicit and explicit task performance may be misleading when the informational features tested require such binding. For instance, using a repaired-voice design, one might have concluded that amnesics do not store any voice information, but the evidence for a specificity effect in the new-voice design suggests a binding deficit rather than a storage deficit. More generally, we do not take the view that whenever amnesic patients exhibit an impairment on an implicit test, a storage deficit can be automatically assumed. If performance on the particular implicit task is enhanced by access to associations between qualitatively different kinds of information (e.g. word and voice), then amnesics may have stored individual information attributes but failed to bind them together into an integrated representation.

Mayes and Downes imply that the distinction between implicit and explicit memory may reduce to a distinction between different retrieval operations that act on common memory representations. We certainly agree that retrieval differences are key to the implicit/explicit distinction. Indeed, the original formulations of the distinction (e.g. Graf & Schacter, 1985; Schacter, 1987) emphasised that it is concerned with different ways in which the effects of past experience can be expressed. Subsequent discussions noted the need to distinguish between two important dimensions of the implicit/explicit distinction: retrieval intentionality (unintentional retrieval vs. intentional retrieval) and subjective recollective experience (aware vs. unaware; see Schacter, Bowers, & Booker, 1989; for related discussion, see Richardson-Klavehn & Bjork, 1988). Implicit memory reflects primarily the bottom-up, nonconscious effects of prior experience on single brain subsystems, and may also involve interactions between a limited number of brain subsystems. Explicit memory reflects the top-down, simultaneous retrieval of information from multiple information-processing brain mechanisms. This massive integration of information (e.g. perceptual, semantic, temporal, spatial, etc.) may be necessary to support conscious recollection of previous experiences. Thus, when priming or similar phenomena are driven largely by individual brain subsystems, retrieval is involuntary and there is no conscious experience of remembering. Limited interactions that we have hypothesised are involved in certain kinds of priming effects (e.g. perceptual and word form features) may be sufficient for influencing behaviour involuntarily, but may not be sufficient for coherent conscious recollection. Alternatively, these kinds of priming effects may constitute an example of what has been called "involuntary conscious memory" (cf Richardson-Klavehn, Gardiner, & Java, 1994; Richardson-Klavehn, Lee, Joubran, & Bjork, 1994; Schacter, 1987, 1994). We think that it is reasonable to hypothesise that as more and more brain systems contribute to a particular retrieval effect, the expressed knowledge becomes more "explicit" and less "implicit".

To summarise, we agree with many of Mayes and Downes' arguments concerning implicit memory, but we have tried to point out and elucidate a number of phenomena and issues that are especially relevant to amnesia. Implicit memory phenomena such as priming are normally spared in amnesia, but deficits may become apparent under conditions in which normal subjects are able to integrate different types of information that are associated with a target stimulus. These ideas are somewhat speculative, still evolving, and based primarily on the results of a few experiments that need replication and extension. Nevertheless, we think that there are still many lessons to be learned by studying implicit memory in amnesic patients, and hope that we have identified a few that merit serious attention in future research.

REFERENCES

Bowers, J., & Schacter, D.L. (1993). Priming of novel information in amnesic patients: Issues and data. In P. Graf & M. Masson (Eds.), *Implicit Memory* (pp.303–326). Hillsdale, NJ: Lawrence Erlbaum Associates Inc.

Carlesimo, G.A. (1994). Perceptual and conceptual priming in amnesic and alcoholic patients. *Neuropsychologia, 32*, 903–921.

Chapman, L.J., Chapman, J.P., Curran, T., & Miller, M.B. (1994). Do children and the elderly show heightened semantic priming? How to answer the question. *Developmental Review, 14*, 159–185.

Church, B.A., & Schacter, D.L. (1994). Perceptual specificity of auditory priming: Implicit memory for voice intonation and fundamental frequency. *Journal of Experimental Psychology: Learning, Memory, and Cognition, 20*, 521–533.

Cohen, N.J., & Eichenbaum, H. (1993). *Memory, amnesia, and the hippocampal system.* Cambridge, MA: MIT Press.

Cohen, N.J., Poldrack, R.A., & Eichenbaum, H. (this issue). Memory for items and memory for relations in the procedural/declarative memory framework. *Memory, 5*(1/2).

Gabrieli, J.D.E., Milberg, W., Keane, M.M., & Corkin, S. (1990). Intact priming of patterns despite impaired memory. *Neuropsychologia, 28* (414–427).

Graf, P., & Schacter, D.L. (1985). Implicit and explicit memory for new associations in normal and amnesic subjects. *Journal of Experimental Psychology: Learning, Memory, and Cognition, 11*, 501–518.

Graf, P., Shimamura, A.P., & Squire, L.R. (1985). Priming across the modalities and priming across category levels: Extending the domain of preserved function in amnesia. *Journal of Experimental Psychology: Learning, Memory, and Cognition, 11*, 386–396.

Haist, F., Musen, G., & Squire, L.R. (1992). Intact priming of words and nonwords in amnesia. *Psychobiology, 19*, 275–285.

Hamann, S.B., Squire, L.R., & Schacter, D.L. (1995). Perceptual thresholds and priming in amnesia. *Neuropsychology, 9*, 3–15.

Humphreys, M.S., Bain, J.D., & Pike, R. (1989). Difference ways to cue a coherent memory system: A theory for episodic, semantic, and procedural tasks. *Psychological Review, 96*, 208–233.

Johnson, M.K., & Chalfonte, B.L. (1994). Binding complex memories: The role of reactivation and the hippocampus. In D.L. Schacter & E. Tulving (Eds.), *Memory Systems 1994* (pp.311–350). Cambridge, MA: MIT Press.

Kinoshita, S., & Wayland, S.V. (1993). Effects of surface features on word-fragment completion in amnesic subjects. *American Journal of Psychology, 106*, 67–80.

Marsolek, C.J., Kosslyn, S.M., & Squire, L.R. (1992). Form-specific visual priming in the right cerebral hemisphere. *Journal of Experimental Psychology: Learning, Memory, and Cognition, 18*, 492–508.

Mayes, A.R., & Downes, J.J. (this issue). What do theories of the functional deficit(s) underlying amnesia have to explain? *Memory, 5*(1/2).

McClelland, J.L., McNaughton, B.L., & O'Reilly, R.C. (1995). Why there are complimentary learning systems in the hippocampus and neocortex: Insights from the successes and failures of connectionist models of learning and memory. *Psychological Review, 102*, 419–457.

Moscovitch, M. (1994). Memory and working with memory: Evaluation of a component process model and comparisons with other models. In D.L. Schacter & E. Tulving (Eds.), *Memory Systems 1994* (pp.269–310). Cambridge, MA: MIT Press.

Musen, G., & Squire, L.R. (1991). Normal acquisition of novel verbal information in amnesia. *Journal of Experimental Psychology: Learning, Memory, and Cognition, 17*, 1095–1104.

Musen, G., & Squire, L.R. (1992). Nonverbal priming in amnesia. *Memory & Cognition, 20*, 441–448.

O'Reilly, R.C., & McClelland, J.L. (1994). Hippocampal conjunctive encoding, storage, and recall: Avoiding a tradeoff. *Hippocampus*, *4*, 661–682.

Ostergaard, A.L. (1994). Dissociations between word priming effects in normal subjects and patients with memory disorders: Multiple memory systems or retrieval. *Quarterly Journal of Experimental Psychology*, *47*A, 331–364.

Ostergaard, A.L., & Jernigan, T.L. (1993). Are word priming and explicit memory mediated by different brain structures? In P. Graf & M.E.J. Masson (Eds.), *Implicit memory* (pp.327–349). Hillsdale, NJ: Lawrence Erlbaum Associates Inc.

Ratcliff, R., & McKoon, G. (1988). A retrieval theory of priming in memory. *Psychological Review*, *95*, 385–408.

Richardson-Klavehn, A., & Bjork, R.A. (1988). Measures of memory. *Annual Review of Psychology*, *39*, 475–543.

Richardson-Klavehn, A., Gardiner, J.M., & Java, R.I. (1994). Involuntary conscious memory and the method of opposition. *Memory*, *2*, 1–29.

Richardson-Klavehn, A., Lee, M.G. Joubran, R., & Bjork, R. (1994). Intention and awareness in perceptual identification priming. *Memory & Cognition*, *22*, 293–312.

Roediger, H.L., & McDermott, K.B. (1993). Implicit memory in normal human subjects. In H. Spinnler & F. Boller (Eds.), *Handbook of neuropsychology* (pp.63–131). Amsterdam: Elsevier.

Schacter, D.L. (1987). Implicit memory: History and current status. *Journal of Experimental Psychology: Learning, Memory, and Cognition*, *13*, 501–518.

Schacter, D.L. (1990a). Perceptual representation systems and implicit memory: Toward a resolution of the multiple memory system debate. In A. Diamond (Ed.), *The development and neural bases of higher cognitive functions* (pp.543–571). New York: Annals of the New York Academy of Sciences.

Schacter, D.L. (1990b). Toward a cognitive neuropsychology of awareness: Implicit knowledge and anosagnosia. *Journal of Clinical and Experimental Neuropsychology*, *12*, 155–178.

Schacter, D.L. (1994). Priming and multiple memory systems: Perceptual mechanisms of implicit memory. In D.L. Schacter & E. Tulving (Eds.), *Memory systems 1994* (pp.233–268). Cambridge, MA: MIT Press.

Schacter, D.L., Bowers, J., & Booker, J. (1989). Intention, awareness, and implicit memory: The retrieval intentionality criterion. In S. Lewandowsky, J.C. Dunn, & K. Kirsner (Eds.), *Implicit memory: Theoretical issues* (pp.47–65). Hillsdale, NJ: Lawrence Erlbaum Associates Inc.

Schacter, D.L., & Church, B.A. (1995). Implicit memory in amnesic patients: When is auditory priming spared? *Journal of the International Neuropsychological Society*, *1*, 434–442.

Schacter, D.L., Church, B., & Bolton, E. (1995). Implicit memory in amnesic patients: Impairment of voice-specific priming. *Psychological Science*, *6*, 20–25.

Schacter, D.L., Cooper, L.A., Tharan, M., & Rubens, A. (1991). Preserved priming of novel objects in patients with memory disorders. *Journal of Cognitive Neuroscience*, *3*, 117–130.

Schacter, D.L., Cooper, L.A., & Treadwell, J. (1993). Preserved priming of novel objects across size transformation in amnesic patients. *Psychological Science*, *4*, 331–335.

Schacter, D.L., & Graf, P. (1986). Preserved learning in amnesic patients: Perspectives from research on direct priming. *Journal of Clinical and Experimental Neuropsychology*, *8*, 727–743.

Schacter, D.L., & Tulving, E. (Eds.). (1994). *Memory systems 1994*. Cambridge, MA: MIT Press.

Shimamura, A.P., & Squire, L.R. (1989). Impaired priming of new associations in amnesia. *Journal of Experimental Psychology: Learning, Memory, and Cognition*, *15*, 721–728.

Squire, L.R. (1994). Declarative and nondeclarative memory: Multiple brain systems supporting learning and memory. In D.L. Schacter & E. Tulving (Eds.), *Memory systems 1994* (pp.203–231). Cambridge, MA: MIT Press.

Tulving, E., & Schacter, D.L. (1990). Priming and human memory systems. *Science*, *247*, 301–305.

MEMORY, 1997, 5 (1/2), 49–71

The Relationships Between Temporal Lobe and Diencephalic Structures Implicated in Anterograde Amnesia

John P. Aggleton

University of Wales, College of Cardiff, UK

Richard C. Saunders

National Institute for Mental Health, Maryland, USA

The relationship between the anterograde amnesic syndromes associated with diencephalic and temporal lobe pathology is examined in the light of recent findings. It is proposed that a common feature of anterograde amnesia is damage to part of an "extended hippocampal system" comprising the hippocampus, the fornix, the mammillary bodies, and the anterior thalamic nuclei. Damage to this system results in deficits in the recall of episodic information, the core symptom of anterograde amnesia. In contrast, lesions in this system need not disrupt tests of recognition memory when they primarily tax familiarity judgements. It is assumed that familiarity judgements depend on other regions (e.g. the rhinal cortex in the case of temporal lobe amnesia) and that the extended hippocampal system is principally involved in those aspects of recognition that are retrieval-based rather than familiarity-based. These proposals arise from new evidence on the performance of delayed nonmatching-to-sample by animals, from a meta-analysis of the performance of amnesic subjects on a test of recognition memory, and from new research into the pattern of connections between the medial temporal lobe and the medial diencephalon in primates.

INTRODUCTION

The review by Mayes and Downes (this issue) identified several important gaps in our understanding of anterograde amnesia and pointed to future areas of profitable research. One gap concerns the anatomical basis of anterograde amnesia. Although dysfunctions in different brain regions can result in anterograde amnesia, the contribution of individual structures and their inter-relationships still remains a matter of uncertainty and debate. The failure to

Requests for reprints should be sent to John Aggleton, School of Psychology, University of Wales, Cardiff, PO Box 901, Cardiff CF1 3YG, Wales, UK. Email: aggleton@cardiff.ac.uk

Much of the research of one of the authors (JPA) has been supported by the Medical Research Council.

resolve this central issue is partly due to lack of amnesic subjects with specific patterns of pathology, but it may also be due to the complexity of the relationships between those regions contributing to amnesia.

Pathology in various brain regions, most typically in the medial diencephalon of the medial temporal lobe, can result in anterograde amnesia. This finding has been viewed in two quite different ways. One interpretation is that the amnesias associated with these different regions result from damage to the same functional system. This view is supported by the many direct anatomical connections between the regions in question, and the similarities between the respective mnemonic deficits. An alternative view is that a number of largely independent dysfunctions can lead to the memory losses characteristic of amnesia. This view emphasises those dissociations that have been reported between different amnesic states (Parkin & Leng, 1990; Parkin & Leng, 1993). It also predicts that connections, such as those through the fornix, which relay information between the medial temporal lobe and the diencephalon need not be crucial for normal memory (Squire & Zola-Morgan, 1991). Clearly these two views must be resolved before the anatomy of anterograde amnesia can be fully understood. The resolution of this issue will also benefit a longstanding practical problem associated with studies of amnesia, namely how best to allocate amnesic subjects into meaningful groups.

The most obvious grouping of amnesic subjects is between those who have principally suffered temporal lobe damage and those who have principally suffered diencephalic damage. This division can readily be applied to some of the more common causes of amnesia (e.g. Korsakoff's disease, herpes encephalitis, vascular accidents, tumours). Furthermore, reports that damage to the fornix, which links the hippocampal formation with the diencephalon, does not result in amnesia indicates that this grouping represents a qualitative division (Bengochea et al., 1954; Woolsey & Nelson, 1975). Other support has come from evidence that, unlike diencephalic amnesics, temporal lobe amnesics display faster than normal rates of forgetting (Huppert & Piercy, 1979; Squire, 1981). This difference has, however, proved difficult to sustain (Freed, Corkin, & Cohen, 1987). Likewise, the view that fornix damage does not cause amnesia has been strongly challenged (Gaffan & Gaffan, 1991), and there is now growing evidence that fornix transection can lead to pronounced impairments in episodic memory (Gaffan, Gaffan, & Hodges, 1991). Perhaps the strongest evidence for a qualitative difference between diencephalic and temporal lobe amnesia would come from a reliable double association, but as yet none has been forthcoming.

The likely limitation of any simple distinction based on diencephalic pathology versus temporal lobe pathology is indicated by the fact that these two brain regions have extensive anatomical interconnections. Further evidence has come from PET studies showing that quite different pathologies can result in abnormal levels of activity in common diencephalic and temporal regions (Fazio et al., 1992). Such findings highlight the difficulty in separating subjects based on a simple division between temporal lobe and diencephalic pathology.

In this review we wish to propose a different neuropathological grouping of anterograde amnesias. This grouping starts with the assumption that a common feature of all diencephalic and temporal lobe amnesias is the involvement of at least part of the "extended hippocampal system" (i.e. the hippocampus, fornix, mammillary bodies, anterior thalamus, and, possibly, the cingulum bundle), and that damage to different parts of this system produces very similar impairments (Delay & Brion, 1969). It should be added that the term "hippocampus" refers to the hippocampal fields CA1–4, the dentate gyrus, and the subicular complex. The rhinal cortices (perirhinal and entorhinal) are treated separately. Amnesics can then be initially divided into (a), those with memory dysfunctions due almost solely to selective lesions in parts of the extended hippocampal system, and (b), those with additional pathology in certain subcortical and cortical sites that can extend the nature of the memory loss so that it involves other aspects of memory. Within this latter group there are likely to be further divisions based on the locus of the pathology, in particular, the extent of frontal lobe and temporal lobe involvement. The frontal lobe dysfunctions are assumed to result from direct cortical damage, or from pathology in the thalamic nucleus medialis dorsalis, or from a combination of both (e.g. Korsakoff's disease). The temporal lobe dysfunctions are assumed to arise from pathology that involves regions such as the rhinal cortex, the parahippocampal gyrus, the temporal pole, and amygdala. The starting point of this proposal, that all amnesias involve dysfunctions in the extended hippocampal system, helps to explain why it has proved so difficult to demonstrate a reliable double dissociation between different amnesic conditions.

Three strands of evidence point to these proposed distinctions: (1) The effects of selective limbic lesions in animals on the acquisition and performance of delayed nonmatching-to-sample tasks; (2) A comparison between the ability of amnesic subjects to perform tests of recall and tests of recognition; (3) The results of tracing studies that have mapped the pattern of anatomical connections between the temporal lobe and the medial diencephalon.

1. ANIMAL STUDIES

The lack of patients with confirmed, selective pathology has led to numerous studies examining the effects of selective lesions in animals. The favoured approach has been to compare the performance of animals on tests of delayed nonmatching-to-sample (DNMS). In these tests, which tax recognition memory, the animal is first shown a distinctive stimulus (the sample). After the delay of between a few seconds to a few minutes, during which the animal is left in the apparatus, the animal is required to select between two stimuli, the now familiar sample and a novel alternative. Selection of the novel item (i.e. nonmatching) leads to a reward. Typically the stimuli are distinctive, three-dimensional "junk" objects and are "trial-unique" (that is, a given object does not reappear within a series of sessions). The choice of this task arises from the fact that a deficit in recognition memory is regarded as a prominent, core feature of amnesia (Haist, Shimamura, & Squire, 1992; Parkin & Leng, 1993; Squire & Shimamura, 1986). Furthermore, when amnesic patients have been given memory tests closely modelled on the DNMS design they perform poorly (Aggleton, Nicol, Huston, & Fairbairn, 1988; Squire, Zola-Morgan, & Chen, 1988).

Before considering the results of individual experiments it must be pointed out that the surgical method used when making the lesion may be of enormous importance. The favoured technique for research using monkeys has often been aspiration, even for subcortical sites. This is because the target region can be confirmed at the time of surgery, an extremely important factor when studying small-sized groups. On the other hand, stereotaxy has the advantage that it helps to minimise damage to regions outside the target area and it facilitates the use of neurotoxins, so aiding the selectivity of lesions. The importance of distinguishing between these different surgical techniques is highlighted by the fact that the direct surgical approach most often used to aspirate the amygdala or the hippocampus in monkeys results in additional temporal damage (Gaffan & Lim, 1991). This additional damage includes the rhinal cortex, an area of particular importance. Indeed, lesions just restricted to the rhinal cortices can themselves produce very severe DNMS deficits (Meunier, Bachevalier, Mishkin, & Murray, 1993; Murray, 1992; Squire & Zola-Morgan, 1991).

DNMS tasks using trial-unique or session-unique stimuli have been devised for rats as well as monkeys, and the effects of various selective lesions appear to be broadly consistent across the different species. Damage to the perirhinal cortex in monkeys severely impairs DNMS performance (Fig. 1; Meunier et al., 1993; Murray, 1992; Squire & Zola-Morgan, 1991), and there is similar, preliminary evidence from studies of lesions centred in the perirhinal area of rats (Mumby & Pinel, 1994; Otto & Eichenbaum, 1992). Entorhinal damage may also contribute to the rhinal DNMS deficit (Meunier et al., 1993). In contrast to these effects, lesions of the hippocampus have much milder effects (Fig. 1; Mishkin, 1978; Murray, 1992), but it must be remembered that these surgeries also involve caudal parts of the rhinal cortex. Indeed, in those studies where hippocampal lesions result in minimal rhinal damage standard DNMS performance may be largely unaffected (Aggleton, Hunt, & Rawlins, 1986b; Alvarez, Zola-Morgan, & Squire, 1995; O'Boyle, Murray, & Mishkin, 1993; but see Beason-Held, Rosene, & Moss, 1993). As a consequence it appears that selective hippocampal damage is not sufficient to disrupt DNMS performance when it is tested in the standard manner. Consistent with this is the finding that fornix lesions often have little, if any, effect on DNMS performance in monkeys (Gaffan, Gaffan, & Harrison, 1984; Bachevalier, Saunders, & Mishkin, 1985a; Zola-Morgan, Squire,

DNMS (monkeys)

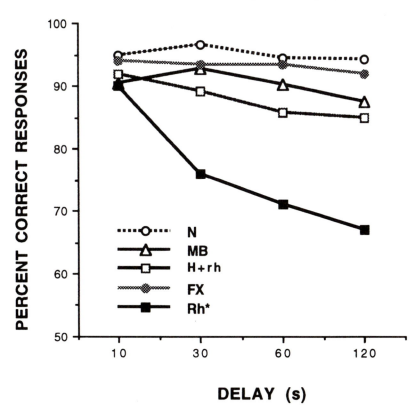

DELAY (s)

FIG. 1. Performance of monkeys on the delayed nonmatching-to-sample task after surgery to remove the fornix (FX), mammillary bodies (MB), hippocampus (H+rh), and rhinal cortex (Rh). Although the data (MB, Aggleton & Mishkin, 1985; FX, Bachevalier et al., 1985a; H+rh, Murray & Mishkin, 1986; Rh, Meunier et al., 1993) come from different studies, they are from the same laboratory in which test procedures have remained constant. The hippocampal surgeries (H+rh) involved the caudal part of the perirhinal cortex, and so may have exaggerated the size of deficit associated with selective hippocampal damage. The mammillary body data came from the four animals in that study with the most complete lesions (Aggleton & Mishkin, 1985). All studies used cynomolgus monkeys (*Macaca fascicularis*) except that by Meunier et al. (1993) in which rhesus monkeys (*Macaca mulatta*) were used. This difference is likely to have reduced the size of the perirhinal deficit when compared with the other groups (Murray, 1992). Normal data (N) from Aggleton and Mishkin (1985).

& Amaral, 1989), and can spare DNMS performance in rats (Aggleton, Hunt, & Shaw, 1990; Rothblat & Kromer, 1991; Shaw & Aggleton, 1993). Fornix damage can, however, exacerbate the effects of other lesions that disrupt DNMS performance (Bachevalier, Parkinson, & Mishkin, 1985b), and so this tract does appear to convey information that can aid performance of the task. Although this may reflect the involvement of hippocampal connections, it might alternatively reflect the involvement of entorhinal–thalamic projections (Meunier et al., 1993), some of which are carried in the fornix (see Section 3).

It now appears that the hippocampal involvement in DNMS performance is very minor compared to that of the adjacent rhinal cortices, a view borne out by single unit recording studies in monkeys and rats (Brown, Wilson, & Riches, 1987; Zhu, Brown, & Aggleton, 1995a) and recent c-fos experiments (Zhu, Brown, McCabe, & Aggleton, 1995b). Although confirmation of this conclusion will have to await the result of more studies into the effects of cytotoxic lesions in the primate perirhinal cortex as well as the hippocampus, it will be seen that this conclusion is largely consistent with what is presently known about the effects of selective damage to the diencephalic targets of the hippocampus.

There has been less research into the effects of diencephalic lesions on DNMS performance in animals. The few studies show that mammillary body lesions do not disrupt DNMS tasks performed by monkeys or rats (Aggleton et al., 1990; Aggleton & Mishkin, 1985; Zola-Morgan et al., 1989a). In contrast, thalamic lesions in the region of nucleus medialis dorsalis (MD) impair both the acquisition and performance of DNMS tasks (Aggleton & Mishkin, 1983b; Hunt & Aggleton, 1991; Zola-Morgan & Squire, 1985b). More anterior thalamic lesions made by aspiration can also disrupt DNMS performance (Aggleton & Mishkin, 1983b), and exacerbate the effects of lesions in the region of medialis dorsalis (Aggleton & Mishkin, 1983a,b). The approach used to reach the anterior thalamus in these studies did, however, result in much fibre damage, and there is a need to re-examine these findings using more discrete lesion techniques. This view is reinforced by recent research showing that selective neurotoxic lesions of the anterior thalamus in rats do not disrupt the spontaneous recognition of novel objects (Aggleton, Neave, Nagle, & Hunt, 1995a).

Taken together, DNMS studies indicate that the hippocampus and its direct diencephalic targets (the mammillary bodies and the anterior thalamus) have only a minor role in recognition memory when it is assessed in this manner. If the DNMS task is truly a benchmark test for anterograde amnesia (Zola-Morgan & Squire, 1985a) then one would have to conclude that pathology in these regions is relatively unimportant for the appearance of anterograde amnesia. In fact it is known that the same set of structures (i.e. the "extended hippocampal system") is vital for other aspects of memory, and this finding might help resolve the anomaly of how hippocampal pathology can seem so central to amnesia but barely affect DNMS performance.

It has long been known that damage to the rat hippocampus can produce striking impairments on a variety of spatial memory tasks (O'Keefe & Nadel, 1978), including delayed forced alternation in a T-maze (Aggleton et al., 1986b). The sensitivity of this task to hippocampal dysfunction allows it to be used as a behavioural assay with which to test the contribution of diencephalic regions to mnemonic tasks dependent on the hippocampus. Such studies show that normal performance depends on the mammillary bodies as well as the hippocampus, fornix, and anterior thalamic nuclei (Aggleton et al., 1995a; Aggleton & Sahgal, 1993), the magnitude of the lesion deficit being greatest after hippocampectomy and least after mammillary body damage. Similar results are found for an automated test of spatial working memory, delayed nonmatching-to-position in an operant chamber (Aggleton et al., 1992; Aggleton & Sahgal, 1993). These findings point to an extended hippocampal system which may not be necessary for recognition memory but which is critical for normal spatial memory in the rat. A comparable series of spatial experiments has yet to be conducted with monkeys, although it has been shown that fornix lesions impair T-maze forced alternation in rhesus monkeys (Murray et al., 1989), and that hippocampal, fornix, and mammillary body lesions can all markedly disrupt place discrimination reversals (Jones & Mishkin, 1972; Mahut, 1972; Holmes, Butters, Jacobson, & Stein, 1983).

These findings suggest that certain diencephalic targets of the hippocampus are very closely involved in the normal functioning of the hippocampus. As a consequence the distinctions based on temporal lobe versus diencephalic amnesia are likely to be misleading if these syndromes are, in part, a result of damage to these closely integrated structures. The difficulty in dissociating between diencephalic and temporal lobe syndromes might be further heightened if it were to be shown that the reciprocal projections back to the temporal lobe from the diencephalon constitute part of this functional system. Preliminary findings indicate that the cingulum bundle, which conveys projections from the anterior thalamic nuclei to the temporal region, may conduct information that is important for allocentric spatial memory in the rat (Aggleton et al., 1995b). This result is consistent with the notion of a partially reciprocal temporal lobe–diencephalic system.

Although these studies have focused on spatial memory there is growing evidence that this same functional system is involved in other, closely related aspects of memory (Gaffan, 1992b, 1994b; Rawlins et al., 1993). An example of this concerns evidence that lesions of the fornix will disrupt the acquisition of concurrent discriminations when the stimuli to be discriminated are complex scenes that often contain common elements (Gaffan, 1992b). This finding has recently been explored in more detail and it appears that the critical feature is whether the task requires the spatial array of the elements in the stimuli to be discriminated (Gaffan, 1994b). These results have been taken to indicate that the fornix, and hence the hippocampus, is important for the scene-specific memory of objects (Gaffan, 1992a, 1994a,b). There is also recent evidence that the mammillary bodies are involved in this same process (Gaffan, Parker, & Gutnikov, 1995). As a consequence the hippocampal system is thought to aid the normal recall of episodic information as it permits the subject to distinguish or recreate the unique scene associated with the to-be-remembered item (Tulving,

1983; Gaffan, 1992a, 1994b), a process that will reduce interference from other similar events (Gaffan, 1994b). From this it can be predicted that anterior thalamic lesions will also disrupt similar concurrent discriminations, although this has yet to be tested. It can be seen that these recent findings are consistent with the notion that damage to the extended hippocampal system will disrupt the normal recall of episodic memory, the hallmark of anterograde amnesia.

If it is accepted that the extended hippocampal system mainly contributes to recall rather than recognition, then the severe DNMS deficits associated with lesions in either the medial temporal lobe or the medial diencephalon (Aggleton & Mishkin, 1983a; Mishkin, 1978; Murray, 1992; Squire & Zola-Morgan, 1991) must involve other structures. In the case of the medial temporal lobe this appears to be the perirhinal cortex (Meunier et al., 1993; Murray, 1992; Squire & Zola-Morgan, 1991) the entorhinal cortex (Meunier et al., 1993), and perhaps the parahippocampal cortex (Squire & Zola-Morgan, 1991, Zola-Morgan, Squire, Amaral, & Suzuki, 1989; but see Ramus, Zola-Morgan, & Squire, 1994). Although the perirhinal region has extensive connections with the hippocampus, its contribution to recognition memory seems to be largely independent of that structure. This conclusion comes from the difference in the severity of the DNMS deficit following rhinal and hippocampal lesions (see Fig. 1) and is reinforced by recent evidence of a double dissociation between the contributions of the perirhinal cortex and the hippocampus to memory (Gaffan, 1994a). In that study it was found that perirhinal lesions produced a much greater disruption of a delayed matching-to-sample task than fornix transection. In contrast, the fornix lesions impaired a spatial task while perirhinal lesions had little or no effect (Gaffan, 1994a).

The origin of the diencephalic DNMS deficit is less certain. Evidence from animal lesion studies indicates that the thalamic nucleus medialis dorsalis (MD) contributes to the deficit (Aggleton & Mishkin, 1983b; Hunt & Aggleton, 1991; Zola-Morgan & Squire, 1985b). This accords with the fact that MD receives direct inputs from the perirhinal cortex, via the inferior thalamic peduncle (Aggleton, Desimone, & Mishkin, 1992; Murray, 1992). It is, however, the case that the magnitude of the MD lesion deficit is insufficient to account for the full extent of the diencephalic DNMS impairment (Aggleton & Mishkin, 1983a,b). This may be because the published studies have failed to destroy all of MD, but it seems more likely that damage to other fibre tracts in the region of the medial thalamus is required in order to produce the full recognition deficit. The latter proposal is consistent with the location of the pathology in thalamic amnesia (Cramon, von Hubel, & Schuri, 1985; Graff-Radford, Tranel, Van Hoesen, & Brandt, 1990; Markowitsch, 1988) and the apparent lack of amnesics with lesions confined to MD (Markowitsch, 1982; Kritechevsy, Graf-Radford, & Damasio, 1987). One possibility is that damage to the mammillothalamic tract not only brings about a recall deficit but also accentuates the recognition impairment associated with MD damage. The mammillothalamic tract effect on recognition memory might be due to the disruption of fornical projections to the mammillary bodies and anterior thalamus, which on their own are often not vital for DNMS performance, but when combined with other damage may potentiate lesion effects. Evidence for this comes from the effect of fornix transection when combined with lesions of the amygdala and temporal stem (Bachevalier et al., 1985b), and from the mild deficit associated with fornix transection on a delayed matching-to-sample task that used complex, naturalistic scenes as stimulus material (Gaffan, 1994a). It should be added that although these fornical effects imply a contribution from the hippocampus, they could prove to result from entorhinal disconnections (Meunier et al., 1993) (see Section 3). It is also possible that damage close to the mammillothalamic tract might involve other important fibre tracts. For example, lesions in this region may increase the disruption of fibres connected with the prefrontal cortex (Bachevalier & Mishkin, 1986; Schacter, 1987), and this might further add to the thalamic recognition deficit. The resolution of these issues will require a systematic analysis of highly selective diencephalic lesions.

2. RECALL AND RECOGNITION IN AMNESIA

One of the most striking conclusions from this brief review of animal studies is that there is a mismatch between those areas often thought to be responsible for anterograde amnesia and those that disrupt DNMS performance. To account for this it is suggested that damage to the hippocampus or its diencephalic targets impairs the recall of episodic information (i.e. produces amnesia) but need not severely affect recognition (i.e. spares DNMS performance). In contrast, those pathologies that affect *both* the extended hippocampal system and other cortical regions may severely disrupt recall and recognition. Because this latter group of subjects is far commoner than those with selective damage, the large majority of amnesic subjects will perform poorly when tested on analogues of DNMS tasks.

Up to now recognition has been considered as if it were a single process. In fact, there is a strong consensus that recognition involves two processes (Gardiner & Parkin, 1990; Horton, Pavlick, & Moulin-Julian, 1993; Jacoby & Dallas, 1981; Mandler, 1980). One of these permits a recognition judgement to be made on the basis of stimulus familiarity (stimulus fluency). The other involves the retrieval of episodic or contextual information associated with the item to be recognised. These processes are seen as additive and separate (Mandler, 1980). Following from the previous discussion concerning the contribution of the extended hippocampal system to episodic memory, it is assumed that damage to this system spares familiarity-based recognition but can disrupt retrieval-based components. As a consequence, hippocampal system damage will be expected to disrupt only certain tests of recognition, i.e. those in which explicit retrieval of information about the target item is used to aid recognition. Related to this it is assumed that the standard DNMS task, as given to monkeys or rats, is essentially a test of familiarity judgements and so is little affected by extended hippocampal system damage. This assumption concerning the DNMS task will, however, require independent support as there is the danger of lapsing into a circular argument.

A clear prediction from the current proposals is that a few amnesics will show disproportionately mild recognition deficits in the face of substantial recall deficits, and that these cases will be those with more selective damage to the hippocampus or its subcortical outputs. There is, however, a major obstacle in testing this prediction. This concerns the relative rarity of amnesic subjects with discrete damage to the hippocampal system. In order to minimise this problem we decided to compare performance on a standard test of recognition that has been administered to many amnesic subjects (Aggleton & Shaw, 1996). We therefore conducted a literature survey of all amnesics who had taken the Recognition Memory Test or RMT (Warrington, 1984). This test is divided into two parts, one a test of word recognition, the other a test of face recognition. In each part the subject is shown a series of 50 sample stimuli (words or faces) and then tested in a forced-choice manner, i.e. each sample is paired with a novel stimulus. The subject must indicate which word or face they previously saw. From this it can be seen that the RMT procedure closely resembles delayed matching-to-sample with a list of 50 items.

The survey produced 33 studies which gave the RMT scores of a total of 112 people described as suffering from anterograde amnesia. These were then placed in 11 groups according to their aetiology and pathology. The groups were: alcoholic Korsakoff (n = 39), Post-encephalitic (n = 19), Anterior Communicating Artery Aneurysm (n = 9), Splenial tumours (n = 7), Bilateral Thalamic infarcts or tumours (n = 8), Left Thalamic infarcts, (n = 4), Fornix (n = 2), Hippocampus (n = 3), Other Temporal Lobe (n = 3), Mammillary Body region (n = 2), and those amnesics who did not fit into any of the preceding groups (Others n = 16). Mean performance levels are shown in Fig. 2.

Comparisons using age-matched, normative data provided by Warrington (1984) revealed that only three amnesic groups failed to show a clear impairment (P > .05, one-tailed tests) on both the Words and the Faces subtests. These were the Hippocampus, Fornix, and Mammillary Body subjects. This lack of impairment for both RMT subtests persisted even when these three groups were combined (n = 7) (Aggleton & Shaw, 1996). These same three groups also performed significantly better than the Post-encephalitic amnesics on the RMT subtests. These findings indicate that damage focused in the hippocampal system can largely spare recognition, as measured by the RMT. Additional support has come from a series of five patients with bilateral fornix damage, reported after the completion of this review (McMackin, Cockburn, Anslow, & Gaffan, 1995). All five cases were described as showing moderate or severe losses of memory, yet of the ten RMT scores (five words and five faces), only one was more than 1.65 standard deviations (P < .05) below the normative scores for that age group (Warrington, 1984). This apparent lack of effect of hippocampal system damage clearly echoes the findings from animal studies using the DNMS task.

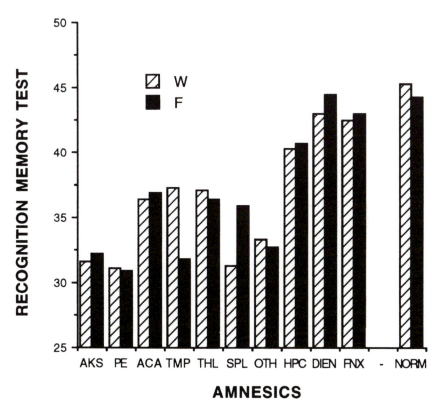

AMNESICS

FIG. 2. Mean performance of groups of amnesics with bilateral damage on the Recognition Memory Test (Warrington, 1984) from literature survey by Aggleton and Shaw (1996). Scores for both the Words (W) and Faces (F) subtests are shown. The normal data (NORM) come from 107 subjects aged 45–54 years (Warrington, 1984). The abbreviations refer to the principal site of pathology or aetiology: ACA, anterior communicating artery aneurysm; AKS, alcoholic Korsakoff syndrome; FNX, fornix: HPC, hippocampus; DIEN, mammillary body region; OTH, other amnesics; PE, post-encephalitic; SPL, splenium; THL, thalamus; TMP, other temporal lobe;

Although the evidence of an unusually mild recognition deficit in those cases with selective hippocampal system damage is consistent with the main proposal outlined in this review, there are other possible explanations for this pattern of results. One possibility is that the criteria for inclusion in these three groups (Hippocampus, Fornix, Mammillary Body) may have led to a bias towards those subjects with only partial damage to the critical region. This is because those subjects with complete or near-complete damage to these structures are the same subjects most likely to have pathology that extended into other, adjacent regions, and so cause them to be placed in different groups. It is therefore possible that the subjects in these three groups only suffered partial damage to the relevant structures and so only suffered a mild amnesia. Given that recognition tasks are typically much easier than tests of recall, this might then explain the apparent lack of an RMT deficit.

This alternative explanation rests on the assumption that the subjects in the Hippocampus, Fornix, and Mammillary Body groups displayed only a mild amnesia. In order to test this possibility we examined that subset of amnesics who had been tested on both subtests of the RMT and on the Wechsler Memory Scale Revised or WMSr (Wechsler, 1987). The WMSr was selected because the Delayed Recall and the General Memory indices that are derived from the test are regarded as valid measures of the severity of amnesia (Butters et al., 1988). This produced a group of five amnesics with Hippocampal System damage and 27 Other Amnesics. As expected, the mean RMT scores of the two groups differed for both the Words [Hippocampal System = 41.4, Other Amnesics = 34.7, $t(30) = 2.14$, $P < .05$] and the Faces [Hippocampal System = 42.2, Other Amnesics = 34.9, $t(30) = 2.40$, $P < .05$] subtests. In contrast, the mean scores of the two groups of amnesics for the Delayed Recall (Hippocampal System = 60.4, Other Amnesics = 56.9) and the General Memory (Hippocampal System = 76.4, Other Amnesics = 68.4) indices did not differ (both $P > .2$). The somewhat lower performance of the Other Amnesics on the General Memory Index is principally due to the alcoholic Korsakoff subjects (n = 14) who comprised the majority of the Other Amnesics and who are known to score particularly poorly on this measure (Butters et al., 1988).

A final comparison examined whether the Hippocampal System subjects showed an unusually large discrepancy between their RMT and WMSr scores. An analysis of variance was used to compared the combined scores for the two RMT tests (Words plus Faces) with the Delayed Recall Index from the WMSr (Fig. 3). The group by test interaction, indicative of a disproportionate difference between the two groups, was found to be close to significance [$F(1,30) = 3.65$, $P = .066$]. Among the Other Amnesics, however, there was one subject who may have suffered damage to the extended hippocampal system but not to other regions that might disrupt memory. This amnesic was diagnosed as having a hypothalamic tumour (Parkin & Hunkin, 1993), which is likely to have directly invaded the mammillary bodies. The precise locus of this tumour was not, however, described. In view of the uncertain status of this subject he was removed from the previous analysis. This resulted in a significant interaction between RMT scores and Delayed Recall Index for the two groups of amnesics [$F(1,29) = 5.47$, $P = .026$]. It should be added that this hypothalamic tumour case could not be included in the Mammillary Body group as the extent of his pathology had not been directly assessed. In contrast, all of the subjects in the three Hippocampal System groups (Hippocampus, Fornix, Mammillary Body) had received at least MRI confirmation of the location of their pathology. In the case of two of the Hippocampus subjects, post-mortem reports (Rempel-Clower, Zola-Morgan, & Squire, 1994) were able to verify that both patients had suffered

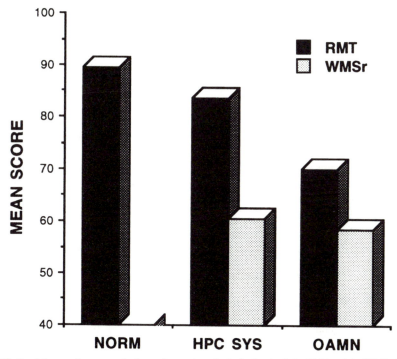

FIG. 3.   Mean performance of subset of amnesics who had taken both the RMT and the WMSr. The amnesics are divided between those with selective, hippocampal system damage (hippocampus or mammillary body, n = 5) and those with other patterns of pathology (n = 27). The RMT scores for the two subtests (Words and Faces) have been combined while the WMSr scores refer to the Delayed Recall index. The normal data (NORM) come from 107 subjects aged 45–54 years (Warrington, 1984).

complete, bilateral lesions of the CA1 field of the hippocampus. In one of these cases there was additional damage in CA3, and minor pathology outside the hippocampal region in both cases. From the pathology in these two cases and that in a third amnesic patient, RB, who had also been carefully studied (Zola-Morgan, Squire, & Amaral, 1986), it would appear that damage in the hippocampal region is sufficient to produce anterograde amnesia.

It can be seen that these analyses are consistent with the conclusion that subjects with selective hippocampal system damage can have an amnesia of standard severity but show relative sparing of recognition memory. The results from the RMT test are, however, preliminary and should at this stage be treated with caution. This is because the pattern of recognition test results might be task-dependent. As has been indicated, the extent to which a particular recognition task taxes familiarity-based judgements may prove to be of critical importance. With this in mind it is relevant to note that the Faces subtest of the RMT (the

Words subtest was not examined) is not susceptible to extreme switches in context between the sample phase and the test phase (Parkinson & Aggleton, 1994). This is consistent with the view that this test, as standardly applied, makes little demand on retrieval-based processes. In addition, there is evidence that changes to the type of stimuli or to the way they are tested (forced-choice versus yes/no) might affect the outcome of recognition tests given to amnesics (Hanley, Davies, Downes, & Mayes, 1994; Parkin, Yeoman, & Bindschaedler, 1994). Further complications arise from the fact that some tests of recognition are prone to ceiling effects. This particular problem was considered in a recent study of an amnesic subject with selective mammillary body damage (Holdstock, Shaw, & Aggleton, 1995). By carefully manipulating task difficulty it was possible to show that this factor could not account for the sparing of forced-choice recognition over those delays tested. Thus, in spite of these issues, it is clear that the RMT results support the proposal that hippocampal system damage is sufficient to induce the severe recall deficit in amnesia and that the main recognition deficit principally arises from dysfunctions in other regions.

3. ANATOMICAL CONSIDERATIONS

The third strand of evidence concerns research into the anatomical connections between the medial temporal lobe and the medial diencephalon in the primate brain. This information principally comes from axonal transport studies in monkeys (rhesus macaque and cynomolgus macaque) as it has not been possible to study the equivalent connections in the human brain in the same detail. In light of the current proposals a number of key anatomical questions emerge.

A central question concerns the extent of the perirhinal cortex projections to the medial diencephalon. This could help to identify that part of the diencephalic amnesic syndrome thought not to depend on the hippocampal system, and also clarify the relationship between the DNMS deficits found in monkeys following certain diencephalic and temporal lobe lesions. It will also be important to discover the route of these rhinal–thalamic connections and the extent to which they rely on the fornix or on other pathways. This is of interest because transection of the fornix appears to disrupt the recall of episodic events but may often have only a small effect on recognition. According to the current proposal this is because the fornix largely carries information from the hippocampus and so does not contribute to familiarity judgements. It is, however, likely that the current proposals would have to be modified if it were found that perirhinal efferents contribute substantially to the fornix or if there were significant hippocampal projections to the mammillary bodies and anterior thalamic nuclei that do not pass through the fornix.

(i) Hippocampal (Subicular) Projections to the Thalamus and Mammillary Bodies

The hippocampal projections to the anterior thalamic nuclei (nuclei AV/AM/ AD) and the mammillary bodies (MB), which originate in the subiculum, all appear to travel through the fornix. Thus if retrograde tracers are placed in the MB or in the anterior thalamic nuclei and the fornix is cut, no labelled cells are found in the subiculum (Saunders, Aggleton, & Mishkin, 1996). Similarly, if the fornix is cut and anterograde tracers are placed in the subiculum no label is found in the mammillary bodies or the anterior thalamic nuclei (Aggleton et al., 1986a). The other major target for hippocampal–thalamic projections is the lateral dorsal nucleus (LD), but this receives both a fornical and a non-fornical component (Aggleton et al., 1986a). Like the projections to the anterior thalamic nuclei, cells in the deep layers of the subiculum contribute to the fornix projection to LD (Saunders et al., 1996). But in addition to this subicular contribution there is a substantial component that arises in the pre- and parasubiculum that does not pass through the fornix (Saunders et al., 1996). This projection appears to course laterally to the temporal stem before passing caudally towards the pulvinar. It then arches around and over the pulvinar before coursing rostrally to reach LD (Aggleton et al., 1986a). It can be seen, therefore, that the fornix carries all of the hippocampal projections to the mammillary bodies and to the anterior thalamic nuclei AM, AV, and AD, but that there is a sizeable alternative projection to LD. As yet, projections from the hippocampus to the medial dorsal nucleus of the thalamus (MD) have not been demonstrated.

(ii) Entorhinal Cortical Projections to the Thalamus

The entorhinal cortex (area 28) is, for the most part, positioned rostral and medial to the hippocampus with the most caudal part, 28M, medially adjacent to the pes hippocampi (Saunders & Rosene, 1988). Area 28 has usually been considered a transitional cortex between the lateral neocortex of the temporal lobe and the archicortex of the hippocampus. It is from the cells of layers 2 and 3 that the perforant path originates and thus provides the major access for cortical information into the hippocampus. Historically its role was considered little more than a relay of cortical information into and out of the hippocampus and is often regarded as part of, or an extension of, the hippocampus. Recent anatomical studies (Aggleton et al., 1986a; Rosene & Saunders, 1987; Russchen, Amaral, & Price, 1987; Suzuki, 1996; Saunders et al., 1996) have demonstrated that this region has a much wider array of subcortical projections than previously thought, and as a consequence its mnemonic contributions may be more diverse than initially proposed.

All divisions of the entorhinal cortex project to the medial thalamic region. Results from injections of both retrograde and anterograde tracers have demonstrated projections to both the anterior thalamic nuclei and the medial dorsal nucleus, as well as the mammillary bodies. The routes of these projections have been determined by cutting the fornix or the central amygdalofugal pathway prior to the injection of tracers in the thalamus or temporal lobe (Aggleton et al., 1986a; Saunders et al., 1996). These manipulations have demonstrated the variability of these routes.

Injections of amino acids in the entorhinal cortex result in light label in AV/ AM (Aggleton et al., 1986a) and this is consistent with the finding of retrogradely labelled cells in area 28 after AV injections (Saunders et al., 1996). The number of these entorhinal cells is, however, considerably less than that seen in the subiculum. Transection of the fornix resulted in a reduction of these labelled cells but did not eliminate all of them, suggesting a very light nonfornical component to the AV/AM projection. Indeed anterograde tracing experiments appear to confirm a very light nonfornical projection via the temporal stem/temporo-pulvinar bundle that passes LD to reach AV/AM. As for the projection to MD, it also appears to arise from all parts of area 28, but it only has one route, that via the inferior thalamic peduncle. Fibres could be traced through and around the amygdala, after which they join the interior thalamic peduncle to enter the rostral thalamus and pass around the mammillothalamic tract before reaching the magnocellular part of MD.

In contrast to the relatively light projections to AV/AM and MD, there is a much denser projection from the entorhinal cortex to the lateral dorsal nucleus. For the most part the source of this projection is located in the medial bank of the rhinal sulcus (28S). This LD projection, like that from the pre- and parasubiculum, does not course through the fornix. These nonfornical LD projections, in some part, appear to follow the same route as the pre- and parasubiculum projections to LD. They might also contribute to the inferior thalamic peduncle and then course caudally to LD.

Thus the entorhinal cortex has connections to rostral (anterior thalamic nuclei) and caudal (MD and LD) parts of the medial thalamus with fibres coursing not only through the fornix but via other routes. Some of these nonfornical projections pass in close proximity to the mammillothalamic tract. In addition to these thalamic projections there is a light projection from all sections of area 28 to the MB. In comparison to the subicular projection to the MB, which arises from an enormous number of cells, the entorhinal projection to the MB arises from a very limited population of cells. This small projection courses through the fornix.

(iii) Perirhinal Cortex Projections to the Thalamus and Mammillary Bodies

The perirhinal cortex is closely associated with the entorhinal cortex and like the entorhinal cortex provides a relay of cortical information into the hippocampus. This region lateral to the rhinal sulcus is composed of areas 35 and 36. Area 35 comprises the lateral bank of the rhinal sulcus and area 36 extends laterally as a transition area between the rhinal cortex and the temporal neocortex. Tract tracing studies, both anterograde and retrograde, have shown no evidence of a projection from the perirhinal cortex to the anterior nuclei of the thalamus. In contrast there appears to be a reasonably dense projection to magnocellular MD (Aggleton et al., 1986a; Russchen et al., 1987). Transection of the VAF path resulted in an absence of retrogradely labelled cells in the perirhinal cortex after injections into MD, thus the route to MD is similar to that from the entorhinal cortex and the amygdala. In contrast to the entorhinal cortex, there was no evidence of a projection from perirhinal cortex to LD.

(iv) Origin of the Fornical Fibres in the Temporal Lobe

A direct way of determining those fields of the temporal lobe that contribute efferent fibres to the fornix is to place HRP gel into a cut section of the fibre tract (Saunders et al., 1996). Retrogradely labelled cells, indicating the origin of the fornix, are found throughout the hippocampus and in the superficial layers of the entorhinal and perirhinal cortex. Once again, this shows that the fornix does carry some non-hippocampal efferents, i.e. those from the entorhinal and perirhinal cortices. Although this technique cannot ascertain where these projections are targeted, it has been shown that the entorhinal cortex has a relatively small number of fornical projections to the MB and AV/AM. The perirhinal cortex does not, however, project via the fornix to medial thalamic regions and these labelled cells may reflect target regions outside the diencephalon.

In conclusion, there are relatively few nonhippocampal and nonfornical projections to AV/AM and LD from the medial temporal lobe. The most robust thalamic projections from outside of the hippocampus are from the entorhinal cortex and perirhinal cortex to LD and MD, respectively. In addition, there is a substantial nonfornical projection from the pre- and parasubiculum to LD. This appears to leave the projections from the rhinal cortex to MD to account for most of the recognition deficit found in diencephalic amnesia, but disconnection studies using monkeys have called this into question by showing that a lesion thought to cut this pathway produces only mild DNMS impairments (Bachevalier et al., 1985a). This study also showed that fornix lesions could exacerbate this mild DNMS deficit, a result that may reflect the transection of the relatively few entorhinal efferents that use the fornix with a loss of the retrieval components of recognition. The relative lack of effect associated with any individual disconnection suggests that the diencephalic recognition deficit stems from a combination of these effects, as well as a disruption of frontal connections (Bachevalier & Mishkin, 1986). Finally, in the light of the current proposal it would be interesting to know whether LD, which is sometimes regarded as part of the anterior thalamic nuclei, contributes to either recognition or recall processes, and whether damage to this region can accentuate other memory deficits.

GENERAL CONCLUSIONS

Evidence from a variety of sources appears consistent with a revised grouping of amnesias. In this formulation, damage to at least one part of the "extended hippocampal system" (hippocampus, fornix, mammillary bodies, anterior thalamic nuclei) is regarded as a common feature of all anterograde amnesias, and is principally responsible for the characteristic recall deficit. For this reason different amnesic conditions will share many features and be difficult to dissociate. Frequently overlaid on this hippocampal system deficit will be additional temporal lobe, frontal lobe, or diencephalic damage. This extra damage leads to other impairments that include a more pronounced recognition deficit. The extent to which this additional damage may also exacerbate the basic recall deficit, or the extent to which the recognition deficit is exacerbated by hippocampal system damage, remains to be determined and these are now issues of high priority. It has, for example, been suggested that the relative sparing of recognition memory after hippocampal system damage reflects the ability of animals or amnesic subjects to make accurate judgements based on familiarity. It is, however, also predicted that hippocampal system damage will disrupt the retrieval-based component of recognition memory and this will require examination.

It is assumed that anterograde amnesia usually results from a combination of different deficits that reflect dysfunctions in more than one functional system. It is hoped, however, that this reformulation of the disorder with its emphasis on the extended hippocampal system will make it easier to interpret the findings from neuropathological studies and to assemble appropriate groups in order to look for meaningful dissociations between different amnesic states. One intriguing issue concerns those amnesias associated with aneurysms of the anterior communicating artery. They are of particular interest as it has been claimed that this disorder does not involve those regions responsible for temporal lobe or diencephalic amnesia (Parkin & Leng, 1993), and they may therefore prove to be an exception to the proposal that all anterograde amnesias involve the extended hippocampal system. In view of the fact that the pathology associated with these aneurysms can involve parts of the fornix, may disturb the cingulum bundle as well as the cingulate cortex, and can on occasions extend into the anterior thalamus (Hanley et al., 1994) it seems more parsimonious to assume that they are another example of an amnesia principally due to disruption of the extended hippocampal system. This can only be confirmed by very careful post-mortem analyses of such cases.

Finally, one important class of evidence that may prove to have a considerable bearing on the details outlined in this proposal comes from studies of functional imaging (Fazio et al., 1992). These studies have helped to show the extent to which discrete diencephalic and discrete temporal lobe lesions can disrupt processing in other brain regions. Initial evidence indicates that in amnesia there may be hypoactivity in areas quite distal to the actual site of pathology and such information is likely to have a significant influence on the future analysis of amnesia.

REFERENCES

Aggleton, J.P., Desimone, R., & Mishkin, M. (1986a). The origin, course, and termination of the hippocampo-thalamic projections in the macaque. *Journal of Comparative Neurology, 243*, 409–421.

Aggleton, J.P., Hunt, P.R., & Rawlins, J.N.P. (1986b). The effects of hippocampal lesions upon spatial and non-spatial tests of working memory. *Behavioural Brain Research, 19*, 133–146.

Aggleton, J.P., Hunt, P.R., & Shaw, C. (1990). The effects of mammillary body and combined amygdalar-fornix lesions on tests of delayed non-matching-to-sample in the rat. *Behavioural Brain Research, 40*, 145–157.

Aggleton, J.P., Keith, A.B., Rawlins, J.N.P., Hunt, P.R., & Sahgal, A. (1992). Removal of the hippocampus and transection of the fornix produce comparable deficits on delayed non-matching to position by rats. *Behavioural Brain Research, 52*, 61–71.

Aggleton, J.P., & Mishkin, M. (1983a). Visual recognition impairment following medial thalamic lesions in monkeys. *Neuropsychologia, 21*, 189–197.

Aggleton, J.P., & Mishkin, M. (1983b). Memory impairments following restricted medial thalamic lesions in monkeys. *Experimental Brain Research, 52*, 199–209.

Aggleton, J.P., & Mishkin, M. (1985). Mammillary-body lesions and visual recognition in monkeys. *Experimental Brain Research, 58*, 190–197.

Aggleton, J.P., Neave, N., Nagle, S., & Hunt, P.R. (1995a). A comparison of effects of anterior thalamic, mammillary body and fornix lesions on reinforced spatial alternation. *Behavioural Brain Research, 68*, 91–101.

Aggleton, J.P., Neave, N., Nagle, S., & Sahgal, A. (1995b). A comparison of the effects of medial prefrontal, cingulate cortex, and cingulum bundle lesions on tests of spatial memory: Evidence of a double dissociation between frontal and cingulum bundle contributions. *Journal of Neuroscience, 15*, 7270–7281.

Aggleton, J.P., Nicol, R.M., Huston, A.E., & Fairbairn, A.F. (1988). The performance of amnesic subjects on tests of experimental amnesia in animals: Delayed matching-to-sample and concurrent learning. *Neuropsychologia, 26*, 265–272.

Aggleton, J.P., & Sahgal, A. (1993). The contribution of the anterior thalamic nuclei to anterograde amnesia. *Neuropsychologia, 31*, 1001–1019.

Aggleton, J.P., & Shaw, C. (1996). Amnesia and recognition memory: A re-analysis of psychometric data. *Neuropsychologia, 34*, 51–62.

Alvarez, P., Zola-Morgan, S., & Squire, L.R. (1995). Damage limited to the hippocampal region produces long-lasting memory impairment in monkeys. *Journal of Neuroscience, 15*, 3796–3807.

Bachevalier, J., & Mishkin, M. (1986). Visual recognition impairment follows ventromedial but not dorsolateral prefrontal lesions in monkeys. *Behavioural Brain Research, 20*, 249–61.

Bachevalier, J., Parkinson, J.K., & Mishkin, M. (1985b). Visual recognition in monkeys: Effects of separate vs. combined transection of fornix and amygdalofugal pathways. *Experimental Brain Research, 57*, 554–561.

Bachevalier, J., Saunders, R.C., & Mishkin, M. (1985a). Visual recognition in monkeys; Effects of transection of fornix. *Experimental Brain Research, 57*, 547–553.

Beason-Held, L., Rosene, D.L., & Moss, M.B. (1993). Memory deficits associated with ibotenic acid lesions of the hippocampal formation in rhesus monkeys. *Society for Neuroscience Abstracts, 19,* 186.5.

Bengochea, F.G., de la Torre, O., Esquival, O., Vieta, R., & Fernandez, C. (1954). The section of the fornix in the surgical treatment of certain epilepsies. *Transaction American Neurological Association, 39,* 176–178.

Brown, M.W., Wilson, F.A.W., & Riches, P. (1987). Neuronal evidence that inferomedial temporal cortex is more important than hippocampus in certain processes underlying recognition memory. *Brain Research, 409,* 158–162.

Butters, N., Salmon, D.P., Munro Cullum, C., Cairns, P., Tröster, A.I., Jacobs, D., Moss, M., & Cermak, L.S. (1988). Differentiation of amnesic and demented patients with the Wechsler Memory Scale–Revised. *Clinical Neuropsychology, 2,* 133–148.

Cramon, D.Y., von Hebel, N., & Schuri, U. (1985). A contribution to the anatomical basis of thalamic amnesia. *Brain, 108,* 993–1008.

Delay, J., & Brion, S. (1969). *Le syndrome de Korsakoff.* Paris: Masson.

Dusoir, H., Kapur, N., Byrnes, D.P., McKinstry, S., & Hoare, R.D. (1990). The role of diencephalic pathology in human memory disorder. *Brain, 113,* 1695–1706.

Fazio, F., Perani, D., Gilardi, M.C., Colombo, F., Cappa, S.F., Vallar, G., Bettinardi, V., Paulesu, E., Alberoni, M., Bressi, S., Franceshci, M., & Lenzi, G.L. (1992). Metabolic impairment in human amnesia: A PET study of memory networks. *Journal of Cerebral Blood Flow and Metabolism, 12,* 353–358.

Freed, D.M., Corkin, S., & Cohen, N.J. (1987). Forgetting in H.M.—A second look. *Neuropsychologia, 25,* 461–472.

Gaffan, D. (1992a). The role of the hippocampus-fornix-mammillary system in episodic memory. In L.R. Squire & N. Butters (Eds.) *Neuropsychology of memory* (2nd edn.). New York: Guilford Press.

Gaffan, D. (1992b). Amnesia for complex naturalistic scenes and for objects following fornix transection in the rhesus monkey. *European Journal of Neuroscience, 4,* 381–388.

Gaffan, D. (1994a). Dissociated effects of perirhinal cortex ablation, fornix transection and amygdalectomy: Evidence for multiple memory systems in the primate temporal lobe. *Experimental Brain Research, 99,* 411–422.

Gaffan, D. (1994b). Scene-specific memory for objects: A model of episodic memory impairment in monkeys with fornix transection. *Journal of Cognitive Neuroscience, 6,* 305–320.

Gaffan, D., & Gaffan, E.A. (1991). Amnesia in man following transection of the fornix. *Brain, 114,* 2611–2618.

Gaffan, E.A., Gaffan, D., & Harrison, S. (1984). Effects of fornix transection on spontaneous and trained non-matching by monkeys. *Quarterly Journal of Experimental Psychology, 36B,* 285–303.

Gaffan, E.A., Gaffan, D., & Hodges, J.R. (1991). Amnesia following damage to the left fornix and to other sites. *Brain, 114,* 1297–1313.

Gaffan, D., & Lim, C. (1991). Hippocampus and the blood supply to TE: Parahippocampal pial section impairs visual discrimination learning in monkeys. *Experimental Brain Research, 87,* 227–231.

Gaffan, D., Parker, A., & Gutnikov, S.A. (1995). Mammillary body lesions in rhesus monkeys impair object-in-place memory and leave the fornix without function. *Society for Neuroscience Abstracts,* 586.9.

Gardiner, J.M. & Parkin, A.J. (1990). Attention and recollective experience in recognition memory. *Memory & Cognition, 18,* 579–583.

Graff-Radford, N.R., Tranel, D., van Hoesen, G.W., & Brandt, J.P. (1990). Diencephalic amnesia. *Brain, 113,* 1–25.

Haist, F., Shimamura, A.P., & Squire, L.R. (1992). On the relationship between recall and recognition memory. *Journal of Experimental Psychology, 18,* 691–702.

Hanley, J.R., Davies, A.D.M., Downes, J.J., & Mayes, A.R. (1994). Impaired recall of verbal material following rupture and repair of an anterior communicating artery aneurysm. *Cognitive Neuropsychology, 11,* 543–578.

Holdstock, J.S., Shaw, C., & Aggleton, J.P. (1995). The performance of amnesic subjects on tests of delayed matching-to-sample and delayed matching-to-position. *Neuropsychologia, 33,* 1583–1596.

Holmes, E.J., Butters, N. Jacobson, S., & Stein, B.M. (1983). An examination of the effects of mammillary-body lesions on reversal learning sets in monkeys. *Physiological Psychology, 3,* 159–165.

Horton, D.L., Pavlick, T.J., Moulin-Julian, M.W. (1993). Retrieval-based and familiarity-based recognition and the quality of information in episodic memory. *Journal of Memory and Language, 32,* 39–55.

Hunt, P.R., & Aggleton, J.A. (1991). Medial dorsal thalamic lesions and working memory in the rat. *Behavioural and Neural Biology, 55,* 227–246.

Huppert, F.A., & Piercy, M. (1979). Normal and abnormal forgetting in organic amnesia: Effect of locus of lesion. *Cortex, 15,* 385–390.

Jacoby, L.L., & Dallas, M. (1981). On the relationship between autobiographical memory and perceptual learning. *Journal of Experimental Psychology: General, 110,* 306–340.

Jones, B., & Mishkin, M. (1972). Limbic lesions and the problem of stimulus-reinforcement associations. *Experimental Neurology, 36,* 362–377.

Kritchevsky, M., Graf-Radford, N.R., & Damasio, A.R. (1987). Normal memory after damage to medial thalamus. *Archives of Neurology, 44,* 959–964.

Mahut, H. (1972). A selective spatial deficit in monkeys after transection of the fornix. *Neuropsychologia, 10,* 65–74.

Mandler, G. (1980). Recognizing: The judgment of previous occurrence. *Psychology Review, 87,* 252–271.

Markowitsch, H.J. (1982). Thalamic mediodorsal nucleus and memory: A critical evaluation of studies in animals and man. *Neuroscience and Biobehavioural Reviews, 6,* 351–380.

Markowitsch, H.J. (1988). Diencephalic amnesia: A reorientation towards tracts? *Brain Research Reviews, 13,* 351–370.

Mayes, A.R., & Downes, J.J. (this issue). What do theories of the functional deficit(s) underlying amnesia have to explain? *Memory, 5(1/2).*

McMackin, D., Cockburn, J., Anslow, P., & Gaffan, D. (1995). Correlation of fornix damage with memory impairment in six cases of colloid cyst removal. *Acta Neurochir, 135,* 12–18.

Meunier, M., Bachevalier, J., Mishkin, M., & Murray, E.A. (1993). Effects on visual recognition of combined and separate ablations of the entorhinal and perirhinal cortex in rhesus monkeys. *Journal of Neuroscience, 12,* 5418–5432.

Mishkin, M. (1978). Memory in monkeys severely impaired by combined, but not by separate removal of amygdala and hippocampus. *Nature, 273,* 297–298.

Mumby, D.G., & Pinel, J.P.J. (1994). Rhinal cortex lesions and object recognition in rats. *Behavioural Neuroscience, 108,* 1–8.

Murray, E.A. (1992). Medial temporal lobe structures contributing to recognition memory: The amygdaloid complex versus the rhinal cortex. In J.P. Aggleton (Ed.), *The amygdala: Neurobiological aspects of emotion, memory, and mental dysfunction.* New York: Wiley-Liss.

Murray, E.A., Davidson, M., Gaffan, D., Olton, D.S., & Suomi, S. (1989). Effects of fornix transection and cingulate cortical ablation on spatial memory in rhesus monkeys. *Experimental Brain Research, 74,* 173–186.

Murray, E.A., & Mishkin, M. (1986). Visual recognition in monkeys following rhinal cortical ablations combined with either amygdalectomy or hippocampectomy. *The Journal of Neuroscience, 7,* 1991–2003.

O'Boyle, V.J., Murray, E.A., & Mishkin, M. (1993). Effects of excitotoxic amygdalo-hippocampal lesions on visual recognition in rhesus monkeys. *Society for Neuroscience Abstracts, 19,* 186.4.

O'Keefe, J., & Nadel, L. (1978). *The hippocampus as a cognitive map.* Oxford: Oxford University Press.

Otto, T., & Eichenbaum, H. (1992). Complementary roles of the orbital prefrontal cortex and the perirhinal-entorhinal cortices in an odor-guided delayed-nonmatching-to-sample task. *Behavioural Neuroscience, 106,* 762–775.

Parkin, A.J., & Hunkin, N.M. (1993). Impaired temporal context memory on anterograde but not retrograde tests in the absence of frontal pathology. *Cortex, 29,* 267–280.

Parkin, A.J., & Leng, N.R.C. (1993). *Neuropsychology of the amnesic syndrome.* Hove, UK: Lawrence Erlbaum Associates Ltd.

Parkin, A.J., Leng, N.R.C., & Hunkin, N.M. (1990). Differential sensitivity to context in diencephalic and temporal lobe amnesia. *Cortex, 26,* 373–380.

Parkin, A.J., Yeomans, J., & Bindschaedler, C. (1994). Further characterization of the executive memory impairment following frontal lobe lesions. *Brain and Cognition, 26,* 23–42.

Parkinson, J.A., & Aggleton, J.P. (1994). The failure of context shifts to alter the recognition of faces: Implications for contextual deficits in amnesia. *Cortex, 30,* 351–354.

Ramus, S.J., Zola-Morgan, S., & Squire, L.R. (1994). Effects of lesions of perirhinal cortex or parahippocampal cortex on memory in monkeys. *Society for Neuroscience Abstracts, 20,* 1074.

Rawlins, J.N.P., Lyford, G.L., Seferiades, A., Deacon, R.M.J., & Cassaday, H.J. (1993). Critical determinants of nonspatial working memory deficits in rats with conventional lesions of the hippocampus or fornix. *Behavioural Neuroscience, 107,* 420–433.

Rempel-Clower, N.L., Zola-Morgan, S., & Squire, L.R. (1994). Damage to the hippocampal region in human amnesia: Neuropsychological and neuroanatomical findings from two new cases. *Society for Neuroscience Abstracts, 20,* 444.9.

Rosene, D.L., & Saunders, R.C. (1987). Subcortical projections of the entorhinal cortex in the macaque. *Society for Neuroscience Abstracts, 11,* 886.

Rothblat, L.A., & Kromer, L.F. (1991). Object recognition memory in the rat: The role of the hippocampus. *Behavioural Brain Research, 42,* 25–32.

Russchen, F.T., Amaral, D.G., & Price, J.L. (1987). The afferent input to the magnocellular division of the mediodorsal thalamic nucleus in the monkey *Macaca fascicularis. Journal of Comparative Neurology, 256,* 175–210.

Saunders, R.C., Aggleton, J.P., & Mishkin, M. (1996). *Projections from the entorhinal and perirhinal cortices to the medial thalamus in macaque monkeys; identifying different pathways using disconnection techniques.* Unpublished findings.

Saunders, R.C., & Rosene, D.L. (1988). A comparison of the efferents of the amygdala and the hippocampal formation in the rhesus monkey: I. Convergence in the entorhinal, prorhinal and perirhinal cortices. *Journal of Comparative Neurology, 271,* 153–184.

Schacter, D.L. (1987). Memory, amnesia, and front lobe dysfunction. *Psychobiology, 15,* 21–36.

Shaw, C., & Aggleton, J.P. (1993). The effects of fornix and medial prefrontal lesions on delayed non-matching-to-sample by rats. *Behavioural Brain Research, 54,* 91–102.

Squire, L.R. (1981). Two forms of human amnesia: An analysis of forgetting. *Journal of Neuroscience, 1,* 635–640.

Squire, L.R., & Shimamura, A.P. (1986). Characterizing amnesic patients for neurobehavioural study. *Behavioural Neuroscience, 100,* 866–877.

Squire, L.R., & Zola-Morgan, S. (1991). The medial temporal lobe memory system. *Science, 253,* 1380–1386.

Squire, L.R., Zola-Morgan, S., & Chen, K.S. (1988). Human amnesia and animal models of amnesia: Performance of amnesic patients on tests designed for the monkey. *Behavioural Neuroscience, 102,* 210–221.

Suzuki, W.A. (1996). The anatomy, physiology and functions of the perirhinal cortex. *Current Opinions in Neurobiology, 6,* 179–186.

Tulving, E. (1983). *Elements of episodic memory.* Oxford: Clarendon Press.

Warrington, E.K. (1984). *The Recognition Memory Test.* Windsor, UK: NFER-Nelson.

Wechsler, D. (1987). *Wechsler Memory Scale–Revised.* New York: Psychological Corporation.

Woolsey, R.M., & Nelson, J.S. (1975). Asymptomatic destruction of the fornix in man. *Archives of Neurology, 32,* 566–568.

Zola-Morgan, S., & Squire, L.R. (1985a). Medial temporal lesions in monkeys impair memory on a variety of tasks sensitive to human amnesia. *Behavioural Neuroscience, 99,* 22–34.

Zola-Morgan, S., & Squire, L.R. (1985b). Amnesia in monkeys after lesions of the mediodorsal nucleus of the thalamus. *Annals of Neurology, 17,* 558–564.

Zola-Morgan, S., Squire, L.R., & Amaral, D.G. (1986). Human amnesia and the medial temporal region: Enduring memory impairment following a bilateral lesion limited to field CA1 of the hippocampus. *Journal of Neuroscience, 10,* 2950–2967.

Zola-Morgan, S., Squire, L.R., & Amaral, D.G. (1989a). Lesions of the hippocampal formation but not lesions of the fornix or the mammillary nuclei produce long-lasting memory impairment in monkeys. *Journal of Neuroscience, 9,* 898–913.

Zola-Morgan, S., Squire, L.R., Amaral, D.G., & Suzuki, W.A. (1989b). Lesions of perirhinal and parahippocampal cortex that spare the amygdala and hippocampal formation produce severe memory impairment. *Journal of Neuroscience, 9,* 4355–4370.

Zhu, X.O., Brown, M.W., & Aggleton, J.P. (1995a). Neuronal signalling of information important to visual recognition memory in rat rhinal and neighbouring cortices. *European Journal of Neuroscience, 7,* 753–765.

Zhu, X.O., Brown, M.W., McCabe, B.J., & Aggleton, J.P. (1995b). Effects of the novelty or familiarity of visual stimuli on the expressions of the immediate early gene c-fos in rat brain. *Neuroscience, 69,* 821–829.

MEMORY, 1997, 5 (1/2), 73–88

Consolidating Dispersed Neocortical Memories: The Missing Link in Amnesia

Ken A. Paller

Northwestern University, Illinois, USA

Consolidation is often conceptualised as a general process by which memory traces can be strengthened in the brain. An alternative idea, developed here, is that a particular sort of consolidation is required for establishing memories belonging to a neurobiologically defined category—memories dispersed across multiple distinct neocortical zones. These memories are consolidated via the formation of a neocortical cell assembly that confers coherence to the set of scattered neocortical memory traces. A set of memory traces linked in this manner can subsequently serve as the basis for conscious recollection. A disruption of this neocortical consolidation process is held to be responsible for the patterns of preserved and impaired memory observed in amnesic patients. A suitable strategy for empirically testing this sort of theory requires an examination of evidence from neuropsychological studies of amnesia and from studies of the neural substrates of memory functions in normal subjects.

INTRODUCTION

In an influential paper published in 1976, Paul Rozin systematically contrasted various theories of human amnesia and came to a conclusion that may still be appropriate today. Rozin proposed that the core defect in amnesia is a severe consolidation block with normal memory-activation processes, and furthermore, he ended his review (1976, p.42) by expressing the hope that by 1990, "the intervening advances in the psychological understanding of human memory will permit someone to organize materials on the amnesic syndromes so that they can be covered in a few pages." The literature on amnesia, however, has steadily expanded, as Mayes & Downes (this issue) demonstrated in their survey of the evidence that theories of amnesia must address. The number of theoretical positions has also expanded, but a clear consensus on which theory can best explain the evidence has not yet emerged.

Requests for reprints should be sent to Ken Paller, Department of Psychology, Northwestern University, 2029 Sheridan Road, Evanston, IL 60208-2710, USA. Email: kap@nwu.edu

I acknowledge support from NINDS grant #NS34639 and thank the many memory theorists who have influenced the ideas expressed here. Special thanks to Larry Squire and Andrew Mayes, who provided useful feedback on previous versions of this paper.

In this article I describe a new version of a consolidation theory and examine how well it can handle the challenge of explaining the evidence from amnesia. In addition, I argue that a reasonable goal is to seek connections between theories of amnesia and theories of normal memory so as to foster their synergistic development. This can be accomplished by considering the neuropsychological evidence from amnesia together with evidence about the neural substrates of normal memory functions. To support this view, the penultimate section summarises recent research using neuroimaging and neuromonitoring techniques to study memory functions in normal subjects, building on the knowledge gained through the study of amnesia.

In amnesia, brain damage undermines the ability to recollect previously experienced episodes and facts. In some cases of amnesia, a memory deficit occurs in the absence of other intellectual dysfunctions.[1] The selectivity of the memory deficit affords two key conclusions: (1) the preserved intellectual abilities do not require the integrity of the damaged brain areas, and (2) these brain areas contribute a function that is critical for the type of memory that is impaired. But what is the nature of this critical function?

Although it is possible to investigate the *functional deficit* of amnesia without regard to the nature of the *neural dysfunction*, the most suitable strategy for understanding amnesia is to simultaneously seek to understand the disorder from both perspectives. Thus, an adequate theoretical account of amnesia would include:

1. a psychological description of the disrupted memory function;
2. a biological description of the neural disruption;
3. a mapping between the psychological dysfunction and the brain dysfunction with reference to the neural implementation of memory functions in normal subjects.

Whereas psychological and biological aspects of a theory can be listed separately, they are highly interdependent. Ultimately it will be important to bridge the gap between these two levels of description—a key goal of the field of cognitive neuroscience.

---

[1] Mayes & Downes (this issue) note the lack of agreement about whether amnesia should be considered a heterogeneous syndrome. Indeed, amnesia often occurs together with additional symptoms that are dissociable from the memory impairment (e.g. confabulation, anosognosia, disorientation, perseveration, and remote memory loss). Despite this controversy, a working hypothesis is adopted here that the disruption of a single memory function gives rise to a set of core memory impairments.

CONSOLIDATION OF DISPERSED NEOCORTICAL MEMORIES

The idea that amnesia arises because of the disruption of a consolidation process is not new. The construct of consolidation—the process whereby memories change to become stronger over time—has a long history in the study of memory, both in human and nonhuman subjects (Squire, Cohen, & Nadel, 1984). Early theorising by Burnham (1903, p. 396) construed consolidation as "a physical process of organization and a psychological process of repetition and association." The view that human amnesia reflects a consolidation deficit was advocated by Brenda Milner in explaining the pattern of deficits in patient HM, who received a bilateral surgical excision to the hippocampus and adjacent temporal lobe regions (Scoville & Milner, 1957). Milner (1965) referred to this area as "the hippocampal zone" and suggested that it made possible the storage of information beyond the immediate present via the consolidation process. Milner also concluded that the hippocampal zone was not necessary for forming temporary associations between stimuli or for the variety of intellectual abilities that patients retained, including many uses of past learning. These abilities were thought to depend primarily on cell assemblies within the cerebral cortex (Hebb, 1949). Temporary associations could be recalled if attention was continuously maintained on the information. After attention was diverted, recall was thought to depend on the simultaneous activity of cortical and hippocampal cells. Furthermore, Milner explained the intact remote memories of amnesic patients by supposing that cortical cell assemblies could eventually mediate recall autonomously, without the hippocampus.

The present consolidation theory of amnesia extends these ideas in several directions. Some similarities to other theories in the literature are discussed in a subsequent section. The theory can be summarised by eight chief propositions, as follows:

1. Episodes are experienced when a set of neocortical neurons representing relevant events and states are activated. This requires the participation of neocortical regions specialised for representing different types of information (various visual areas, various auditory areas, and so on). The term *neocortical zone* will be used to refer to these functionally distinct regions. Aspects of spatiotemporal context are essential features of episodes that depend on a large set of neocortical zones. Thus, encoding and storage of episodic information characteristically involves multiple neocortical zones. Likewise, many sorts of facts also rely on representations distributed across multiple neocortical zones. A set of neurons within each neocortical zone can function to represent a single memory feature (or "memory attribute" as described by Underwood, 1969). This set of neurons will be termed a *neocortical ensemble*. The collection of neocortical ensembles that represents factual or episodic

information dispersed across multiple neocortical zones will be termed a *neocortical consortium.*

2. Re-experiencing an episode as a memory requires the participation of the same neocortical consortium that was activated during the original experience. Consolidation of a dispersed neocortical memory (henceforth referred to simply as consolidation) involves a process whereby the constituent parts of the memory are linked together in an enduring way. Remembering an episode or fact is facilitated by consolidation because successful retrieval depends on the extent to which the individual elements of the memory are strongly integrated as a unit.

3. The consolidation process is accomplished via an interplay between the hippocampal zone and the neocortex. The retrieval of facts and episodes is made possible because this interplay results in the modification of synaptic connections at memory storage sites distributed across multiple neocortical regions. The contribution of the hippocampal–neocortical interaction is twofold. First, hippocampal neurons are instrumental in the re-activation of a dispersed neocortical memory at the time of retrieval. Second, the same hippocampal neurons function over extended time periods to promote the formation of what will be referred to as a *coherence ensemble.* Each coherence ensemble has connections to the constituent parts of a neocortical consortium and facilitates the activation of that consortium as a unit. Eventually, the coherence ensemble takes over the role of facilitating the re-activation of the neocortical consortium such that the hippocampal connections are no longer required.

4. Memory storage can be facilitated by consolidation for memories that rely on representations dispersed across multiple neocortical zones, and this can apply for episodes, facts, and perhaps for some associative priming effects. Brain mechanisms responsible for these memories can collectively be termed the *declarative memory* system. Varieties of *nondeclarative memory* are accomplished without the necessary participation of the declarative memory system and are intact in amnesia either because (a) the memories are stored in places other than the neocortex or (b) plasticity within individual neocortical zones is sufficient for memory storage.

5. Consolidation proceeds in proportion to the extent to which the neocortical consortium is re-activated as a unit. Processes critical for consolidation—memory access, association, and integration—are active processes and are markedly promoted during dreaming. Consolidation is not a passive process inexorably set into motion at encoding, but rather it is determined by the continuing relevance of the memorial information and relationships to other information in an individual's ongoing cognitive activities.

6. Consolidation depends on the concurrent re-activation of neocortical consortia through two neuronal routes. One pathway involves hippocampal connections through transitional cortex in the temporal lobe. The second pathway involves diencephalic projections to neocortical regions, along with

prefrontal interconnections. After consolidation is complete, coherence ensembles in anterior temporal and orbitofrontal cortex participate in the re-activation of neocortical consortia through direct cortical–cortical connections.

7. Hippocampal plasticity is rapidly and indiscriminately available to provide coherence to dispersed neocortical memories. The formation of coherence ensembles takes longer to achieve, but provides coherence to neocortical memories less indiscriminately and fades more slowly.

8. Consolidation and recollection occur under the supervision of prefrontal areas that provide critical activation of posterior regions in the service of memory retrieval. This prefrontal activation is instrumental for memory search operations that can selectively access coherence ensembles as well as individual neocortical ensembles that comprise declarative memories.

Given this theoretical framework, how can the central findings from amnesia be explained? Table 1 lists the chief characteristics of amnesia and

TABLE 1
Accounting for the Chief Characteristics of Amnesia as the Outcome of a Defect in Consolidating Dispersed Neocortical Memories

Impaired recall and recognition of facts and episodes (anterograde)	In the absence of consolidation, re-activation of the scattered components comprising the memorial information occurs only inefficiently.
Preserved immediate memory	Once activated, dispersed neocortical representations can be maintained in an activated state via prefrontal connections.
Preserved retrieval of remote memories	Remote memories can be efficiently accessed via previously established coherence ensembles.
Temporal gradient of retrograde amnesia	The temporal gradient corresponds to the protracted timespan of consolidation, which varies greatly from one memory to another.
Preserved motor skills, conditioning, and nonassociative learning	These types of learning are not mediated cortically but instead depend on other brain regions such as the cerebellum and basal ganglia. Different sorts of consolidation may be required.
Preserved semantic memory	General knowledge of the world is available because it is already consolidated or because it is contained within a single neocortical zone.
Preserved item-specific priming	This type of priming depends on the storage of information within a single neocortical zone. Temporary effects of the activation of these representations do not require consolidation.
Impaired association-specific priming	New associations across multiple neocortical zones are facilitated by consolidation, and so are stored less efficiently in the absence of normal consolidation.

corresponding explanations based on the core deficit proposed in the present theory. A salient feature of this theory is that neurobiological criteria are used to define declarative memory, the type of memory impaired in amnesia. Declarative memories are those that rely on dispersed neocortical memory traces, and furthermore, the process of consolidation specified here is taken to apply only to this type of memory. One shortcoming of this approach is that these neurobiological criteria are not transparent from the behaviour of the subject, although in essence these distinctions pertain to the brain. Memory distinctions *are* biological distinctions. Furthermore, tying well-established psychological conceptualisations to the biology of cortical storage has the virtue of connecting them to a long tradition of neuroscience research concerned with understanding the physiology of nervous systems (Squire, Knowlton, & Musen, 1993).

The theory posits that consolidation confers coherence to elements of a declarative memory. The elemental unit of information is thought to be contained within a single neocortical zone. The plasticity takes the form of changes in synaptic connection strengths such that the memorial information is represented using a large number of neurons, as in a Hebbian cell assembly. The cell assembly, or neocortical ensemble, might involve neurons in more than one cortical column, but these columns would share common representational principles and would be considered part of the same neocortical zone. Although general methods for empirically delineating neocortical zones cannot be given, presumably there are distinct zones for each of the ways in which sensory input is analysed. For example, within the arena of representing facial information, a variety of visual analyses may be conducted, and there may be corresponding zones for representing the results of these different analyses. Judging from the number of distinct visual areas found in the neocortex, the sum total of neocortical zones may be quite large.

The nature of a neocortical zone is central here because consolidation is defined as a process that links neocortical information *across* zones. Declarative memories are fundamentally characterised by a dependence on connections among neocortical ensembles in multiple zones. Preserved priming effects in amnesia are characterised by a dependence on plasticity within single neocortical zones. Consider item-specific and association-specific priming. An example of the former is enhanced identification for studied words compared to nonstudied words; an example of the latter is enhanced identification for studied word pairs compared to studied words combined to form new pairings (Paller & Mayes, 1994). Item-specific priming is preserved because the relevant plasticity occurs within a neocortical zone concerned with representing one aspect of an item, such as visual word-form. Such representations involve a large number of neurons, but the crucial factor concerns the scale of the distributed representations—whether they are distributed within versus across neocortical zones. Association-specific priming is generally impaired because the relevant plasticity occurs with respect to connections among multiple neocortical ensembles not restricted to a single zone, as in the semantic associations formed between words. Schacter (1987) used the term "free fragments" to denote the isolated memory components that an amnesic patient can retain. Representations maintained within a single neocortical zone may correspond to so-called unitised representations or free fragments (Hayes-Roth, 1977; Schacter & McGlynn, 1989).

Retrieval factors can have a strong influence on whether a priming effect relies on within-zone plasticity or across-zone plasticity. A given test of association-specific priming that yields impaired performance in amnesia could be construed as a test that relies on across-zone plasticity. Similarly, disproportionate deficits in recall versus recognition can arise if the circumstances are such that the recall test places relatively more demands on across-zone plasticity. Unfortunately, an independent metric for within- versus across-zone plasticity has not been identified. In addition, the situation is complicated by the possibility that behavioural priming effects may depend more on one or the other type of plasticity as a function of subtly different retrieval circumstances. In any event, further research is needed to more precisely specify the boundaries of preserved priming in amnesia. Note that the use of an implicit memory test does not guarantee a preserved priming effect in amnesia. Therefore, the contrast between implicit and explicit memory is not adequate for defining the categories of preserved and impaired memory functions in amnesia.

Burnham's (1903) description of consolidation cited both physical and psychological processes. One way to construe the physical or neural mechanism of consolidation is as an automatic firming up of neural connections necessary for long-term storage. Many have speculated on how long such a process would require. The completion of such a process might indeed require a constant time period due to some passive molecular process. In contrast, consolidation in the present formulation is considered an active process that depends on intervening rehearsal and association; it does not inexorably run its course. Consolidation can be thought of as the reorganisation of memory traces that occurs when information is rehearsed and also when any portion of the memory is accessed. By this view, consolidation takes place at many points in time after the initial experience. The time span of consolidation depends on the complexity and meaningfulness of the memorial information, the number of times the memory is accessed, and the nature of concomitant reorganisation.

A prime opportunity for this memory access is in the context of the retrieval of the memory in question. Significantly, retrieval does not only occur in the waking state. In all likelihood, consolidation regularly occurs in the context of retrieval that takes place during sleep. In dreams, a multitude of memories are accessed, particularly recent memories. Consolidation may occur whether or not there is any lasting memory for the dream. Indeed, a peculiar characteristic of dreams—that they are quickly forgotten upon awakening unless rehearsed during the waking state—suggests that memory functions have switched to another mode. Winson (1985) and others have shown that changes in the functional connectivity of hippocampal subregions correlate with sleep stage (e.g. hippocampal gating patterns change such that output from CA3 neurons is enhanced during slow-wave sleep). Furthermore, firing patterns of ensembles of rat hippocampal neurons demonstrate a degree of synchrony during waking that is specifically maintained during subsequent slow-wave sleep (Wilson & McNaughton, 1994). Thus, dream sleep may be a vital time for the "off-line" processing of memories (e.g. Marr, 1971; Winson, 1985). In this way, memories can be retrieved and integrated with the individuals' long-term plans and goals, although this is not necessarily apparent in dream content. Associations thus forged among recent memories and old, well-established memories provide a critical part of the consolidation process. Importantly, the reorganisation of memories does not happen randomly but is regulated according to higher-level goals such that certain memories are more likely to be accessed and thus more readily consolidated.

Another fundamental issue that theories of amnesia must address is whether the impairment applies to only certain types of information or to all types of information. Cohen and Squire (1980) suggested that consolidation is preferentially required for the particular type of information termed *declarative knowledge*, which includes autobiographical episodes as well as facts and is directly accessible to conscious recollection. Others have emphasised configurational processing, in the sense that some memories require relational connections among multiple informational elements (Eichenbaum, Otto, & Cohen, 1992; Sutherland & Rudy, 1989). I also place central importance on configurational connections, but not fundamentally with respect to informational elements. Rather, representations that exist within discrete neocortical zones constitute the elements that must be associated via consolidation. Thus, consolidation operates by strengthening connections among a set of neocortical ensembles, each localised within a single neocortical zone. In the absence of consolidation, not all types of information are lost. The boundary between impaired and preserved memory depends on the biology—memory is impaired when it depends on connections among neocortical ensembles. A lingering problem is to be able to determine whether or not connections among neocortical ensembles are required for any given instance of memory performance.

In addition to specifying the functional characteristics of consolidation, it is also necessary to specify the outcome of consolidation. What is it that changes over the course of consolidation? So far I have speculated that a new declarative memory requires a special sort of neocortical plasticity that is capable of linking memory traces from disparate neocortical regions. The key change is the formation of a new neocortical ensemble in the anterior temporal region and/or associated orbitofrontal regions. This newly formed coherence ensemble differs from the proverbial "grandmother cell" in that it does not operate independently. It maintains the integrity of the consortium of neocortical ensembles but it does not redundantly re-represent all the same information. Global aspects of a fact or event may be represented by the coherence ensemble, whereas the consortium of neocortical ensembles represents the various components of the memory. Neocortical ensembles can also be used concurrently in other memories (just as neurons participating in each neocortical ensemble can also be used concurrently in other neocortical ensembles). Recollection thus involves the conjoint activation of the coherence ensemble and the consortium of neocortical ensembles. In short, consolidation can be conceptualised as the transfer of the coherence contribution from a set of neurons in the hippocampus to a set of interconnected neocortical neurons constituting a coherence ensemble. This neocortical coherence function takes some time to develop, whereas the hippocampal coherence function develops more quickly, perhaps even in a single trial, but also fades more rapidly with disuse (see McClelland, McNaughton, & O'Reilly, 1995; Milner, 1989).

The present proposal accounts for the common coexistence of anterograde and retrograde amnesia, while it also allows for dissociations between anterograde and retrograde amnesia, as follows. First, hippocampal damage causes anterograde amnesia because new coherence ensembles can only be created slowly and inefficiently. Hippocampal damage also produces some retrograde amnesia because of incomplete consolidation of recent memories— the formation of coherence ensembles occurs over a time period that depends on the extent to which the memories are retrieved, integrated, and associated. Second, damage to anterior portions of temporal and/or orbitofrontal cortex can lead to retrograde amnesia (see reviews by Kapur, 1993; Markowitsch, 1995) because some of the storage sites of coherence ensembles have been destroyed such that retrieval of the formerly associated neocortical consortia is inefficient. Third, a more severe amnesia is produced after damage to both the hippocampus and anterior temporal areas because neocortical consolidation is more severely hampered without either the hippocampus to promote the formation of coherence ensembles or anterior temporal regions to act as the substrate for these new ensembles.

THE NEURAL DYSFUNCTION OF AMNESIA

Each of the multifarious neurological conditions associated with amnesia disrupts function in one or more of a set of brain structures generally regarded as components of the limbic system. Prominent among these structures are the hippocampus, neighbouring cortical areas in the temporal lobe, structures in the diencephalon (the mammillary bodies and certain midline thalamic loci, although precisely which is controversial), and the basal forebrain. An exhaustive list of the critical brain lesions might thus include a large number of areas that may or may not comprise a single functional system. For present purposes, a key question is how these areas function in the service of consolidation.

One difficulty in identifying the lesions that are critical for the emergence of amnesia is that many of the conditions that produce it cause additional damage to other regions. These additional lesions can cause memory and cognitive disturbances that are dissociable from the deficits caused by the critical lesions. Patients with amnesia due to Korsakoff's syndrome, for example, usually have brain damage that superimposes additional symptoms on the amnesia. Even taking such superimposed deficits into account, the available neuropsychological evidence is insufficient to support firm conclusions about whether the core deficits of amnesia differ as a function of qualitatively different configurations of brain damage.

Although the anatomy of amnesia has been studied intensively for many years, *in vivo* neuroimaging technology now provides a significant source of information that was not previously available. Moreover, functional neuroimaging can provide a vital new perspective on the neural dysfunction. The majority of the extant evidence on the neuroanatomy of amnesia specifies only structural damage, whereas functional alterations can also be highly relevant for understanding amnesia. This point can be made more concretely with reference to a study of alcoholic Korsakoff's syndrome (Paller et al., in press). Functional neuroimaging of glucose utilisation with positron emission tomography was used to investigate the neural dysfunction responsible for the amnesic impairment. Results suggested that the known diencephalic lesions in these patients had remote effects on other brain areas. In particular, metabolic abnormalities were found in the frontal lobe, the parietal lobe, and both anterior and posterior cingulate regions. In contrast, abnormalities were not found in temporal lobe areas, including the hippocampus. Therefore, the idea that amnesia reflects an across-the-board disruption of processing within the medial temporal region and parts of the diencephalon must be supplanted by a theory that confers a degree of independence to these two brain areas.

A likely alternative is that hippocampal–neocortical interaction is not the sole factor mediating consolidation. Specifically it can be hypothesised that midline thalamic nuclei function to activate widespread cortical regions such that two types of interactions with neocortical storage sites can occur simultaneously. One is mediated by projections from the hippocampus to posterior neocortical regions via entorhinal cortex. The other is mediated by projections from several midline thalamic nuclei to prefrontal cortex and to other parts of the cerebral cortex. Prefrontal projections to posterior cortical regions also figure in related mechanisms for immediate or working memory (e.g. Fuster, 1995). In short, two types of interactions must be active in order for neocortical ensembles to store declarative memories normally. Synaptic alterations may occur through Hebbian principles such that concurrent input from both sources is required. This speculation is consistent with the notion that many different configurations of brain damage produce basically the same sort of memory defect.

COMPARISONS WITH OTHER CONSOLIDATION VIEWS

Neural interactions between the hippocampus and distributed neocortical locations in the service of consolidation have been emphasised in many more theories than can be cited in the space available here. For example, the need for linking information from multiple cortical regions was recognised in a proposal developed by Damasio (1989), although that formulation did not include specifics about consolidation. Squire et al. (1984) described a consolidation process in which neocortical activity was modified by input from the hippocampal region, leading to neocortical reorganisation. Importantly, reorganisation was portrayed as occurring in concert with forgetting, in that some connectivity is improved while some is lost. Several computational models of hippocampal consolidation have been developed (McClelland et al., 1995; Squire & Alvarez, 1995; Treves & Rolls, 1994). Halgren (1984) postulated that the hippocampus contributes to the retrieval of recent memories and to the experience of familiarity though reciprocal connections between hippocampus and neocortex forming positive feedback loops. Highly specific connections would thus be required such that particular hippocampal and neocortical cells mutually excite each other. A different sort of hippocampal–neocortical interaction was proposed in the memory-indexing theory of Teyler and DiScenna (1986). The information stored in the hippocampus was thought to provide a map or index of the sets of neocortical ensembles representing particular experiences. Thus, reactivation of a hippocampal index would lead to the reactivation of an array of neocortical loci and thereby a memorial experience. Consolidation was conceived of as a process of continual reactivation of a hippocampal index, leading to incremental effects on the associated cortical circuitry and the establishment of a cortically based memory trace. Squire, Shimamura, and Amaral (1989) argued for an alternative view based on anatomical evidence suggesting that specific reciprocal feedback between the hippocampus and neocortex is not anatomically possible. Instead, hippocampal output was hypothesised to act nonspecifically. Whether hippocampal output can topologically access specific neocortical ensembles remains a point of contention. The present theoretical stance does not solve this controversy, but it does emphasise the idea that temporal lobe pathways and diencephalic/frontal pathways function together in mediating neocortical consolidation. Wickelgren (1979) described a learning process in which the hippocampus regulates how new representations are assigned to neuronal ensembles. The present concept of the formation of coherence ensembles has much in common with Wickelgren's use of the concept of "chunking" and is also related to the idea of unitised representations discussed by Schacter and McGlynn (1989) and others.

RECOLLECTION, NEUROIMAGING, AND NEUROMONITORING

Consolidation theories of amnesia generally postulate that retrieval processes are not directly disrupted. However, the memory loss that amnesic patients experience is a failure of recollection, so some comments on the subjective experience of remembering are in order. The feeling of familiarity is not a function solely of memory retrieval. Jacoby and colleagues have argued that familiarity arises as an unconscious inference based on current situational factors as well as on retrieved memories (e.g. Jacoby, Kelley, & Dywan, 1989; for a related view see Mandler, 1989). Unconscious inferences can also give rise to priming effects in paradigms wherein prior experience with studied material is not attributed to familiarity with the material but is instead attributed to another factor (e.g. the fame of a face or name, the loudness of a sound, or the duration of a visual presentation). Amnesic patients are not deficient in making inferences in these priming paradigms, yet they are deficient when it comes to inferences regarding recognition (Paller et al., 1991; Squire & McKee, 1992). The functional deficit of amnesia is clearly not in the ability to make these inferences. Nonetheless, it can be useful to consider recollection as an outcome of an inference process, rather than as an inherent characteristic of memory. It remains to conceptualise the neural processes whereby memory retrieval events can provoke the type of inference that is critical for recollective experience.

Research on amnesia has taught us that the recollection of facts and events is associated with a type of memory distinctly different from priming phenomena, although both types of memory rely on neocortical storage mechanisms. These two types of memory are biologically dissociable in their dependence on nonidentical brain regions. Configurations of brain damage that give rise to circumscribed amnesia spare priming, whereas particular types of priming can be disrupted in the absence of declarative memory deficits (e.g. Gabrieli et al., 1995). The distinct neural correlates of these two types of memory can also be studied in normal subjects.

Neuroimaging studies using positron emission tomography (PET) have begun to examine cerebral blood-flow changes correlated with recollective processing. These blood-flow changes are used as a proxy for neuronal activity. For example, studies using a stem-completion paradigm showed that frontal lobe areas were activated more strongly during recall than during baseline conditions (Buckner et al., 1995). Results from other PET studies are also consistent with the conclusion that the frontal lobe plays an important role in recollection (e.g. Grasby et al., 1993; Schacter et al., 1996; Shallice et al., 1994; Tulving et al.,

1994). In contrast, a bilateral blood-flow reduction in occipito-temporal neocortex was shown in the priming relative to the control condition (Buckner et al., 1995). This effect was interpreted as supporting the idea that sensory-specific areas necessary for representing visual word-form are important for priming, in that they are activated less by words when those words have been recently encountered compared to when they have not. These results readily accord with prior ideas on the neural substrates of recollection and priming.

Neuromonitoring studies using electrophysiological measures called event-related potential (ERPs) offer a different perspective on memory functions of the brain. Whereas neuroimaging techniques can be used to show which brain areas are active during particular types of cognitive processing, neuromonitoring techniques—in which the electrical activity of the brain is monitored with high temporal resolution—can be used to find out more precisely when and in what circumstances these memory functions come into play. In this manner, it may be possible to use ERPs to monitor the neural events underlying recollection as they unfold (for review, see Rugg, 1995). For example, Paller and Kutas (1992) isolated an ERP correlate of recollection that occurred during a word-identification priming test. This ERP measure was recorded 500–900ms after words were flashed and was evident at all scalp locations examined. The intracranial sources of this ERP effect have not been established, but scalp topographic evidence suggests that frontal lobe activity was likely to have made a contribution. Moreover, the ERP effect was evident over the frontal lobe 100ms prior to being evident at other locations. In contrast, qualitatively different results were found in experiments wherein ERP correlates of visual word-form priming were isolated (Paller & Gross, submitted; Paller et al., submitted), indicating that ERPs are selectively sensitive to the different retrieval processing underlying recollection and priming.

The process of consolidating dispersed neocortical memories cuts across encoding–retrieval distinctions because it begins when encoding occurs and it continues with subsequent retrieval events so that the neocortical memory becomes self-sufficient. Most memory studies with neuroimaging or neuro-monitoring have focused on encoding or retrieval. Intracranial ERP recordings have suggested that the hippocampus is active both during initial stimulus presentation and at retrieval when retention intervals are fairly short (Paller, Roessler, & McCarthy, 1990). In future, it may be possible to investigate consolidation by probing the intervening events of rehearsal. This is when retrieval happens—and also when consolidation happens.

With future technical advances, evidence from neuromonitoring and neuroimaging will probably become increasingly more relevant for under-standing the neural substrates of recollection and other memory functions. Hypotheses that once appeared untestable in human subjects may thus turn out to be subject to empirical test. The use of these techniques in memory research may be most advantageous when neuropsychology provides a foundation upon which neuroimaging and neuromonitoring can build more elaborate and comprehensive theoretical structures.

TOWARDS A PSYCHOBIOLOGICAL UNDERSTANDING OF HUMAN MEMORY

Combining the multiple perspectives of neuropsychology, neuroimaging, and neuromonitoring provides a way to approach both the psychological and biological aspects of human memory in an integrated manner. The theoretical stance taken here to address the evidence from human amnesia, along with evidence concerning the neural substrates of memory functions in normal subjects, is at once psychological and biological. The consolidation theory that I have articulated includes many aspects borrowed from prior theories, and yet it is still incomplete and in need of additional empirical support. Obviously there is much more to learn about the neural substrates of human memory functions. Optimistically, attention to theory should guide future research, and new evidence guide theory development, such that the consolidation view may continue to change and improve—like a ship that is rebuilt plank by plank on the open sea, all the while staying afloat (paraphrasing Neurath, 1932).

REFERENCES

Buckner, R.L., Petersen, S.E., Ojemann, J.G., Miezin, F.M., Squire, L.R., & Raichle, M.E. (1995). Functional anatomical studies of explicit and implicit memory retrieval tasks. *Journal of Neuroscience, 15*, 12–29.

Burnham, W.H. (1903). Retroactive amnesia: Illustrative cases and a tentative explanation. *American Journal of Psychology, 14*, 382–396.

Cohen, N.J., & Squire, L.R. (1980). Preserved learning and retention of pattern analyzing skill in amnesia: Dissociation of knowing how and know that. *Science, 210*, 207–209.

Damasio, A.R. (1989). Time-locked multiregional retroactivation: A systems-level proposal for the neural substrates of recall and recognition. *Cognition, 33*, 25–62.

Eichenbaum, H., Otto, T., & Cohen, N.J. (1992). The hippocampus—What does it do? *Behavioral and Neural Biology, 57*, 2–36.

Fuster, J.M. (1995). *Memory in the cerebral cortex: An empirical approach to neural networks in the human and nonhuman primate.* Cambridge, MA: MIT Press.

Gabrieli, J.D.E., Fleischman, D.A., Keane, M.M., Reminger, S.L., & Morrell, F. (1995). Double dissociation between memory systems underlying explicit and implicit memory in the human brain. *Psychological Science, 6*, 76–82.

Grasby, P.M., Frith, C.D., Friston, K.J., Bench, C., Frackowiak, R.S.J., & Dolan, R.J. (1993). Functional mapping of brain areas implicated in auditory–verbal memory function. *Brain, 116*, 1–20.

Halgren, E. (1984). Human hippocampal and amygdala recording and stimulation: Evidence for a neural model of recent memory. In L.R. Squire & N. Butters (Eds.), *Neuropsychology of memory* (pp.165–182). New York: Guilford Press.

Hayes-Roth, B. (1977). Evolution of cognitive structures and processes. *Psychological Review, 84*, 260–278.

Hebb, D.O. (1949). *Organization of behavior.* New York: Wiley & Sons.

Jacoby, L.L., Kelley, C.M., & Dywan, J. (1989). Memory attributions. In H.L. Roediger, III & F.I.M. Craik (Eds.), *Varieties of memory and consciousness: Essays in honour of Endel Tulving* (pp.391–422). Hillsdale, NJ: Lawrence Erlbaum Associates Inc.

Kapur, N. (1993). Focal retrograde amnesia in neurological disease: A critical review. *Cortex, 29,* 217–234.

Mandler, G. (1989). Memory: Conscious and unconscious. In P.R. Solomon, G.R. Goethals, C.M. Kelley, & B.R. Stephens (Eds.), *Memory: Interdisciplinary approaches* (pp.84–106). New York: Springer-Verlag.

Markowitsch, H.J. (1995). Which brain regions are critically involved in the retrieval of old episodic memory? *Brain Research Reviews, 21,* 117–127.

Marr, D. (1971). Simple memory: A theory for archicortex. *The Philosophical Transactions of the Royal Society of London, 262* (Series B), 23–81.

Mayes, A.R., & Downes, J.J. (this issue). What do theories of the functional deficit(s) underlying amnesia have to explain? *Memory, 5*(1/2).

McClelland, J.L., McNaughton, B.L., & O'Reilly, R.C. (1995). Why there are complementary learning systems in the hippocampus and neocortex: Insights from the successes and failures of connectionist models of learning and memory. *Psychological Review, 102,* 419–457.

Milner, B. (1965). Memory disturbance after bilateral hippocampal lesions. In P.M. Milner & S.E. Glickman (Eds.), *Cognitive processes and the brain* (pp.97–111). Princeton, NJ: Van Nostrand.

Milner, P.M. (1989). A cell ensemble theory of hippocampal amnesia. *Neuropsychologia, 27,* 23–30.

Neurath, O. (1932). Protokollsätz. *Erkenntnis, 3,* 204–212. [Translated by G. Schlick and reprinted as "Protocol sentences" in A.J. Ayer (Ed.) (1959). *Logical positivism.* New York: Macmillan.]

Paller, K.A., Acharya, A., Richardson, B.C., Plaisant, O., Shimamura, A.P., Reed, B.R., & Jagust, W.J. (in press). Functional neuroimaging of cortical dysfunction in alcoholic Korsakoff's syndrome. *Journal of Cognitive Neuroscience.*

Paller, K.A., & Gross, M. (submitted). *Brain potentials associated with perceptual priming versus explicit remembering during the repetition of visual word-form.*

Paller, K.A., & Kutas, M. (1992). Brain potentials during memory retrieval provide neurophysiological support for the distinction between conscious recollection and priming. *Journal of Cognitive Neuroscience, 4,* 375–391.

Paller, K.A., Kutas, M., & McIsaac, H.K. (submitted). *An electrophysiological measure of priming of visual word-form.*

Paller, K.A., & Mayes, A.R. (1994). New-association priming of word identification in normal and amnesic subjects. *Cortex, 30,* 53–73.

Paller, K.A., Mayes, A.R., McDermott, M., Pickering, A.D., & Meudell, P.R. (1991). Indirect measures of memory in a duration-judgement task are normal in amnesic patients. *Neuropsychologia, 29,* 1007–1018.

Paller, K.A., Roessler, E., & McCarthy, G. (1990). Potentials recorded from the scalp and from the hippocampus in humans performing a visual recognition memory test. *Journal of Clinical and Experimental Neuropsychology, 12,* 401.

Rozin, P. (1976). The psychobiological approach to human memory. In M.R. Rosenzweig & E.L. Bennett (Eds.), *Neural mechanisms of learning and memory* (pp.3–48). Cambridge, MA: MIT Press.

Rugg, M.D. (1995). Event-related potential studies of human memory. In M.S. Gazzaniga (Ed.), *The cognitive neurosciences* (pp.789–801). Cambridge, MA: MIT Press.

Schacter, D.L. (1987). Implicit expressions of memory in organic amnesia: Learning of new facts and associations. *Human Neurobiology, 6,* 107–118.

Schacter, D.L., Alpert, N.M., Savage, C.R., Rauch, S.L., & Albert, M.S. (1996). Conscious recollection and the human hippocampal formation: Evidence from positron emission tomography. *Proceedings of the National Academy of Sciences, USA, 93,* 321–325.

Schacter, D.L., & McGlynn, S.M. (1989). Implicit memory: Effects of elaboration depend on unitization. *American Journal of Psychology, 102,* 151–181.

Scoville, W.G., & Milner, B. (1957). Loss of recent memory after bilateral hippocampal lesions. *Journal of Neurology, Neurosurgery and Psychiatry, 20,* 11–21.

Shallice, T., Fletcher, F., Frith, C.D., Grasby, P., Frackowiak, R.S.J., & Dolan, R.J. (1994). Brain regions associated with acquisition and retrieval of verbal episodic memory. *Nature, 368,* 633–635.

Squire, L.R., & Alvarez, P. (1995). Retrograde amnesia and memory consolidation: A neurobiological perspective. *Current Opinion in Neurobiology, 5,* 169–177.

Squire, L.R., Cohen, N.J., & Nadel, L. (1984). The medial temporal region and memory consolidation: A new hypothesis. In H. Weingartner & E. Parder (Eds.), *Memory consolidation* (pp.185–210). Hillsdale, NJ: Lawrence Erlbaum Associates Inc.

Squire, L.R., Knowlton, B., & Musen, G. (1993). The structure and organization of memory. *Annual Review of Psychology, 44,* 453–495.

Squire, L.R., & McKee, R. (1992). Influence of prior events on cognitive judgments in amnesia. *Journal of Experimental Psychology: Learning, Memory, and Cognition, 18,* 106–115.

Squire, L.R., Shimamura, A.P., & Amaral, D.G. (1989). Memory and the hippocampus. In J. Byrne & W. Berry (Eds.), *Neural models of plasticity* (pp. 208–239). New York: Academic Press.

Sutherland, R.J., & Rudy, J.W. (1989). Configural association theory: The role of the hippocampal formation in learning, memory, and amnesia. *Psychobiology, 17,* 129–144.

Teyler, T.J., & DiScenna, P. (1986). The hippocampal memory indexing theory. *Behavioral Neuroscience, 100,* 147–154.

Treves, A., & Rolls, E.T. (1994). Computational analysis of the role of the hippocampus in memory. *Hippocampus, 4,* 374–391.

Tulving, E., Kapur, S., Markowitsch, H.J., Craik, F.I.M., Habib, R., & Houle, S. (1994). Neuro-anatomical correlates of retrieval in episodic memory: Auditory sentence recognition. *Proceedings of the National Academy of Science, USA, 91,* 2012–2015.

Underwood, B.J. (1969). Attributes of memory. *Psychological Review, 76,* 559–573.

Wickelgren, W.A. (1979). Chunking and consolidation: A theoretical synthesis of semantic networks, configuring in conditioning, S–R versus cognitive learning, normal forgetting, the amnesic syndrome, and the hippocampal arousal system. *Psychological Review, 86,* 44–60.

Wilson, M.A., & McNaughton, B.L. (1994). Reactivation of hippocampal ensemble memories during sleep. *Science, 265,* 676–679.

Winson, J. (1985). *Brain and psyche: The biology of the unconscious.* New York: Vintage Books.

MEMORY, 1997, 5 (1/2), 89–98

A Positive Approach to Viewing Processing Deficit Theories of Amnesia

Laird S. Cermak

Boston University School of Medicine and Boston Department of Veterans Affairs Medical Center, USA

This reply is admittedly a defence of the encoding-deficits theory of amnesia. However, it attempts to go further by proposing that this deficit, which was originally designed just to explain amnesics' explicit episodic memory disorder, might be viewed as being but one instance of a more general disorder characteristic of all aspects of amnesic patients' information processing. It is proposed that amnesic patients' inability to perform more consciously controlled conceptual analyses results not only in explicit recall deficits, but sometimes also in instances of below normal implicit memory and recognition ability. Their ability to perform automatic, perceptual-level processing produces normal performance on some implicit and some recognition tasks, but it is not sufficient for all tasks.

INTRODUCTION

Mayes and Downes (this issue) are certainly correct in stating that no one theory has been able to straddle the entire spectrum of disorders that they feel it is necessary to incorporate into an all-encompassing theory of amnesia. On the other hand, it could as easily be concluded, after reading the array of disorders they wish to place under one umbrella, that the abundance of dissociated disabilities preclude the necessity for a master theory. From my point of view, encoding-deficits theory was never intended to explain anything other than anterograde "explicit" memory. However, if encoding-deficits theory is viewed as one example of the general class of processing theories, then impairments in other forms of processing can be proposed as contributors to deficits in areas such as implicit memory or recognition memory. This will be the thesis of the present reply, with the emphasis on encoding because that was the area under attack in the target article and because it is still the best example of a processing theory's approach to an explanation of amnesia.

Requests for reprints should be sent to Laird S. Cermak, Boston University Medical Center, Psychology Research (151-A), 150 South Huntington Avenue, Boston, MA 02130, USA.

I begin, perhaps a bit defensively, by responding to Mayes and Downes' assertion (pp.18–19) that encoding theory fails to provide an adequate accounting of anterograde "explicit" amnesia, the very area it was targeted to explain. The defence will be brief, because a full portrayal of the development of this line of research can be found in the newly published text "Neuropsychological explorations of memory and cognition: A tribute to Nelson Butters" (Cermak, 1994). For our present purposes, all comments will be directed specifically towards the representation of the theory on pp.18–19 of the target article. There Mayes and Downes depict encoding theory as it was originally presented during the early 1970s, a rather outmoded characterisation that does not need to be defended, because the theory has evolved so much since that time. To casual readers each transformation may have appeared relatively obscure in isolation, and for that I have to take full responsibility; but the foundation of the present theory has not changed for at least a decade. The fact that misconceptions continue to exist means that the final depiction is not completely clear. Consequently, I am pleased to take this opportunity to be more explicit.

Mayes and Downes do not appear to realise that encoding-deficits theory of amnesia was originally conceived of as a form of a storage theory prior to evolving into a subtype of transfer-appropriate theories: one with greater emphasis on input than output. It is true that much of the emphasis in research has been on the abstraction, analysis, and manipulation of the perceptual and semantic features of information prior to their storage, but it has always been the ability to retain and utilise this "encoding" that has been under question in amnesia. Some patients, most notably Korsakoff patients, do have considerable trouble "attending" to the features of verbal information that promote adequate storage of the information on the basis of these features; but, *all* amnesics have trouble "storing" the features of this verbal information in such a way that cues directed towards feature representation can evoke the desired item directly. Every amnesic patient has difficulty utilising feature representation, most notably semantic feature representation, to guide his or her search for the desired stimulus item. The theory proposes that this is because the patient has lost those features that usually promote normal storage, differentiation, and retrieval. Thus although I feel that amnesia is not produced by a loss of a specific area of storage (such as declarative memory), I still feel that the loss of a specific processing ability does result in a storage deficit. As with others (e.g. Dunn & Kirsner, 1989; Jacoby, Toth, Lindsay, & Debner, 1992; Masson & MacLeod, 1992), I feel that processing abilities might well span across direct and indirect tasks and only appear to differentiate or support specific systems of memory. Systems are useful in subdividing these process and lending structure to their investigation as well as in helping to understand processing functions, interactions, and purposes, but systems are "packages" that need to be unpacked into their constituent and associate processes.

With this definition of encoding in mind, some of the data that Mayes and Downes utilise in submitting their rejection of encoding deficits theory of amnesia can be put in perspective: beginning with one of the most frequently cited paradigms, the Wickens' (1970) release from PI paradigm. Originally this paradigm was designed to demonstrate a subject's ability to utilise specific features of words to store and retrieve that information. Words drawn from the same semantic category are presented on consecutive trials. When the subject becomes overwhelmed with similarly analysed words, search for a specific item among these similarly represented items is increasingly impaired. When material from a new category is introduced, the subject has the opportunity to store this material on the basis of that new feature. These words then become more easily retrievable because their representation is no longer saturated at the time of retrieval. Mayes and Downes are uneasy about attributing this increase in performance to encoding because the subject is clearly tested at the time of retrieval whereas encoding occurs at initial presentation. However, Wickens emphasised that since the only paradigmatic change that occurs takes place during item presentation, and it involves the nature of the words' categorical representation, the only aspect of the paradigm that could produce a change in behaviour has to occur at the time of input. In addition, Wickens demonstrated that an *independent* rating of feature salience (e.g. Osgood's semantic differential ratings) was able to predict the degree of retrieval probability. This provided converging evidence that feature representation differentiation in storage determines recall ability in this paradigm. The ability to perform this differential feature representation was Wickens' very definition of "encoding" and its demonstration earned him the Warren Medal for excellence in research from the Society of Experimental Psychologists. Now, his original definition may have been obscured within our encoding deficits theory by the emphasis on the semantic analytic skills of Korsakoff patients, as opposed to the storage difficulties of other amnesics. But none of this should obscure the notion that encoding occurs at input. Deficits in encoding may occur at different stages of processing for different populations of amnesics but the end result is that storage on the basis of differential feature representation is impaired for all amnesics.

Mayes and Downes turn next to the suggestion that even if it is granted that PI release results from encoding at input, such encoding is *not* deficient for any amnesics. To support their contention they cite the finding that Korsakoff patients show both a "delayed" release from PI (Winocur, Kinsbourne, & Moscovitch, 1981) when a second trial from the new class of material is presented, and release when they are cued at retrieval (Kinsbourne & Wood, 1975). However, both delayed and cued release findings can just as easily (I contend *more* easily) be interpreted as evidence that encoding does *not* occur on a normal level for these patients. In the first place, the delayed release of PI that occurs is *extremely* small relative to that seen on a release trial for normals. Second, if patients were encoding normally, a "decrease" should occur on this trial because the material presented on this trial is the same as that from the preceding trial. What could be happening is that amnesics demonstrate a small increase in performance because time has passed since the majority of interference occurred and although the patients may not differentially encode at presentation they may have been aware of similar material in their small set of correct responses. Allowing a little time to pass has been shown to produce a small increment in performance for normals even when the encoding category does not change. This increment, therefore, occurs not because of differential encoding but because of the dissipation, over time, of retrieval interference (Cermak, 1970).

The second area of successful PI release that Mayes and Downes cite as existing for amnesics involves the presentation of cues at retrieval. I have always felt that this alters the task so sufficiently that it changes the question that one is asking about amnesics' abilities. Improvement on the cueing task could occur from the partial reinstantiation of the original presentation and may be the result of activating the most fluent item of that particular category in the same manner as it does for implicit memory tasks. The patient has the ability to realise that an item belongs to a certain category and will give it when it is the most fluent. His problem is to automatically use knowledge of that category inclusion during the time the word is being presented. That disability is no longer being investigated in the cueing at retrieval task cited by Mayes and Downes.

This direct attack on encoding now deflected, we turn our attention to applying the more general model of processing-deficits theory (remember that I prefer to see encoding as just one facet of processing) to some of the other issues demarcated by Mayes and Downes. To cover all the topics would rival the target article in length; therefore, two areas that highlight the major points of disagreement among amnesia theories today will receive direct attention. I begin by exploring how differential processing affects implicit memory and the circumstances under which normal performance occurs for amnesics and when it does not. Then I will explore the phenomena of recognition memory and describe the processing requirements for obtaining normal recognition memory in amnesia.

IMPLICIT MEMORY PERFORMANCE

Mandler (1980) and Jacoby (1984) were among the first to suggest that more than one form of processing might exist during an item's presentation. Jacoby describes one form as being strategic and conceptual, producing a level of awareness that includes knowledge of the existence of the episode. By the encoding-deficits theory espoused here, we would predict that amnesics should not be able to perform this kind of processing. Jacoby considers the second form of processing to be more automatic and probably perceptually based. This form of processing does not produce nor require awareness, therefore amnesic patients' processing, which has been proposed as existing on a purely automatic perceptual level, should be sufficient to support normal performance. By this reasoning, it could be predicted that if performance on an implicit task could be made to depend on strategic processing then amnesics might be impaired even though they show normal implicit task performance when it is based on more automatic processing.

We (Cermak, Talbot, Chandler, & Wolbarst, 1985) have used a perceptual identification task with pseudowords as stimuli to highlight instances in which amnesics do not demonstrate normal implicit priming, because it was widely assumed that amnesics would evidence normal performance on any perceptual identification priming task. We found impaired priming by amnesics for this novel material and interpreted it as occurring because the pseudowords lacked semantic representation, and thus probably demanded greater processing during presentation. Encoding of pseudowords might necessitate some kind of strategy as they have no preformed representation. In an attempt to determine the level at which strategy became necessary in these tasks, we designed two further perceptual identification experiments which used ''pseudohomonyms'' as stimuli (Cermak et al., 1991). Pseudohomonyms are unique relative to pseudowords because, like pseudowords, pseudohomonyms have no existing orthographic representation, but they do share a phonology with an existing real word (e.g. ''phaire'', ''fair''). Thus, their phonological representation does exist even though their specific orthographics do not. Using these words, we felt we could separate performance on the basis of encoding on two separate levels: orthography (necessitating strategy) and phonology (perhaps automatic). We found that amnesics demonstrated normal priming for pseudohomonyms, suggesting that the existence of phonological representation bypassed further need for more strategic encoding. To investigate this further, a second experiment was designed which presented pseudowords, pseudohomonyms, and real words within one study list. We felt that if phonological activation occurred automatically then the mixed-list design should produce the same pattern of results as that for the unmixed design. However, what we found was that priming for pseudohomonyms in the mixed list not only became significantly less than normal; in fact, it was nearly nonexistent. Even though pseudohomonyms have a familiar auditory word form, realisation of this fact seemed to be concealed by the unfamiliar orthography of *all* stimuli on the list. Pseudohomonyms seemed to lose their semantic salience and simply looked like pseudowords. When pseudohomonyms were mixed with real words, Korsakoff patients' priming for pseudohomonyms also became significantly lower than was the case for the alcoholic controls. This implied that normal pseudohomo-nym priming in this paradigm must have *depended* on the salience of those words' phonological similarity to real words. For real words, access to representation might always occur automatically, resulting in normal priming effects irrespective of task manipulations. But for pseudohomonyms, the presence and magnitude of priming effects seems to be affected by contextual variables which influence the manner in which the information is processed. This means that when automatic processing is sufficient to support implicit performance, amnesics are normal, and when contextual conditions lead to pre-existing representations, performance can also be normal. But when strategic (and conceptual) processing is required, amnesics are not spontaneously capable of such controlled processing and do not demonstrate normal implicit performance.

Many readers must be aware that this proposal is identical to one Nelson Butters and I espoused years ago to explain amnesics' explicit memory performance. We demonstrated frequently that although amnesic Korsakoff patients are capable of semantic analysis, they do not perform this level of analysis when left to their own devices (Butters & Cermak, 1980). Consequently, they have no ability to reconstruct the verbal information they were explicitly asked to retain on the basis of semantic features. In an implicit perceptual identification task, it again appears that when all the stimuli are directed towards one form of analysis, the patients can use this feature to improve their performance. But such analysis has to be controlled *for* the patient as it does not seem to occur automatically. Normals must be able to control their own processing and seem to ''analyse'' the stimulus features that make a verbal item unique. Amnesics, on the other hand, seem capable of perceptual processing because it occurs automatically, but they are not capable of strategic processing because it requires control of their own processing beyond the automatic level. This finding that performance on an implicit task may be mediated by a combination of automatic and controlled processes raises the possibility that even when amnesics and controls perform equivalently on any given memory task, their performance may be produced differently. Thus, it becomes important to try to separate the effects of such automatic processes and controlled processes within the same task, so as to isolate the contribution of each to the performance of amnesics and control subjects.

Following Jacoby and Kelley (1991), we have recently attempted to make such a separation by creating a situation in which the effects of familiarity (felt to be an automatic process) and conscious recollection (a controlled process) were directly opposed to one another (Cermak, Verfaellie, Sweeney, & Jacoby, 1992). In this task, patients participated in a word-stem completion task in which they were told *not* to use the words that had just been presented on the study list to complete the word stems. Under these instructions, amnesic patients completed more word stems with list items than did the alcoholic controls. Comparing performance on this exclusion task with that on a standard word-completion task, we found that instructions to exclude had very little effect on the performance of amnesics, whereas it sharply decreased the number of study list completions for the alcoholic controls. It appeared that the amnesics were unable to attribute the familiarity generated by a particular word used to complete a stem to its recent presentation. Precisely why this is so is still under investigation but it fits with the notion that the patients may have been forced to respond purely on the basis of the fluency produced by the very low level of automatic processing they accomplished at input. Had the patients been able to achieve high levels of analysis (including context), they may have become more cognisant of the locus of the fluency; and, thus, more capable of discarding responses produced by items included in the critical list.

EXPLICIT (RECOGNITION) MEMORY IN AMNESIA

A similar interpretation can be invoked to explain amnesics' performance on explicit recognition tasks where for some time now a controversy over the normalcy of amnesic patients' recognition memory has existed. Huppert and Piercy (1976) and Hirst et al. (1986) have demonstrated recognition abilities in amnesic patients that exceed their free recall abilities, while Shimamura and Squire (1988) and Haist, Shimamura, and Squire (1992) report that recognition memory is always as impaired as free recall. One way that has been used to reconcile these two views is to explore recognition memory in terms of the underlying processing demanded by the task. In this way it can be determined whether or not amnesics' recognition performance is normal when a rudimentary level of processing is sufficient to support recognition and below normal when more controlled, conceptual, processing is required. Normal subjects could base their recognition response on an intentional act of reconstruction (conceptual processing) or on the more automatic effect of the fluency produced by the repetition of processing during the recognition task depending on the task demands (Jacoby, 1983; Mandler, 1980). Given the theory that amnesics rely almost exclusively on the fluency provided by automatic, perceptual, processing to achieve normal performance on implicit tasks, it stands to reason that they may also have to rely on this type of processing to perform any recognition task regardless of task demand. When the task demands reliance on this automatic processing component, amnesics' performance may be normal; when it relies on reconstruction, it may be impaired.

To support this conclusion Verfaellie and Treadwell (1993) examined amnesics' recognition performance under several conditions within an oppositional strategy paradigm. In the first phase of their experiment, patients read words or solved anagrams. In a second phase they were asked to try to remember a list of words that was presented to them auditorily. This was then followed by a recognition test which included items from both phase I and II. In the inclusion condition, patients were told to respond "old" to all previous items. In the exclusion condition they were told to respond "old" only to words presented during phase II. Verfaellie and Treadwell found that normal controls endorsed more items in the inclusion than in the exclusion condition from Phase I of the experiment, whereas amnesics did not differ in the number of responses they gave under these two conditions. In other words, amnesics could *not* use conscious reconstruction as a basis for their recognition, but instead relied almost exclusively on the fluency produced by prior processing. Separating these two contributors using the formulas developed by Jacoby (1991) revealed that amnesics' level of fluency was actually identical to that seen for normals, but their reconstructive ability was totally impaired. All the patient could rely on was the intact fluency generated by his or her own processing to "recognise" a prior item. The patient was simply attributing his or her sensation of fluency to the possibility that it may have been produced by a prior presentation of the word and not to any reconstructive ability to actually place that word in the context of the experiment. Thus, the same process underlying successful implicit task performance can be postulated as underlying successful performance on this explicit task. This argues against the usual interpretation that results on these two types of tasks support a distinction between two different types of memory.

FINAL THOUGHTS

As I stated at the outset, this commentary is largely a defence of the application of processing theory to the study of amnesia with encoding-deficits theory as the cornerstone. No-one is more keenly aware than I of the fluctuations of the zeitgeist from processing theories to systems theories over the past few decades. The pendulum seems to swing from an emphasis on one theory to the other, probably because both have something different to contribute to our knowledge of memory and amnesia. My own bias has been towards processing theory, primarily because it places the onus for understanding on what the subject is "doing" at the time of the task rather than where, theoretically or neurologically, he or she is doing it. It encourages us to explore the subject's "on-line" performance rather than his or her "off-line" capacity. It relies more extensively on converging operations to decipher what is occurring during a multitude of similar tasks rather than resorting simply to the alignment of tasks performed well and those failed. It suggests that processes might exist that support transfer from reception to expression rather than static storehouses containing, or not containing, material dispatched to that vicinity. It emphasises the control the subject has over the destiny of a bit of remembered information instead of a predetermined fate based on system utilised. It is dynamic, not static. In short, it appears more human than computer-like; which makes it an intrinsically more interesting framework as far as I am concerned.

This belief is clearly biased and I understand totally that a devout neuropsychologist would recoil from its sudden resurrection. By its very nature it remains elusive and difficult to pin down. It shifts with the nature of the task and even changes with instructions within the same task. Unlike systems theories, it is not amenable to single-task, single-function hypotheses. It is impossible to localise and predict that specific lesion sites will have specific consequences. Understandably, it holds less appeal among neuropsychologists than it does among cognitive theorists or philosophers. But ignoring the possibility that processing completely determines retrieval probability means overlooking a potential source of explanation for neurobehavioural phenomena. The tendency among systems theorists to rely on behavioural outcomes of specific tasks to postulate localisation of function may not work in the long run simply because correlating performance levels on a particular task with areas of damage must almost by definition remain on a purely "descriptive" level of science. It can never attain the level of explanation provided by a processing approach. It may be easier to achieve "system localisation" because description is always easier than explanation, but this approach will always hold us back from achieving a full knowledge of brain operation. Remaining within a systems framework produces a mechanistic, computational approach that seems to lack the very essence of memory. Memory and cognition theorists for the most part tend to resist this pull towards reductionism and I believe neuropsychologists should frequently refresh themselves with changes in the cognitive approach towards the study of memory. Currently the emphasis is returning to the study of processing, and neuropsychology needs to be cognisant of that fact.

REFERENCES

Butters, N., & Cermak, L.S. (1980). *Alcoholic Korsakoff's syndrome: An information processing approach to amnesia.* New York: Academic Press.

Cermak, L.S. (1970). Decay of interference as a function of the intertrial interval in short-term memory. *Journal of Experimental Psychology, 84*, 499–501.

Cermak, L.S., Talbot, N., Chandler, K., & Wolbarst, L.R. (1985). The perceptual priming phenomenon in amnesia. *Neuropsychologia, 23*, 615–622.

Cermak, L.S., Verfaellie, M., Milberg, W., Letourneau, L., & Blackford, S. (1991). A further analysis of perceptual identification priming in alcoholic Korsakoff patients. *Neuropsychologia, 29*, 725–736.

Cermak, L.S., Verfaellile, M., Sweeney, M., & Jacoby, L.L. (1992). Fluency versus conscious recollection in the word completion performance of amnesic patients. *Brain and Cognition, 20*, 367–377.

Cermak, L.S. (1994). *Neuropsychological explorations of memory and cognition: Essays in Honor of Nelson Buffers.* New York: Plenum Press.

Dunn, J.C., & Kirsner, K. (1989). Implicit memory: Task or process? In S. Lewandowsky, J.C. Dunn, & K. Kirsner (Eds.), *Implicit memory: Theoretical issues* (pp. 17–32). Hillsdale, NJ: Lawrence Erlbaum Associates Inc.

Haist, F., Shimamura, A.P., & Squire, L.R. (1992). On the relationship between recall and recognition memory. *Journal of Experimental Psychology: Learning, Memory and Cognition, 18*, 691–702.

Hirst, W., Johnson, M.K., Kim, J.K., Phelps, E.A., Risse, G., & Volpe, B.T. (1986). Recognition and recall in amnesics. *Journal of Experimental Psychology: Learning, Memory and Cognition, 12*, 445–451.

Huppert, F.., & Piercy, M. (1976). Recognition memory in amnesic patients: Effect of temporal context and familiarity of material. *Cortex, 12*, 3–20.

Jacoby, L.L. (1983). Remembering the data: Analyzing interactive processes in reading. *Journal of Verbal Learning and Verbal Behavior, 22,* 485–508.

Jacoby, L.L. (1984). Incidental versus intentional retrieval: Remembering and awareness as separate issues. In L.R. Squire & N. Butters (Eds.), *Neuropsychology of memory* (pp.145–156). New York: Guilford Press.

Jacoby, L.L. (1991). A process dissociation framework: Separating automatic from intentional uses of memory. *Journal of Memory and Language, 30,* 513–541.

Jacoby, L.L., & Kelley, C. (1991). Unconscious influences of memory: Dissociations and automaticity. In D. Milner & M. Rugg (Eds.), *Consciousness and cognition: Neuropsychological perspectives* (pp.201–234). New York: Academic Press.

Jacoby, L.L., Toth, J.P., Lindsay, D.S., & Debner, J.A. (1992). Lectures for a layperson: Methods for revealing unconscious processes. In R. Bornstein & T. Pitman (Eds.), *Perception without awareness.* New York: Guilford Press.

Kinsbourne, M., & Wood, F. (1975). Short-term memory processes and the amnesic syndrome. In D.D. Deutsch & J.A. Deutsch (Eds.), *Short-term memory* (pp.257–291). New York: Academic Press.

Mandler, G. (1980). Recognizing: The judgement of previous occurrence. *Psychological Review, 87* 252–271.

Masson, M.E.J., & MacLeod, C.M. (1992). Reenacting the route to interpretation: Enhanced perceptual identification without prior perception. *Journal of Experimental Psychology: General, 121,* 145–176.

Mayes, A.R., & Downes, J.J. (this issue). What do theories of the functional deficits underlying amnesia have to explain? *Memory, 5*(1/2).

Shimamura, A.P., & Squire, L.L. (1988). Long-term memory in amnesia: Cued recall, recognition memory, and confidence ratings. *Journal of Experimental Psychology: Learning, Memory and Cognition, 14,* 763–770.

Verfaellie, M., & Treadwell, J.R. (1993). Status of recognition memory in amnesia. *Neuropsychology, 7,* 5–13.

Wickens, D.D. (1970). Encoding categories of words: An empirical approach to meaning. *Psychological Review, 77,* 1–15.

Winocur, G., Kinsbourne, M., & Moscovitch, M. (1981). The effect of cueing on release from proactive interference in Korsakoff amnesic patients. *Journal of Experimental Psychology: Human Learning and Memory, 7,* 56–65.

MEMORY, 1997, 5 (1/2), 99–104

How Should a Database on Human Amnesia Evolve? Comments on Mayes and Downes "What Do Theories of the Functional Deficit(s) Underlying Amnesia Have to Explain?"

Alan J. Parkin and Nicola M. Hunkin

University of Sussex, UK

Mayes and Downes have provided an interesting snapshot of the current state of research into amnesia. However, in the light of their conclusions, the immediate prospects for amnesia research seem daunting. It appears that there is little agreement on anything concerning the nature and explanation of amnesia. In this article we will explore one dimension of what we believe to be the cause of this difficulty.

An undoubted stumbling block is the term "amnesia" as a means of classifying a disorder and, more importantly, as a criterion for averaging the performance of a group of patients similarly classified. It is curious that this practice has continued largely unabated within amnesia research despite its widespread condemnation within other areas of cognitive neuropsychology (e.g. McCloskey, 1993). No-one, for example, works on groups of "acquired dyslexics" or "agnosics". These general clinical classifications have been replaced by finer-grained, theoretically driven, distinctions such as surface and deep dyslexia, integrative and semantic access agnosia, and so on. Research in these areas would have been severely curtailed without these refinements, and one must ask whether a similar type of refinement is necessary to improve the status of amnesia research.

At the outset of the target article the basis for assuming that "amnesia" is something to explain is laid out in terms of amnesia being a *syndrome*. On this

Requests for reprints should be sent to Alan J. Parkin, Laboratory of Experimental Psychology, University of Sussex, Brighton, Sussex BN1 9QG, UK.

This work was partly supported by The Wellcome Trust. Nicola Hunkin is now at the Department of Clinical Neurology, Royal Hallamshire Hospital, Sheffield, UK.

count, we believe there is an argument on clinical grounds: If a clinician refers a patient with the amnesic syndrome we will, on the presumption that they are clinically competent, have no doubts as to what to expect in general terms. The problem, however, is whether the manner in which the syndrome is specified is a sufficiently precise basis on which to investigate scientific hypotheses.

Unless completely blinkered, any cognitive neuropsychologist reading this article will be aware that the preceding argument is far from novel and that the subject has been riven by debates concerning the value of syndromes (Caramazza, 1986, 1988; McCloskey, 1993; Robertson, Knight, Rafal, & Shimamura, 1993). Nowhere is this more marked than in the study of aphasia. Here there is no dispute that categories such as Broca's and Wernicke's aphasia have value as clinical diagnostics, but their value as theoretically oriented descriptions has come under increasing scrutiny. More specifically it is argued that these clinical syndromes mask a variation in underlying deficits that defies any attempt to produce a unitary theory (Badecker & Caramazza, 1985).

Within amnesia research, as Mayes and Downes illustrate, there are still many attempts to produce unitary theories of amnesia by, for example, explaining amnesia as a contextual encoding deficit or an impairment of retrieval. However, we would minimally contend that an enterprise of this type is undermined because it should, at the very least, acknowledge a degree of heterogeneity in amnesic patients. A question arises, therefore, as to how research may accommodate this heterogeneity.

Our initial stance has been to acknowledge a fundamental anatomical feature of the amnesic syndrome: its persistent association with lesions in either the midline diencephalic nuclei or the medial temporal lobe. We have suggested on many occasions that this fact is *prima facie* evidence for some functional dissociation between forms of amnesia (e.g. Parkin, 1992). Although not widely stated it would seem that the commonest objection to this view is the involvement of these two brain regions in the limbic system. Here it is proposed that the limbic system provides a "memory circuit" such that damage to any part of it can result in the same pattern of disturbed behaviour. However, this proposal seems naïve. It is much more likely that progression from one component of the limbic system to another is coextensive with some significant change in the nature of information processing being undertaken, as is the case with other pathways in the brain (e.g. the geniculo-striate pathway).

Following this view we have shown, over a series of experiments comparing patients with diencephalic vs. medial temporal lobe damage, that a single theoretical framework for explaining anterograde amnesia seems untenable. Briefly, we have examined the value of the contextual deficit hypothesis as a means of explaining amnesia and have shown that a contextual processing deficit only offers a means of explaining diencephalic amnesia (Hunkin & Parkin, 1993; Hunkin, Parkin, & Longmore, 1994; Parkin, Leng, & Hunkin,

1990). This work is briefly acknowledged by Mayes and Downes but its implications are not even discussed.

There are at least two alternative explanations for our results. First, our findings may simply be unreliable. We would dispute this on the simple grounds that our primary result—differential sensitivity to contextual information in the recency judgement task—has been extensively replicated twice following our initial study. Second, it may be that the differences we have found between the groups are due to coincidental group differences such as different patterns of associated functional lobe deficits. We would concede that the absence of correlations between estimates of frontal dysfunction and measures of contextual encoding deficit hardly constitutes strong evidence. However, our attendant demonstration of confirmatory evidence in patients with discrete diencephalic lesions and no frontal impairment is, we feel, a sufficiently strong argument (Parkin & Hunkin, 1993; Parkin, Rees, Hunkin, & Rose, 1994).

Our position, therefore, is that aetiology, in so much as it relates to proven differences in underlying brain pathology, is an essential variable in amnesia research. However, those persuaded by the "ultra-cognitive" viewpoint (e.g. Caramazza & Badecker, 1989; McCloskey, 1993) would argue that even this modified position is naïve because, in effect, we have replaced one syndrome with two. The ultra-cognitive position stems from the belief that lesions and their relation to cognitive processes are not yet specifiable in such precise terms as to allow the construction of patient groups.

One important counterargument in favour of maintaining group studies is that the enormous advances in neuroimaging will enable patient groups to be specified more accurately. Thus, when groups of patients are classified with diencephalic or temporal lobe amnesia in the future, it is hoped that this will be minimally confirmed by structural MRI. We would also argue against the ultra-cognitive position by proposing that the usefulness of group studies depends on the nature and precision of the hypothesis under consideration. Thus, a group study would allow differentiation between patients with left hemisphere damage presenting with pure word deafness who, nevertheless, are able to extract affective information from speech, and those with right hemisphere damage who can comprehend speech but who may be unable to deduce the affective state of the speaker from their voice. However, where the dissociation under consideration is extremely fine-grained, a case study approach may be the only valid one. A good example here is the distinction between viewer-centred and object-centred stages of visual word recognition (Caramazza & Hillis, 1990). In cases such as this it may be unreasonable, with the limitations of currently available technology, to determine precise anatomical loci for these stages of information processing.

However, when we consider a hypothesis such as the contextual deficit hypothesis, we are undoubtedly dealing with a theory that is less precise. Thus it may be possible, within current technological capabilities, to relate a deficit in this broader kind of memorial process to a particular brain region. This does not mean, however, that the anatomical relationship would not break down when the contextual deficit theory is explored in more detail. The undoubted complexity of what is meant by context will be revealed as the characteristics of patients are specified more fully. Nonetheless it would remain the case that, at one level of specification, the retention of contextual information appears more strongly associated with one region of the brain than another and that, *ipso facto*, anatomical considerations should be involved at some stage in investigations of the contextual deficit theory.

Using these anatomical considerations and the examination of group differences, we should be able to construct, in Mayes and Downes' terminology, a *level one* model of memory. This model would delineate the proposed stages of memory (e.g. consolidation, storage, retrieval) and allow us to hypothesise subcomponents of these processes (e.g. the ability to process contextual information at each of the three stages). Consideration of the model would allow us to make predictions about the functional deficits observed in patients with differing neuropathology. For example, diencephalic patients with a proposed deficit in contextual processing should show a different pattern of performance from patients with temporal lobe pathology who, it has been proposed (Hunkin & Parkin, 1993), may have problems in consolidating the products of contextual processing.

As indicated earlier, however, it is likely that the complexity of what constitutes context will become apparent as research in this area develops. Thus, as the model becomes more sophisticated and our theorising overtakes our imaging prowess, group studies will lose their validity and single case studies may yield more useful information. In terms of memory research, a good illustration of this is the recently defined disorder of focal retrograde amnesia (Kapur, 1992). This is a form of amnesia in which the primary deficit appears to be retrograde rather than anterograde. Although the study of focal retrograde amnesia is still in its infancy, it has already emerged that aspects of remote memory show dissociation (Hodges & McCarthy, 1993; McCarthy & Warrington, 1992). For example, Kapur et al. (1989) report a patient with an impairment on tests of public semantic memory accompanied by relative preservation of autobiographical memory. In contrast, O'Connor, Butters, Miliotis, Eslinger, & Cermak (1992) report a patient with the converse—poor autobiographical memory with better performance on tests of public semantic memory. Dissociations have not only been found on behavioural measures, but also in terms of neuropathology. Several studies of focal retrograde amnesia have related remote memory deficits to temporal lobe pathology (DeRenzi & Lucelli, 1993; Kapur et al., 1992; Markovitsch et al., 1993). However, we have recently reported focal retrograde amnesia in a patient in whom temporal lobe structures appeared to be intact. This patient, DH, had a right parieto-occipital lesion together with bilateral occipital lesions. This pattern of pathology prompted an explanation of DH's retrograde deficit based on an impairment in accessing stored information, as opposed to the storage deficit account that one can offer for patients with temporal lobe lesions (Hunkin, Parkin, Bradley, Jansari, & Aldrich, 1995).

These examples of fractionation in retrograde amnesia suggest that the single case approach, in which neuropsychological evidence is used to build models of cognitive function, can be effective in memory disorders research. We believe this is both likely to continue and increase as memory disorders research falls more into line with other areas of cognitive neuropsychology. The limitations of group studies need to be appreciated, and it is foreseen that this latter type of study will become increasingly dependent on accurate neuroimaging, thereby allowing for dissociation of patterns of neuropathology.

REFERENCES

Bedecker, W., & Caramazza, A. (1985). On considerations of method and theory governing the use of clinical categories in neurolinguists and cognitive neuropsychology: The case against agrammatism. *Cognition*, *20*, 97–125.

Caramazza, A. (1986). On drawing inferences about the structure of normal cognitive systems from the analysis of patterns of impaired performance: The case for single-patient studies. *Brain and Cognition*, *5*, 41–66.

Caramazza, A. (1988). When is enough, enough? A comment on Grodzinsky and Marek's "Algorithic and heuristic processes revisited". *Brain and Language*, *33*, 390–399.

Caramazza, A., & Badecker, W. (1989). Patient classification in neuropsychological research. *Brain and Cognition*, *10*, 256–295.

Caramazza, A., & Hillis, A.E. (1990). Levels of representation, co-ordinate frames, and unilateral neglect. *Cognitive Neuropsychology*, *5/6*, 391–445.

DeRenzi, E., & Lucelli, F. (1993). Dense retrograde amnesia, intact learning capability and abnormal forgetting rate: A consolidation defect? *Cortex*, *29*, 449–466.

Hodges, J., & McCarthy, R.A. (1993). Autobiographical amnesia resulting from bilateral paramedian thalamic infarction. *Brain*, *116*, 921–940.

Hunkin, N.M., & Parkin, A.J. (1993). Recency judgments in Wernicke-Korsakoff and Post-encephalitic Amnesia: Influences of proactive interference and retention interval. *Cortex*, *29*, 485–500.

Hunkin, N.M., Parkin, A.J., Bradley, V.A., Jansari, A., & Aldrich, F.K. (1995). Focal retrograde amnesia following closed head injury: A case study and theoretical account. *Neuropsychologia*, *33*, 509–523.

Hunkin, N.M., Parkin, A.J., & Longmore, B.E. (1994). Aetiological variation in the amnesic syndrome. *Neuropsychologia*, *32*, 819–825.

Kapur, N. (1992). Focal retrograde amnesia in neurological disease: A critical review. *Cortex*, *29*, 217–234.

Kapur, N., Young, A.W., Bateman, D., Kennedy, P. (1989). A long-term clinical and neuropsychological follow-up of focal retrograde amnesia. *Cortex*, *25*, 387–402.

Kapur, N., Ellison, D., Smith, M., McClellan, L., & Burrows, D.H. (1992). Focal retrograde amnesia: A long-term clinical and neuropsychological follow-up. *Brain*, *115*, 73–85.

Markovitsch, H.J., Calabrese, P., Liess, P., Haupts, M., Durwen, H.F., & Gehlen, W. (1993). Retrograde amnesia after traumatic injury of the fronto–temporal cortex. *Journal of Neurology, Neurosurgery and Psychiatry*, *56*, 988–992.

McCarthy, R.A., & Warrington, E.K. (1992). Actors but not scripts: The dissociation of people and events in retrograde amnesia. *Neuropsychologia, 30,* 633–644.

McCloskey, M. (1993). Theory and evidence in cognitive neuropsychology: A "radical" response to Robertson, Knight, Rafal, and Shimamura (1993). *Journal of Experimental Psychology: Learning, Memory and Cognition, 19*(3), 718–734.

O'Connor, M., Butters, N., Miliotis, P., Eslinger, P., & Cermak, L.S. (1992). The dissociation of anterograde and retrograde amnesia in a patient with Herpes encephalitis. *Journal of Clinical and Experimental Neuropsychology, 14,* 159–178.

Parkin, A.J. (1992). Functional significance of etiological factors in human amnesia. In L.R. Squire & N. Butters (Eds.), *Neuropsychology of memory* New York: Guilford Press.

Parkin, A.J., & Hunkin, N.M. (1993). Impaired temporal context memory on anterograde but not retrograde tests in the absence of frontal pathology. *Cortex, 29,* 267–280.

Parkin, A.J., Leng, N.R.C., & Hunkin, N.M. (1990). Differential sensitivity to contextual information in diencephalic and temporal lobe amnesia. *Cortex, 26,* 373–380.

Parkin, A.J., Rees, J.E., Hunkin, N.M., & Rose, P.E. (1994). Impairment of memory following discrete thalamic infarction. *Neuropsychologia, 32,* 39–51.

Robertson, L.C., Knight, R.T., Rafal, R., & Shimamura, A.P. (1993). Cognitive neuropsychology is more than single case studies. *Journal of Experimental Psychology: Learning, Memory, and Cognition, 19,* 710–717.

MEMORY, 1997, 5 (1/2), 105–114

Comments on Mayes and Downes: "What Do Theories of the Functional Deficit(s) Underlying Amnesia Have to Explain?"

Michael D. Kopelman

Guy's and St Thomas's Hospitals, London, UK

INTRODUCTION

Mayes and Downes's characteristically thoughtful paper clearly outlines the criteria within which theories of amnesia must operate. This is timely. During the last 10 or 15 years, theorists have sometimes appeared to forget what they have been trying to explain. Mayes and Downes (this issue) have put the fundamental deficit (or deficits) underlying amnesia back into the centre-stage of theory.

Fifteen years ago in a series of publications, Warrington and Weiskrantz (e.g. 1970, 1982) put forward various arguments against a simple "consolidation" theory of amnesia, such as that advocated by Milner (1966, 1972). However, their own interference-based retrieval hypothesis also came to grief as an explanation of the disorder (for review, see e.g. Meudell & Mayes, 1982), as they themselves tacitly acknowledged (Warrington & Weiskrantz, 1982). At much the same time, Butters and Cermak (1980) were postulating a fundamental deficit in semantic encoding as the basis of the alcoholic Korsakoff syndrome, which also failed to fulfil its predictions (McDowell 1981; Meudell & Mayes, 1982). Consequently, around 1980, memory researchers started to turn their attention *away* from the underlying deficit in amnesia towards what was *preserved* in organic amnesia, its delineation and characterisation. The identification of unimpaired implicit or procedural memory was usually

Requests for reprints should be sent to Dr. M.D. Kopelman, The Neuropsychiatry and Memory Disorders Clinic, Division of Psychiatry and Psychology, United Medical and Dental Schools of Guy's and St Thomas's Hospitals, St Thomas's Campus, London SE1 7EH, UK.

Nicola Stanhope's research was supported by the Wellcome Trust to Drs. M.D. Kopelman, J. Wade, and B. Kendall.

interpreted as evidence of multiple systems in memory (e.g. Tulving & Schacter, 1990), rather than implying anything about the issues (concerning encoding, storage, and retrieval) that had so preoccupied psychologists before 1980.

IMPLICIT MEMORY

Mayes and Downes (this issue) have changed the ground rules, arguing that *impaired* item-specific implicit memory would imply a storage deficit in amnesia, whereas *intact* item-specific implicit memory would be consistent with a deficit in retrieval. More particularly, they have argued (p.9) that the "two system" account of explicit and implicit memory is "highly implausible ... The assumption of two memory systems for the same information is redundant, and the theorists wishing to retain it need to provide a strong argument to explain the redundancy." This should ruffle a few feathers. However, it is equally incumbent upon Mayes and Downes to show that their account (storage or retrieval) can deal parsimoniously with a partial disruption of implicit memory, where it arises. An impairment in implicit memory may not be all-or-none, but, in certain circumstances, amnesic patients may show a *relative* decline in implicit memory performance after suitable controls for baseline have been made (Ostergaard, 1994). A partial disruption of implicit memory could arise from a retrieval deficit, a partial degradation of the store, or some combination of the two. A further complication arises from recent observations that amnesic patients may show priming for some types of novel information but not others (Schacter, 1994). It is not clear that Mayes and Downes's argument addresses these issues.

THE NOTION OF "STORAGE"

"Storage" is an ambiguous term, which can imply "putting into store" as well as "maintenance in the store", and these may or may not be related. "Putting into the store" is what I understand by "acquisition", and it encompasses a whole range of actual or postulated processes at differing levels of explanation. These include (i) "psychological" encoding of semantic or contextual information; (ii) hypothesised physiological processes such as either "consolidation" (Milner, 1966, 1972), "reverberating cell assemblies" and "phase sequences" resulting in synaptic enlargement (Hebb, 1949), or a gain in "synaptic weights" within distributed parallel neural networks (Rumelhart & McClelland, 1986); and (iii) physiological processes that are, in principle, measurable, such as either long-term potentiation (Lynch & Baudry, 1988) or cholinergic/serotoninergic neurotransmission (Kopelman & Corn, 1988; Martin et al., 1989). Consequently, if evidence is produced which appears to exclude a role for a semantic encoding deficit (for example) as the basis of amnesia, that does not in itself eliminate the possibility that a dysfunction at some other level of explanation results in a fundamental disruption of acquisition, "putting into store'', or new learning. Unfortunately, an acquisition deficit is often extremely hard to test directly if specified *only* at the level of hypothesised (pseudo-) or even measurable physiological processes, although psychopharmacological manipulations (for example) do offer some leeway into this issue.

Mayes and Downes (this issue) appear to identify acquisition deficits with impairments in "psychological" encoding processes and to employ the term "storage" to refer to some kind of maintenance storage over relatively short intervals (although they themselves use the term "maintenance" storage to refer to delays of weeks or months). I think that their notion of "storage" does need to be clarified. Moreover, the authors appear to play down any potential contribution of deficits in encoding-retrieval interactions in the production of amnesia, perhaps justifiably, but this needs to be made explicit.

RATE OF FORGETTING

In this paper, Mayes and Downes (this issue) argued that the Huppert and Piercy (1978) procedure underestimates the forgetting rate for amnesic patients, as control subjects will have been measured at a point where their forgetting was relatively steep. Control subjects (given briefer exposure times per slide) are presented with the initial stimuli over a shorter total duration than are amnesic patients, and, as forgetting rates are usually assumed to occur at an inverse exponential rate (Ebbinghaus, 1885), the controls will have been tested at an earlier and therefore steeper point on their forgetting curves. This argument has been made before (Mayes, 1986, 1988), but I think that it is extremely unlikely to have accounted for the result in most studies. First, in my own (Kopelman, 1985) experiment, the forgetting by controls over the first 24 hours fell by a mean of only about 10% from a 10-minute score of 82%: extrapolating from that finding, it seems to me that, if presentation of the stimuli to the controls had been more spread out over just a few more minutes, any change to the overall finding (that controls, Korsakoff, and Alzheimer patients forgot at the same rate) would almost certainly have been minimal. Second, all methods of measuring forgetting rates are potentially flawed: the one proposed by the authors in their footnote can be viewed as producing an *artefactual* or averaged forgetting curve for the amnesic patients from a number of *different* forgetting curves (one for each occasion of presentation). Third, comparisons between different methods of stimulus presentation in pilot studies by my own team (and also, I believe, by Freed and Corkin) failed to show any difference in the result according to different methods of presentation (when comparing prolonged exposure on one occasion of presentation per slide versus briefer exposures of slides presented on multiple occasions).

The significance of this is that Mayes and Downes (this issue) are curtly dismissive of the findings using this procedure. They write (p.25): "results have been inconsistent so that it would be unsafe to conclude that any group of amnesics reliably shows evidence of forgetting pathologically fast at delays beyond 10 minutes''. An alternative way of summarising the findings would be ''results have in fact been so consistent using this procedure that it is as safe as anything ever is in neuropsychology (admittedly, not terribly safe) to say that forgetting rates in patients with focal structural lesions are normal using this procedure''. This is, of course, somewhat embarrassing for the Mayes and Downes (this issue) theory that amnesic patients exhibit a deficit in retaining information in storage; but the findings of Huppert and Piercy (1978), Squire (1981), Kopelman (1985), Martone, Butters, and Trauner (1986), Freed et al. (1987, 1989), and McKee and Squire (1992) are highly consistent. Moreover, these results contrast strikingly with those obtained from patients in confusional states following ECT, or head injury patients who are still within the period of post-traumatic amnesia (Levin, High, & Eisenberg, 1988; Lewis & Kopelman, in preparation; Squire, 1981). These latter three studies demonstrated that confusional-state patients do exhibit accelerated forgetting on this task (perhaps resulting from gross metabolic disruption), and that the Huppert-Piercy procedure *is* sensitive to changes in forgetting rate, where pronounced abnormalities are present.

What is certainly true is that these studies have all used a *recognition* task to focus attention on forgetting at 10 minutes and beyond. However, there is suggestive evidence in the literature that, where *recall* tasks are employed, forgetting rates may differ between amnesic patients and healthy subjects during intervals from 1 to 10 minutes after stimulus presentation, although virtually all the relevant studies have been flawed until recently (for review, see Kopelman, 1992a, b). The recent findings reported in Mayes and Downes (this issue) that amnesic patients may forget organised verbal material faster than healthy subjects between about 20 seconds and 10 minutes when tested by free recall is complemented by a similar finding by Nicola Stanhope and myself that amnesic patients show faster forgetting in the recall of pictorial material between 20 seconds and 10 minutes. In this latter study (Kopelman & Stanhope, submitted-a), the difference in forgetting on recall tasks occurred even though the subjects' performance on recognition and cued recall tasks over the same intervals did not differ between groups.

These findings need to be incorporated into any theory of the functional deficit in amnesia, and they may indeed reflect some failure in ''consolidation''. Mayes and Downes (this issue) may be correct in postulating two separate deficits in organic amnesia; but the sheer difficulty in demonstrating differences in forgetting in studies of patients with focal structural lesions, and the very specific conditions in which those differences occur, indicate that accelerated forgetting alone is extremely unlikely to account for the amnesic syndrome.

RETROGRADE AMNESIA

Patient RB had a retrograde amnesia of about two years (Zola-Morgan, Squire, & Amaral, 1986), and in the earlier studies patient HM had a retrograde amnesia of about three years (Marslen-Wilson & Teuber, 1975). Both these patients had lesions largely confined to the medial temporal lobes, and their relatively brief periods of retrograde memory loss contrasted with the much more extensive retrograde amnesia (extending over years or decades) commonly seen in Korsakoff and Alzheimer patients, for example. Both HM and RB had a severe anterograde amnesia accompanying their brief retrograde loss, whereas the status of the opposite pattern—disproportionate retrograde amnesia—is much more controversial. In a subsequent review, I will be arguing that some of the patients so described had a memory impairment that might be better conceived in other ways (e.g. in "effortful" or visual memory), whereas in other patients there have been indications that psychiatric factors may not have been examined in sufficient detail.

As Mayes and Downes (this issue) point out, different patients appear to have varying degrees of impairment in factual and autobiographical memory, and implicit processes in retrograde memory have hardly been explored (an exception being a psychogenic patient described by Kopelman, Christensen, Puffett, & Stanhope, 1994). However, (i) the evidence of a possible discrepancy between recognition and recall memory in retrograde amnesia (Kopelman, 1989; Kritchevsky, 1992), (ii) the response to cueing (Kopelman, Stanhope, & Kingsley, submitted-a; Warrington & McCarthy, 1988), and (iii) the faster recovery of retrograde memory compared with anterograde memory in head injury and some cases of transient global amnesia (TGA) do all suggest the possible contribution of a retrieval deficit in retrograde amnesia. Like Mayes et al. (1994), Kopelman (1989) found that memory for dates and temporal order appeared to be particularly severely impaired in retrograde memory, as well as in anterograde memory: it is possible that the retrieval deficit in retrograde amnesia relates, in part, to the loss of these temporal markers.

COMPARISON OF THE EFFECTS OF DIFFERENT LESION SITES

Earlier research emphasised putative differences between patients whose amnesia resulted from diencephalic or temporal lobe pathology, particularly in forgetting rates or the extent of retrograde amnesia (e.g. Butters & Cermak, 1980; Huppert & Piercy, 1979; Parkin & Leng, 1988; Squire, 1981). By contrast, it was the view of Warrington and Weiskrantz that the pattern of amnesia from such lesions was essentially similar (Warrington, 1982; Weiskrantz, 1985). More recently, emphasis has been placed on the ways in which memory impairment resulting from lesions in the frontal lobes differs from that resulting from pathology within the limbic-diencephalic circuits (for review, see e.g.

Milner, 1982; Shimamura, Janowsky, & Squire, 1991, 1994; Stuss, Eskes, & Foster 1994).

In a series of papers, Nicola Stanhope and I have found that similarities between these groups of patients are, in many ways, more striking than differences, even when comparing patients with frontal lobe lesions and those with diencephalic or temporal lobe lesions. Differences do exist, but they are relatively subtle across groups; and the more important differences may sometimes occur within groups. This does not provide an argument in favour of either single-case studies or group studies, although it does emphasise the need to examine variance and its determinants within groups, and to be cautious about attributing particular patterns of cognitive performance to specific sites of pathology in single-case studies.

For example, we found that all three groups performed the same on measures of verbal and nonverbal short-term forgetting and, in fact, they did not differ in our study from healthy controls (Kopelman & Stanhope, submitted-a). Likewise, on measures of recognition memory and cued recall, the groups did not differ in terms of forgetting rates for picture, word, or design stimuli, measured over delays from 1 minute to 20 or 30 minutes; and this was true after controlling for the factors raised by Mayes (1986, 1988). As mentioned earlier, the groups did differ in forgetting rates when the free recall of pictorial material was assessed between 20 seconds and 10 minutes. In this case, patients with diencephalic or temporal lobe lesions forgot significantly faster than healthy subjects or patients with frontal lesions, and Green and Kopelman (1996) found a similar result when examining forgetting rates in the free recall of word lists. Moreover, in the Kopelman and Stanhope (submitted-a) study, patients with focal frontal lesions, and (to a lesser extent) patients who had had a recent frontal tractotomy, also showed some evidence of forgetting faster than controls.

As already mentioned, the differences that do exist between lesion groups are sometimes relatively subtle. For example, in a comparison of recall and recognition memory, 30 seconds after the end of stimuli presentation and after matching for recognition memory performance, we found no differences between the groups in terms of overall findings (Kopelman & Stanhope, submitted-b). On the other hand, on examining the recall of categorised versus uncategorised words, we found that patients with frontal lesions were able to benefit markedly from the words being organised for them into blocks of semantic categories, whereas the diencephalic and temporal lobe amnesia patients were not helped by this. On measures of context memory (Kopelman, Stanhope, & Kingsley, submitted-b), we found that patients with either diencephalic or temporal lobe lesions were impaired on measures of temporal context, and that this was not correlated significantly with their performance on executive/frontal tasks, whereas only the temporal lobe group were significantly impaired at a measure of spatial context and, in this case, patients with right temporal lesions performed significantly worse than patients with left temporal lesions. Most interestingly, patients with frontal lesions penetrating to the dorso-lateral cortex showed very severe impairment on the temporal context task, whereas patients with more medially placed frontal lesions were relatively intact. Subjective evaluations of memory (Kopelman & Stanhope, submitted-c) were more closely related to sites of pathology—patients with frontal lobe lesions in isolation, or with diencephalic pathology also implicating the frontal lobes, showing a severe lack of awareness of their memory deficits. On the other hand, it was not the site of the lesion alone that determined subjective evaluations: these evaluations were correlated with how well or badly the most remote memories were affected—loss of early remote memories producing low self-evaluations, and the longer a subject had been amnesic, the more aware he or she became of the memory deficit.

Perhaps the most striking differences between the groups occurred in retrograde memory (Kopelman, Stanhope, & Kingsley, submitted-a). Even here, the patient groups showed many features in common. They were impaired in their retrieval of autobiographical memories and in their knowledge of public events but, in terms of the latter, all the groups showed benefit from the use of recognition cues and/or word-completion cues. The only exceptions to these findings were two patients who had very focal lesions to their diencephalon following irradiation for pituitary tumours. These two patients had minimal pathology elsewhere and, despite a severe anterograde amnesia (a 49-point IQ–MQ discrepancy in one case), these two patients were virtually intact in terms of retrograde memory. All the remaining patient groups had a severe and extensive (going back many years or decades) retrograde amnesia, the main difference between them being that Korsakoff patients showed a steeper temporal gradient than did patients with frontal or temporal lobe pathology. From these findings, we concluded that the extensive retrograde loss in the main patient groups resulted from cortical pathology; that there was a retrieval component to the deficit, indicated by the responsiveness to recognition and word-completion cues; and that the involvement of semantic memory may contribute to the flatter temporal gradient in patients with temporal lobe lesions compared with Korsakoff patients.

Returning to the debate in the early 1980s between those who argued that there was a specific amnesic syndrome (principally Warrington and Weiskrantz) and those who argued for specific deficits related to particular sites of pathology, it seems that both parties may have captured an element of truth. Many of the distinctions postulated at that time have not proved resilient, and our own recent research argues for commonalities in the patterns of memory deficit between different lesion groups. On the other hand, differences do exist, albeit at a relatively subtle level. Perhaps the situation is closer to that described in the older literature on intelligence and personality than has hitherto been suspected; namely, we need to examine for the more general effects of a memory disorder (the "g" or core syndrome or commonality) as well as the more specific factors (or deficits), relating to particular lesions. In this respect, I am somewhat more cautious than Mayes and Downes (this issue) that we will be able to advance rapidly from what they call the "level 1" to "level 2" explanations of organic amnesia, despite the revolution in neuroimaging in recent years, both structural and functional.

CONCLUDING COMMENTS

In brief, we probably need to distinguish, first, the retrograde and anterograde memory deficits, which are poorly correlated. Disruption of (frontal and/or temporal) cortical circuits is critical to the former, whereas involvement of limbic-diencephalic and/or basal forebrain circuits is characteristic of the latter. Having said this, we may need to distinguish, within anterograde amnesia, between what I have called, on the one hand, the general factor, core syndrome, or commonality and, on the other, more specific deficits (for example, in context memory, subjective evaluations, or aspects of semantic memory). A severe impairment in acquisition remains characteristic of the "core syndrome" (evident across measures of recognition memory and cued recall as well as free recall), but there may be a subtler deficit in retention across particular delays (1 minute to 10 minutes approximately), evident only on measures of free recall.

I have argued for greater clarity in the use of the notion of "storage". To some degree, attempts to formulate "acquisition", "binding", or "consolidation" deficits more closely in psychological terms have proved very disappointing, but psychopharmacological manipulations and the use of neuroimaging activation studies may provide greater elucidation (in terms of brain physiology) of what I have called the core syndrome in the memory deficits of amnesic patients. The more specific deficits, which some amnesic patients display, may indeed be more closely related to particular sites of pathology, although my suspicion remains that the correspondence between "level 1" and "level 2" explanations may be more complex than Mayes and Downes (this issue) assume. Nevertheless, their review has clearly laid out the territory that studies of organic amnesia now encompass, as well as some of the difficulties; and they are to be congratulated on putting the fundamental deficit(s) of amnesia back into the centre-stage of memory theorising.

REFERENCES

Butters, N., & Cermak, L.S. (1980). *Alcoholic Korsakoff's syndrome: An Information-processing approach to amnesia.* New York and London: Academic Press.

Ebbinghaus, H. (1885). Über das Gedächtnis. Leipsig: Dunker. [Translated by H. Ruyer & C.E. Bussenius, (1913), *Memory*, New York, Teachers College, Columbia University.]

Freed, D.M., Corkin, S., & Cohen, N.J. (1987). Forgetting in HM: A second look. *Neuropsychologia, 25*, 461–472.

Freed, D.M., Corkin, S., Growdon, J.H., & Nissen, M.J. (1989). Selective attention in Alzheimer's disease: Characterizing cognitive subgroups of patients. *Neuropsychologia, 27*, 325–339.

Green, R., & Kopelman, M.D. (1996). *Contribution of context dependent memory and familiarity judgment to forgetting rates in organic amnesia.* Manuscript in preparation.

Hebb, D.O. (1949). *Organization of behavior.* New York: John Wiley.

Huppert, F.A., & Piercy, M. (1978). Dissociation between learning and remembering in organic amnesia. *Nature, 275,* 317–318.

Huppert, F.A., & Piercy, M. (1979). Normal and abnormal forgetting in organic amnesia: Effects of locus of lesion. *Cortex, 15,* 385–390.

Kopelman, M.D. (1985). Rates of forgetting in Alzheimer-type dementia and Korsakoff's syndrome. *Neuropsychologia, 23,* 623–638.

Kopelman, M.D. (1989). Remote and autobiographical memory, temporal context memory, and frontal atrophy in Korsakoff and Alzheimer patients. *Neuropsychologia, 27,* 437–460.

Kopelman, M.D. (1992a). Storage, forgetting, and retrieval in the anterograde and retrograde amnesia of Alzheimer dementia. In L. Backman (Ed.), *Memory functioning in dementia* (pp.45–71). Amsterdam: Elsevier Science Publishers.

Kopelman, M.D. (1992b). The 'new' and the 'old': Components of the anterograde and retrograde memory loss in Korsakoff and Alzheimer patients. In L.R. Squire & N. Butters (Eds.), *The neuropsychology of memory, 2nd edn* (pp.130–146). New York: Guilford Press.

Kopelman, M.D., Christensen, H., Puffett, A., & Stanhope, N. (1994). The Great Escape: A neuropsychological study of psychogenic amnesia. *Neuropsychologia, 32,* 675–691.

Kopelman, M.D., & Corn, T.H. (1988). Cholinergic 'blockade' as a model for cholinergic depletion: A comparison of the memory deficits with those of Alzheimer-type dementia and the alcoholic Korsakoff syndrome. *Brain, 11,* 1079–1110.

Kopelman, M.D., & Stanhope, N. (submitted-a). Rates of forgetting in organic amnesia following temporal lobe, diencephalic, or frontal lobe lesions.

Kopelman, M.D., & Stanhope, N. (submitted-b). Recall and recognition memory in patients with focal frontal, temporal lobe, and diencephalic lesions.

Kopelman, M.D., & Stanhope, N. (submitted-c). Subjective memory evaluations in patients with focal frontal, diencephalic and temporal lobe lesions.

Kopelman, M.D., Stanhope, N., & Kingsley, D. (submitted-a). The nature of retrograde amnesia in patients with focal diencephalic, temporal lobe or frontal lesions.

Kopelman, M.D., Stanhope, N., & Kingsley, D. (submitted-b). Temporal and spatial context memory in patients with focal frontal, temporal lobe, and diencephalic lesions.

Kritchevsky, M. (1992). Transient global amnesia. In L.R. Squire & N. Butters (Eds.), *The neuropsychology of memory, 2nd edn* (pp.147–155). New York: Guilford Press.

Levin, H., High, W.M., & Eisenberg, H.M. (1988). Learning and forgetting during post-traumatic amnesia in head-injured patients. *Journal of Neurology, Neurosurgery and Psychiatry, 51,* 14–20.

Lewis, P., Kopelman, M.D. (1996). *Rates of forgetting in psychiatric disorders.* Manuscript in preparation.

Lynch, G., & Baudry, M. (1988). Structure–function relationships in the organization of memory. In M.S. Gazzaniga (Ed.), *Perspectives in memory research.* Cambridge, MA: MIT press.

Marslen-Wilson, W., & Teuber, H.-L. (1975). Memory for remote events in anterograde amnesia. *Neuropsychologia, 13,* 353–364.

Martin, P.R., Adinoff, B., Eckardt, M.J., Stapleton, J.M., Bone, G.H., Rubinow, D.R., Lane, E.A., & Linnoila, M. (1989). Effective pharmacotherapy of alcoholic amnesic disorder with fluvoxamine. *Archives of General Psychiatry, 46,* 617–621.

Martone, E., Butters, N., & Trauner, D. (1986). Some analyses of forgetting of pictorial material in amnesic and demented patients. *Journal of Clinical and Experimental Neuropsychology, 8,* 161–178.

Mayers, A.R. (1986). Learning and memory disorders and their assessment. *Neuropsychologia, 24,* 25–50.

Mayes, A.R. (1988). *Human organic memory disorders.* Cambridge: Cambridge University Press.

Mayes, A.R., & Downes, J.J. (this issue). What do theories of the functional deficit(s) underlying amnesia have to explain? *Memory, 5*(1/2).

Mayes, A.R., Downes, J.J., MacDonald, C., Poole, V., Rooke, S., Sagar, H.J., & Meudell, P.R. (1994). Two tests for assessing remote public knowledge: A tool for assessing retrograde amnesia. *Memory, 2*, 183–210.

McDowell, J. (1981). Effects of encoding instructions on recall and recognition in Korsakoff patients. *Neuropsychologia, 19*, 43–48.

McKee, R.D., & Squire, L.R. (1992). Equivalent forgetting rates in long-term memory for diencephalic and medial temporal lobe amnesia. *Journal of Neuroscience, 12*, 3765–3772.

Meudell, P., & Mayes, A. (1982). Normal and abnormal forgetting: Some comments on the human amnesic syndrome. In A.W. Ellis (Ed.), *Normality and pathology in cognitive functions.* London: Academic Press.

Milner, B. (1966). Amnesia following operation on the temporal lobes. In C.W.M. Whitty & O. Zangwill (Eds.), *Amnesia* (1st edn). London: Butterworths.

Milner, B. (1972). Disorders of learning and memory after temporal lobe lesions in man. *Clinical Neurosurgery, 19*, 421–426.

Milner, B. (1982). Some cognitive effects of frontal-lobe lesions in man. *Philosophical Transactions of the Royal Society of London, B, 298*, 211–226.

Ostergaard, A.L. (1994). Dissociations between word priming effects in normal subjects and patients with memory disorders: Multiple memory systems or retrieval? *Quarterly Journal of Experimental Psychology: Section A: Human Experimental Psychology, 47*, 331–364.

Parkin, A.J., & Leng, N.R.C. (1988). Comparative studies of human amnesia: Syndrome or syndromes? In H. Markowitsch (Ed.), *Information processing by the brain.* Toronto: Hans Huber.

Rumelhart, D.E., & McClelland, J.L. (Eds). (1986). *Parallel distributed processing: Explorations in the microstructure of cognition.* Cambridge, MA: MIT Press.

Schacter, D.L. (1994). Paper presented at the 3rd International Conference on Practical Aspects of Memory, Maryland, USA.

Shimamura, A.P. (1994). Memory and frontal lobe function. In M.S. Gazzaniga (Ed.) *The cognitive neurosciences.* Cambridge MA: MIT Press.

Shimamura, A.P., Janowsky, J.S., & Squire, L.R. (1991). What is the role of frontal lobe damage in memory disorders? In H.S. Levin, H.M. Eisenberg, & A.L. Benton (Eds.), *Frontal lobe function and injury.* Oxford: Oxford University Press.

Squire, L.R. (1981). Two forms of human amnesia: An analysis of forgetting. *Journal of Neuroscience, 1*, 635–640.

Stuss, D.T., Eskes, G.A., & Foster, J.K. (1994). Experimental neuropsychological studies of frontal lobe functions. In F. Boller & J. Grafman (Eds.), *Handbook of neuropsychology, Vol. 9.* Amsterdam: Elsevier Science BV.

Tulving, E., & Schacter, D.L. (1990). Priming and human memory systems. *Science, 247*, 301–306.

Warrington, E.K. (1982). The double dissociation of short-term and long-term memory deficits. In L.S. Cermak (Ed.), *Human memory and amnesia.* Hillsdale, NJ: Lawrence Erlbaum Associates Inc.

Warrington, E.K., & McCarthy, R. (1988). The fractionation of retrograde amnesia. *Brain and Cognition, 7*, 184–200.

Warrington, E.K., & Weiskrantz, L. (1970). Amnesic syndrome: Consolidation or retrieval? *Nature, 228*, 628–630.

Warrington, E.K., & Weiskrantz, L. (1982). Amnesia—a disconnection syndrome? *Neuropsychologia, 20*, 233–248.

Weiskrantz, L. (1985). On issues and theories of the human amnesic syndrome. In N.M. Weinberger, J.L. McGaugh, & G. Lunch (Eds.), *Memory systems of the brain.* New York and London: Guilford Press.

Zola-Morgan, S., Squire, L.R. & Amaral, D.G. (1986). Human amnesia and the medial temporal region: Enduring memory impairment following a bilateral lesion limited to field CA1 of the hippocampus. *Journal of Neuroscience, 6*, 2950–2967.

MEMORY, 1997, 5 (1/2), 115–129

How Can We Best Explain Retrograde Amnesia in Human Memory Disorder?

Narinder Kapur

Wessex Neurological Centre, Southampton, UK,
Department of Psychology, University of Southampton, UK

I firstly consider general issues relating to our attempts to understand retrograde amnesia. Three main hypotheses are reviewed that have been proposed to account for retrograde amnesia. A theory is outlined to explain the dense autobiographical amnesia that is a focal phenomenon in some cases of severe head injury. This theory postulates that autobiographical retrieval requires the activation of a distributed network of cognitive operations, and that autobiographical amnesia results from the occurrence of multiple areas of pathology, distributed over both space and time.

INTRODUCTION

A number of implicit and explicit assumptions are often made during discussions of retrograde amnesia. Although most researchers will be aware of many of these assumptions, the assumptions may sometimes be taken on board in theoretical formulations without qualification, or they may be forgotten or deliberately played down. If the quality of data from amnesic patients is compromised by lack of care given to specific assumptions, then it follows that there will be a knock-on effect on attempts to understand amnesia. Good data may give rise to bad theories, but good theories cannot be built on bad data.

I will set out some of the factors of which I am aware, and which I think are important, in any consideration of how to explain functional deficits associated with retrograde amnesia. I will then focus on three attempts to understand retrograde amnesia. Finally, I will propose a formulation that I think is best able to account for some aspects of retrograde amnesia.

Requests for reprints should be sent to Narinder Kapur, Wessex Neurological Centre, Southampton General Hospital, Southampton SO16 6YD, UK.

I thank Mrs Pat Abbott for her assistance. I am grateful to the Wellcome Trust for financial support.

Functional Domains

The functional domains that lie within the province of retrograde memory need to be clearly specified. Over a lifetime, human beings build up an enormous store of knowledge, experience, and skills. Much of this may be amenable to conscious awareness, although some of it is probably governed by unconscious mechanisms. The term "retrograde amnesia" has a long and checkered history (Levin, Peters, & Hulkonen, 1983). Until recent years, it has most commonly been used to refer to the loss of memory for events that had preceded a head injury, and formed the complement of the term "post-traumatic amnesia". Thus, the term usually referred to loss of memory for personally experienced events, rather than loss of knowledge or skills that had been acquired prior to the injury. At the other extreme, consider for a moment those patients who suffer a language disturbance following an illness such as a stroke. They now do not have access to knowledge and skills relating to a language that they could use fluently before their stroke. If one subsumes knowledge and skills along with personally experienced events within the domain of retrograde memory, then such patients could be described as suffering from "retrograde amnesia". Similarly, one could argue that patients with visual agnosia suffer from a form of retrograde amnesia. For the purposes of the present discussion, I will include within the domain of retrograde amnesia those personally experienced events that had occurred during all of the person's life before the onset of the brain illness/injury, and those facts and skills that had been normally acquired during adulthood before the onset of the brain illness/injury. Thus, I would specifically exclude general knowledge about the world, and knowledge and use of the individual's primary language—areas that would tend to be subsumed under the terms "semantic memory". The decision to exclude such domains is more of a pragmatic one, rather than a statement as to the relationship between the various domains of knowledge. It is quite possible that similar mechanisms operate for superficially different domains of knowledge, and that impairment in one set will generally lead to impairments on some other set.

Although most discussions of retrograde amnesia have concentrated on permanent retrograde amnesia, we should not ignore the transient retrograde amnesias. These may present as spontaneous events, due to aetiologies such as cerebrovascular disease, epilepsy, etc. or they may be associated with interventions by the clinician—as in the case of retrograde amnesia induced by electroconvulsive therapy or by direct electrical stimulation of the brain. A further aspect of retrograde amnesia, one that I will *not* be considering, relates to functional retrograde amnesia. This phenomenon, which probably reflects a variety of conditions, is interesting in its own right but entails a distinct set of assumptions and explanations.

Time of Onset

The time of onset of amnesia needs to be clearly specified in relation to knowledge deficits. As retrograde amnesia should refer to loss of memories for events, knowledge, or skills that were acquired in a normal fashion before the patient's illness/injury, the latter needs to be clearly specified. For illnesses such as a primary degenerative dementia, it may be difficult to indicate the exact time of onset of the brain pathology. It is clear that where the illness onset is not known with any degree of certainty, it will be difficult to make statements about retrograde memory loss.

Exposure Period(s)

The period(s) when retrograde memory test items have received exposure needs to be clearly specified. Retrograde amnesia should ideally refer to loss of memory for information that was normally acquired during a specific time period before the brain illness/injury, and which has never occurred/been rehearsed since the illness/injury. In the case of public event test items, the particular dating of the ''exposure period'' for items may be easy for certain news events, but it may be more difficult for items such as new words that entered into the vocabulary or faces of famous personalities. It may be almost impossible to be sure that items have not recurred since the illness/injury of the patient, and this problem is the more acute if a long period has elapsed since the onset of the patient's amnesia (see later).

Patient's Age

The age of the patient at the time of occurrence of amnesia may be critical. This factor is often ignored in discussions of patterns of retrograde memory loss found in particular case studies. If the process of consolidation goes on over a number of years, then a young patient in their teens/early twenties will possess memories that have a different pattern and strength from someone in their seventies. There will be differences in the degree of consolidation and rehearsal of memories, and the amount and type of autobiographical and factual knowledge that can be meaningfully assessed in the two age-groups. Statements about the presence/absence of gradients of memory loss will generally be easier to make in the older than the younger patients.

Time Since Onset

Time since onset of retrograde amnesia may be a critical factor. As it is inevitable that at least some items relating to pre-illness knowledge will have recurred during the post-illness period, then in those patients with a major anterograde amnesia there will be a tendency for the apparent severity of retrograde amnesia to be related to the length of time that has elapsed since the onset of the amnesia. This may result in a paradoxical deterioration in retrograde memory over the years after the onset of the amnesia, simply because control subjects have been able to use re-exposure/rehearsal of items to their benefit, whereas for amnesic patients such opportunities for continued consolidation of past memories cannot be realised.

In the case of patients with focal retrograde amnesia, that is without a major anterograde memory loss, it has to be remembered that in the post-illness period they will have used opportunities to "relearn" memories from their past. Autobiographical memories will have been rehearsed as a result of family members discussing such items with the patient, and this may also apply to a lesser extent with factual knowledge. Skills (such as driving a car, swimming, etc.) that the patient does not remember performing will be practised again. Although patients with such a focal retrograde amnesia seldom recover the vividness or authenticity of their past memories, it may nevertheless sometimes be difficult to tease out which memories were never lost in the first place and which have been relearned.

As a general rule, the longer the period that has elapsed since the onset of the patient's amnesia, the more difficult it will be to obtain a pure, reliable index of the patient's retrograde amnesia. This applies to patients such as the famous amnesic patient H.M. (Ogden & Corkin, 1991), who suffered the onset of his severe amnesia in 1953.

HOW CAN RETROGRADE AMNESIA BEST BE EXPLAINED?

Three hypotheses

Although no global, all-inclusive theory of retrograde amnesia has yet been systematically formulated, three conceptual frameworks have been offered in an attempt to understand retrograde amnesia. I will briefly outline these. I will then propose my own formulation that attempts to explain some of the retrograde amnesia phenomena seen in memory disordered patients. The three main conceptual frameworks that have been published are:

1. An hypothesis that comprises the concept of "time-locked multiregional retroactivation" (Damasio, 1989a,b and later papers).
2. A neocortical consolidation hypothesis (Squire, 1992).
3. A disconnection hypothesis (Hodges & McCarthy, 1993).

Some other formulations are similar to elements of these three frameworks— e.g. some of the components of the model proposed by Johnson and Chalfonte (1994) have certain similarities with the framework suggested by Damasio

(1989a,b), and some of the ideas put forward by Milner (1989) and by Mishkin (1993) are similar to those of Squire (1992). However, for the sake of exposition, I will limit my discussion to the three proposals listed.

A limitation with all three hypotheses, and with my own hypothesis, is the relative lack of specific, distinctive predictions that emerge and which could yield data that could falsify the hypotheses. As our database of information on retrograde amnesia increases, with more refined neuropsychological and anatomical tools, this situation will probably change in the coming years.

(1) "Time-locked Multiregional Retroactivation" (Damasio, 1989a,b; Damasio & Damasio, 1989, 1993, 1994). Damasio has proposed that different features of an event are stored as representations in sensory-motor cortices, both primary sensory and first-order association cortices, where the event was originally registered. Further downstream are local "convergence zones", which comprise amodal records of the combinatorial arrangement of feature fragments that occurred synchronously during the initial experience, and also "non-local convergence zones", which comprise amodal records of the synchronous combinatorial arrangement of local convergence zones. Damasio has postulated that these convergence zones store binding codes, or patterns of neural activity, through which information stored in sensory-motor and multimodal cortices is accessed. The binding code ensures that neural activity that is generated in unimodal and multimodal cortices is time-locked, i.e. that the activity has the same temporal and spatial resolution as that which occurred when the event was experienced. Subsequent recall of experiences depends on "time-locked" neuronal activation of neuronal ensembles within the sensory-motor cortices, with synchronous activations being directed from various sets of convergence zones. Different levels of convergence zones are hypothesised. Low-level convergence zones bind signals relative to entity categories (e.g. the colour and shape of an object), and are located in association cortices immediately downstream from primary sensory/motor cortex or first-order association cortices whose activity defines feature representations. Higher-level convergence zones would be more critically involved in typical retrograde memory tasks, as they would bind signals relating to complex combinations of feature representations.

Damasio rejects a single anatomical locus for the storage or retrieval of memories relating to events. He has, however, indicated four anatomical regions that may form substrates for the cognitive structures in his model:

1. Primary and early association cortices, both sensory and motor, that comprise the substrate for the features of an experience;

2. Higher-order association cortices, some limbic structures, the neostriatum and the cerebellum—these contain the substrate for "binding code records";

3. Feed-forward and feedback connectivity interrelating structures in (1) and (2);

4. "Servosystem structures" in the thalamus, basal forebrain, hypothalamus, and brain stem nuclei.

Meaningful recall appears to depend on "time-locked multiregional retro-activation of widespread fragment records". Damasio has suggested that some of the higher-order convergence zones are located in anterior-most temporal and frontal regions.

Damasio's model has been derived from a range of lesion studies, not just those concerned with retrograde amnesia. A specific application of the model to a case of focal retrograde amnesia has been offered by Hunkin et al. (1995). They studied a patient who suffered a severe head injury, and who lost most autobiographical memories for events that occurred before his injury. By contrast, anterograde memory functioning and post-injury autobiographical memories were relatively preserved or much less affected. Their patient had major pathology, as shown on MRI scans, in posterior cortical and white matter areas, with no major pathology evident in the temporal lobes. Hunkin et al. proposed that their patient's lesions disrupted transmission of information to the convergence zones from visual/imagery activity in the posterior cortex, or to the posterior cortex from convergence zones. This would therefore lead to disruption of the synchronised neural activity that would appear from Damasio's model to underlie failure to recall past events. Hunkin et al. explained the relative preservation of post-injury autobiographical memories by assuming that, if disruption of such processes was not total, residual activity in the pathways would enable the visual cortex and convergence zones to communicate efficiently to set up new, albeit less efficient, binding codes and to allow storage and retrieval of new memories.

(2) A Neocortical Consolidation Hypothesis (Squire, 1992). This hypothesis has been less explicitly related to specific sets of retrograde amnesia data than the other two hypotheses. It is well summarised by Squire (1992) in his comprehensive review of amnesia in humans, rodents and primates (1992, p.222):

The facts of retrograde amnesia, as they are now understood, require a gradual process of reorganization or consolidation within declarative memory, whereby the contribution of the hippocampus and related structures gradually diminishes and the neocortex alone gradually becomes capable of supporting usable, permanent memory. This reorganization could depend on the development of effective cortico–cortical connections between the separate sites in neocortex, which together constitute the whole memory, or it could require the development of new representations. In either case, it would seem that slow changes in synaptic connectivity must be involved. One possibility is that consolidation is a part of the biologic process of forgetting and that the connections between some elements of representations are lost over time, whereas other connections grow stronger.

Thus, according to this hypothesis, memory is gradually reorganised or consolidated over time, and storage in the neocortex eventually becomes independent of the limbic-diencephalic system. This hypothesis would therefore predict temporally graded retrograde amnesia after focal limbic–diencephalic pathology, but an absence of such a gradient following neocortical damage.

(3) Disconnection Hypothesis (Hodges & McCarthy, 1993). Hodges and McCarthy presented a case of marked anterograde and retrograde amnesia following bilateral thalamic lesions. The retrograde amnesia was characterised by major confabulation, whereby the patient thought that he was still on active naval service (he had in fact served in the navy around 50 years previously). In addition to his memory deficits, he also showed impairments on tests of frontal lobe functioning. Similar to Damasio, Hodges and McCarthy propose a distinction between the feature representation of records of experiences and mechanisms that act on these to bring about autobiographical memories. Thus, retrieval of memories is thought of as being mediated via a hierarchical program structure. At the lowest level are elements of autobiographical records, which may be relatively fragmentary and cognitively unstructured. At the highest level of the program are retrieval "frameworks". The major role of these frameworks is to provide a basic organisational structure for guiding retrieval and integration of the lower-level records. The higher-level frameworks are thought to be organised thematically, in terms of major life events or lifetime periods. Hodges and McCarthy considered that their patient's retrograde amnesia was due to a major disruption of the thematic retrieval framework. Thus he appeared to have lost, or to be unable to access, an adequate set of frameworks to index his autobiographical memory records, and appeared to have got "stuck" on a framework relating to his navy life. Hodges and McCarthy further considered that their patient's disproportionate impairment of autobiographical events, compared to a lesser impairment for knowledge of people or knowledge of public events, could be explained by two further assumptions. First, there are alternative means of accessing and constructing memories at a level below that of thematic retrieval frameworks. Second, there may be subschemes that can be used to retrieve and reconstruct information under alternative headings. At the anatomical level, Hodges and McCarthy proposed that their patient's memory loss could be explained by a disconnection syndrome that involved a failure to link anterior and posterior cerebral processing systems via thalamo-frontal neural tracts. It is interesting to note that an earlier case of dense retrograde amnesia had been reported to show major frontal lobe dysfunction, and this frontal lobe dysfunction was attributed to a disconnection syndrome, in this case between mesencephalic and prefrontal areas (Goldberg et al., 1981, 1989).

OVERVIEW

I would suggest that the question "How can we explain retrograde amnesia?" may in fact be a misleading one. Retrograde amnesia comprises such a heterogeneous range of functional deficits, many of which are dissociable, that it is probably more meaningful (though less glamorous) to ask questions in relation to specific retrograde memory deficits rather than try to develop an all-encompassing theory of retrograde amnesia. Functional deficits that are often subsumed under the rubric of retrograde amnesia include:

1. Failure to retrieve information about personally experienced events.
2. Failure to retrieve knowledge about the facts of one's personal past.
3. Failure to identify, or to recognise as familiar, scenes, routes or photographs relating to personally experienced events.
4. Failure to identify, or to recognise as familiar, famous faces or other stimuli such as monuments, cars, etc.
5. Failure to identify, or to recognise as familiar, photographs relating to famous news events.
6. Failure to retrieve information about, or to recognise as familiar, verbal material such as famous names, recently introduced terminology/vocabulary, etc.
7. Failure to retrieve information about, or to recognise as familiar, verbal knowledge relating to famous news events.

Such functional deficits may occur in clinical domains that include:

(i)   retrograde amnesia associated with the various aetiologies that give rise to the classical amnesic syndrome;
(ii)   focal retrograde amnesia;
(iii) retrograde amnesia associated with transient states such as transient global amnesia;
(iv)   transient epileptic amnesia;
(v)   electroconvulsive therapy;
(vi)   the short period of pre-traumatic amnesia frequently seen after mild or moderate cases of closed head injury.

Some of these clinical domains could be further fractionated into distinct pathological and anatomical conditions—e.g. the retrograde amnesia seen in the classical amnesic syndrome may be different after herpes simplex encephalitis and after hypoxia, or it may be different after discrete vascular lesions in the thalamus and discrete vascular lesions in the basal forebrain.

It remains possible that a global theory of knowledge storage and retrieval, similar to that outlined by Damasio, will be able to explain all manifestations of retrograde memory loss. However, for the remainder of this article I will limit my own exposition to one particular functional deficit that has been found in one particular aetiology—focal autobiographical memory loss that has been observed in some cases of severe head injury. In most of the cases of focal retrograde amnesia that have been reported, a severe head injury has resulted in a dense memory loss for personally experienced events. Even though patients may relearn information relating to these events, they still do not retain any sense of vividness or authenticity. How can such retrograde amnesia best be explained? I will frame my discussion in the form of anatomical hypotheses, but will also try to relate these to a particular conceptual framework.

The retrieval of personally experienced events from many years previously is undoubtedly a complex task—complex in terms of the number and connectivity of neural networks that are likely to be involved. There are as yet few clues from functional imaging studies of normal subjects as to the neural mechanisms that underlie autobiographical memory. In a pilot activation study, Tulving (1989) reported that activation of anterior brain structures was found in a retrieval task that required the subject to think about a particular autobiographical episode. It would seem logical to assume that when asked to retrieve a complex event, such as a wedding or a holiday that occurred several years earlier, a number of different neural mechanisms are brought into play—a frontal lobe mechanism that designs, selects, and implements strategies for retrieving particular episodes; verbally encoded representations of some episodes within the event, probably in the temporal lobe (these representations might be at a broad "thematic" level and also at a more specific level of entities within an event); structures in the frontal or temporal lobes that contain temporal and spatial codes that were formed at the time of the event and that are used as index markers to assist in the retrieval of the event; areas in posterior association cortex and other association areas that have stored visual images (e.g. scenes) in relation to the event; language areas that help to translate the results of the search through episodic memory into a meaningful verbal description; and frontal/thalamic/mesencephalic mechanisms that help to integrate these various sets of neural activities so that a meaningful response can be made.

I will consider in turn plausible anatomical hypotheses, and then suggest a framework that aims to take into account the current data sets, both anatomical and neuropsychological, that have been published.

Can a Focal Brain Stem Lesion Result in Retrograde Amnesia?

Goldberg et al. (1981) suggested that a mesencephalic lesion may have played a critical role in the autobiographical amnesia of their patient, although as has been pointed out (Kapur, 1993) this patient also suffered other pathology such as temporal lobe damage. It is possible that marked "executive deficits" displayed by this patient may have played a part in his poor performance on some retrograde memory tasks. Goldberg et al. (1989) later suggested that this patient's "disexecutive syndrome" may have been due to a disconnection between reticular and frontal lobe structures. Unfortunately, this patient appears to have been lost to follow-up, such that MRI scanning does not seem to have been carried out.

Can Focal Temporal Lobe Pathology Result in Dense Autobiographical Amnesia?

Of all the lesion locations in the brain associated with memory loss, the temporal lobes have probably been the subject of more published reports than other areas. If focal temporal lobe lesions alone were to result in autobiographical amnesia, then this should have been evident in many of these reports, but such reports are conspicuous by the absence of any such data. Allowing for Teuber's famous dictum, "Absence of evidence is not evidence of absence", it is unlikely that major autobiographical amnesia would fail to be manifest at the clinical level. What about the other side of the coin—patients with dense autobiographical amnesia and intact temporal lobes? One possible case has recently been reported (Hunkin et al., 1995). This was a patient with a severe head injury, where MR imaging primarily showed bilateral posterior occipital lesions. The important proviso must be made that, as this was a case of severe head injury, temporal lobe damage may well have occurred but did not show up on brain imaging. Allowing for the possibility that mild forms of autobiographical memory loss may pass unnoticed and that cases such as the one described by Hunkin et al. are the exception, we would have to conclude on the basis of the available evidence that temporal lobe mechanisms alone are unlikely to result in major loss of memory for personally experienced past events.

Can Focal Frontal Lobe Pathology Result in Dense Autobiographical Amnesia?

Tulving et al. (1994) have recently linked retrieval from episodic memory to activation of right frontal lobe structures in normal subjects, but it remains to be seen if such findings represent an epiphenomenon related to the generation of retrieval strategies/cognitive effort for a difficult retrieval task or reflect the operation of specific memory processes. At the clinical level, very few cases of focal, dense retrograde amnesia, similar to those that have been reported in cases of temporal lobe pathology after severe head injury, have been documented where lesions have been solely or predominantly in the frontal lobes. Apart from the report of Della Salla, Laiacona, Spinnler, and Trivelli (1993), who suggested that significant autobiographical memory loss may accompany some cases of bilateral frontal lobe damage, most of the literature on frontal lobe lesions and memory functioning (e.g. Levin, Eisenberg, & Benton, 1991) has failed to indicate that frontal lobe lesions will do any more than exacerbate retrograde amnesia due to other causes or contribute to impairments on retrograde memory tasks where there is a complex retrieval/temporal dating component.

Can Damage to Pathways That Connect Anterior to Posterior Brain Areas Result in Dense Autobiographical Amnesia?

Disconnection theories of cognitive functioning in general, and of memory in particular, are relatively easy to generate but are more difficult to refute. They are seldom couched in terms that are precise enough at the neural level to result in specific predictions that can be tested by the presence or absence of particular brain–behaviour relationships. However, it would seem that some forms of disconnection hypothesis would predict that lesions to white matter structures that link anterior temporal lobe or frontal lobe areas with posterior association cortex may well result in major autobiographical memory loss. The arcuate fasciculus, which links the frontal lobe with the occipito-temporal cortex, and the inferior longitudinal fasciculus, which links the occipital and temporal lobes, would seem to be particularly strong candidates in this respect. Selective lesions to such connecting pathways have seldom been described. It could be argued that diseases that result in major white matter pathology, such as multiple sclerosis (e.g. Damian et al., 1994), or subcortical infarction (Corbett, Bennet, & Kos, 1994), should result in short disconnecting lesions, but major autobio-graphical memory loss has seldom been reported in these or similar conditions. Again, it is important to note that few such studies have formally tested autobiographical memory. Mild or even moderate autobiographical memory loss may have been present but escaped clinical attention, but it is unlikely that severe memory loss for past events would have passed unnoticed.

Can Damage to Posterior Association Cortices Result in Dense Autobiographical Amnesia?

As much of autobiographical retrieval relating to specific events could be argued to involve the generation of visual images such as pictorial scenes relating to these events, a link between damage to posterior association cortex and autobiographical memory would seem to be plausible. The study by Hunkin et al. (1995) reported dense autobiographical amnesia after lesions that were primarily to posterior cerebral structures, and Case 6 reported by Kapur (in press) also had damage that was largely confined to left posterior temporo-occipital cortex and white matter. The case of prosopagnosia and autobio-graphical amnesia reported by Ogden (1993) also had lesions that were primarily to posterior brain areas. However, these case studies appear to be the exception rather than the rule. In most reports of patients with bilateral posterior cerebral lesions, loss of memory such as prosopagnosia has been reported, but a loss of autobiographical memory has seldom been noted (Sergent & Signoret, 1992). It would seem, therefore, that damage that is solely or predominantly to posterior brain areas cannot lead to a dense autobiographical amnesia.

AN HYPOTHESIS

Most of the hypotheses that have been discussed here have proposed either single lesions to a particular structure or to connecting pathways that link that structure to other structures. The hypothesis that I would like to propose is one where dense autobiographical amnesia is considered to be due to lesions that are distributed over space and over time. There are overlaps between this model and those that have been discussed earlier, and also the proposal put forward by Teyler and Discenna (1986). My hypothesis primarily relates to autobiographical amnesia. Although there may be overlap with mechanisms that account for loss of general factual knowledge, such as famous faces (Eslinger et al., 1996), I think it likely that theories for such memory loss may end up being specific to the particular sets of functional deficits in question.

If we assume, as was outlined earlier, that the act of retrieval of a personally experienced past event involves multiple cognitive processes, then a single lesion in one of the critical areas—frontal, thalamic, temporal lobe, etc.—may result in some degree of diminution of the capacity to retrieve such episodes. However, a dense autobiographical amnesia will probably require more than a single lesion.

In common with other conceptual frameworks, I would distinguish between activation memory mechanisms and representation memory mechanisms. The former would be involved in tasks such as retrieval of past memories and would act on stored representations in a dynamic and flexible fashion in order to bring about a set of memories that met the requirements of the particular memory task. My hypothesis further entails the assumption of two sets of representation memory units—those that store perceptual and other elementary features of past events or ''feature codes'', and those that store contextual markers or ''index codes''. These index codes provide temporal and spatial frames of reference for each event, and are laid down at the time of the initial experience. I would propose that, for dense autobiographical amnesia to occur, significant damage must take place to both the representation units and to the index codes. I would propose that the feature codes are located throughout association areas of cortex, mainly in temporal lobe areas, but also in parietal and occipital areas. I further propose that the index codes are stored in the inferior and anterior parts of the temporal lobe and perhaps also in rhinal cortices and parahippocampal gyri. At present it is not possible to be more precise as to the anatomical structures that may be involved.

A final but important part of the conceptual framework that I am proposing concerns the pathological mechanisms by which such damage comes about. A variety of aetiologies may bring about an insult to the brain that results in retrograde amnesia. In cases such as ECT, severe trauma, or ischaemia associated with major vasospasm, the destruction that ensues may be significant, even though the duration of the insult is brief. In the case of chronic, subclinical epilepsy the intensity of insult may be mild but the duration may be months or years. If one assumes (as has been argued by researchers such as Squire, 1986) that reorganisation of memories takes place for years after an event has been experienced, then a chronic pathological process, however mild, may well interfere with this reorganisation and result in destruction of "engrams" or destruction of the index codes that bind such engrams to contextual markers. My hypothesis would account for the dense, relatively focal retrograde amnesia seen in some cases of severe head injury by postulating two pathophysiological mechanisms—(1) destruction to index codes, these probably being stored in inferior-anterior regions of the left temporal lobe; (2) destruction over a period of months, due to a prolonged period of coma/post-traumatic confusion, of feature codes which represent engrams that store features of particular experiences. I would hypothesise that this distribution of pathology over time is a necessary prerequisite for most types of cerebral insult, although it is possible that a more limited degree of significant autobiographical amnesia may result from an insult that may be very severe but that is limited in the duration of its pathophysiological effect. It is possible that only one of these two types of pathology may result in dense autobiographical amnesia if it is associated with damage to neural units that form connecting pathways from (1) to (2). This would explain cases such as that of Hunkin et al. (1995) and Case 6 of Kapur (in press) where dense, relatively focal autobiographical amnesia was associated with lesions that on MR imaging appeared to be restricted to posterior areas of the brain.

Although limbic-diencephalic structures may be critical for the initial acquisition and laying-down of memories, it would seem to be the case that more lateral temporal lobe structures are critical for the longer-term storage of memories. In general, these areas will govern the storage of both pre-illness onset memories and the storage of post-illness onset memories. Damage to neural mechanisms that underlie index codes or engrams that store features of past events may therefore in some instances result in loss of past memories without any loss of memory for some features of new learning. Thus, one may be able to explain instances where memory for material that is a few hours old is relatively normal, whereas pre-injury memories are lost—as in cases of focal retrograde amnesia, or where memory for material that is a few hours old is relatively normal but where very long-term retention of new information is impaired (Ahern et al., 1994; Kapur et al., in press).

CONCLUSION

Retrograde amnesia provides a probe with which we can examine one of the key questions in neural science—how is information stored in the brain? A detailed understanding of retrograde amnesia will require convergence from a variety of approaches, with data from clinical as well as normal subjects. Some of the data from non-human subjects, an area that was not covered in this paper, may also prove to be valuable in pointing us in particular directions. Clinical neuropsychology has its role to play in developing better test procedures for probing retrograde memory functioning and in selecting cases that offer unique opportunities to address certain issues in retrograde amnesia. The contribution of functional brain imaging procedures in normal and clinical populations remains to be determined, but these too may yield important data.

REFERENCES

Ahern, G.L., O'Connor, M., Dalmau, D., Coleman, A., Posner, J.B., Schomer, D.L., Herzog, A.G., Kolb, D.A., & Mesulam, M.M. (1994). Paraneoplastic temporal lobe epilepsy with testicular neoplasm and atypical amnesia. *Neurology, 44*, 1270–1274.

Corbett, A., Bennett, H., & Kos, S. (1994). Cognitive dysfunction following subcortical infarction. *Archives of Neurology, 51*, 999–1007.

Damasio, A.R. (1989a). The brain binds entities and events by multiregional activation from convergence zones. *Neural Computation, 1*, 123–132.

Damasio, A.R. (1989b). Time-locked multiregional retroactivation: A systems-level proposal for the neural substrates of recall and recognition. *Cognition, 33*, 25–62.

Damasio, A.R., & Damasio, H. (1989). *Lesion analysis in neuropsychology.* New York: Oxford University Press.

Damasio, A.R., & Damasio, H. (1993). Cortical systems for retrieval of concrete knowledge: The convergence zone framework. In C. Koch & J.L. Davis (Eds.), *Large-scale neuronal theories of the brain.* London: MIT.

Damasio, A.R., & Damasio, H. (1994). Cortical systems underlying knowledge retrieval: Evidence from human lesion studies. In T.A. Poggio & D.A. Glaser (Eds.), *Exploring brain functions: Models in neuroscience.* New York: John Wiley.

Damian, M.S., Schilling, G., Bachmann, G., Simon, C., Stoppler, S., & Dorndorf, W. (1994). White matter lesions and cognitive deficits: Relevance of lesion pattern? *Acta Neurological Scandanavica, 90*, 430–436.

Della Salla, S., Laiacona, M., Spinnler, H., & Trivelli, C. (1993). Autobiographical recollection and frontal damage. *Neuropsychologia, 31*, 823–839.

Eslinger, P.J., Easton, A., Grattan, L.M., & Van Hoesen, G.W. (1996). Distinctive forms of partial retrograde amnesia after asymmetric temporal lobe lesions. Possible role of occipitotemporal gyri in memory. *Cerebral Cortex, 6*, 530–539.

Goldberg, E., Antin, S.P., Bilder, R.M., Gerstmann, L.J., Hughes, J.E.O., & Mattis, S. (1981). Retrograde amnesia: Possible role of mesencephalic reticular formation in long-term memory. *Science, 213*, 1392–1394.

Goldberg, E., Bilder, R.M., Hughes, J.E.O., Antin, S.P., & Mattis, S. (1989). A reticulo-frontal disconnection syndrome. *Cortex, 25*, 687–695.

Hodges, J.R., & McCarthy, R.A. (1993). Autobiographical amnesia resulting from paramedian thalamic infarction. *Brain, 116*, 921–940.

Hunkin, N.M., Parkin, A.J., Bradley, V.A., Burrows, E.H., Aldrich, F.K., Jansari, A., & Burdon-Cooper, C. (1995). Focal retrograde amnesia following closed head injury: A case study and theoretical account. *Neuropsychologia, 33*, 509–523.

Johnson, M.K., & Chalfonte, B.L. (1994). Binding complex memories: The role of reactivation and the hippocampus. In E. Tulving & D. Schacter (Eds.), *Memory systems 1994* (pp. 311–350). Cambridge: MIT Press.

Kapur, N. (1993). Focal retrograde amnesia: A critical review. *Cortex, 29,* 217–234.

Kapur, N. (in press). Autobiographical amnesia and temporal lobe pathology. In A.J. Parkin (Ed.), *Classic case studies in the neuropsychology of memory.* Hove, UK: Lawrence Erlbaum Associates Ltd.

Kapur, N., Millar, J., Colbourn, C., Abbott, P., Kennedy, P., & Doherty, T. (in press). Very long-term amnesia in association with temporal lobe epilepsy: Evidence for multiple-stage consolidation processes. *Brain and Cognition.*

Levin, H., Eisenberg, H.M., & Benton, A.L. (Eds.). (1991). *Frontal lobe function and injury.* Oxford: Oxford University Press.

Levin, H.S., Peters, B.H., & Hulkonen, D.A. (1983). Early concepts of anterograde and retrograde amnesia. *Cortex, 19,* 427–440.

Milner, P.M. (1989). A cell assembly theory of hippocampal amnesia. *Neuropsychologia, 27,* 23–30.

Mishkin, M. (1993). Cerebral memory circuits. In T.A. Poggio, & D.A. Glaser (Eds.), *Exploring brain functions: Models in neuroscience* (pp. 113–125). New York: John Wiley.

Ogden, J., & Corkin, S. (1991). Memories of H.M. In W.C. Abraham, M. Corballis, & K. White (Eds.), *Memory mechanisms* (pp. 200–205). Hillsdale, NJ: Lawrence Erlbaum Associates Inc.

Ogden, J.A. (1993). Visual object agnosia, prosopagnosia, achromatopsia, loss of visual imagery, and autobiographical amnesia following recovery from cortical blindness: Case MH. *Neuropsychologia, 31,* 571–589.

Sergeant, J., & Signoret, J. (1992). Variety of functional deficits in prosopagnosia. *Cerebral Cortex, 2,* 375–378.

Squire, L.R. (1986). Mechanisms of memory. *Science, 232,* 1612–1619.

Squire, L.R. (1992). Memory and the hippocampus: A synthesis from findings with rats, monkeys, and humans. *Psychological Review, 99,* 195–231.

Teyler, T.J., & Discenna, P. (1986). The hippocampal memory indexing theory. *Behavioural Neuroscience, 100,* 147–154.

Tulving, E. (1989). Memory: Performance, knowledge and experience. *European Journal of Cognitive Psychology, 1,* 3–26.

Tulving, E., Kapur, S., Craik, F., Moscovitch, M., & Houle, S. (1994). Hemispheric encoding/retrieval asymmetry in episodic memory: Positron emission tomography findings. *Proceedings of the National Academy of Sciences, 91,* 2016–2020.

MEMORY, 1997, 5 (1/2), 131–178

Memory for Items and Memory for Relations in the Procedural/Declarative Memory Framework

Neal J. Cohen and Russell A. Poldrack

University of Illinois at Urbana-Champaign, USA

Howard Eichenbaum

Boston University, USA

A major area of research in memory and amnesia concerns the item specificity of implicit memory. In this paper we address several issues about the nature of implicit memory phenomena and about what constitutes an "item", using the procedural/declarative memory theory to guide us. We consider the nature of memory for items and of memory for relations among items, within the context of the procedural/declarative framework, providing us with the foundation necessary to analyse the basis for item-specific implicit memory phenomena. We review recent work from our laboratories demonstrating the fundamentally relational and flexible nature of declarative memory representation, in both humans and animals, and the essential role of the hippocampal system in relational memory processing. We show, further, that the memory representations supporting implicit memory phenomena are inflexible and nonrelational, and are tied to specific processing modules. Finally, we introduce empirical approaches that blur the distinction between skill learning and repetition priming, and show computational modelling results that demonstrate how these two implicit memory phenomena can be mediated by a single incremental learning mechanism, in accord with the claims of the procedural-declarative theory. Taken together, these various analyses of memory for items and memory for relations help to illuminate the nature of the functional deficit in amnesia and the memory systems of the brain.

INTRODUCTION

A major theme in the Mayes and Downes target article (this issue), and in the literature on memory and amnesia upon which it comments, is the *item specificity of implicit memory*. Exploring the item specificity of implicit memory would seem, at first blush, a straightforward empirical matter—having identified an important memory phenomenon, the field moves to explore its nature and characteristics. However, as we hope to make clear here, progress on this front

Requests for reprints should be sent to Neal J. Cohen, Amnesia Research Lab, Beckman Institute, University of Illinois, 405 N. Mathews, Urbana, IL 61801, USA. E-mail: njc@uiuc.edu

Russell A. Poldrack is now at Stanford University, CA, USA.

requires that we address some important issues about just what implicit memory is and about what an item is.

In this paper, we consider these issues at some length. Starting with implicit memory, we address the questions: To what level of description does the term implicit memory apply? How apt a characterisation of preserved learning in amnesia does it provide? and What aspects of normal memory does it best help illuminate? We then go on to consider the nature and implications of the claimed item specificity of implicit memory, asking: What is an item? and Where does the item specificity derive from and what are its implications?

It will be the central point of this paper that, rather than being a purely empirical matter, serious inquiry into the item specificity of implicit memory benefits greatly from a commitment to one or another theoretical approach to memory and amnesia. In our work, and in the analysis offered here, we are guided by the view that implicit memory phenomena, and the dissociation between spared and impaired memory abilities in amnesia, are best explained by distinguishing between *procedural* and *declarative* memory systems, and that the functional deficit in amnesia is the selective disruption of declarative memory. Using this framework, in this paper we discuss memory for items and memory for relations among items, in an attempt to illuminate a set of issues about the nature of amnesia and the organisation of normal memory.

IMPLICIT MEMORY

The distinction between explicit and implicit memory offered by Schacter and Graf (Graf & Schacter, 1985; Schacter, 1987; Schacter & Graf, 1986) revolves around whether or not conscious recollection of a "prior study episode" is necessary for memory performance. Tests of explicit memory depend on conscious recollection of the learning event, and refer the subject to some particular study episode or learning event (e.g. in the query: "What did you have for breakfast yesterday?" or in the instructions for a multiple-choice recognition memory test: "Which of the following items did you see on the previous list?"). Tests of implicit memory refer subjects to some processing task (e.g. "What is the first word that comes to mind that completes the stem *mot____*?"), and then measure the extent to which previous exposure to the to-be-tested stimulus materials changes the speed or accuracy of performance on the processing task. No conscious recollection of the learning event is required. As applied to amnesia, the claim is that amnesia is a selective deficit of explicit memory, leaving implicit memory fully intact. This conception of memory has been very popular, and is featured throughout Mayes and Downes' presentation.

We believe, however, that the use of these terms leads to confusion about the organisation of memory and the nature of amnesia because, as has been argued by Johnson and Hasher (1987) and Richardson-Klavehn and Bjork (1988), it conflates *types of memory tests* with *types of memory*. So far as we can see, these terms are still used indiscriminately by many authors to describe both memory tests and types of memory, except for those authors who now use the terms direct and indirect to describe memory tests, following Richardson-Klavehn and Bjork (1988), as we shall do here.

Levels of Description

In our discussion here of memory and amnesia, we distinguish among three levels of description: memory tests, memory phenomena, and memory mechanisms. We shall describe these three levels and consider what it is that "implicit memory" refers to at each level. *Memory tests* elicit the operation of, and assess, particular memory processes and mechanisms, requiring particular kinds of information for their successful completion. Some tests of memory direct subjects to gain access to specific prior learning events, requiring conscious recollection; others do not. Some memory tests require the ability to relate or bind together multiple, perceptually distinct objects or events; others do not. Some memory tests invoke only working memory capacities, while others require both working memory and long-term memory mechanisms. At this level of description implicit memory equates to indirect tests of memory, for which performance does not require conscious recollection of prior learning events.

Memory phenomena are manifestations of the operation of particular memory mechanisms, seen in the form of empirical findings. They are what we capture in memory tests and what we invoke hypothetical memory mechanisms to explain. Implicit memory phenomena include repetition priming, skill learning, nonrecollective (as opposed to recollective) memory, and preserved learning in profoundly amnesic patients. Priming is the benefit that accrues to the processing of a specific stimulus when it is repeated in a task; skill learning is the acquisition of ability that extends to new items in a task; nonrecollective memory refers to memory phenomena in which the subject just *knows* that a given item was presented previously but without recalling the context; preserved learning refers to the set of memory abilities that remain intact following brain damage that results in amnesia.

Memory mechanisms are the underlying (cognitive and neural) entities that *produce* the memory phenomena. What is implicit memory at this level of description? The implicit/explicit memory distinction, as proposed in the literature, offers no theory about or characterisation of the underlying memory mechanisms. It is less a proposal about memory mechanisms than it is a statement of the conditions necessary, or the tests best suited, for eliciting different memory performances. It speaks about different kinds of memory only in the sense of saying that there exists one kind of memory that is elicited with explicit (direct) tests, i.e. when directed towards conscious recollection of the learning event, and another kind of memory that is elicited with implicit (indirect) tests, i.e. when not directed towards conscious recollection.

Different classes of theories about the memory mechanisms supporting implicit memory phenomena, and explicit memory phenomena, include the view that there are functionally distinct *memory systems*, such as procedural and declarative memory (Cohen 1981, 1984; Cohen & Eichenbaum 1993; Eichenbaum, Otto, & Cohen, 1992, 1994; Squire, 1987, 1992; Squire & Cohen, 1984), or semantic and episodic memory (Tulving, 1972, 1983, 1991; Tulving & Schacter, 1990; Schacter & Tulving, 1994), and an opposing view that proposes a unitary memory system with functionally separable *memory processes*, such as the data-driven and conceptually driven processing view of Roediger and colleagues (e.g. Roediger, 1990). Note that, as argued persuasively by Jacoby (1991), multiple memory mechanisms can be involved in performance on a given memory test or in the production of a particular memory phenomenon.

It is easy to see how confusion could be engendered by not clearly disambiguating the meaning of implicit memory at the different levels of description just discussed. Accordingly, we find it useful to reserve the term implicit memory for referring to a class of memory phenomena. Like Richardson-Klavehn and Bjork (1988), we favour the terms direct and indirect to refer to tests of memory. Finally, as will be apparent later, we offer an explanation of implicit memory phenomena in terms of procedural memory mechanisms from within the declarative-procedural memory theory.

The Implicit/Explicit Memory Distinction and the Nature of Amnesia

The finding that patients, whose profound amnesias produce severe impairments in recall of the events of daily life and marked deficits in recognition of individuals and of objects with which these patients come into contact, nonetheless exhibit fully normal performance on a variety of indirect tests of memory, constitutes one of the most compelling phenomena in neuropsychology. Amnesic patients have demonstrated normal repetition priming effects and normal skill learning on any number of tasks for which their direct memory performance is grossly impaired (for reviews see Cohen & Eichenbaum, 1993; Squire, 1992; Tulving & Schacter, 1990). Is conceiving of the dissociation between spared and impaired memory abilities in amnesia in terms of the implicit/explicit memory distinction helpful in illuminating the nature of amnesia? We think not.

As noted earlier, the implicit/explicit memory distinction is not an account of memory mechanisms and hence cannot afford an explanation of *why*, given the nature of the impairment sustained in amnesia, the acquisition and expression of skilled performance remains intact in amnesia while explicit remembering is so profoundly affected. Moreover, even when conceiving of the implicit/explicit memory distinction only at the level of memory phenomena, there are serious shortcomings with a description of spared versus impaired memory abilities in amnesia in terms of implicit versus explicit memory, i.e. in terms of whether or not the tasks direct subjects towards conscious recollection of prior training events. One problem is that it provides no ability to make contact with the literature on animal models of amnesia. Although the animal literature has had little influence on the cognitive psychology literature on human memory, the animal model literature can and has been very illuminating with respect to the nature of human amnesia. Damage to the hippocampal system in rodents and nonhuman primates produces an amnesia that, like human amnesia, exhibits selectivity in the aspects of memory that are impaired. Such animals show impairments in learning and remembering of spatial relations among environ-mental cues, configurations of multiple perceptually independent cues, contextual or conditional relations, and comparisons among temporally discontinuous events. They are impaired when information learned in a given context must be expressed in or related to novel contexts. Yet the same animals can show normal learning and remembering of a large variety of conditioning, discrimination, and skill tasks. This dissociation among memory capacities is every bit as compelling as that seen in human amnesia and, in fact, parallels closely the dissociation in human amnesia (see Cohen & Eichenbaum, 1993; Eichenbaum et al., 1994). Theories of memory and amnesia unable to make any contact with this memory dissociation from the animal literature seem unduly limited in scope.

The second problem is that, even for the human amnesia literature, the implicit/explicit memory distinction is not adequate to correctly categorise all of the relevant behavioural data. More specifically, it turns out that the critical difference between the memory spared and the memory impaired in amnesia is not about conscious recollection after all, but rather about the ability to relate or bind together into a compositional representation any set of perceptually distinct objects or events. We will give two examples from our own work to illustrate.

Vocabulary Learning.   Gabrieli, Cohen, and Corkin (1988) attempted to teach new vocabulary to the patient HM and to normal subjects. Subjects were given implicit memory test instructions in conformance with the implicit/explicit memory framework, in that they were directed away from conscious recollection of the previous learning events, and memory was assessed in terms of improvement in performance across multiple trials. Subjects were trained and tested in a five-phase procedure. They studied eight vocabulary words (e.g. tyro, cupidity, manumit, anchorite) each with a one-line definition (e.g. cupidity—an inordinate desire for wealth) in an initial *definition-study* phase, and in a subsequent *synonym-study* phase, the same eight vocabulary words were paired with synonyms (e.g. cupidity–greed).

There were three testing phases—of definitions, synonyms, and the use of the words to complete sentence frames. In the *definition-test* and the *synonym-test*, subjects were shown a list of the definitions or the synonyms in a random order, with each of the eight vocabulary words appearing at the bottom of the screen, one at a time. For each word, subjects were asked to indicate which of the definitions or synonyms in the list "goes best with" the word at the bottom of the screen. Performance was assessed for each of the eight words in a series of trials with different random-order listings of the definitions or synonyms and different random presentations of the words until correct responses were given to all eight words on a single trial. In the *sentence-test*, the eight vocabulary words appeared in a random-order listing in the centre of the display, and sentence frames appeared one at a time (e.g. The king demanded excessive taxes from the people in order to satisfy his____) at the bottom of the display. Subjects were asked to indicate which of the words on the list "best completes" the sentence shown at the bottom of the screen. The procedure was identical to that used in the definition-test and synonym-test, involving the presentation of as many trials as necessary for subjects to attain errorless performance.

The results were striking: Whereas normal subjects learned the new vocabulary words readily, producing errorless choices of definitions within an average of 2.2 trials, of synonyms within 1.9 trials, and of sentence frame completions within 2.3 trials, HM was grossly impaired and, indeed, showed no measurable learning. He ended up receiving 20 trials of definition testing, producing over 200 errors, without showing improvement; then 20 trials of synonym testing, producing over 200 errors, without showing improvement; and then 20 trials of the sentence completion test, again without showing improvement.

The fact that his performance was basically at zero is not what is important here; no claim is being made about total inability to acquire new vocabulary. There is other work, by Glisky, Schacter, and Tulving (1986) and by Tulving, Hayman, and MacDonald (1991) demonstrating some slow, painstaking acquisition in some amnesic patients using rather different methods from those noted here. What is important is the profound impairment shown by HM, and by the patients studied by Glisky et al. (1986) and Tulving et al. (1991), despite using exactly the kind of indirect testing methods that usually produce normal implicit memory phenomena in amnesia.

Apparently, using an indirect (or implicit) test of memory, and hence obviating the requirement to gain access to some previous learning episode, is *not* sufficient to guarantee normal performance in amnesia. Accordingly, the issue of whether or not the test has a requirement for conscious recollection does *not* seem to be the critical determinant of whether memory is impaired versus spared in amnesia, after all. What is required in the vocabulary experiment, and what cannot be accomplished by HM, is the formation of memories for the seemingly arbitrary relations between words and their meanings (or synonyms). Studies of priming for word pairs have also shown that the performance of amnesic patients does not measure up to the performance of normal controls when the words are arbitrarily paired (see later). We believe that this is a crucial factor—that the ability to learn such relationships depends uniquely on a particular kind of memory, namely declarative memory, a fundamentally relational form of memory; and that amnesic patients will be impaired on such learning *no matter whether direct (explicit) or indirect (implicit) tests of memory are employed.* Another more recent example of work from our lab demonstrates this point even more clearly.

Eye Movements as an Indirect Measure of Memory.   Much work using indirect measures of memory has shown that prior familiarity with (i.e. exposure to) stimuli changes the efficacy with which these stimuli are processed, in terms of increased accuracy and/or shortened reaction times, when they are encountered on subsequent occasions. In recent eye movement monitoring experiments in our lab, we have been able to show that previous viewing of faces changes the *nature* of subjects' subsequent processing, changing the way in which people later visually explore these stimuli with their eyes. Using measures of the number and duration of eye fixations, and Markov-based measures of the predictability or constraint on transitions among successive fixation locations, it was possible to classify individual stimuli as having been previously viewed versus not having been previously viewed by individual viewers on the basis solely of his or her eye movements (Althoff, Maciukenas, & Cohen, 1993; Cohen et al., 1996). Moreover, in work with two well-characterised amnesic patients tested on faces that they could not distinguish on standard, direct tests of memory, we found the same differences in the way amnesic patients viewed famous faces compared to nonfamous faces as we saw in unimpaired college-aged subjects. Having developed these eye movement monitoring methods as an indirect (or implicit) measure of memory for faces, we assessed memory for the arbitrary relations among objects in scenes in amnesia (Whitlow, Althoff, & Cohen, 1995). Subjects saw real-world scenes and answered questions to each scene that required examination of the relevant object relations (e.g. ''Is there a chair behind the oranges?''). They viewed each of 40 scenes twice, and then viewed half of them for a third time and half of them in a manipulated version in which the relations among objects in the scene were changed (e.g. for the example given, the chair or the oranges may have had their positions changed). The scenes containing relational manipulations were perfectly perceptually coherent scenes; i.e. whether the chair was behind and to the left of the oranges as opposed to being behind and to the right of the oranges. But, because the manipulated scenes were altered with respect to a previous version of the scene, it was expected that, *to the extent that subjects had some memory representation of the relations among the critical objects from the previous version of the scene,* there would be a change in eye movement behaviour as well as in the reaction times necessary to answer the questions to the manipulated scenes versus repeats of the old scenes.

Reaction time data for unimpaired college-aged subjects showed a repetition effect, distinguishing between old and new items, and a relational manipulation effect, distinguishing between repeated old and manipulated old items. The same two amnesic patients mentioned earlier were run in this paradigm and showed a normal repetition effect but *no* relational manipulation effect (see Fig. 1).

The same pattern of results was seen in the eye movement data. Normal subjects showed a difference between old and new items, constituting a repetition effect. They also showed a relational manipulation effect, shown in Fig. 1 as a higher percentage of viewing time in critical regions (the regions in which manipulations occurred) in manipulated versions of the scenes compared to original (unchanged) versions of the scenes. The amnesic patients failed to show *any* relational manipulation effect, with no difference in viewing of the critical regions of repeated old versus manipulated old items.

The implicit/explicit memory distinction can offer nothing towards understanding why the repetition effect was preserved while the relational manipulation effect was impaired in amnesia despite both effects being measured indirectly (implicitly). If the critical determinant of performance in amnesia concerns the requirement for conscious recollection, i.e. whether the task involves implicit or explicit memory phenomena, then performance of amnesic patients on indirect tests of memory should be normal, even for relations among objects. If, however, the critical determinant concerns the requirement to learn arbitrary relationships, as suggested earlier, then performance of amnesic patients on tests of memory for arbitrary relations should be impaired, even when testing directly (or implicitly). This latter outcome is what was observed, both in the eye movement study just described and in the vocabulary learning experiment described earlier, suggesting that a different theory of memory is required in order to fully account for the pattern of impairment and sparing in amnesia.

The Procedural/Declarative Memory Theory

We have offered a different view, that we believe provides a straightforward account of these data. This view distinguishes between declarative and procedural memory (Cohen, 1981, 1984; Cohen & Eichenbaum, 1993; Eichenbaum et al., 1992, 1994; see also Squire & Cohen, 1984; Squire, 1987, 1992 for a related version). On this view, *the functional deficit in amnesia is the selective disruption of declarative memory*, i.e. of a fundamentally relational representation system supporting memory for the relationships among perceptually distinct objects that constitute the outcomes of processing of events. This system is to be contrasted with procedural memory, which accomplishes experience-based tuning and modification of individual processors, and involves fundamentally inflexible, individual (i.e. nonrelational) representations. We shall elaborate on this account in the next section of the

A) RT

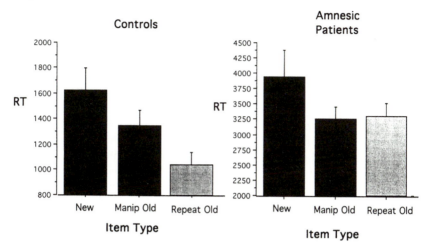

B) Eye Movements

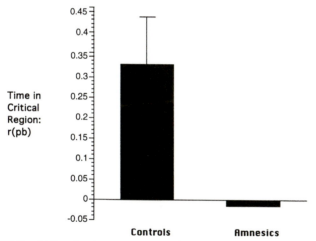

FIG. 1. (a) Reaction times to answer questions about new scenes, manipulated scenes, and repeated old scenes in the relational manipulation test for controls (left) and amnesic patients (right). Both control subjects and amnesic patients showed a repetition effect (repeated old vs. new scenes), but only the control subjects showed a relational manipulation effect (repeated old vs. manipulated scenes). (b) Point biserial correlations indicating the amount of viewing time during which eye movements were directed to the critical regions of the scenes in which relational manipulations occurred, comparing the manipulated items versus the repeated old items. The positive value on this measure for control subjects indicates that they spent more time in the critical regions for the manipulated items than for the repeated old items; the near-zero value for amnesic patients indicates that they failed to show this relational manipulation effect.

paper, first offering more description of the two kinds of memory (for a more complete treatment see Cohen & Eichanbaum, 1993 and Eichenbaum et al., 1994), then outlining some of the data that supports this view, and then discussing how its framework gives us some insight into the nature of memory for items and memory for relations among items.

Declarative memory is concerned with the accumulation of facts and data derived from learning experiences. This system represents the *outcomes* of processing by various modules engaged in identifying, appreciating, and responding appropriately to the objects and persons we encounter, and to the events in which we participate. Declarative memory serves to "chunk" or "bind" together the converging processing outcomes reflecting the learning event, providing a solution to the "binding problem" for memory.

Any complex event will involve information about the various visual objects present during the learning event, information about the sounds in the environment during that event, information about odours present, and so forth. The "binding problem" for memory concerns how these separate perceptual objects—separate constituents of the original event, each processed by different processing modules (visual, auditory, olfactory)—get bound together into a coherent representation of the event that captures all the information about the relations among them. The way in which this is accomplished seems to depend critically on the interaction of the declarative memory system with the various processing modules. The binding process seems to depend on the hippocampal system—the brain system whose damage in HM and other patients causes amnesia—and its reciprocal interconnections with all of the highest-order cortical processing networks of the brain. Co-activations of the various cortical networks constituting processing of the learning event converge onto the hippocampal network, providing the ability to represent in a single memory space the converging outcomes of processors that could not otherwise communicate. These cortical networks are still essential in providing the outcomes that undergo binding or chunking through the participation of the hippocampal system, and are the necessary storage sites of the (distributed attributes of the) memories that are thus formed. But it is the hippocampal system that provides the relational memory space in which the binding and chunking of the cortical outputs leads to the construction of declarative representations.

These outcomes of processing, represented in highly interconnected networks that capture various possible relations, provide the fundamentally *relational* character of declarative memory. Activation of any given declarative memory, i.e. activation of any given element or set of elements in declarative networks, automatically gives rise to activation of other related memories (i.e. of other connected elements), revealing or producing all manner of relations among the stored items. This in turn, gives rise to *representational flexibility and promiscuity*. That is, the full interconnectedness of such a representational system produces the ability of information to be activated regardless of the current context, i.e. by all manner of external sensory or even purely internal inputs. As a consequence, the representations are promiscuously accessible to— can be activated by—various processes and processing modules; and they can be manipulated and flexibly expressed in any number of novel situations, independent of the circumstances in which the information was initially acquired.

A crucial feature of the relational representation we propose for declarative memory is the property of *compositionality*: the representation of some scene or event, and the thinking or grasping of some complex idea, entails simultaneous representation both of the separate constituent pieces of knowledge and the larger structure they serve. Thus, for example, representation of an office entails both its office-ness (as opposed to, say, a bedroom or closet or auditorium), and its being composed of desk, chairs, windows, phone, books, and stacks of papers. Likewise, representation of an event such as a ball game involves simultaneously representing the event as distinct from other possible events, and also representing its constituent events and objects, such as parking the car, buying a hotdog, finding the seats, the players being introduced, and so forth. The important point is that a relational representation of scenes, events, and complex ideas in declarative memory is *not* as blends, or configurals, and does *not* involve conjoining of the multiple individual stimuli or constituent pieces of knowledge into unified knowledge structures (see later discussion of configurals and other unified knowledge structures). Rather, a relational representation preserves the status of the constituents of the larger structure while still permitting the larger structure to be appreciated.

This property of compositionality is critical to the generativity of language and, presumably, of thinking. Language and thought depend on the fact that the same constituent pieces of knowledge can be used to construct any number of larger structures (complex ideas, sentences, even book chapters), while still maintaining their own identity; an identity that must remain systematic across the different larger structures they help to form (see Fodor & Pylyshyn, 1988). It is the compositionality of relational representations that contributes so much to the ability of declarative memory to be *manipulated* in our heads and thereby contributes to (at least one aspect of) its characteristic feature of representational flexibility. These properties of declarative memory representation are also crucial to the exercise of consciousness and conscious recollection, as will be elaborated later.

By contrast, procedural memory involves memory representations that are *in*flexible and *non*relational, residing within and inextricably tied to the processing modules that were engaged during initial learning. This type of memory involves tuning of and changes in the way those operations actually run—that is, modification of the processing elements themselves. This accounts for the *in*flexibility and the nonrelational nature of procedural memory: The experience-dependent changes mediated by procedural memory occur only to those processing elements engaged during the initial learning event, and are accessible only to those processing modules involved and only when they are again engaged. The representations therefore can only be expressed or otherwise exert their influence under testing conditions that so closely mirror the circumstances of original learning as to constitute a repetition of the original learning situation.

Procedural memory can support performance whenever there is in place the processing machinery to derive a solution to the problem at hand; with practice, the processing machinery that is used will be tuned and biased by experience, gradually optimising its performance, producing facilitation when the same processors are again called on to derive a solution. Current views of learning algorithms capable of modifying neural networks in accordance with experience provide us with at least one way of understanding this type of memory mechanism: incremental changes occur in the strengths or weights of connections among the network elements, tuning and shaping the networks to gradually transform the way in which they operate.

Evidence for the Procedural-declarative Account

Converging evidence from various sources indicate that declarative memory, and the hippocampal system that supports it, mediates a fundamentally relational and flexible memory system that is selectively compromised in amnesia.

Neuropsychological.   A comprehensive analysis of the nature of preserved versus impaired memory abilities in amnesic patients and in animals with experimental lesions to the same brain systems damaged in human amnesia shows that amnesic patients are impaired on those tasks (or components of tasks) that depend on or benefit greatly from the ability to learn new relationships, and/ or that depend on or benefit greatly from the ability to manipulate and flexibly express memory in novel situations (see Cohen & Eichenbaum, 1993 for an extended treatment). This includes the recall or recognition of specific items (people, words, places, tunes, etc.), recollection of events, learning and remembering of arbitrarily associated items (e.g. names with faces, words with definitions, people or things that happened arbitrarily to be in the same place at the same time), and conscious introspection. As seen earlier, the deficit in memory for relational information occurs even when tested indirectly (implicitly). A recent, very interesting piece of neuropsychological evidence for the role of hippocampal-dependent declarative memory in the binding of items into a relational representation comes from findings of conjunction errors (false recognition of new objects composed of conjunctions of elements of previously seen objects) in patients with hippocampal amnesia (Kroll et al., 1995).

By contrast, normal learning occurs in amnesia on those tasks in which successful performance can be mediated by the tuning or biasing of processors and the incremental adaptation of behavioural performance in accordance with the regularities across learning events. These conditions are met in skill learning and repetition priming tasks, in which there is repetition of the original processing circumstances, and when experience-based modifications of these processors can impact on subsequent performance.

Functional Neuroimaging.   Despite the overwhelming evidence linking the hippocampal system to memory, many previous functional neuroimaging studies have been largely unsuccessful in finding reliable hippocampal activation during memory tasks, typically in attempts to compare conditions involving explicit versus implicit memory performances (see Buckner et al., 1995). One functional magnetic resonance imaging (fMRI) study examined hippocampal involvement in a task that, for the first time in functional imaging studies, required binding of multiple streams of information, in accordance with the procedural-declarative account described earlier (Cohen et al., 1994). Seven normal volunteers participated in two tasks involving the processing of colour images of computer-digitised faces, with names and occupation-related icons superimposed, rear-projected onto a high-contrast screen. In the baseline task, subjects made gender decisions about each face; information provided by the names or icons were irrelevant. In the memory task, subjects had a series of alternating study and test conditions requiring the binding together of the three different streams of information. The declarative-memory dependence of this task was verified in behavioural testing of two well-characterised amnesic patients who performed at chance levels (compared to 78% correct for the normal subjects) but normally on the gender decision task. Using a TURBO FLASH gradient-echo pulse sequence, 18 sagittal slices of the brain were collected at the rate of one per second throughout the entire 30-minute (baselines and memory task) session. In each of the seven subjects, activation (increased signal intensity on 99%-confidence T-maps) was observed in hippocampal regions in a comparison of baseline task versus memory task (see Fig. 2). Activation was initiated at the outset of the study phase of the first memory test condition and stayed elevated above baseline levels throughout the eight relational memory (study + test) task conditions.

Neuroanatomical and Neurophysiological.   The hippocampal system possesses the requisite anatomical connections and physiological machinery to perform the binding of converging inputs into relational representations. This evidence is discussed in detail elsewhere (see Cohen & Eichenbaum, 1993; Eichenbaum & Cohen, 1988; Eichenbaum et al., 1992); it will be outlined briefly here. The anatomical connections of the hippocampal system place it in a position to receive and to compute the relationships among converging inputs

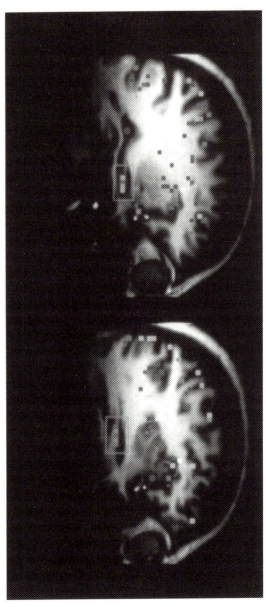

FIG. 2. Two consecutive sagittal slices through the brain of a subject in fMRI study, showing those areas with increased signal intensity, at the 99%-confidence level, for the condition requiring relational processing or binding of the face-name-icon streams of information versus the condition requiring only gender decisions. The box shows the hippocampal region. The overlap in the areas activated in the two slices, because the slices are consecutive, represent a 3-D volume of activation (From Cohen et al., 1994).

from multiple higher-order associational areas that convey information about the functional characteristics of "objects", "events", and "actions". That is, the hippocampal system receives as input the outcomes of processing of the brain's various processing modules, placing the hippocampal network in a position to process the conjunctions or associations of objects and events, and of their relative behavioural significance or task relevance.

Hippocampal neurons are activated by and seem to participate in the encoding or representation of all manner of relationships and conjunctions of significant events or objects. Hippocampal neural activity has long been known to reflect the processing of relationships among spatial cues, leading to a description of hippocampal neurons as "place cells" (O'Keefe, 1976). The observation of hippocampal place cells forms a major line of evidence used in support of the view that the hippocampus is dedicated to spatial processing. However, most studies demonstrating the spatial properties of hippocampal unit activity have employed tasks that emphasise spatial cues but minimise nonspatial cues. In studies that permit nonspatial cues to have prominence, other (nonspatial) relational properties of hippocampal neurons can be demonstrated. The relationships encoded by hippocampal neurons include relations among objects and their spatial locations (e.g. when a particular odour is produced at a specific location in the environment), and among objects or events and the task-defined relevance or significance of those objects or events (e.g. at a particular odour port when, and only when, the presentation of an olfactory cue needs to be sampled in order to get a reward). Confronted with different task environments on different occasions, the same hippocampal networks process different relationships among the events and objects they receive as inputs. We have argued that hippocampal neurons are more properly conceived of as "relational cells" (see Eichenbaum & Cohen, 1988).

Results from a study by Young, Fox, and Eichenbaum (1994) illustrate nicely this broader conceptualisation of relational cells. In this study, we recorded the activity of hippocampal complex-spike cells from rats performing a nonspatial radial maze task, in which performance was guided by local visual-tactile cues on the maze arms (distal spatial cues were made irrelevant). Of the units recorded, almost one fifth were classified as *cue cells* in that their activity was associated with cue type but not spatial location. A similar proportion of the units was classified as *place cells* in that their activity was associated with location, but not cue type. For yet a third similarly sized proportion of units, firing was influenced only by relative position and not by local cues or spatial locations. For the majority of units, however, firing was related to combinations of these three variables, indicating that most hippocampal neurons encoded conjunctions or relations between spatial and local cue information.

One final piece of evidence for the notion that the hippocampal system supports a fundamentally relational form of memory is the presence in hippocampus of a powerful associative learning mechanism (LTP) capable of mediating the representation of relationships. This form of synaptic plasticity is best elicited by activation of multiple inputs arriving in close temporal proximity—just the conditions required to support the relational processing that we propose is characteristic of hippocampal-mediated declarative memory. More generally, LTP is preferentially induced by patterns of conjunctive neural activity that occur naturally during hippocampal-dependent declarative learning.

There is another class of converging data that supports the declarative-procedural theory of memory, this evidence demonstrating the existence of *non*-hippocampal-based systems that support *non*relational forms of memory. Abundant evidence now exists documenting the plasticity of cortical processing areas, supporting procedural-like "tuning" mechanisms that operate throughout the lifetime of an animal to change the receptivity of the individual processing units within the basic processors of the brain.

Anatomical and Physiological Changes in Cortical Systems of Animals. Anatomical and physiological plasticity has been shown in primary visual cortex by manipulating the early visual experience of cats during a critical developmental period, producing changes in certain basic properties of visual cortex neurons (e.g. Blakemore, 1974; Hubel, Wiesel, & LeVay, 1977; Wiesel & Hubel, 1963, 1965). Rearrangements of the representation in primary somatosensory cortex of the body surface has been shown in monkeys following traumatic and more natural interventions in somatosensory input and in response to behavioural training (Merzenich, Recanzone, Jenkins, & Grajski, 1990; Recanzone, Allard, Jenkins, & Merzenich, 1990; Recanzone et al., 1992). Similar changes in the receptive field patterns as a result of specific training experience have been demonstrated in the auditory cortex of rats trained in a tone discrimination (Diamond & Weinberger, 1986). These and the aforementioned cortical rearrangements may be a general consequence of experiences that support learning and memory.

Plasticity in Humans as a Result of Learning and Memory.   With the advent of functional imaging technologies it has become possible to search for experience-based changes of cortical networks in humans. A series of PET studies have shown that repetitions of words in conditions that produce word priming result in changes (*decreases* in activation) in the occipital-lobe visual processing areas engaged by the reading task. Changes in the activity of neural networks accompanying implicit memory phenomena are also seen in recent fMRI studies. Perceptual learning resulted in changes in activation seen in the visual cortical areas that were engaged in the original perceptual processing (Ungerleider, 1994). The learning of specific finger movement sequences resulted in changes in the distribution of activation in motor cortex (Karni et al., 1994) and cerebellum (Kim, Ugurbil, & Stick, 1994) compared to that seen during the initial performance of the sequences. Finally, regions in left prefrontal cortex that were activated when performing semantic encoding of words showed a decrease in activation for repeated (already processed) words compared to new words (Demb et al., 1995).

All of these changes seem to occur as tunings or modifications of the actual processing elements in specific cortical (or subcortical) processors, dedicated to the particular processing systems engaged by the task just as predicted by the procedural-declarative theory. These examples of plasticity, and related cortical plasticities, are the substrate of procedural memory.

Neuropsychological Evidence.   When the cortical processors whose activity exhibits change accompanying implicit memory are damaged in certain neuropsychological patients, implicit memory phenomena are selectively compromised. Studies of two patients with damage to right occipital lobe areas, LH (Keane, Clarke, & Corkin, 1992) and MS (Gabrieli et al., 1995) show a selective deficit of visual word priming. The priming tasks on which they are impaired are the same ones that elicit activation of right occipital lobe areas in the PET studies mentioned earlier. These patients do not have deficits of explicit remembering of words or, for that matter, of other items. These data provide further support for the claim that implicit memory phenomena are mediated by procedural-memory modifications of specific cortical processing networks.

Consciousness and Recollective Experience

The issue of conscious recollection is a central one in human amnesia research. More than one investigator has commented on the ability of amnesic patients to exhibit what seems to be "memory without awareness" (e.g. Jacoby, 1984; Moscovitch, 1994). Moreover, the findings of dissociation between the ability of amnesic patients to exhibit normal acquisition and expression of skilled performance versus an inability to consciously recollect their learning experiences or to consciously introspect about the contents of their knowledge (Cohen, 1981, 1984; Cohen & Squire, 1980; Milner, 1962) can be fairly said to have irrevocably changed the direction of amnesia research. The implicit/ explicit memory distinction (Graf & Schacter, 1985; Schacter, 1987; Schacter & Graf, 1986) emphasises conscious recollection precisely because of this dissociation. Among other researchers, Gardiner (1988) has followed up these findings with research on the nature of recollective versus nonrecollective memory, defined as whether subjects can *recollect* the actual learning event in which a given item was presented as opposed to simply *knowing* that an item was presented previously without being able to get recollective access to any specific learning event. However, as noted earlier, the emphasis of the implicit/

explicit memory theory on conscious recollection prevents it from being able to make any contact with the animal work.

We can nonetheless ask to what extent are consciousness and recollective experience related to hippocampal function, declarative memory, and the nature of the deficit in amnesia? Notwithstanding Moscovitch's (1994) and Gray's (1995) claims about the essential role of the hippocampal system in consciousness, it seems that the hippocampal system neither produces conscious awareness nor is it critical for such. Large lesions of the hippocampal region, resulting in profound impairments of memory, have no demonstrable effect on consciousness in humans and no effect on "conscious" reactions to stimuli in animals, to the extent that such can be determined. Furthermore, hippocampal system damage has no effect on conscious recollection of remote memories.

In our theorising about the hippocampal system, declarative memory (explicit remembering), and conscious experience, we have proposed (Cohen & Eichenbaum, 1993; Eichenbaum et al., 1994) that the hippocampal system mediates the organisation of memory representations in widespread neocortical regions. The hippocampal system uses the outcomes of item comparisons to create and update networks of cortical memory representations to capture important relationships among the items, and these cortical memory representations can be used by a variety of processors. For example, in humans, the brain's verbal systems can access, manipulate, and express declarative memories of even wholly nonverbal events. Among those processors with access to declarative memory representations are whichever (not yet fully specified, but likely to include prefrontal cortex) extra-hippocampal brain systems are involved in conscious recollection and cognitively mediated processing.

Conscious recollection is envisioned, then, as another very powerful example of access to and manipulations within relational networks by high-order cognitive systems in humans and in animals. Thus, on our view, the hippocampal system plays only an indirect role in consciousness—it organises the database, so to speak, on which other brain systems may operate and, in so doing, determines the structure and range of conscious recollections.

Also, the importance of the hippocampal system in conscious recollection is limited: hippocampal damage prevents the establishment of new memory representations that are subject to conscious access but does not prevent access to memory representations consolidated prior to the damage. Because the hippocampus has a time-limited role in the establishment and updating of cortical relational representations, eventually the cortical networks can be accessed, and, in humans, conscious recollection of remote memories can be accomplished without hippocampal support. Accordingly, the hippocampal system is neither the place where consciousness occurs nor the system critical for its occurrence. Instead, it has evolved to support a particular kind of memory (declarative memory) that supports a variety of cognitively mediated and recollective processing tasks (see Eichenbaum & Cohen, 1995).

An Aside.   In light of the particular view we have offered about the relationality and flexibility of declarative memory, it seems likely that both awareness in humans and spatial memory in rodents are species-critical aspects of cognitive processing enabled by declarative memory. Rather than conscious awareness and spatial memory constituting the central functional role of the hippocampal system in humans and rats, respectively, it is declarative memory, providing the foundation for these and other cognitive activities, that constitutes the core of hippocampal functioning.

ITEM-SPECIFICITY

We turn now to the issue of item-specificity of implicit memory phenomena. Before we can begin to discuss the nature and implications of item-specificity, however, we must point out that there is a difficult question of just what an "item" is—an issue that is crucial to theoretical development in this area. Furthermore, considering the importance to our view of representations of the relations among perceptually distinct items, we must not only come to terms with what constitutes an item, but also with what are relations among items.

This is an area that appears to be fraught with confusion. However, there are two aspects of our theory of declarative and procedural memory that provide some guidance. One concerns the issue of the processing loci of procedural learning, and the other concerns the issue of when an item is part of a relational representation. We shall consider each of these in turn.

The Processing Loci of Procedural Learning

The notion of procedural memory that we have proposed takes very seriously the view that the brain and cognition have a modular architecture (e.g. see Fodor, 1983). Performance on any given task undoubtedly involves the processing contributions of a large number of distinct modules or processors; and, as a result of having been engaged by the task, the neural networks supporting each module will experience incremental tuning or other modification of its connection weights. These changes, which *are* procedural memory, can occur at multiple points in the stream of processing, from perceptual processors (leading to perceptual priming) to lexical processors (leading to word-level priming) to semantic processors (leading to conceptual priming).

This conceptualisation of procedural memory leads us to search for the specific processing loci of repetition priming effects or of other implicit memory phenomena, such as skill learning. That is, given behavioural facilitation on a task, we are interested in specifying the points at which processing has been changed due to experience. This view has important consequences for the question of what constitutes an item in any given task. Take, for example, a word priming task in which subjects study words and later perform a fragment completion test. According to our view of procedural memory, facilitation for previously studied words can occur at any of the processors involved in performance of the study task, including those processors specific to perceptual features, to letters, to orthographic subunits, to whole words, or to elaboration from words. Thus, even though to the subjects in the experiment it is the words on the study list that are being treated as items here, certainly when performance on this task is compared to performance on a task in which the study list is composed of word pairs, our view of procedural memory suggests that it may be more complicated than that.

Following from this notion of procedural memory, we can define an item as the functional unit of repetition in a task *with respect to a given processing module.* The definition of an item thus varies across processing modules. With respect to the word priming example given earlier, a perceptual feature (e.g. a vertical line) is an item from the point of view of the feature detectors in visual cortex, letters may be items from the point of view of the neural networks supporting letter recognition, and whole words may be items from the point of view of the networks effecting lexical recognition.

Processing Considerations

An immediate consequence of our conceptualisation of procedural memory is that we are in rare accord with critics of the multiple memory systems approach (e.g. Jacoby & Kelley, 1991) when they reject any notion that tasks could be classified as "process-pure". Performance on any task involves a (frequently large) number of processing modules, and thus can be expected to include variable contributions from different (processing and memory) systems. Any view that takes seriously the nature of neural information processing cannot help but reject the notion of process-purity; in fact, even the dual-process notions like those proposed by opponents of process-purity (e.g. Jacoby, 1991) seem rather implausible given highly modular neural organisation and the multiple levels at which performance can be altered by experience.

Another consequence of this conceptualisation is that the principle of transfer-appropriate processing (Roediger, 1990) falls out directly from the theory. The amount of performance facilitation caused by study depends on the degree to which study and test engage the same processing modules, and the degree to which those modules are used in the same way. That is, facilitation will be larger as a function of the extent to which the processors engaged at study and test view the stimulus materials as the same "items" at study as at test. The procedural/declarative theory gives a neurally plausible explanation for this well-established fact about memory performance, and helps us to see how it is tied to the issue of what constitutes an item.

Skill Learning and Repetition Priming

There has been much recent interest in the relationship between skill learning and repetition priming, which are both examples of implicit memory phenomena spared in amnesic patients (see Cohen, 1984; Cohen & Eichenbaum, 1993). What is taken to differentiate skill learning from repetition priming, definitionally, is item-specificity. Repetition priming refers to the beneficial effects of repeating the actual to-be-tested items; it is measured as the performance advantage for repeated over nonrepeated items; and is taken to be highly specific to the processing operations invoked while processing a given item (hence "item-specific implicit memory"; cf. Roediger, Weldon, & Challis, 1989; Tulving & Schacter, 1990). Skill learning refers to the generally beneficial effect that practice on a set of items has on nonstudied items in the same processing domain (e.g. the skill of reading extends to all well-formed sentences in a language). So, if skill learning and repetition priming are distinguished on the basis of item-specificity, then we had better be clear about just what an item is. As we shall see, later, ambiguity about what constitutes an item confuses attempts to explore the relationship between skill learning and repetition priming.

Our view of procedural and declarative memory makes the strong claim that skill learning and repetition priming are both supported by a single learning mechanism, namely procedural memory. Skill learning and repetition priming have in common their reliance on the same kind of incremental learning mechanism and share the same representation properties (i.e. inflexibility and nonrelationality). Skill learning is taken to be the sum total of all the individual repetition priming effects (Cohen & Eichenbaum, 1993). Note that this view of a common procedural memory mechanism for skill learning and repetition priming is at odds with Squire's (1992) description of "nondeclarative memory", embodying what he suggests is a collection of dissociable phenomena including skill learning, repetition priming, and other preserved learning phenomena, such as adaptation-level effects and some types of classical conditioning.

The relationship between skill learning and priming has recently been the subject of empirical inquiry, with a number of reports emerging of dissociations between skill learning and priming, both between neuropsychological groups and within normal subjects. In the next section we shall evaluate the dissociation evidence, concluding that the empirical evidence just does *not* make a compelling case for separate memory mechanisms underlying skill learning and priming. We base our conclusion on two considerations: one is new modelling data from our lab indicating that a single learning mechanism can produce both skill learning and priming, and, more to the point, can reproduce the various empirical relationships between skill learning and priming that have been used to argue for separate memory mechanisms. The second involves new empirical approaches in which items can be treated at multiple levels, blurring the distinction between skill learning and priming.

Dissociations? Neuropsychological Findings

A well-known finding from Heindel et al. (1989), who examined skill learning and priming in patients with Alzheimer's disease and patients with Huntington's disease, is that patients with Alzheimer's disease exhibited normal skill learning on the rotary pursuit task but impaired priming on the word completion test; patients with Huntington's disease exhibited an opposite pattern of spared priming and impaired skill learning. The Heindel et al. (1989) findings clearly demonstrate a dissociation. But what is the nature of this dissociation? The two tasks used to examine skill learning and priming differ quite clearly, with one based on motor processing and the other based on lexical/semantic processing. Given the motor deficits that occur in patients with Huntington's disease and the cognitive (including verbal processing) deficits that accompany Alzheimer's disease, it is not surprising that these patient groups would demonstrate the pattern of data observed by Heindel et al. (1989). The observed deficits need not have anything to do with skill learning and priming *per se*. In order to show that a fundamental dissociation between skill learning and priming is driving the observed differences between patient groups, it is necessary to test skill learning and priming within a single task—in either the motor domain or the lexical domain. Particularly with the new functional imaging and neuropsychological data described earlier, indicating implicit memory phenomena being tied to specific neural processors, it seems prudent for tests of possible differences between various implicit memory phenomena to be performed within a single domain tied to a specific neural processing system. Such a test has not yet been performed.

Dissociations? Studies With Normal Subjects

Dissociations between skill learning and priming have also been noted in normal subjects. Schwartz and Hashtroudi (1991) found that the amount of priming and the amount of skill learning exhibited by subjects were uncorrelated in both mirror-reading and word identification tasks, and that word frequency affected the amount of priming but did not affect skill learning. Kirsner and Speelman (1995) found that priming remained constant across a number of training blocks while skill learning increased. It has been suggested that these findings constitute dissociations between skill learning and priming that necessitate separate underlying memory systems to support them.

In order to examine whether these empirical findings do indeed suggest the operation of separate underlying systems, we explored a number of computational models, assessing the extent to which single-system models could accommodate the dissociation data (Poldrack & Cohen, 1996a). We used two different classes of models, a connectionist model and a model based on Logan's (1988) instance theory, in both of which a single learning mechanism was used to model both skill learning and priming. In a series of simulations, exploring the effects of a variety of parameter manipulations, we were able to reproduce the various patterns of data claimed to necessitate separate skill learning and priming mechanisms. We demonstrated a constant level of priming across various levels of skill learning, and a lack of correlation between skill learning and priming, in systems with just a single memory mechanism. The fact that the various relationships between skill learning and priming thought to indicate memory systems could be reproduced in two different classes of single-memory-system computational models casts serious doubt on claims of separate underlying memory systems for these two memory phenomena. In these modelling results, as in our procedural-declarative memory theory, skill learning and repetition priming seem to be different manifestations of a single memory system.

Ambiguity About What Constitutes an Item: Implications for Skill Learning and Repetition Priming

As we have noted, procedural memory mechanisms operate on whichever neural networks are involved in performance on a given task and work to tune or bias these networks incrementally over time so that they function optimally in the immediate stimulus environment. The determination of whether a given implicit memory phenomenon represents skill learning or repetition priming must depend, we believe, on an analysis of the processing loci of facilitation in performance. Suppose, in a task involving reading of individually presented mirror-reversed words, there is tuning at both of two different levels—the level encoding the regularities in the visual features that constitute mirror-reversed letters, and the level encoding the regularities of the letters composing mirror-reversed words. In such a case, the same experience-based tunings of those levels will produce both repetition priming for the specific words that had been presented previously (repeated items would have an advantage at the letter-to-word level) and a generalised skill learning effect (because, given enough study items, all letters will have been "primed" at the features-to-letter level). Accordingly, the distinction between skill learning and repetition priming becomes rather artificial.

An Empirical Example: Digit Entering Task

Recent work from our laboratory (Poldrack, Selco, Field, & Cohen, 1996) has examined skill learning and repetition priming together in a single task, which will serve to demonstrate some ways in which multiple levels of facilitation can coexist to determine task performance, making the distinction between skill learning and repetition priming seem artificial. Subjects were presented with five-digit numbers (e.g. ''49218''), and entered these numbers onto a numeric computer keypad. They performed three sessions of the task, with 512 trials in each session. The stimuli were constructed using a set of rules that constrained the possible transitions between digits; for example, the digit 5 might be followed exclusively by the digits 1, 3, 7, or 8 (see Fig. 3). In each block of 48 trials, some numbers were unique (i.e. presented only once in the entire experiment) and some were repeated (i.e. presented in every block). Extensive balancing was performed to control for the frequency of occurrence of each digit in each position in the numeral and the frequency of each digit-to-digit transition, so that repetition effects (the difference between repeated and unique items) could be reasonably attributed to memory for whole numbers.

In a third session, subjects were also presented with numbers constructed from a transition rule set complementary to the one used to construct the training numbers: e.g. if 5 had been followed by 1, 3, 6, or 8 in the training numbers, it would be followed by 2, 4, 7, or 9 in the new number set. The stimulus number remained on the screen until the subject entered the first digit, and response times were measured for the response latency (time from stimulus onset until the first response) and interkeystroke interval (IKI; the average time between successive keystrokes).

Reflection on this task reveals multiple levels at which learning could (and likely would) occur. At the level of general skill learning alone, there are many possible sources of facilitation. Number recognition, stimulus–response mapping, and spatial response learning (i.e. learning key locations) are all possible sources of general learning. In addition, specific fragmentary number knowledge (e.g. two- or three-digit number chunks) could result in general facilitation to the extent that the entire item set shares those same subunits. At the level of whole numbers, there are both perceptual and motoric levels at which memory could influence performance.

The results of the experiment are presented in Fig. 3; IKI data are shown for brevity, but initial latencies exhibited the same patterns. Subjects exhibited significant skill learning, as seen by a decrease in IKI on unique items across training blocks. There was an additional increase in performance for repeated items, showing that subjects acquired number-specific information. Performance in the third session was reduced for items from the complementary rule set, suggesting that some portion of skill learning in the task comprised transition-specific knowledge; however, the fact that performance on the new-transition items did not return to the level of initial performance suggests that skill learning also comprised more general learning (e.g. perceptual-motor mapping of numbers to number keys). The transition rule results are quite similar to those presented by Masson (1986) for mirror-reversed reading, in which skill learning in the task was specific to only those letters and letter groups actually present in training.

5-Digit Number Construction

Transition Rule Set 1 Stimuli

13794
81526
92184
39619

Transition Rule Set 2 Stimuli

12836
61469
36162
97317

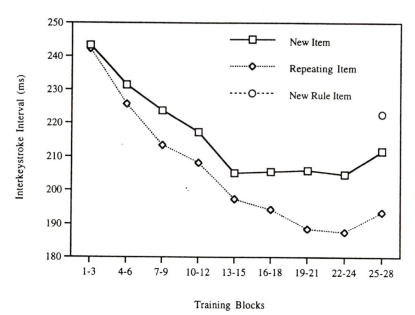

FIG. 3. (top) Examples of transition rules for constructing the five-digit stimuli in the digit-entering task. (bottom) Interkeystroke interval data from the digit-entering experiment for new and repeating items, and, for blocks 25–28, for new, repeating, and new rule items. Repeating items were responded to faster than new (same rule) items which were, in turn, faster than new rule items. (Adapted from Poldrack et al., 1996).

These results prove difficult to account for if one attempts to draw a strict distinction between skill learning and repetition priming. For example, take the transition-specific transfer effects seen in session 3 of the experiment. To the extent that these effects contributed to performance on a wide range of stimuli (i.e. all numbers constructed from that transition rule set), this can be construed as an instance of skill learning. However, the effects were specific to components (transitions) of the stimuli, so they might also be construed as repetition effects. We interpret these results as demonstrating that performance on the task must be understood in terms of multiple loci of learning. The contribution of the various loci can then be assessed through transfer tests which examine the contribution to performance of each locus. However, in general it will be difficult to account for all possible loci of learning, and analysis of performance will have to be guided by a theory of the task that states which levels are important for performance.

When is an "Item" in Memory Part of a "Relational Representation"?

On the view we have offered, declarative memory involves relational representations of scenes and events, exhibiting the crucial property of compositionality, in which there is maintained both the elements of the scene or event and the relevant relations among the elements (Cohen & Eichenbaum, 1993). Procedural memory entails a form of representation in which, rather than the constituent elements of a complex scene or event being represented in a relational, compositional way, instead the elements may be combined into blends, or configurals, involving conjoining of the constituent elements of the scene or event into unified, nonrelational knowledge structures.

What we mean by an item is an independent percept, or conceptual unit, that constitutes the outcome of processing of one or another processing module. One example of an item is a particular face. Faces are quite complex, of course, yet we perceive a face as an independent percept and indeed judge it to be the same conceptual unit through a large variety and range of changes in size, contrast, orientation, and other perceptual transformations. Faces could, at least in principle, be broken down into an organisation of elements and described by the relations (distances and angles) between smaller items like eyes, ears, mouth, and nose. But to the extent that such calculations (and decompositions) are made, it seems they are accomplished at *early* stages of visual processing. But the neurophysiological machinery that is at the end-point of the visual processing stream for object recognition, and that then goes on to feed its computed outcome to the hippocampal system, has been shown to encode a face as an item: cells in inferotemporal cortex show strong constancy in their response to a face throughout the large variety and range of transformations (Perret, Mistlin, & Chitty, 1987).

Note that this finding clearly goes beyond issues of the "binding problem" in perception. It is not only that the elements of a face are perceived as a composite because of parallel motion, continuous contour, and other strict perceptual features. In the case of a particular face, the concept is constant across many reoccurrences and a very broad range of perceptual transformations that exceed simply holding together the set of elements; grandma's face is "grandma" no matter what hairdo and hat she wears, with make-up or not, etc. Thus a conceptual item involves much more than the binding of elemental perceptual features.

Still, a face is a relatively "easy" example of an item, one that we can all easily accommodate by stretching our notions of perceptual processing. How about yet more complex things? Is it possible, for example, that an item can involve a set of faces? Let us begin to answer this question with an analogy that we suggested some years ago (Eichenbaum, Cohen, Otto, & Wible, 1991). Imagine viewing a photograph of some family gathering, say a barbeque in the back yard. If you are a member of that family, even this isolated photo will be capable of evoking a sense of familiarity for, and a heartwarming memory of, the occasion captured in the photo. You may well be able to reconstruct many of the events that occurred that day, and will probably be reminded of similar events. In remembering these related events, you may find it much like perusing a family photo album stored in your memory. The various entries in the "memory photo album" are all interconnected, or, as discussed earlier, compositionally linked, in one way or another. Each of them helps trigger related memories of other scenes and events. Thinking about the individual people and places featured in any one of these events will probably remind you of other events and scenes in which they also participated and to which they are also connected. That is, they exhibit compositionality, permitting memory to be maintained not only of the whole event (the barbeque) itself, but also of the various constituent elements (the various family members, pets, etc. in attendance that day). The various "items" depicted in the photograph are clearly part of a larger relational, compositional representation.

But to someone who is not a member of the family, all you have is a snapshot without the album—just an isolated, complex scene that is outside the temporal and spatial context of your own life's scenes and events. The scene depicted is not familiar, and may not be connected or related at all to the rich network of your own personal memories. The individual people and places captured in the scene have no independent meaning to you outside the scene. All in all there is little you can do with the depicted scene with respect to the scenes and events stored in your memory. A memory of this "snapshot without an album" is likely to be maintained as a single conjoined or configural "item" of the kind that does not involve declarative memory.

The Experimental Analysis of Compositionality

These properties of declarative and procedural memory should permit us to discern whether items in memory have been incorporated into relational representations, linked compositionally to any number of other relational representations, or whether they remain individual memories. In making this distinction in experimental analyses, we rely on the property of "flexibility" that defines compositionality, and conversely the inflexibility characteristic of nonrelational representation of items. It is this nonrelational, inflexible form of representation that seems analogous in some respects to the analogy of the snapshot without an album.

Schacter (1985, see also Tulving & Schacter, 1990) has also written about the "hyperspecific" nature of memories supporting preserved skill learning and priming in human amnesic patients. For example, Glisky and Schacter's (1987, 1989) studies on teaching amnesic patients certain job-relevant terms to use on a computer revealed that patients could, after a great deal of painstaking repetitive practice, learn to enter relevant computer commands, but their knowledge was "hyperspecific"—it could be expressed only when the training conditions were reproduced. Moreover, it has been amply documented that skill learning and repetition priming are so sensitive to changes between training and test conditions that the modality of stimulus presentation and even the specific type font of verbal stimuli become critical variables.

Beyond these examples, it is important that direct, operational methods be used to determine whether a memory has been stored as an isolated item or in a relational representation of the organisation of the elemental items. Our experimental strategy involves two stages: first, we train patients or animals with hippocampal system damage on tasks that involve learning specific associations, assessing the learning performance of amnesic subjects versus controls. Second, we probe the representations acquired by all subjects during training, assessing just how relational the stored memories are and how flexibly they can be expressed. Patients or animals with damage to the hippocampal-dependent declarative memory system should have only isolated, hyperspecific, inflexible situation-dependent representations, and should learn only those tasks for which such representations provide an adequate solution. These representations would be, and are, capable of capturing certain "associations", but as configurals or blends, i.e. in a noncompositional form. To determine the general applicability of this experimental strategy we have applied it to several different categories of materials.

New Associations in Human Amnesia?

The question of whether human amnesics can acquire memory for new associations has been quite contentious. As amnesic patients are by definition impaired on direct tests of memory for new associations (e.g. the delayed paired associates section of the Wechsler Memory Scale), interest has centred on the examination of memory for new associations on indirect tests. We will describe three tasks that have been used to examine this question: word completion with word pairs, reading time, and the Stroop task. In each case we will consider whether new associations can be learned, and the degree to which the putative representations are hyperspecific and inflexible versus flexible and compositional.

Word Completion with Word Pairs.   The first reported finding of memory for new associations on an indirect test of memory was presented by Graf and Schacter (1985). In their experiment, subjects first studied normatively unrelated word pairs (e.g. WINDOW–REASON). They were then tested using word-stem completion as an indirect test of memory; subjects were told to complete the stem with the "first word that comes to mind". In the same-context test condition, subjects were presented with a context word that matched the one presented with the target at study (e.g. WINDOW–REA____). In the different-context condition, subjects were presented with a different context word from the one presented with the target at study, but which occurred elsewhere in the study list (e.g. CLIENT–REA____). Graf and Schacter (1985) found that, for both normal subjects and amnesic patients, the target was completed with the studied word more often in the same-context condition than in the different-context condition. This result suggested to them that amnesic subjects could acquire memory for new associations in a normal manner when tested indirectly.

This result did not survive further scrutiny, however, as noted by Mayes and Downes (this issue). Several subsequent studies with this task failed to replicate the same-context effect in severely amnesic patients (Cermak, Bleich, & Blackford, 1988; Mayes & Gooding, 1989; Shimamura & Squire, 1989). More important, two studies (Mayes & Gooding, 1989; Shimamura & Squire, 1989), both of which found no group effects of the context manipulation in amnesics, nevertheless found significant correlations between individual context effects and residual declarative memory in amnesic patients. These findings suggest that the same-context effect was not mediated by an intact hippocampal-independent learning mechanisms in amnesic patients.

Reading Time.   When a passage of text is read multiple times, the reading time for the text is decreased (see Levy, 1993, for a review). This text-specific benefit has been shown in amnesic patients (Musen, Shimamura, & Squire, 1990) and subjects with Alzheimer's disease (Monti et al., 1994), and is thought to involve both semantic and structural levels of the text. A related method has been developed by Moscovitch, Winocur, and McLachan (1986) that can support finer-grained hypotheses about the nature of learning in text rereading. In this task, subjects read a list of normatively unrelated word pairs rather than paragraphs of text. Pairing-specific information can then be manipulated without changing the semantic organisation of the stimuli.

Moscovitch et al. (1986, Experiment 3) presented 30 unrelated word pairs individually at study, and then presented three test lists, containing 10 studied word pairs, 10 recombined pairs of studied words, and 10 new word pairs respectively; reading time for each list was measured with a stopwatch. Young subjects, matched elderly control subjects, and a group of memory-disordered subjects (predominantly patients with early-stage Alzheimer's disease) were tested. An overall planned comparison on the reading time data for all groups showed a significant difference between old and recombined word lists, suggesting that the memory-disordered subjects acquired memory for word pairs. However, separate statistics were not reported for each group, and it is not clear from the data that the difference in reading times for old and recombined items in the memory-disordered patients is as large as the difference for control subjects.

Musen and Squire (1993b) attempted to replicate the Moscovitch et al. findings in a set of well-characterised amnesic patients and matched control subjects. In an experiment that closely followed the method used by Moscovitch et al., Musen and Squire (1993b) failed to replicate the pairing-specific reading time effect; there was no difference between old and recombined word pairs for amnesic or control subjects after a single study trial. Musen and Squire speculated that the difference in findings could have been due to the way in which reading times were measured (Moscovitch et al. used a stopwatch, whereas Musen & Squire used a speech digitiser for more accurate measurement), or in the nature of the tested subject populations. In other experiments, Musen and Squire (1993b) found that pairing-specific repetition effects for normal subjects and amnesic subjects only occurred after multiple (10) study trials. They concluded that memory for new associations can be acquired by amnesic subjects in an incremental fashion, different from what happens in normal subjects, although they may be acquired in a single trial under some circumstances.

The importance of reading time studies for our understanding of amnesia depends crucially on what is learned that can mediate the facilitation for new associations. If subjects learn new abstract relationships between words, theories of amnesia that postulate a deficit in relational (Cohen & Eichenbaum, 1993) or contextual (Mayes, 1988) processes will have difficulty explaining the data. If the facilitation for new associations is due to tuning of existing processes or procedures for perceiving and producing letter (or sound) combinations—i.e. if the "item" is letters, letter combinations, or sound transitions rather than words—these theories need not be challenged by findings of memory for new associations.

Recent studies from our laboratory (Poldrack & Cohen, 1996b) have examined the nature of learning in the word pair rereading task, and suggest that learning in the task does *not* involve the acquisition of new abstract relational knowledge. We presented six lists of 20 word pairs for three presentations each; on the first two presentations, the word pairs and positions within the pair remained constant, but the order of pairs in the list was random. On the third presentation, some of the word pairs were manipulated. Three manipulations were used. In Experiment 1, the words were re-paired for three of the word lists; this conceptually replicated Experiment 3 from Moscovitch et al. (1986), but with an extra study presentation. In this experiment, we found a significant difference between old pairings and changed pairings on the third presentation (see Fig. 4).

Experiment 2 examined whether changes that left pairings intact but changed the production operations at test would result in reductions in facilitation. In this experiment, on the third presentation word pairings were left intact but the (left–right) positions of the words were changed within the pair. If the pairing-specific facilitation is due to the acquisition of abstract pairing knowledge, then this change should have no effect. However, a significant effect of position change was found in Experiment 2; indeed, this effect was similar in size to the effect of pairing changes in Experiment 1 (see Fig. 4).

In response to Experiment 2, it might be argued that subjects acquired directional abstract associations between words in each pair; the position change would thus disrupt the retrieval of directional associational information. In Experiment 3, we tested this argument by inserting the word "and" between the paired words, and then examining the difference between old and new pairs. If subjects acquire abstract associational knowledge, then the insertion of "and" should not interfere with the pairing-specific repetition effect. We found, however, that the insertion of "and" *eliminated* the pairing-specific effect (see Fig. 4). These findings suggest that the pairing-specific repetition effect lies in the facilitation of specific production operations, for example in producing the sound transitions necessary to say word pairs fluently. The repetition effect in this task is *not* supported by a compositional, relational representation, but instead appears to be supported by an inflexible, procedural memory representation. Accordingly, the ability of amnesic patients to show such a repetition effect would be fully consistent with our view that the functional deficit in amnesia is a selective disruption of relational memory processing.

Colour–word Associations.   Musen and Squire (1993a) examined the learning of new colour–word associations in a Stroop task. Subjects were presented with conflicting Stroop stimuli (e.g. the word "RED" drawn in blue), and named the colour in which the word was written (i.e. the correct response in the previous example would be "blue"). A set of six stimuli were presented for four blocks with the same conflicting colour–word pairings. Colour-naming time was reduced across these four blocks for normal subjects and amnesic patients.

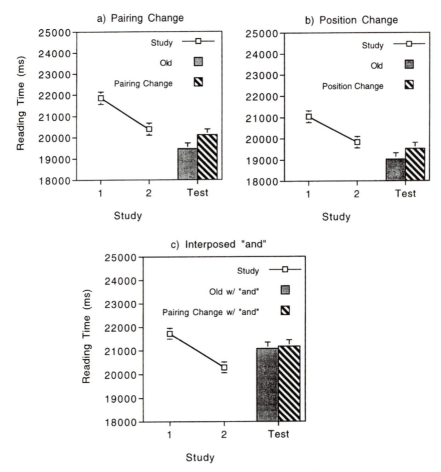

FIG. 4.   Reading time data for word-pair reading experiments. For all three panels, performance is shown for the two study presentations and for a third presentation in which either the same word pairs are re-presented or are presented with some change. (a) Experiment 1: changed pairings; changing the pairings slowed reading time. (b) Experiment 2: changed position; changing the left–right positions of the words within a pair slowed reading times. (c) Experiment 3: interposed "and" plus changed pairings; interposing "and" between the words of a pair slowed reading times equally for the same versus changed-pairings presentations. (Adapted from Poldrack & Cohen, 1996b).

Subjects were then presented with newly re-paired colour–word stimuli, in order to assess the degree to which the facilitation in the first four blocks was pairing-specific. Both amnesic subjects and normal subjects exhibited negative transfer when the colour–word pairings were changed, suggesting that both had acquired new colour–word associations. Amnesic subjects were impaired, however, on a recognition test for these associations.

Importantly this spared associative learning by amnesics occurred when multiple training trials were given, i.e. when an incremental learning process of the sort we attribute to procedural memory can manifest itself, and, based on further analyses of this phenomenon by Musen and O'Neil (1994), only when the colour and word are presented as readily fusable or unitised composites. There is no evidence that this form of learning is supported by compositional, relational representations.

The Nature of Items and Relations in Rodents

In this section, we shall examine memory in odour discrimination learning and in spatial learning tasks; we will then move to discussion of whether or not amnesic animals can learn new associations, considering, as with our treatment of the human amnesia literature, the nature of the relations that can and cannot be learned.

Hippocampal Representation in Odour Discrimination Learning.   After disconnection of the hippocampal system by transection of the fornix, impairment was observed when the discriminative cues were presented simultaneously and in close juxtaposition, encouraging the comparison of multiple cues and a memory representation of the relations among them. Yet *facilitation* of learning was observed when the same odour cues were presented successively across trials, hindering their comparison and encouraging individual representations for each odour (Eichenbaum, Fagan, Mathews, & Cohen, 1988). In a follow-up experiment using the simultaneous discrimination task we explored the nature of relational learning (Eichenbaum, Mathews, & Cohen, 1989). We had observed that despite the severe impairment on this task, rats with hippocampal system damage occasionally learned (some) new discrimination problems at a normal rate. Accordingly, we trained pairs of intact rats and rats with fornix lesions on an extensive series of odour discrimination problems, until the rats with fornix transections succeeded in learning two problems at a normal rate. This required presentation of up to 10 problems for some subjects with fornix lesions. When all rats were performing consistently well in overtraining on the instruction problems, we challenged their memory representations with probe trials composed of novel "mispairings" of the rewarded odour from one problem and the nonrewarded odour from the other (Fig. 5). These probes were presented only occasionally, intermingled among frequent repetitions of the original instruction trials. Intact rats performed as well on probe trials as on instruction trials, as these were all odours that had been previously presented and they all maintained their original reward valence. But rats with fornix lesions, while maintaining good performance on repetitions of the instruction trials, performed at *chance* levels on the probe trials, as if presented with novel stimuli. They demonstrated the same "inflexibility" of responding, and hence the same absence of compositional representations, that we observed in human amnesia in the experiments described earlier.

Hippocampal Representation in Place Learning.   Probe testing of the presence or absence of relational representation and flexibility was extended to performance in the water maze task, in which rats must use distal visual cues to find the location of a hidden escape platform from various starting points (Morris, Garrud, Rawlins, & O'Keefe, 1982). On our view, the procedure of releasing animals from different start locations during instruction introduces conflicts among the individual associations of views along the different trajectories towards the constant goal location, making it advantageous to represent the place of escape according to positional relations among these cues. Consistent with this view, rats with hippocampal system damage are severely impaired in the standard version of this task.

In our variant of the standard procedure, we circumvented the confusions arising from the variable-start procedure by releasing rats from a constant position on each trial, with a constant goal location, thus making the association of cues observed along a single trajectory unambiguous. Comparing performance under both conditions, we found that rats with fornix lesions failed to learn the water maze with a variable-start position, but succeeded in place learning guided by the same distal cues in the constant-start condition (Eichenbaum, Stewart, & Morris, 1990).

Analogous to our strategy in the odour discrimination experiments, we assessed the flexibility of place representations by presenting probe trials that challenged rats to locate the escape site from novel start positions. These probe trials were presented occasionally among frequent repetitions of the instruction trial. Normal rats performed well on repetitions of the instruction trial given just before each probe trial, and also swam directly to the goal location from *novel* start positions. In contrast, rats with fornix lesions, while continuing to perform well on repetitions of the instruction trials, often headed out in the wrong direction and required considerably more time to locate the goal location when starting from *novel* start positions (see Fig. 6).

A further observation on the pattern of behaviour in rats with fornix lesions gave additional insight into the nature of their place memory representation. We identified two salient cues that were directly in the line of view towards the escape site along the route taken on instruction trials, and rotated these cues 180 degrees. On another probe trial using these rotated cues, we also started rats in a

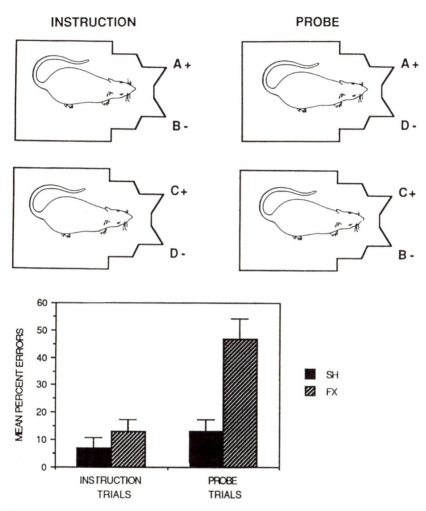

INSTRUCTION   PROBE

A +

B -

C +

D -

A +

D -

C +

B -

FIG. 5. Assessment of flexible use of odour memory representation. (top) Schematic diagrams on the left illustrate examples of trials on two instructional problems (odours A+ vs. B– and C+ vs. D–) that rats with lesions of the fornix (FX) learned as rapidly as sham-operated (SH) rats. Flexible use of their representations was assessed by challenging them to identify the same odours ''mispaired'' in rare probe trials, illustrated on the right. (bottom) SH and FX rats had low error scores on repetitions of instruction trials, and SH rats also performed well on probe trials, but FX rats performed at chance level on the probes. (From Eichenbaum et al., 1989).

PLACE LEARNING

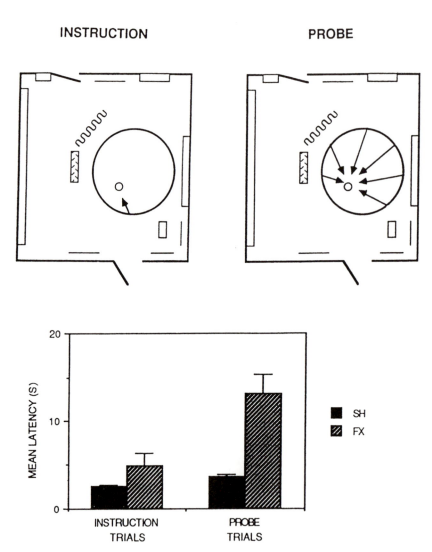

FIG. 6. Assessment of flexible use of place memory representations. (top) As indicated in the schematic diagram of the water maze and test room on the left, rats were instructed to locate the escape site (a platform shown here as a circle) from a constant start location along the perimeter of the maze (denoted by the arrow). Flexible use of their memory representations was assessed by challenging them to locate the escape site from novel start positions (denoted by arrows) on rare probe trials (right). (bottom) Both SH and FX rats had short escape latencies on repetitions of instruction trials, and SH rats also performed well on probe trials, but FX rats had elevated escape latencies on the probes. (From Eichenbaum et al., 1990).

166

position 180 degrees from that of the instruction trials so that, if the rat's behaviour was guided only by those particular cues, one would expect it to swim directly across a location corresponding to a 180-degree rotation of the escape site. Conversely, if the rat's behaviour was guided predominantly by the remaining cues, one would expect it to swim directly to the standard escape location. Consistent with the latter prediction, all normal rats swam directly to the original escape location, as they had on the novel start probe trials (see Fig. 7). In contrast, the swim pattern of most of the rats with fornix lesions was partially, although not completely, consistent with cue-rotation. They headed initially towards the rotated cues but stopped short of the escape location that would be predicted by rotation, then swam in diverse directions. One rat with a fornix lesion behaved completely in accordance with the rotation of cues, swimming directly across the escape location that would be predicted by rotation. However, two other rats with fornix lesions headed towards neither the trained nor the rotated escape location initially, but seemed "lost". These findings indicated that the swim trajectories of normal rats are influenced mainly by the majority of constant cues regardless of start locus. In contrast, most rats with fornix lesions are abnormally dependent on a few salient cues, although they do not use these cues exclusively.

Paired Associate Learning in Rodents

We have suggested that animals with hippocampal system damage are inordinately likely to "fuse" cues together, binding them into single representations that cannot be employed to respond to the separate elements—i.e. relying on *non*compositional representations. Intact animals, by contrast, can store stimulus elements as part of compositional, relational representations, as evidenced in their ability to both respond appropriately to repetitions of the original learning situation and to presentations of elements of the original scene in novel configurations. We have previously (Cohen & Eichenbaum, 1993) used this account of hippocampal-independent and hippocampal-dependent representation to explain findings across a large domain of evidence on discrimination learning in animals, including the data on context-shifts (Winocur & Olds, 1978), on configural learning (Sutherland & Rudy, 1989) and on conditional discrimination in monkeys (Saunders & Weiskrantz, 1989).

A more direct approach to studying how stimulus elements are fused together into a single unitised representation or instead are stored in a compositional, relational representation is to employ the "paired associate" paradigm—tasks in which subjects are specifically required to associate two previously unassociated stimulus elements. This consideration led us to examine the role of the hippocampal system in paired associated paradigms designed for animals.

But before considering the results of our experiments on paired associate learning, it is important to understand some background on the anatomical

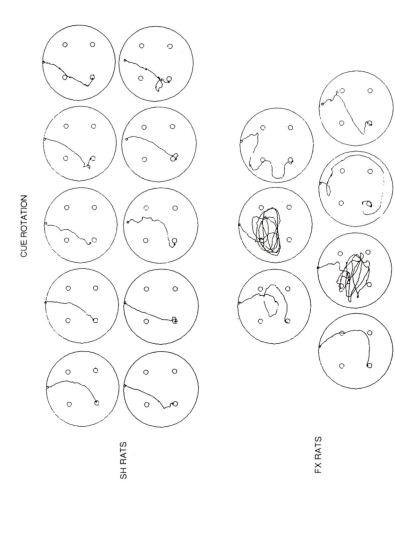

CUE ROTATION

SH RATS

FX RATS

FIG. 7.   Assessment of stimulus representation on a probe trial of the place memory (water maze) task in which two salient cues and the start position were rotated 180 degrees. Tracings of individual swim paths for SH rats (top) and FX rats (bottom) are presented, starting the trial from the north. The escape location (a platform indicated here by the small circle) predicted by cue-rotation is in the northeast quadrant; the training escape position is in the southwest quadrant. (From Eichenbaum et al., 1990).

subdivisions of the hippocampal system and its connections with the cortex (see Fig. 8). The outcomes of sensory processing by distinct neocortical systems converge on the hippocampal system in the parahippocampal region, a collection of cortical areas immediately surrounding the hippocampus. The parahippocampal region is in a position to merge this information and provides the primary source of cortical input to the hippocampus. Following several stages of serial and parallel processing within the hippocampal formation, the outputs of hippocampal processing are sent back to the final cortical processing stages, using the parahippocampal region as the conduit in the return direction as well.

This arrangement of serial bi-directional connections among cortical and hippocampal structures renders hippocampal function dependent on parahippo-campal processing, but the parahippocampal region is directly interconnected with the cortex and so may subserve some functions and exert influences on cortical function independent of hippocampal processing. Recent studies have confirmed that the parahippocampal region does indeed serve an important, albeit unclearly defined, function in memory (Eichenbaum et al., 1994). Thus,

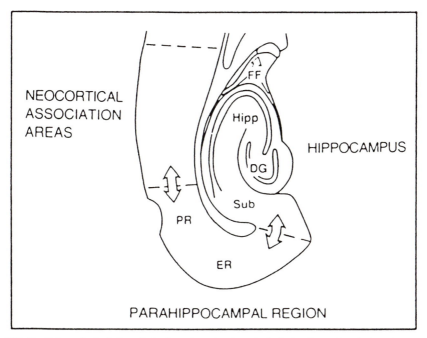

NEOCORTICAL ASSOCIATION AREAS

HIPPOCAMPUS

FF

Hipp

DG

Sub

PR

ER

PARAHIPPOCAMPAL REGION

FIG. 8.   Schematic depiction of a horizontal section through the brain, illustrating the locations and flow of information to the hippocampus via the parahippocampal region and adjacent neocortical areas. DG = dentate gyrus; ER = entorhinal cortex; FF = fimbria-fornix; Hip = hippocampus proper; PR = perirhinal cortex; Sub = subiculum.

our aims in studying paired associate learning included not only a further attempt to show the parallels between human and animal amnesia in terms of memory for items and memory for relations, but also to examine the potentially distinct contributions of the hippocampus and parahippocampal region to these different kinds of memory.

We designed a task using odour stimuli and a recognition format that required subjects to distinguish appropriate odour pairs from a large number of foils (Bunsey & Eichenbaum, 1993). Rats were trained to perform a nose poke into a sniff port when a signal light was illuminated. They sniffed two odours presented in rapid succession, separated by a period when airflow was reversed to prevent stimulus blending. Four rewarded odour sequences (paired associates) were composed out of eight different odours (A–B, C–D, E–F, G–H). When the rat smelled a rewarded pair (e.g. A–B or B–A), it could obtain a sweetened water reward from the water port.

There were two kinds of unrewarded "foil" odour sequences. One kind (mispairings) was composed of the same odours used to form the paired associates but presented in different combinations (e.g. A–C). There were 48 such mispair sequences. To distinguish a mispairing from a paired associate, the rat had to learn the arbitrarily assigned association between the odours. The other type of foil (nonrelational sequences) involved one of the odours A through H combined with one of four other odours that was never associated with reward (W through Z). There were 64 of these nonrelational sequences. To distinguish a nonrelational sequence from a paired associate, the rat was required only to recognise the never-rewarded odour in the sequence. The inclusion of both types of foils allowed us to examine in the same subjects the effects of hippocampal system damage on associative and nonassociative learning.

Sham-operated rats and rats with lesions of the parahippocampal area (effectively eliminating the contributions of both that area and the hippocampus itself) learned to distinguish nonrelational pairs from paired associates at the same rate. In addition, normal rats gradually learned to distinguish paired associates from odour mispairings. By contrast, rats with parahippocampal lesions could not learn to distinguish paired associates from mispairings, even when given nearly twice as many training trials as normal rats. Examination of the patterns of performance during learning also indicated qualitative differences for the two types of foils. Both groups acquired appropriate responses to the nonrelational sequences relatively rapidly, although learning these items was not immediate for either group. Normal rats learned more incrementally to distinguish mispairings from paired associates, but rats with parahippocampal lesions remained at near-chance levels of performance with respect to mispairings throughout testing. Taken together these observations indicate a specific deficit in learning the appropriate stimulus relationships following parahippocampal lesions.

In a subsequent study (see Eichenbaum & Bunsey, 1995) we found that selective neurotoxic lesions of the hippocampus significantly affected paired associated learning and had no effect on learning nonrelational sequences. However, by contrast to the severe impairment observed after parahippocampal region lesions, hippocampal lesions resulted in a significant *facilitation* in distinguishing paired associates from mispairings. Needless to say, this result came as a surprise, but one that might be quite illuminating regarding the different roles of the paraphippocampal region and the hippocampus. This combination of findings indicates that both areas normally contribute to paired associate learning, and suggests that their functions are different and apparently antagonistic. The results led us to speculate that stimulus representations involved in paired associate learning could be encoded in two fundamentally different—indeed opposing—ways, one subserved by the parahippocampal region and another mediated by the hippocampus.

One form of encoding could involve the fusion of the two odour representations as might occur when the items are not conceptually distinct. We have suggested that the parahippocampal region has the capacity to hold stimulus representations for extended periods and, in doing so, can combine items that occur sequentially as well as simultaneously (Eichenbaum et al., 1994). In this way the parahippocampal region could mediate the encoding of the elements of paired associates as fused (*non*compositional). Alternatively, stimulus elements in paired associates could be separately encoded and then have their representations associated in memory. An "association" of this type differs from a fused representation in that it maintains the compositionality of the elemental representations and organises them according to the relevant relationships among the items. We have previously argued that such relational representations are mediated by the hippocampal system; based on the findings on paired associate learning, our current view is that relational memory processing is mediated specifically by the hippocampus itself.

We envision the parahippocampal region and hippocampus as in competition with one another to control the expression of learning paired associates via fused or relational representations, respectively. In normal animals, we suggest that the hippocampus "wins" the competition between the representational strategies and, consequently, the odours are stored separately in terms of their pairing relationships. In rats with selective damage to the hippocampal formation, processing by the parahippocampal region and its connections with cortical areas remains intact, supporting performance based on storage of fused odour-pair representations. By contrast, after damage to the parahippocampal region neither the fused nor the relational form of representation is intact. The ability of the parahippocampal region to make fused representations is directly eliminated and this lesion disconnects the hippocampus with cortical inputs carrying the odour information, also effectively preventing the hippocampus from mediating a relational representation of odour pairings.

Notably, other forms of learning, such as the acquisition of response biases to individual stimuli, do not require either component of the hippocampal system. In these experiments, neither hippocampal nor parahippocampal ablation affected the acquisition of appropriate responses to the nonrelational sequences.

"Natural" Paired Associate Learning.   One curious aspect of this accounting of our findings is that the acquisition of odour-guided paired associates by intact animals using a relational representation was slower than the acquisition of the task by rats with hippocampal lesions using fused stimulus representations. This suggests there is little to be gained by a relational representation, at least for this sort of paired associate learning. But might rats be more likely to employ such a relational representation—and hence show impaired performance after hippocampal damage—if the stimuli were familiar odours presented in a natural context? Some results from studies on a "natural" form of paired associate learning by rats are consistent with this prediction. Galaf (1990) has shown that rats learn from conspecifics which foods are preferable by experiencing the pairing of a distinctive (not necessarily novel) food odour with an odorous constituent of rat's breath (carbon disulfide). We have recently found this form of paired associate learning is blocked by selective neurotoxic lesions of the hippocampus, indicating that the learning of paired associates does depend on the hippocampus itself in a situation where the relevant stimulus relationships are set in a "natural" context. An important issue here may be that in "natural" paired associate learning, as in the typical verbal paired associate task used in humans, at least one of the elements of the association (carbon disulfide) has long-standing familiarity and independent significance to the subject.

CONCLUDING REMARKS

The procedural-declarative theory distinguishes between procedural and declarative memory systems on representational, processing, and anatomical grounds. It characterises declarative memory as supporting relational memory processing and binding of stimulus elements, and identifies these aspects of memory as the functional deficit in amnesia.

Studies based on this framework have revealed that amnesic and normal subjects, both human and animal, may solve logically equivalent problems in radically different ways, depending on their conceptions of what an item is. The fundamental difference between these strategies is the extent to which they make use of the compositional, relational representations supported by the hippocampal-dependent declarative memory system. To the extent that successful performance on a task requires a compositional representation of the relations among items, amnesic subjects are impaired no matter how directly (explicitly) or indirectly (implicitly) they are tested. Conversely, when amnesic subjects are successful in learning, probe tests of the nature of the knowledge supporting their performance show the absence of compositional, relational representations; instead their performance can be shown to depend on inflexible, unitised representations of items.

Applying the procedural-declarative framework to the phenomenon of item-specific implicit memory, we see the critical importance of analysing performance in terms of the loci of processing facilitation in the specific processors that are involved in procedural learning. The procedural-declarative framework has also led us to examine the relationship between different implicit memory phenomena, specifically skill learning and repetition priming. Computational modelling, together with analysis of the levels or "loci" of learning effects in empirical studies, suggests that the skill learning and priming phenomena have their basis in a single (procedural) incremental learning system. These phenomena are best understood as different manifestations of the same experience-based tuning and modifying of specific cortical processors.

Finally, extending the analyses of memory to normal and amnesic animals permits examination of the role of hippocampal and nonhippocampal systems in memory for items and memory for relations. The human amnesia and animal model literatures are now in close correspondence with regard to the nature of the functional deficit in amnesia and nature of the contribution of the hippocampal system to memory. Inclusion of the animal work provides an opportunity to understand the way in which different structures within the hippocampal system and in other brain regions construct relational and nonrelational memory representations.

REFERENCES

Althoff, R.R., Maciukenas, M., & Cohen, N.J. (1993). Indirect assessment of memory using eye movement monitoring. *Society for Neuroscience Abstracts, 19*, 439.

Blakemore, C. (1974). Developmental factors in the formation of feature-extracting neurons. In F.O. Schmitt & F.G. Worden (Eds.), *The neurosciences: Third study program* (pp.105–113). Cambridge, MA: MIT Press.

Buckner, R., Peterson, S.E., Ojemann, J.G., Miezin, F.M., Squire, L.R., & Raichle, M.E. (1995). Functional anatomical studies of explicit and implicit memory retrieval tasks. *Journal of Neuroscience, 15*, 12–29.

Bunsey, M., & Eichenbaum, H. (1993). Paired associate learning in rats: Critical involvement of the parahippocampal region. *Behavioral Neuroscience, 107*, 740–747.

Cermak, L.S., Bleich, R.P., & Blackford, S.P. (1988). Deficits in the implicit retention of new associations by alcoholic Korsakoff patients. *Brain and Cognition, 7*(3), 312–323.

Cohen, N.J. (1981). *Neuropsychological evidence for a distinction between procedural and declarative knowledge in human memory and amnesia.* Unpublished doctoral dissertation, University of California, San Diego.

Cohen, N.J. (1984). Preserved learning capacity in amnesia: Evidence for multiple memory systems. In L.R. Squire & N. Butters (Eds.), *Neuropsychology of memory* (pp.83–103). New York: Guilford Press.

Cohen, N.J., Althoff, R.R., Webb, J.M., McConkie, G.W., Holden, J.A., & Noll, E.L. (1996). *Eye movement monitoring as an indirect measure of memory.* Unpublished manuscript.

Cohen, N.J., & Eichenbaum, H.E. (1993). *Memory, amnesia, and the hippocampal system.* Cambridge, MA: MIT Press.

Cohen, N.J., Ramzy, C., Hut, Z., Tomaso, H., Strupp, J., Erhard, P., Anderson, P., & Ugurbil, K. (1994). Hippocampal activation in fMRI evoked by demand for declarative memory-based bindings of multiple streams of information. *Society for Neuroscience Abstracts, 20,* 1290.

Cohen, N.J., & Squire, L.R. (1980). Preserved learning and retention of pattern-analyzing skill in amnesia: Dissociation of knowing how and know that. *Science, 210*(4466), 207–210.

Demb, J.B., Desmond, J.E., Wagner, A.D., Stone, M., Lee, A.T., Glover, G.H., & Gabrieli, J.D.E. (1995). Semantic encoding and retrieval in the left inferior prefrontal cortex: A functional MRI study of task difficulty and process specificity. *Journal of Neuroscience, 15,* 5870–5878.

Diamond, D.M., & Weinberger, N.M. (1986). Classical conditioning rapidly induces specific changes in frequency receptive fields of single neurons in secondary and ventral ectosylvian cortical fields. *Brain Research, 372,* 357–360.

Eichenbaum, H., & Bunsey, M. (1995). On the binding of associations in memory: Clues from studies on the role of the hippocampal region in paired associate learning. *Current Directions in Psychological Science, 4,* 19–23.

Eichenbaum, H., & Cohen, N.J. (1988). Representation in the hippocampus: What do hippocampal neurons code? *Trends in Neurosciences, 11*(6), 244–248.

Eichenbaum, H., & Cohen, N.J. (1995). Consciousness, memory, and the hippocampal system: What kind of connections can we make? *Behavioral and Brain Sciences, 18,* 680–681.

Eichenbaum, H., Cohen, N.J., Otto, T., & Wible C. (1991). A snapshot without the album. *Brain Research Reviews, 16,* 209–215.

Eichenbaum, H., Fagan, A., Mathews, P., & Cohen, N.J. (1988). Hippocampal system dysfunction and odor discrimination learning in rats: Impairment of facilitation depending on representational demands. *Behavioral Neuroscience, 102,* 331–339.

Eichenbaum, H., Mathews, P., & Cohen, N.J. (1989). Further studies of hippocampal representation during odor discrimination learning. *Behavioral Neuroscience, 103*(6), 1207–1216.

Eichenbaum, H., Otto, T., & Cohen, N.J. (1992). The hippocampus: What does it do? *Behavioral and Neural Biology, 57*(1), 2–36.

Eichenbaum, H., Otto, T., & Cohen, N.J. (1994). Two component functions of the hippocampal memory system. *Behavioral and Brain Sciences, 17,* 449–517.

Eichenbaum, H., Stewart, C., & Morris, R.G.M. (1990). Hippocampal representation in spatial learning. *Journal of Neuroscience, 10,* 331–339.

Fodor, J.A. (1983). *Modularity of mind.* Cambridge, MA: MIT Press.

Fodor, J.A., & Pylyshyn, Z. (1988). Connectionism and cognitive architecture: A critical analysis. *Cognition, 28,* 3–71.

Gabrieli, J.D., Cohen, N.J., & Corkin, S. (1988). The impaired learning of semantic knowledge following bilateral medial temporal-lobe resection. Special Issue: Single-case studies in amnesia: Theoretical advances. *Brain and Cognition, 7*(2), 157–177.

Gabrieli, J.D.E., Fleischman, D.A., Keane, M.A., Reminger, S.L., & Morrell, F. (1995). Double dissociation between memory systems underlying explicit and implicit memory in the human brain. *Psychological Science, 6,* 76–82.

Galef, B.G. (1990). An adaptionist perspective on social learning, social feeding, and social foraging in Norway rats. In D.A. Dewsbury (Ed.), *Contemporary issues in comparative psychology* (pp.55–79). Sunderland, MA: Sinauer.

Gardiner, J.M. (1988). Functional aspects of recollective experience. *Memory and Cognition, 16*(4), 309–313.

Glisky, E.L., & Schacter, D.L. (1987). Acquisition of domain-specific knowledge in organic amnesia: Training for computer-related work. *Neuropsychologia, 25*(6), 893–906.

Glisky, E.L., & Schacter, D.L. (1989). Extending the limits of complex learning in organic amnesia: Computer training in a vocational domain. Special Issue: Memory. *Neuropsychologia, 27*(1), 107–120.

Glisky, E.L., Schacter, D.L., & Tulving, E. (1986). Learning and retention of computer-related vocabulary in memory-impaired patients: Method of vanishing cues. *Journal of Clinical and Experimental Neuropsychology, 8*(3), 292–312.

Graf, P., & Schacter, D.L. (1985). Implicit and explicit memory for new associations in normal and amnesic subjects. *Journal of Experimental Psychology: Learning, Memory, and Cognition, 11*(3), 501–518.

Gray, J.A. (1995). The contents of consciousness: A neuropsychological conjecture. *Behavioral and Brain Science, 18*, 659–722.

Heindel, W.C., Salmon, D.P., Shults, C.W., Wallicke, P.A., & Butters, N. (1989). Neuropsychological evidence for multiple implicit memory systems: A comparison of Alzheimer's and Parkinson's disease patients. *Journal of Neuroscience, 9*, 582–587.

Hubel, D.H., Wiesel, T.N., & LeVay, S. (1977). Plasticity of ocular dominance columns in the monkey striate cortex. *Philosophical Transactions of the Royal Society of London: Biology, 278*, 377–409.

Jacoby, L.L. (1984). Incidental versus intentional retrieval: Remembering and awareness as separate issues. In L.R. Squire & N. Butters (Eds.), *Neuropsychology of memory* (pp.145–156). New York: Guilford Press.

Jacoby, L.L. (1991). A process dissociation framework: Separating automatic from intentional uses of memory. *Journal of Memory and Language, 30*(5), 513–541.

Jacoby, L.L., & Kelley, C.M. (1991). Unconscious influences of memory: Dissociations and automaticity. In D.M. & M. Rugg (Eds.), *Consciousness and cognition: Neuropsychological perspectives* (pp.201–234). New York: Academic Press.

Johnson, M.K., & Hasher, L. (1987). Human learning and memory. *Annual Review of Psychology, 38*, 631–668.

Karni, A., Meyer, G., Jezzard, P., Adams, M., Turner, R., Ungerleider, L.G. (1994). The acquisition and retention of a motor skill: A functional MRI study of long-term motor cortex plasticity. *Society for Neuroscience Abstracts, 20*, 1291.

Keane, M.M., Clarke, H., & Corkin, S. (1992). Impaired perceptual priming and intact conceptual priming in a patient with bilateral posterior cerebral lesions. *Society for Neuroscience Abstracts, 18*, 386.

Kim, S.G., Ugurbil, K., & Strick, P.L. (1994). Activation of a cerebellar output nucleus during cognitive processing. *Science, 265*, 949–951.

Kirsner, K., & Speelman, P. (1996). Skill acquisition and repetition priming: One principle, many processes? *Journal of Experimental Psychology: Learning, Memory, and Cognition, 22*, 563–575.

Kroll, N.E., Knight, R.T., Metcalfe, J., Wolf, E.S., & Tulving, E. (1996). Cohesion failure as a source of memory illusions. *Journal of Memory and Language, 35*, 176–196.

Levy, B.A. (1993). Fluent rereading: An implicit indicator of reading skill development. In P. Graf & M.E.J. Masson (Eds.), *Implicit memory: New directions in cognition, development and neuropsychology* (pp.49–74). Hillsdale, NJ: Lawrence Erlbaum Associates Inc.

Logan, G.D. (1988). Toward an instance theory of automatization. *Psychological Review, 95*(4), 492–527.

Masson, M.E. (1986). Identification of typographically transformed words: Instance-based skill acquisition. *Journal of Experimental Psychology: Learning, Memory, and Cognition, 12*(4), 479–488.

Mayes, A.R. (1988). *Human organic memory disorders.* Cambridge: Cambridge University Press.

Mayes, A.R., & Downes, J.J. (this issue). What do theories of the functional deficit(s) underlying amnesia have to explain? *Memory, 5*(1/2).

Mayes, A.R., & Gooding, P. (1989). Enhancement of word completion priming in amnesics by cueing with previously novel associates. *Neuropsychologia, 27,* 1057–1072.

Merzenich, M.M., Recanzone, G.H., Jenkins, W.M., & Grajski, K.A. (1990). Adaptive mechanisms in cortical networks underlying cortical contributions to learning and nondeclarative memory. In *Cold Spring Harbor symposia on quantitative biology, Vol. 55: The Brain.* New York: Cold Spring Harbor Laboratory.

Milner, B. (1962). Les troubles de la memoire accompagnant des lesions hippocampiques bilaterales. In P. Passouant (Ed.), *Physiologie de l'hippocampe.* Paris: Centre de la Recherche Scientifique.

Monti, L.A., Gabrieli, J.D.E., Wilson, R.S., & Reminger, S.L. (1994). Intact text-specific implicit memory in patients with Alzheimer's disease. *Psychology and Aging, 9*(1), 64–71.

Morris, R.G., Garrud, P., Rawlins, J.N., & O'Keefe, J. (1982). Place navigation impaired in rats with hippocampal lesions. *Nature, 297,* 681–683.

Moscovitch, M. (1994). Memory and working-with-memory: A component process model based on modules and central systems. In D.L. Schacter & E. Tulving (Eds.), *Memory systems 1994.* Cambridge, MA: MIT Press.

Moscovitch, M., Winocur, G., & McLachlan, D. (1986). Memory as assessed by recognition and reading time in normal and memory-impaired people with Alzheimer's disease and other neurological disorders. *Journal of Experimental Psychology: General, 115*(4), 331–347.

Musen, G., Shimamura, A.P., & Squire, L.R. (1990). Intact text-specific reading skill in amnesia. *Journal of Experimental Psychology: Learning, Memory, and Cognition, 16*(6), 1068–1076.

Musen, G., & Squire, L.R. (1993a). Implicit learning of color–word associations using a Stroop paradigm. *Journal of Experimental Psychology: Learning, Memory, & Cognition, 19,* 789–798.

Musen, G., & Squire, L.R. (1993b). On the implicit learning of novel associations by amnesic patients and normal subjects. *Neuropsychology, 7*(2), 119–135.

Musen, G., & O'Neill, J.E. (1994). *Implicit memory for nonverbal associations.* Paper presented at the annual meeting of the Psychonomics Society, St. Louis.

O'Keefe, J.A. (1976). Place units in the hippocampus of the freely moving rat. *Experimental Neurology, 51,* 78–109.

Perret, D.I., Mistlin, A.J., & Chitty, A.J. (1987). Visual neurones responsive to faces. *Trends in Neuroscience, 10,* 358–364.

Poldrack, R.A., & Cohen, N.J. (1996a). The relationship between skill learning and repetition priming. II: Evidence from computational models. Manuscript submitted for publication.

Poldrack, R.A., & Cohen, N.J. (1996b). *Priming of new associations in reading time is inflexible.* Unpublished manuscript.

Poldrack, R.A., Selco, S.L., Field, J.E., & Cohen, N.J. (1996). *The relationship between skill learning and repetition priming. I: Observations from a digit entering task.* Manuscript submitted for publication.

Recanzone, G.H., Allard, T.T., Jenkins, W.M., & Merzenich, M.M. (1990). Receptive-field changes induced by peripheral nerve stimulation in SI of adult cats. *Journal of Neurophysiology, 63,* 1213–1225.

Recanzone, G.H., Merzenich, M.M., Jenkins, W.M., Grajski, K.A., & Dinse, H.R. (1992). Topographic reorganization of the hand representation in cortical area 3b of owl monkeys trained in a frequency discrimination task. *Journal of Neurophysiology, 67,* 1031–1056.

Richardson-Klavehn, A., & Bjork, R.A. (1988). Measures of memory. *Annual Review of Psychology, 39,* 475–543.

Roediger, H.L. (1990). Implicit memory: Retention without remembering. *American Psychologist, 45*(9), 1043–1056.

Roediger, H.L. III, Weldon, M.S., & Challis, B. (1989). Explaining dissociations between implicit and explicit measures of retention: A processing account. In H.L. Roediger III & F.I.M. Craik (Eds.), *Varieties of memory and consciousness: Essays in honour of Endel Tulving* (pp.3–42). Hillsdale, NJ: Lawrence Erlbaum Associates Inc.

Saunders, R.C., & Weiskrantz, L. (1989). The effects of fornix transection and combined fornix transection, mammillary body lesions and hippocampal ablations on object pair association memory in the rhesus monkey. *Behavioral Brain Research, 35,* 85–94.

Schacter, D.L. (1985). Priming of old and new knowledge in amnesic patients and normal subjects. *Annals of the New York Academic of Sciences, 444,* 41–53.

Schacter, D.L. (1987). Implicit memory: History and current status. *Journal of Experimental Psychology: Learning, Memory, and Cognition, 13*(3), 501–518.

Schacter, D.L. (1990). Perceptual representation systems and implicit memory: Toward a resolution of the multiple memory systems debate. Conference of the National Institute of Mental Health et al: The development and neural bases of higher cognitive functions (1989, Philadelphia, Pennsylvania). *Annals of the New York Academy of Sciences, 608,* 543–571.

Schacter, D.L., & Graf, P. (1986). Effects of elaborative processing on implicit and explicit memory for new associations. *Journal of Experimental Psychology: Learning, Memory, and Cognition, 12*(3), 432–444.

Schacter, D.L., & Tulving, E. (1994). *Memory systems 1994.* Cambridge, MA: MIT Press.

Schwartz, B.L., & Hashtroudi, S. (1991). Priming is independent of skill learning. *Journal of Experimental Psychology: Learning, Memory, and Cognition, 17*(6), 1177–1187.

Shimamura, S.P., & Squire, L.R. (1989). Impaired priming of new associations in amnesia. *Journal of Experimental Psychology: Learning, Memory, and Cognition, 15*(4), 721–728.

Squire, L.R. (1987). *Memory and brain.* New York: Oxford University Press.

Squire, L.R. (1992). Memory and the hippocampus: A synthesis from findings with rats, monkeys, and humans. *Psychological Review, 99*(2), 195–231.

Squire, L.R., & Cohen, N.J. (1984). Human memory and amnesia. In G. Lynch, J.L. McGaugh, & N.M. Weinberger (Eds.), *Neurobiology of learning and memory* (pp. 3–64). New York: Guilford Press.

Squire, L.R., Cohen, N.J., & Nadel, L. (1984). The medial temporal region and memory consolidation: A new hypothesis. In H. Weingartner & E. Parker (Eds.), *Memory consolidation* (pp.185–210). Hillsdale, NJ: Lawrence Erlbaum Associates Inc.

Squire, L.R., Ojemann, J.G., Miezin, F.M., Peterson, S.E. Videen, T.O., & Raichle, M.E. (1992). Activation of the hippocampus in normal humans: A functional anatomical study of memory. *Proceedings of the National Academy of Sciences, USA, 89,* 1837–1841.

Sutherland, R.J., & Rudy, J.W. (1989). Configural association theory: The role of the hippocampal formation in learning, memory, and amnesia. *Psychobiology, 17,* 129–144.

Tulving, E. (1972). Episodic and semantic memory. In E. Tulving & W. Donaldson (Eds.), *Organization of memory* (pp.382–403). New York: Academic Press.

Tulving, E. (1983). *Elements of episodic memory.* Cambridge: Cambridge University Press.

Tulving, E. (1991). Concepts of human memory. In L.R. Squire, G. Lynch, N.M. Weinberger, & J.L. McGaugh (Eds.), *Memory: Organization and locus of change.* New York: Oxford University Press.

Tulving, E., Hayman, C.A., & Macdonald, C.A. (1991). Long-lasting perceptual priming and semantic learning in amnesia: A case experiment. *Journal of Experimental Psychology: Learning, Memory, and Cognition, 17*(4), 595–617.

Tulving, E., & Schacter, D.L. (1990). Priming and human memory systems. *Science, 247*(4940), 301–306.

Ungerleider, L.G. (1994). Transient and enduring effects of experience: Functional studies of visual and motor cortex. *Society for Neuroscience Abstracts, 20,* viii.

Whitlow, S.D., Althoff, R.R., & Cohen, N.J. (1995). Deficit in relational (declarative) memory in amnesia. *Society for Neuroscience Abstracts, 21,* 754.

Wiesel, T.N., & Hubel, D.H. (1963). Single cell response in striate cortex of kittens deprived of vision in one eye. *Journal of Neurophysiology, 26,* 1003–1017.

Wiesel, T.N., & Hubel, D.H. (1965). Comparison of the effects of unilateral and bilateral eye closure on cortical unit responses in kittens. *Journal of Neurophysiology, 28,* 1029–1040.

Winocur, G., & Olds, J. (1978). Effects of context manipulation on memory and reversal learning in rats with hippocampal lesions. *Journal of Comparative and Physiological Psychology, 92*(312–321).

Young, B.J., Fox, G.D., & Eichenbaum, H. (1994). Correlates of hippocampal complex spike cell activity in rats performing a non-spatial radial arm maze task. *Journal of Neuroscience, 14,* 6553–6563.

MEMORY, 1997, 5 (1/2), 179–212

Extending Models of Hippocampal Function in Animal Conditioning to Human Amnesia

Mark A. Gluck and Brandon R. Ermita

Rutgers University, USA

Lindsay M. Oliver

Glasgow Caledonian University, UK

Catherine E. Myers

Rutgers University, USA

Although most analyses of amnesia have focused on the loss of explicit declarative and episodic memories following hippocampal-region damage, considerable insights into amnesia can also be realised by studying hippocampal function in simple procedural, or habit-based, associative learning tasks. Although many simple forms of associative learning are unimpaired by hippocampal damage, more complex tasks which require sensitivity to unreinforced stimuli, configurations of multiple stimuli, or contextual information are impaired by hippocampal damage. In several recent papers we have developed a computational theory of hippocampal function which argues that this brain region plays a critical role in the formation of new stimulus representations during learning (Gluck & Myers, 1993, 1995; Myers & Gluck, 1996; Myers, Gluck, & Granger, 1995). We have applied this theory to a broad range of empirical data from studies of classical conditioning in both intact and hippocampal-lesioned animals, and the model correctly accounts for these data. The classical conditioning paradigm can be adapted for use in humans, and similar results for acquisition are obtained in both normal and hippocampal-damaged humans. More recently, we have begun to address an important set of category learning studies in both normals and hippocampal-damaged amnesics. This work integrates experimental studies of amnesic category learning (Knowlton, Squire, & Gluck, 1994) with theoretical accounts of associative learning, and builds on previously established behavioural correspondences between animal conditioning and human category learning (Gluck & Bower, 1988a). Our work to

Requests for reprints should be sent to Mark A. Gluck, Center for Molecular and Behavioral Neuroscience, Rutgers University, 197 University Avenue, Newark, New Jersey 07102, USA. Email: gluck@pavlov.rutgers.edu or see web page www.archtype.com/gluck

This research was supported by an NIMH National Research Service Award 1-F32-MH10351-01 (CM), by a McDonnell-Pew Foundation for Cognitive Neuroscience Grant-in-Aid (MC & CM), and by the Office of Naval Research through the Young Investigator program (MG) and grant N00014-88-K-0112 (MG).

date illustrates some initial progress towards a more integrative understanding of hippocampal function in both animal and human learning, which may be useful in guiding further empirical and theoretical research in human memory and amnesia.

1. INTRODUCTION

In several recent papers, we have argued that the hippocampal region plays an essential role in the formation of novel stimulus representations in the formation of new associations and memories (Gluck & Myers, 1993, 1995; Myers & Gluck, 1996; Myers et al., 1995a). As shown in Fig. 1.1, the hippocampal region comprises a group of structures located deep within the brain, and includes the hippocampus itself as well as the nearby dentate gyrus, subiculum, and entorhinal cortex. The outermost of these structures, the entorhinal cortex, receives highly processed information from the entire spectrum of sensory modalities, as well as from multimodal cortical association areas. Information flows in a roughly unidirectional fashion from the entorhinal cortex to the dentate gyrus, to hippocampus, to the subiculum, and back to the entorhinal

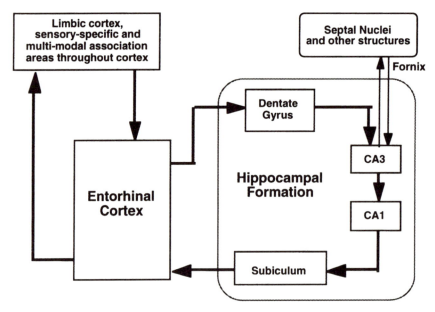

FIG. 1.1. Schematic of major information flow pathways in the hippocampal region. Highly processed, multimodal inputs enter entorhinal cortex, and proceed in a largely unidirectional pathway through the hippocampal formation (dentate gyrus, hippocampal fields CA3 and CA1 and subiculum) before returning to entorhinal cortex and thence back to the same cortical areas where they arose. There is also a bi-directional pathway through the fornix connecting the hippocampus with subcortical areas such as the septal nuclei. Many other connections exist in addition to the major ones shown here.

cortex before returning to the same sensory areas where it originally arose. In addition to this basic pathway, there are a large number of direct connections between the structures of the region. The hippocampus has another input and output pathway through the fornix, a fibre bundle connecting it with subcortical structures (e.g. basal forebrain) which modulate hippocampal functioning.

Damage to the hippocampal region in humans produces a characteristic anterograde amnesia syndrome, strongly impairing the learning of new information (Squire, 1987). Human hippocampal damage can result from a variety of etiologies, ranging from ischemia, viral encephalitis, and aneurysm/ embolism to the arteries that vascularise the hippocampal region. Damage to other related structures, such as the basal forebrain, can also result in an amnesic syndrome which shares features with hippocampal amnesia, presumably because such damage indirectly interferes with normal hippocampal-region processing (see Myers et al., 1996).

The anterograde amnesia that follows human hippocampal-region damage is generally characterised by an inability to acquire new episodic or declarative information, the kind of information about individual events and experiences that is accessible to conscious control. These patients may also show some degree of retrograde amnesia, or disruption of previously acquired information, but this is usually limited to information acquired shortly before the trauma, and tends to lessen in a time-graded fashion for older information (Ribot, 1982; Squire, 1987).

In contrast to episodic or declarative memories that are often acquired in a single exposure, other kinds of memory are incrementally acquired over many exposures. These types of memory are not necessarily accessible to conscious recollection, and often involve learning skills or procedures rather than facts (Squire, 1987). This dissociation between episodic memory and procedural memory is often summarised as a difference between "knowing that" and "knowing how". Many simple forms of procedural memory survive hippocampal-region damage relatively intact. The animal learning literature is full of studies showing how animals with hippocampal-region damage can show normal acquisition of a variety of tasks such as the acquisition of classically conditioned responses to a single stimulus (Akase, Alkon, & Disterhoft, 1989; Schmajuk, 1994; Solomon, 1977; Solomon & Moore, 1975), the ability to choose the novel of a pair of objects where one object was seen immediately before (Zola-Morgan & Squire, 1992) simple discriminations of singly presented odour stimuli in an operant task (Eichenbaum, Fagan, Mathews, & Cohen, 1988), and learning to navigate to an escape platform when started from a constant location in a pool (Eichenbaum, Otto, Wible, & Piper, 1991). Similarly, human hippocampal-damaged amnesics are not impaired at learning a conditioned motor-reflex response (Daum, Channon, & Canavan, 1989; Gabrieli et al., 1995; Woodruff-Pak, 1993), learning simple classification tasks (Knowlton et al., 1994), or learning new motor skills such as mirror drawing (Cohen, 1984). All of these spared tasks can be solved by incremental formation of habits or tendencies, without requiring episodic memories of any individual learning trial.

There are, however, other tasks that seem superficially to be just as procedural or implicit as those noted here, but which are impaired after hippocampal-region damage. For example, although the acquisition of a classically conditioned response to a single CS is not impaired by hippocampal-region damage, there may be severe impairments in classical-conditioning tasks that require learning about unreinforced stimuli (Kaye & Pearce, 1987; Solomon & Moore, 1975), configurations or combinations of stimuli (Sutherland & Rudy, 1989), contextual information (Hirsh, 1974), or relationships that span short delays (Eichenbaum, Otto, & Cohen, 1994; Moyer, Deyo, & Disterhoft, 1990; Port, Romano & Patterson, 1986; Rawlins, 1985; Zola-Morgan & Squire, 1992). These findings imply that the hippocampal-region does indeed participate in information processing during apparently procedural tasks, although this participation may not necessarily be evident from studying whether animals or people can—or cannot—acquire a simple associative response.

In Gluck and Myers (1993) we presented a computational model of hippocampal-region function in associative learning, which suggests that the hippocampal region is involved in the formation of new stimulus representations during normal procedural learning. Learning that depends on new representations is expected to be hippocampal-dependent, whereas learning that can make use of pre-existing representations may be hippocampal-independent. Section 2 of this paper presents this model. We have applied this model to a broad range of empirical data from studies of classical conditioning in intact and hippocampal-lesioned animals, as discussed in Section 3, and the model correctly accounts for these data. Additionally, the classical conditioning paradigm can be adapted for use in humans, and similar results for acquisition training appear to be obtained in both normal and hippocampal-damaged amnesic humans, much as in animals during conditioning. Finally, in Section 4, we note that the model can be easily extended to address an example of probabilistic category learning in both normals and hippocampal-damaged amnesics.

2. STIMULUS REPRESENTATION AND HIPPOCAMPAL FUNCTION

Many previous characterisations of hippocampal-region function in animal learning have been proposed which are task-centred: noting that a particular class of task is hippocampal-dependent, and then seeking to characterise the hippocampus as a processor that implements that kind of function. These task-centred descriptions have implicated the hippocampal region in spatial learning (O'Keefe & Nadel, 1978), contextual processing (Hirsh, 1974; Nadel & Willner, 1980), configural learning (Sutherland & Rudy, 1989), and more. The hippocampal region also appears to be involved in temporal processing such as sequence learning (Buzsaki, 1989), response timing (Akase et al., 1989; Moyer et al., 1990) and intermediate-term memory (Eichenbaum et al., 1994; Olton, 1983; Rawlins, 1985; Zola-Morgan, Squire, & Amaral, 1989).

Instead of a task-specific characterisation of hippocampal function, it may be possible to try and describe an information-processing role for the hippocampal region, and, from this, derive a wider range of task-specific deficits which arise from interfering with this information-processing function. For example, it has been proposed that the hippocampal region is involved in the flexible use of learned information in novel situations (Eichenbaum & Buckingham, 1990; Eichenbaum, Cohen, Otto, & Wible, 1992); attentional control through a process of inhibiting responses to irrelevant cues (Douglas & Pribram, 1966; Schmajuk & Moore, 1985); and providing "contextual tags" to learned information (Penick & Solomon, 1991; Winocur, Rawlins, & Gray, 1987).

In our work, we have focused on a putative role for the hippocampal region in forming new stimulus representations to assist learning. This suggestion builds on many of the earlier information-processing characterisations of hippocampal-region function listed previously, and also on the psychological idea of stimulus representations (Anderson, 1977; James, 1896; Shepard, 1958). The emphasis on representation in psychological modelling has been particularly salient in recent years as simple rule-based models of cognitive function have given way to connectionist models that emphasise how associative networks re-represent stimuli within a multi-layer network (Hanson & Burr, 1990; Rumelhart, Hinton, & Williams, 1986). These connectionist networks are generally assumed to implement abstract characterisations of underlying neural processes, providing a framework for expressing theories about both animal learning (Barto & Sutton, 1982; Kehoe, 1988; Schmajuk & DiCarlo, 1990) and human learning and memory (Gluck & Bower, 1988a; Kruschke, 1992; Shanks & Gluck, 1994; McClelland, McNaughton, & O'Reilly, 1994).

In the remainder of this section, we will briefly review the idea of stimulus representation within the framework of connectionist models, and then present our own computational model of hippocampal-region function in learning.

Connectionist Models of Representation and Learning

Within a typical connectionist network (Fig. 2.1), the internal stimulus representation is characterised as a pattern of activations over a set of "hidden nodes" which recode a stimulus input. These hidden nodes represent the network's internal representation of the stimulus pattern, and are roughly analogous to what psychologists refer to as a psychological representation (or the "psychological space"), as distinct from a sensory representation which primarily reflects the physical qualities of the stimulus input (Shepard, 1958).

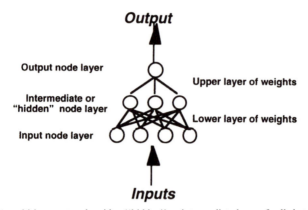

FIG. 2.1.   A multi-layer network, with a "hidden" or intermediate layer of cells between the input and output cell layer, and weighted connections between layers. The hidden layer activations represent a re-coding or re-representation of the inputs. The output layer activations are interpreted as the behavioural response. All connection weights are adaptive.

The hidden layer activations depend on weighted connections between the input and hidden layers, and thus changes to this lower layer of weights are equivalent to changing the stimulus representation. The hidden layer activations feed through weighted connections to an output layer, and the output layer activation determines the behavioural response of the system. The network is trained by adapting the weights in both layers until the system generates the desired output in response to a given input.

The connectionist network in Fig. 2.1 can be trained to give the desired output to each of a set of different inputs. How easily (quickly) this is done depends in part on the hidden layer representations. For example, suppose that a particular input pattern generates the hidden layer activations schematised in the top of Fig. 2.2A. In order to learn the correct response to the first pattern, a set of weights will evolve mapping that hidden layer representation to the correct output activations. Now suppose a second input pattern generates the hidden layer activations schematised at the bottom of Fig. 2.2A. Note that the activation pattern at the top of Fig. 2.2A has considerable overlap (similarity) with the pattern at the bottom of Fig. 2.2A. This implies that the network in Fig. 2.1 will tend to generalise from one pattern to the other or, in other words, it will generate output to the second pattern that is similar to what is learned for the first pattern. If the desired outputs for the two patterns are the same, then this generalisation will be helpful; if the desired outputs for the two patterns are different, this generalisation will cause unwanted interference and hinder the mapping of these similar representations to different outputs. In contrast, two input patterns that evoke very different hidden layer activations (as shown in Fig. 2.2B) will engender far less generalisation, resulting in more facilitation for learning different outputs to these two patterns, but less facilitation for learning the same output to both.

(A)   **(B)**

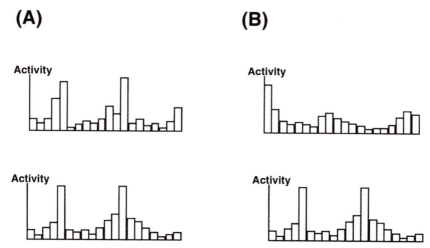

FIG. 2.2.   Schematic of activations evoked in the hidden layer nodes of a connectionist network such as the one shown in Fig. 2.1, by presentation of four different input patterns. These activity patterns constitute stimulus representations in the network. (A) If the hidden-layer representations evoked by two input patterns are very similar, it will be difficult to train the network to respond differently to each. (B) If the representations evoked are very dissimilar, it will be easier to map each to a different response. Conversely, generalisation between inputs is aided by similarity in representation and made difficult by differentiated representations.

In this way, learning the correct responses to a set of input patterns can be affected greatly by changes in stimulus representations. The exact details of these representations are, in general, less important than the varying degree of similarity or overlap between representations of different input patterns.

The Cortico-hippocampal Model

The core idea of Gluck and Myers' (1993) theory of cortico-hippocampal function is that the hippocampal region facilitates learning by constructing internal stimulus representations that are biased in two ways. The first bias, *redundancy compression*, is a tendency to make more similar the representations of stimuli that co-occur or are to be associated with similar outputs; this bias ensures high generalisation between these stimuli. The second bias, *predictive differentiation*, is a tendency to differentiate, or make less similar, the representations of stimuli that are to be mapped to different outputs; this bias decreases generalisation between such stimuli. These two biases to compress and differentiate are partially opposing, and may often interact in complex ways, depending on stimulus–stimulus relationships within the training environment.

Hippocampal Processing.   How can this postulated representational role for hippocampal-region function be implemented? Gluck and Myers (1993) show

how a simple connectionist architecture gives rise to just these sorts of representations. They model hippocampal-region processing as a *predictive autoencoder* (Hinton, 1989), as shown in Fig. 2.3. A predictive autoencoder maps input activations through a hidden layer to two classes of outputs: a reconstruction of the input pattern as well as a prediction for classifying the input pattern. Such a network may be trained via the error backpropagation learning algorithm (Parker, 1985; Rumelhart et al., 1986; Werbos, 1974); this algorithm allows development of representations across the internal layer of nodes that compress redundancies while emphasising predictive information— exactly as required by our theory. The details of the learning procedure are not particularly critical in that many alternative learning procedures are equally able to accomplish the required representational changes (see Myers et al., 1995a, for further discussion of this point).

Intact Cortico-hippocampal Processing.   This hippocampal-region network is assumed to interact with other cortical regions which are the sites of long-term storage. One such network is shown in the intact model of Fig. 2.4A. The cortical network on the left in Fig. 2.4A represents a highly simplified model of some aspects of long-term memory in cerebral and cerebellar cortices. This network takes the stimulus input, and maps it through weighted connections to a hidden node layer and then to an output node; the activation of this output node is interpreted as the system's behavioural response to the input. This cortical network adapts its weighted connection strengths according to the LMS learning algorithm (Widrow & Hoff, 1960), which is related to psychological descriptions

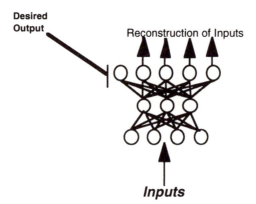

FIG. 2.3.   A predictive autoencoder network, like that assumed in the cortico-hippocampal model to represent hippocampal-region processing. This network maps inputs through a hidden node layer to outputs that learn to reconstruct the input pattern as well as classifying the input. To accomplish this, representations are developed in the hidden node layer which compress redundancies in the input while maintaining and differentiating enough predictive information to allow generation of the desired outputs.

of learning (Gluck & Bower, 1988a; Rescorla & Wagner, 1972; Sutton & Barto, 1981) and also to biological mechanisms of plasticity such as LTP (Bliss & Lomo, 1973; Levy, Brassel & Moore, 1983; Stanton & Sejnowski, 1989).

The hippocampal-region autoencoder, and a simpler multi-layer network representing a cortical module, are combined into the intact model shown in Fig. 2.4A. Within this two-part model of intact cortico-hippocampal processing, new representations are developed first in the hippocampal region and then incrementally transferred, throughout the learning process, to the internal-layer nodes of cortical (or cerebellar) networks. The LMS rule calculates the error at a node as the difference between the desired and actual output at that node, and distributes this error among the weights feeding into the node. For the output layer node in the cortical network, the desired output is simply a prediction of the US arrival, and, thus, the LMS rule can be used to train the upper layer of weights in the cortical network. However, the desired output is not externally defined for the internal layer nodes of the cortical network.

However, the activations of the internal layer of the hippocampal-region network can be used as the desired activations for corresponding internal layer nodes in the cortical network. Thus, a second application of the LMS rule can be used to train the lower layer of cortical weights. Over time, the internal layer of the cortical network will come to mirror the representations developed in the hippocampal network—even though the cortical network alone, using the LMS algorithm, would be incapable of devising these representations. We note that it is not necessary for there to be a one-to-one mapping between the internal-layer nodes of the hippocampal-region and cortical networks; the cortical network

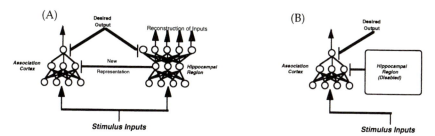

FIG. 2.4. The cortico-hippocampal model (Gluck & Myers, 1993). (A) The intact system is assumed to include a predictive autoencoder, representing hippocampal-region processing, that constructs new stimulus representations in its hidden layer which are biased to compress redundancies while differentiating predictive information. These stimulus representations are acquired by long-term storage sites in the cortex, represented as a multi-layer network which learns to predict US arrival. The cortical network uses the Rescorla-Wagner rule to map from inputs to the hippocampal-mediated internal representations, and again to map from the internal layer to output activations. (B) Hippocampal-region lesion is assumed to disable the hippocampal network, in which cases the cortical network can no longer acquire new internal representations, but can acquire new behavioural responses based on its pre-existing (and now fixed) internal representations.

nodes can be mapped to a fixed, random linear recombination of the hippocampal network activations, and this will maintain most of the relevant information, especially if the cortical hidden layer is larger than the hippocampal hidden layer.

Learning in the hippocampal-region network, and in both layers of the long-term memory cortical network, is assumed to proceed incrementally and in parallel. At this time, we have not made any attempt to clarify the relative speeds of learning in the two networks, nor the time course of transfer of information from one network to the other; however, this general two-component architecture for learning would certainly allow for a consolidation period during which information is slowly transferred from hippocampal-region to long-term memory (see Alvarez & Squire, 1994; McClelland et al., 1994; Murre, 1994; Squire, 1987; Winocur, 1990).

Although it is important to understand the aggregate functional role of the hippocampal region, ultimately we would like to know how the proposed behavioural processes map onto more detailed anatomical structures. Of particular importance is the parahippocampal region, comprising entorhinal, perirhinal, and parahippocampal cortices; these structures are the primary sites through which sensory information both enters and leaves the hippocampal formation. Later, in the Discussion section, we will briefly note more recent work by Myers, Gluck, and Granger (1995) which suggests how Gluck and Myers' (1993) aggregate hippocampal region might be distributed among hippocampal and parahippocampal regions. Other more recent work of ours (Myers, Ermita, Harris, Hasselmo, Solomon, & Gluck, 1996) extends the model to incorporate subcortical inputs, specifically the cholinergic inputs from the septum. For the moment, however, this aggregate characterisation of hippocampal-region function will suffice for describing the relevant mappings from animal learning to human amnesia.

Hippocampal-lesioned Processing.   The lesioned model shown in Fig. 2.4B represents the processing that remains after total removal of all hippocampal-region mediated processes. In this case, the cortical modules are assumed to be unable to acquire new representations, although they can still learn new behavioural responses based on their pre-existing (and now fixed) stimulus representations. Our lesioned model therefore predicts that hippocampal-region damage will be most deleterious to those tasks that require new stimulus representations, but less evident in those tasks for which pre-existing or random stimulus representations suffice.

As described in the next section, the Gluck and Myers' model of Fig. 2.4 can be applied to classical conditioning, and captures many of the trial-level aspects of the behaviour of intact and hippocampal-lesioned animals. Later, in Section 4, we will illustrate how the model can also be applied to some aspects of normal and amnesic human learning.

3. APPLICATION OF MODEL TO CLASSICAL CONDITIONING

Classical Conditioning

Classical Pavlovian conditioning is one of the simplest forms of associative learning: a previously neutral cue (the conditioned stimulus or CS) is repeatedly paired with a response-evoking cue (the unconditioned stimulus or US) and comes itself to evoke an anticipatory response (the conditioned response or CR). Since Pavlov's seminal studies, almost 80 years of detailed behavioural studies and theoretical analyses of classical conditioning have been accumulated. There now exist several detailed mathematical and computational models for classical conditioning which illustrate how a wide range of conditioning behaviours could emerge from a small set of underlying processing and representational assumptions (Mackintosh, 1983; Pearce & Hall, 1980; Rescorla & Wagner, 1972; Sutherland & Mackintosh, 1971). No form of animal or human learning has been better characterised, or more successfully modelled, than classical conditioning. These behavioural models provide an important starting point for understanding and characterising what is missing or different in hippocampal lesioned animals.

Pavlovian conditioning techniques have been applied to several natural reflexes including salivation, knee-jerking, galvanic skin response, and heart rate conditioning. The most popular and widely adopted preparation has been the eyeblink reflex generated in response to an aversive corneal airpuff or paraorbital shock (Fig. 3.1A). If the airpuff or shock US is reliably preceded by a tone or light CS, subjects learn to generate a protective eyeblink to the CS, and time their blinks so that the eye is maximally closed at the time of expected US arrival (Fig. 3.1B; Gormezano, Kehoe, & Marshall, 1983). Eyeblink conditioning has been studied most extensively in rabbits, but also in frogs, rats, cats, and dogs. The neural circuits underlying the mammalian eyeblink response have been delineated in greatest detail in the rabbit (Thompson, 1986, 1990), suggesting that the long-term storage of CS–US associations occurs in the cerebellar cortex and underlying nuclei. Cerebellar lesion permanently abolishes new conditioned eyeblink learning in animals (Clark, McCormick, Lavond, & Thompson, 1984; Glickstein, Hardiman, & Yeo, 1983).

Hippocampal lesion, however, does not impair the acquisition of simple delay-conditioning in animals (Akase et al., 1989; Berger & Orr, 1983; Port & Patterson, 1984; Schmaltz & Theios, 1972; Solomon & Moore, 1975). However, during learning of the conditioned response, hippocampal activity does change, as indicated through neurophysiological recordings (Berger, Rinaldi, Weisz & Thompson, 1983; Disterhoft, Coulter & Alkon, 1988) and human positron emission tomography (PET) scans (Blaxton et al., 1996; Molchan et al., 1994). This implies that, although the hippocampus may not be strictly required for conditioned learning, it is normally active during such learning. Furthermore, in

(A)   **(B)**

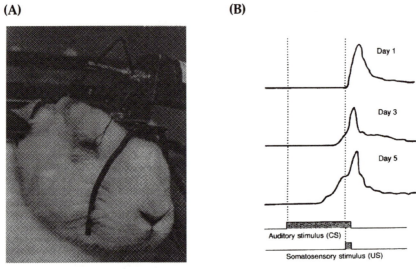

FIG. 3.1.   (A) Eyeblink conditioning in rabbits. The unconditioned stimulus (US) is a blink-evoking corneal airpuff or paraorbital shock. If the US is reliably preceded by a tone or light conditioned stimulus (CS), the animal comes to generate a conditioned blink to the CS alone. Conditioned responding is recorded by noting the displacement of a wire sutured to the subject's eyelid. (B) A CS–US pairing trial consists of a presentation of the CS, followed by US presentations; CS and US co-terminate. Initially (day 1), there is blink responding to the US but not the CS; with repeated CS–US pairings (day 5), a conditioned blink is evoked in response to the CS which anticipates US arrival. Figures reprinted from Carlson, 1991.

conditioning paradigms where there are complex temporal relationships between the CS and US, or complex relationships among multiple CSs and the US, eyeblink conditioning is generally disrupted by hippocampal-region damage (e.g. Moyer et al., 1990; Solomon & Moore, 1975).

   Given the extensive available data on classical conditioning for both intact and hippocampal-lesion animals, together with the existence of formal models which characterise normal classical conditioning behaviours, it would seem that a mechanistic interpretation of hippocampal function might be most clearly revealed within this elementary form of associative learning. As such, we began our computational modelling of hippocampal function in a "top-down" fashion, with a well-defined computational model that accounts for a wide range of behavioural phenomena in classical conditioning, and accurately predicts how behaviour should be affected by hippocampal-region damage (Gluck & Myers, 1993; Myers & Gluck, 1994). In particular, we have suggested that the hippocampus is required to form new stimulus representations to facilitate learning, but not necessarily for simpler stimulus-response learning (Gluck & Myers, 1993). The most salient result from our analyses has been a formal characterisation of how lesioned animals solve tasks differently from normal intact animals, even if this is not always evident from comparing performance on the initial learning task. Later we will note how this account of hippocampal function is broadly compatible with the previous suggestion by Eichenbaum and Cohen that animals with hippocampal lesions are characterised by an inability to apply learned knowledge flexibly in a new situation (Eichenbaum et al., 1992).

Application to Animal Data

Evidence for Redundancy Compression.   Our theory's first bias, redundancy compression, is a bias to compress—or make more similar—the representations of co-occurring or redundant stimuli. Perhaps the simplest paradigm in which redundancy compression is expected in *sensory preconditioning.* Consider two stimulus cues, A and B, perhaps a light and a tone. If these two cues are highly salient, then we would expect the representations they evoke in the hippocampal network hidden layer to be highly distinct—like the examples shown in Fig. 2.2A. As such, there should be very little generalisation between A and B; if A is subsequently paired with the US ("A+ training"), a test presentation of B should evoke very little response. However, if prior to the A + training, there are repeated nonreinforced trials pairing A and B ("AB-pre-exposure"), the situation changes. Redundancy compression makes the representations of co-occurring cues A and B more similar, as in the example of Fig. 2.2B. This will increase generalisation between A and B, so that subsequent A + training will transfer partially to B, and, thus, a test presentation of B will evoke some conditioned responding. Figure 3.2 shows this sensory preconditioning effect in the intact model (Gluck & Myers, 1993). Sensory preconditioning is likewise seen in intact animals (Thompson, 1972). Because our model assumes that sensory preconditioning arises from hippocampal-dependent representational compression during the pre-exposure phase, the enhanced generalisation transfer is not seen in the hippocampal lesioned model (Fig. 3.2). Similarly, hippocampal damage through fornix-fimbrial lesion eliminates sensory preconditioning in rabbits (Port & Patterson, 1984).

Sensory preconditioning illustrates how the increased similarity of stimulus representations can enhance stimulus generalisation. Earlier we noted another implication of increased similarity of stimulus representations: an expected impairment for discriminability. To the extent that two stimuli have similar representations, we expect that discriminating between these patterns will be slower and more difficult than between stimuli with more distinct representations.

We can test this expectation in the following simple variation on sensory preconditioning. We expect that exposure to the compound AB will retard later learning to discriminate A and B in the intact model, as generalisation between the compressed representations will make it harder to map the stimuli to opposite responses. Figure 3.2B indicates that the intact model indeed shows this

(A)   **(B)**

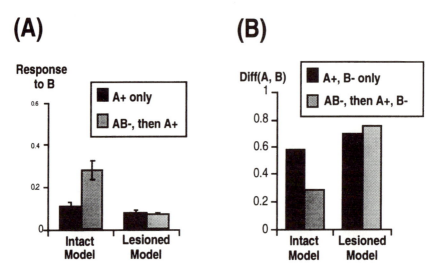

FIG. 3.2. Simulations results with the intact and lesioned models. (A) *Sensory preconditioning*: unreinforced pre-exposure to a compound of two stimuli, AB, followed by training to respond to A, results in stronger responding to B alone than in a control condition with no pre-exposure. The intact but not lesioned model shows this effect; fornix lesion similarly eliminates sensory preconditioning in rabbits (Port & Patterson, 1984). (B) *Compound preconditioning*. Unreinforced pre-exposure to AB slows later training to discriminate A and B, as shown by less relative difference in responding to A and B (Diff{A,B}) after, in the intact model. Intact rats show compound preconditioning (Lubow, et al, 1976); the model predicts hippocampal-region lesions should eliminate the effect.

compound preconditioning effect: the relative difference in responding to A and B, *Diff{A,B}*, following 100 training blocks is reduced if preceded by 20 AB pre-exposure trials, relative to a control condition with no pre-exposure (Gluck & Myers, 1993). In contrast, the lesioned model, with no redundancy compression, shows no difference between the two conditions. This effect is known as the *compound preconditioning* effect, and has been reported both for intact rodents and normal human children (Lubow, Rifkin, & Alek, 1976); this effect has not been tested in hippocampal-lesioned animals (or amnesic humans) and, thus, the elimination of compound preconditioning by hippocampal damage remains a novel prediction of the model.

Note that this is a particularly interesting prediction because we expect a relative enhancement of learning for the lesion group relative to the control group. This is in contrast to the predictions of an expected lesion-related deficit in many other tasks. Such lesion-related deficits can be difficult to interpret because lesion-related deficits can often result from other confounding factors. Thus, a prediction of a lesion-related facilitation is generally more powerful than a predicted lesion-related deficit.

Evidence for Predictive Differentiation.   The second representational bias assumed to depend on hippocampal mediation is predictive differentiation—a bias to decrease the similarity of the representations of stimuli that are to be mapped to different outputs. The simplest paradigm in which differentiation is expected is in a simple discrimination task in which two stimuli, A and B, are associated with different responses (e.g. A+, B– training where A predicts the US but B does not). In the intact model, the hippocampal-region network constructs new internal representations which facilitate this simple discrimination by decreasing the similarity between A and B. These new differentiated representations are acquired by the cortical network's hidden layer, which can then easily map these to different responses, as the task requires. Interestingly, the lesioned model shows no particular deficit on this task, and learns as quickly at the intact model (Fig. 3.3A; Gluck & Myers, 1993). This is because, for this simple task, the pre-existing (fixed) hidden layer representations in the lesioned model's cortical network are likely to at least partially distinguish A and B, and so all the network must do is map these representations to the correct responses.

Consistent with this behaviour, hippocampal lesions do not impair learning a simple discrimination in a variety of preparations (e.g. Good & Honey, 1991; Jarrard, 1993; Jones & Mishkin, 1972; Ross, Orr, Holland, & Berger, 1984; Silveira & Kimble, 1968; Zola-Morgan & Squire, 1986; Zola-Morgan et al., 1992). In some cases, hippocampal-region damage has even been shown to facilitate learning (e.g. Eichenbaum, Fagan & Cohen, 1986; Eichenbaum et al., 1988; Eichenbaum et al., 1991; Port, Mikhail, & Patterson, 1985; Schmaltz & Theios, 1972). These data led to early speculations that the intact hippocampus impaired simple classical conditioning (e.g. Port, Romano & Patterson, 1986). In fact, our lesioned model does show a slight facilitation relative to the intact model (Fig. 3.3A). However, this paradoxical facilitation of simple discrimination learning in the lesioned model results from the fact that the lesioned model learns less than the intact model, which is forming new stimulus representations.

The additional time and effort spent by the intact model (and, presumably, by intact animals) in constructing these new and differentiated stimulus representations can be very helpful if task demands change in a way that preserves which cues are relevant, even if the associations to these relevant cues are different. A simple example of this occurs in the *easy–hard transfer* paradigm, in which animals are first trained on an "easy" discrimination (e.g. black vs. white) and then transferred to a "hard" discrimination along the same stimulus continuum (e.g. dark grey vs. light grey). This transfer facilitates learning even more than an equivalent amount of pre-training on the hard discrimination itself (e.g. Lawrence, 1952; Riley, 1968; Terrace, 1963). The intact model correctly shows this effect (Fig. 3.3b; Gluck & Myers, 1993): in terms of the difference in responding, *Diff(H+, H–)*, between the two hard stimuli in the hard task, pre-training on the easy task leads to better performance

(A)   (B)

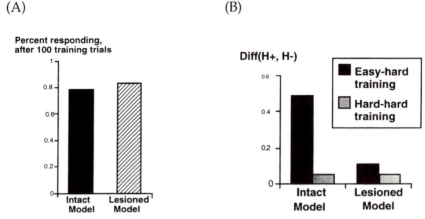

FIG. 3.3.   Simulation results with the intact and lesioned models. (A) *Stimulus discrimination*: training to respond to A but not to B. During this task, the intact model forms new stimulus representations, which differentiate A and B, and then maps them to opposite responses. The lesioned model simply maps from pre-existing (fixed) representations in the cortical network to the correct responses. As a result, there is no impairment in conditioned discrimination learning in the lesioned model. Similarly, there is generally no impairment in simple discrimination learning in hippocampal-damaged animals. Plotted from data presented in Myers et al., 1996. (B) *Easy–hard transfer*: learning a hard discrimination between A and B is facilitated by prior training on an easier discrimination along the same stimulus continuum, in the intact but not lesioned model. This is shown by less relative difference in responding to A and B (Diff(A,B)) after a fixed amount of training in the lesioned model than in the intact model. Intact animals show this effect (e.g. Lawrence, 1952; Riley, 1968; Terrace, 1963); the prediction of hippocampal-dependence remains to be tested in animals. Reprinted from Myers et al., 1995.

than pre-training on the hard task. During pre-training on the easy task, the hippocampal-region network is assumed to differentiate the representations of the two stimuli, which predict different outcomes. As these two stimuli are assumed to differ on only a single feature dimension (such as brightness), that dimension will be differentiated, so that there is decreased generalisation for stimuli with differing values of this feature dimension. This differentiation will help discriminate the stimuli in the subsequent hard task, because they differ along the same dimension. In the control condition, with pre-training on the hard task, the same basic mechanisms operate, but they are slower because the stimuli are harder to distinguish, and therefore the pre-training is not so effective. In the lesioned model, with no differentiation mechanisms, the easy–hard transfer effect is not obtained. This leads us to predict that hippocampal-lesioned animals will not show easy–hard transfer, a novel prediction that remains to be tested.

Contextual Processes.   Many of the learning deficits associated with hippocampal damage can be described as context deficits, as they suggest an inability to incorporate information about the environmental conditions under which an event occurs (cf Hirsh, 1974). In studies of classical conditioning it is possible to manipulate the experimental setup—consisting of the sight, smell, and texture of the training chamber—to explicitly test for the effects of contextual information. The simplest of contextual manipulations involves training an animal respond to a given CS in one context and then testing for responding to the CS in a novel context (Fig. 3.4A). Under these conditions, a normal animal will generally respond less to the CS in the novel context than in the training context (e.g. Hall & Honey, 1989). This context-sensitive decrement in responding suggests that the animal has included some information about the context in the association formed between the experimentally defined CS and the US. In contrast, a hippocampal-lesioned animal does not show this decrement in responding after a context shift (Honey & Good, 1993; Penick & Solomon, 1991). It should be noted that this does not reflect a general inability to perceive contextual cues in the hippocampal-lesioned animal, as lesioned animals can still learn to discriminate contexts (e.g. Good & Honey, 1991; Phillips & Le Doux, 1994). What seems to be disrupted in the lesioned animal is the ability to use context to interpret the meaning of conditioned cues (Myers & Gluck, 1994).

The cortico-hippocampal model provides a framework for understanding why this pattern of preserved and impaired contextual processing might emerge in lesioned animals (Myers & Gluck, 1994). Input to the hippocampal-region autoencoder is assumed to represent not only the presence of any CSs and USs, but also the complete set of background or contextual cues that are present. These contextual cues are "tonic" or unchanging throughout the experiment,

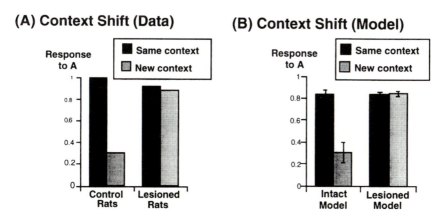

FIG. 3.4.   (A) In normal animals, a conditioned response to A may show a decrement if A is then presented in a new context (Hall & Honey, 1989); hippocampal-lesioned animals do not show this response decrement after a context shift (Honey & Good, 1993; Penick & Solomon, 1991; Figure replotted from data presented in Penick & Solomon, 1991.) (B) The intact but not lesioned model correctly shows this response decrement with context shift (Myers & Gluck, 1994; Figure reprinted from Myers et al., 1995a).

while the CSs and USs are "phasic" and only occur sporadically during training.

As the hippocampal-region autoencoder learns to predict CS–US associations, it also learns to reconstruct its input, including these contextual cues (Fig. 3.5). Thus, contextual information is included in the representations formed in

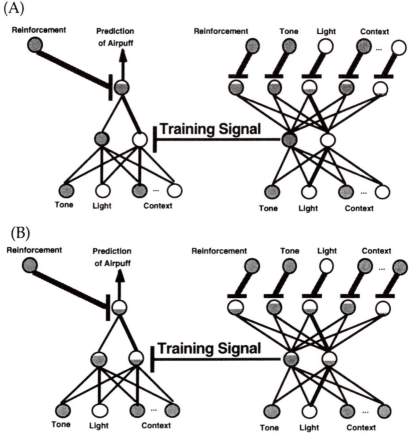

FIG. 3.5.   (A) Schematic of activations in an intact model trained to respond to the presence of a tone stimulus in a particular context (represented by the pattern of input activations). The network has learned to output a strong response at the cortical network output nodes, and a good reconstruction of the input at the hippocampal-region network output nodes. The hidden layer representation that has evolved involves strong activation of one hidden-layer node, and weak activation of the other. (B) Schematic of activations when the tone stimulus is presented in a new context (represented by a different pattern of input activations on the nodes that represent contextual inputs. The hidden layer activation in both networks is more weakly activated than in the trained pattern shown in (A), and the behavioural response output from the cortical network is weaker as well. Thus, the model shows a decremented response when a trained stimulus is presented in a novel context.

the autoencoder's internal layer. As a result, the context influences the internal layer representations in such a way that, if the CS is later presented in a new context, the representation of that CS will be more weakly activated than it was in the training context. Figure 3.4B shows this response decrement after context shift in the intact version of the model, just as observed in the intact animal data of Fig. 3.4A. The model also correctly expects that with extended training the hippocampal representation will exclude irrelevant contextual information and become more and more context-dependent (Myers & Gluck, 1994); there is some evidence of the same kind of time-dependence of contextual sensitivity in animals (Hall & Honey, 1990; see also Myers & Gluck, 1994, for review). In the lesioned version of the model, however, no new internal representations are formed, and so there is no means for incorporating contextual information into the representations of a CS. As a result, the lesioned model is relatively insensitive to context (Fig. 3.4B). This is consistent with the strong responding generally shown by hippocampal-lesioned animals in a new context (Fig. 3.4A). The cortico-hippocampal model can similarly account for results from a range of context studies (Myers & Gluck, 1994) and provides a computational instantiation and elaboration of several existing qualitative theories which have implicated the hippocampus in context learning (Hirsh, 1974; Penick & Solomon, 1991).

Another context-related behavioural phenomenon is *latent inhibition* (Fig. 3.6A) in which unreinforced pre-exposure to a cue slows the rate of subsequent conditioning to that cue (Lubow, 1973). Within the cortico-hippocampal model, latent inhibition can be understood as a variation of compound preconditioning, in which the context is considered as another cue. If we represent the context as a single, compound cue, X, and the CS as another cue A, then conditioning is expressible as learning the discrimination AX+, X–, that is, respond when A is present in context X, but not to X alone. Latent inhibition involves a prior phase of AX–, X– training followed by the AX+, X– training. In the initial phase, where neither AX nor X predicts the US, redundancy compression in the intact model results in an increase in similarity between the representations of A and X, making it more difficult to discriminate AX from X alone. As a result of this, the later phase of learning to respond to AX but not X is made more difficult, which is the observed latent inhibition effect.

This is exactly what we see in simulations of the intact model (Fig. 3.6B). The lesioned model, with no representational changes, does not perform redundancy compression during the pre-exposure phase and therefore learning in the subsequent acquisition phase is not slowed down (Fig. 3.6B). Consistent with the model, broad hippocampal-region damage eliminates latent inhibition (Fig. 3.6A), and these lesioned animals learn about the pre-exposed cue as quickly as a nonpre-exposed cue (Kaye & Pearce, 1987; Solomon & Moore, 1975).

It should be noted that a smaller lesion, limited to the hippocampus but not including surrounding cortices, does not eliminate latent inhibition (Honey &

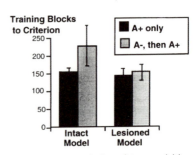

(A) Latent Inhibition (Data)

(B) Latent Inhibition (Model)

FIG. 3.6.   Latent inhibition, in which unreinforced pre-exposure to a cue A slows later acquisition of conditioned responding to A. (A) Intact animals show this effect (Lubow, 1973), reflected in longer training time to learn a strong response to A. Broad hippocampal-region lesion eliminates latent inhibition (Kaye & Pearce, 1987; Solomon & Moore, 1975). Figure plotted from data presented in Solomon & Moore (1975). (B) The intact model correctly shows latent inhibition while the lesioned model does not. Figure reprinted from Myers et al. 1995.

Good, 1993). In more recent work, Myers et al. (1995) have suggested that this result is consistent with a mapping of function to anatomy in which stimulus compression may occur in the entorhinal cortex without requiring the hippocampus proper. Eichenbaum and Bunsey (1995) have argued for a similar functional interpretation of the cortical areas overlaying the hippocampus, especially the entorhinal cortex, in their analyses of intact vs. lesioned animals in olfactory simple discrimination learning.

Summary of Model Performance in Animal Studies.   Given the extensive available data on classical conditioning for both intact and hippocampal-damaged animals, together with the existence of formal models which characterise normal classical conditioning behaviours, we have shown how a mechanistic interpretation of hippocampal function can be clearly revealed within this most elementary form of associative learning. The most salient result from our analyses is a formal characterisation of how lesioned animals solve tasks differently from normal intact animals, even if this is not always evident from comparing performance on the initial learning task. Analyses of sensory preconditioning and compound preconditioning are interpreted as reflecting the hippocampal-dependent bias for *redundancy compression*, while stimulus discrimination and easy–hard transfer are interpreted as reflecting *predictive differentiation*. Further evidence for these hippocampal-dependent representa-tional biases comes from analyses of contextual effects seen in studies of context shifts and latent inhibition.

Human Hippocampal Amnesia and Conditioning

What can all these studies of hippocampal-lesion effects in animals tell us about human medial-temporal lobe (especially hippocampal-based) amnesia? One of the most important reasons for studying classical conditioning is that the neural structures and behavioural properties are very similar across a wide range of species, including humans. Classical conditioning has been extensively studied in humans, using a variety of preparations (cf Daum et al., 1993; Lye, O'Boyle, Ramsden, & Schady, 1988; Solomon, Stowe, & Pendlebury, 1989; Topka, Valls-Sole, Masaquoi, & Hallet, 1993). As with animals, the most popular preparation is the conditioned eyeblink response. Subjects typically wear a hat-type device fitted with tubing to allow light airpuffs to be directed at the cornea; the hat also produces an infrared beam which is reflected off the white of the eyeball and interruption of this beam by an eyeblink is recorded as a response. Just as in animals, repeated pairing of a previously neutral tone or light CS with the blink-evoking airpuff US results in an anticipatory conditioned eyeblink response to the CS alone. At the neural level of analysis, the cerebellum seems to be the necessary substrate for conditioned eyeblink responding in humans as well as in infra-human species (Daum et al., 1993; Lye et al., 1988; Solomon et al., 1989; Topka et al., 1993).

Intact Delay Conditioning in Amnesia

Four studies have examined classical conditioning and human hippocampal amnesia. Weiskrantz and Warrington (1979) first examined eyeblink conditioning in two amnesia patients. One patient had hippocampal damage as characterised by an episode of viral encephalitis, while the other was an alcoholic Korsakoff patient. Although details indicating damage specific to a neuroanatomical focus was not provided, both patients neuropsychologically demonstrated memory defects that are commonly attributable either to pathology to the medial temporal lobe or diencephalic damage. Both amnesic individuals showed clear evidence of conditioned learning without impairment. Interestingly, when later asked to verbalise a declarative account about the experiment they were unaware of their performance.

Daum et al. (1989) investigated eyelid conditioning in three amnesic patients with bilateral temporal damage. Patient 1 had a history of epilepsy and alcohol abuse, patient 2 had a history of encephalitis and epileptic seizures, and patient 3 suffered from epileptic seizures. All three patients showed significant impairments on standard neuropsychological memory tests and indicated hippocampal lesions as supported by EEG or CT measures. As in the amnesics of Weiskrantz and Warrington (1979) all three of these patients were able to condition without impairment using the delay paradigm. However, when assessed on a more complex two-CS, conditional discrimination and reversal experiment, all three failed to effectively learn the task.

Woodruff-Pak (1993) conducted a series of eyeblink studies in the well-studied amnesic, HM. As a result of bilateral removal of medial-temporal lobe structures, including the hippocampus, to relieve the patient's epilepsy, HM because densely amnesic for learning and remembering new information. A second amnesic with medial-temporal-lobe lesions resultant from encephalitis was included for comparison, as were two normal adult controls. It took HM longer (473 trials) to reach learning criterion than a control subject (315 trials). The encephalitic amnesic took 119 trials and his control took 15. In the case of HM, although the extent of his hippocampal removal lesion is well known, some cerebellar atrophy in the vermis and cerebellar hemispheres has recently been noted. Damage to the cerebellum, more so than hippocampal damage, may have been more important as the cause of his slower impairment (yet not abolishment) in conditioning.

Gabrieli et al. (1995) recently tested seven well-characterised amnesic subjects and seven well-matched normal controls. In reviewing the experimental details of the three previous amnesic papers, the studies may be criticised for using inferior eyeblink measurement apparatus and technique, too few amnesic subjects, poor quality of patient diagnoses and characterisation, and not including control subjects for comparisons. In this paper, the amnesic etiologies ranged from encephalitis (n = 2), anoxia (n = 2), aneurysm (n = 1), status epilepticus (n = 1), and closed head injury (n = 1). Five of the patients had neuroimaging data confirming bilateral hippocampal damage. All were densely amnesic in terms of standard neuropsychological memory tests. The subjects were assessed in terms of pseudoconditioning (no pairing of CS and US), conditioning (CS–US pairings) and extinction contingencies (CS alone). In support of the three previous amnesia and delay conditioning studies, no statistical differences were found, with amnesics learning the conditioned response as well as the normal controls (see Fig. 3.7).

Most of the other conditioning paradigms in which hippocampal-lesioned animals are affected, such as simple discrimination reversal, sensory preconditioning, latent inhibition, etc., remain to be tested in human hippocampal amnesics. For example, normal intact humans show latent inhibition of the conditioned eyeblink response (Hulstijn, 1978). It remains to be seen if human hippocampal amnesics will show a similar disruption in latent inhibition as do hippocampal-damaged animals. Similarly, we expect that human hippocampal amnesics may show disruptions in other paradigms (simple discrimination reversal, latent inhibition, etc.) that parallel those seen in hippocampal-lesioned animals.

Having reviewed the evidence for our theory within studies of animal conditioning, and described some preliminary studies of its relevance to human eyeblink conditioning in amnesia, we turn now to consider a more clearly cognitive form of human learning: category learning.

(A)

(B)

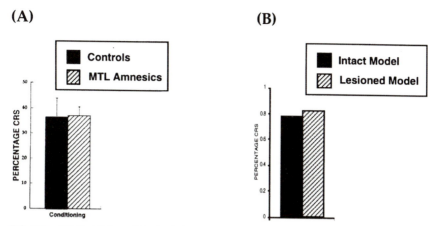

FIG. 3.7.   (A) Eyeblink conditioning in humans is not disrupted by hippocampal damage in human amnesics. Figure reprinted from Gabrieli et al. (1995). (B) Likewise, the lesioned model predicts no deficits. Figure reprinted from Myers et al. (1995b).

4. APPLICATION OF MODEL TO CATEGORY LEARNING

In the previous section of the paper we discussed how the predictions of the cortico-hippocampal model have been tested in both animal and human eyeblink conditioning studies. In this section our focus shifts to human category learning, as we explore the possibility of extending the cortico-hippocampal model further to aid our understanding of higher cognitive processes. Category learning plays a pivotal role in human cognition and has generated a substantial body of empirical and theoretical work (Estes, 1993). By extending a neurobiologically based model of associative learning to account for category learning data we hope to start to establish a bridge over which we can begin to integrate animal and human data from studies of the neural and behavioural bases of cognition.

In a typical category learning experiment, subjects are presented with a series of multidimensional stimuli. The subject's task is to determine to which of two or more categories each stimulus belongs. The subject is then provided with corrective feedback, indicating the correct response.

The behavioural correspondences between animal conditioning and category learning were described by Gluck and Bower (1988a,b) who demonstrated that the Rescorla-Wagner model of conditioning (Rescorla & Wagner, 1972), a simple associative model, can be extended to account for a variety of category learning phenomena in humans. Gluck and Bower's connectionist extension of the Rescorla-Wagner model can account for many fundamental aspects of human category learning (Gluck, Bower, & Hee, 1989) including base-rate neglect (Gluck & Bower, 1988a,b), the interaction of exemplar similarity and linear separability in determining categorisation difficulty (Medin & Schwanen-flugel, 1981), the relationship between classification and recognition memory for instances (Hayes-Roth & Hayes-Roth, 1977), and the impact of correlated attributes on classification (Medin, Altom, Edelson, & Freko, 1982). The modelling of Gluck and Bower as well as other researchers working in a similar vein (Estes, 1993; Shanks, 1991) provide us with an *a priori* basis for believing that there are significant behavioural correspondences between animal conditioning and human category learning. This leads us to ask whether or not there might be neurobiological correspondences, too.

Some preliminary progress in this direction was made by Knowlton et al. (1994) who addressed this issue of neurobiological correspondences between conditioning and category learning in a series of studies in which amnesic patients and control subjects were given a series of multidimensional stimuli and told to classify them into one of two categories. For example, in one task, there were four ''tarot'' cards, each with a unique set of abstract geometric patterns. The stimuli were a drawing of up to four of these cards, and subjects were asked to predict whether there would be ''good'' or ''bad'' weather based on these cards. The actual weather was determined according to a probabilistic rule based on the cards, and each card was therefore a partial predictor of the weather. The probabilistic rule ensured that it was impossible for the subjects to learn the prediction with complete certainty, although it was possible to use the probabilistic card–weather relationships to achieve significantly better-than-chance performance. Two equivalent tasks were also used, with similar underlying logic. These tasks are equivalent to those used by Gluck and Bower (1988b) in an investigation of probabilistic category learning in intact subjects, with the exception that the categories used in the Knowlton et al. study occurred with equal frequency.

In each task, the amnesic patients initially learned to associate the cues with the appropriate outcome at the same rate as control subjects, improving from chance performance (50% correct) to approximately 65% correct (Knowlton et al., 1994). With extended training, however, control subjects eventually outperformed amnesic patients (see Fig. 4.1A). This finding that amnesics outperformed controls only late in training mirrors a similar finding that hippocampal amnesics are initially unimpaired but later impaired at cognitive skill learning (Squire & Frambach, 1990).

As shown in Fig. 4.1B, the cortico-hippocampal model produces learning curves analogous to those observed by Knowlton et al. (Gluck, Oliver, & Myers, in press). In the intact model, the hippocampal-region network develops new stimulus representations to aid learning; these representations may develop over many trials as the model is exposed to a representative subset of training patterns. Early in learning, before these representations develop, the intact

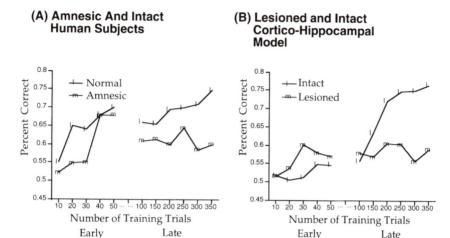

FIG. 4.1. (A) On a probabilistic category learning task (Knowlton et al., 1994), hippocampal amnesics initially learn at the same rate as controls; later in training, the controls continue to improve performance more than the amnesics. Figure reprinted from Knowlton et al. (1994). (B) The cortico-hippocampal model shows a similar effect: the lesioned model initially performs as well as the intact model, but later in training, the lesioned model shows a deficit. Figure reprinted from Gluck and Oliver (in prep.).

model depends on the pre-existing representations in the cortical network, and maps these to (an approximation of) the correct response. Later in training, as the hippocampal representations become available, these new representations are acquired by the cortical network and allow further improvement in performance. In the lesioned model, only the prior cortical representations are ever available. Thus, early in training, performance is similar in the lesioned and intact models; as training progresses, however, and no new representations become available to the lesioned cortical network, the lesioned model shows a deficit relative to the intact model.

The simulation study reported by Gluck, Oliver, and Myers (in press) should be viewed only as preliminary evidence in favour of the cortico-hippocampal model as a model of human category learning. Category learning research has generated a considerable body of data which must be addressed before a model can claim to account for this pervasive aspect of human cognition. Nevertheless, these preliminary analyses point to the possible potential of the cortico-hippocampal model for capturing subtle aspects of amnesic learning which go beyond simply classifying their learning as intact or impaired relative to normals. Moreover, they suggest that careful comparisons of early versus late training difference in learning may be an important factor in understanding the differences between intact and amnesic learning.

5. DISCUSSION

Although most analyses of amnesia have focused on the loss of explicit declarative and episodic memories following hippocampal-region damage, we have tried to show here how insights into amnesia can also be realised by studying hippocampal function in simple procedural, or habit-based, associative learning tasks. Although many simple forms of associative learning are unimpaired by hippocampal damage, more complex tasks that require sensitivity to unreinforced stimuli, configurations of multiple stimuli, or contextual information are impaired by hippocampal damage. We have reviewed here the results of several of our recent papers in which we have argued that these animal conditioning data imply that the hippocampal region plays a critical role in the formation of new stimulus representations during learning (Gluck & Myers, 1993, 1995; Myers & Gluck, 1996; Myers et al., 1995).

Dissociating Hippocampal and Parahippocampal Function

More recently we have begun to extend our modelling efforts to seek a closer rapprochement with the underlying biology. Although the intact model of Fig. 2.4A adopts the simplifying assumption that the hippocampal region functions as a unitary processor, the hippocampal region is, in fact, anatomically divided into several distinct structures—including hippocampal fields CA1 through CA4, dentate gyrus, subiculum, and entorhinal cortex. There are also several inputs to the hippocampal region, including perirhinal and parahippocampal cortices, which provide highly processed polymodal sensory information, as well as a direct connection from unimodal piriform (olfactory) cortex (see Fig. 5.1). In Myers et al. (1995) we hypothesised that the representational function computed in our intact model's hippocampal region may be subdivided, and the subfunctions localised in different anatomical sites around the region; in particular, we proposed that stimulus–stimulus redundancy compression could emerge from the anatomy and physiology of superficial entorhinal cortex. The net result of both entorhinal and hippocampal processing would then be a new stimulus representation constrained by both compression and differentiation biases which could be transferred to long-term storage sites in the cortex.

This hypothesis assumes that a selective hippocampal-lesion (the H-lesion), which does not otherwise damage entorhinal cortex (cf Jarrard & Davidson, 1991), might allow redundancy compression processes to survive. Behaviours that depend mainly on these processes should continue to be exhibited after H-lesion, whereas behaviours that require other representational processes such as predictive differentiation should be disrupted. We can study this situation by constructing a "Selective H-lesioned" model, in which the full hippocampal-region network of Fig. 2.4 is reduced to an enthorhinal network only. The long-

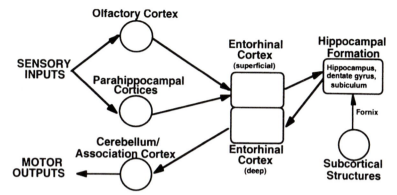

FIG. 5.1.   Schematic of major information flow pathways in the hippocampal region. Inputs are provided directly from unimodal olfactory cortex, as well as polymodal cortices including parahippocampal and perirhinal cortex. Information travels through superficial entorhinal cortex, through the hippocampal formation (including hippocampal fields CA1–CA4, dentate gyrus, and subiculum), and returns through deep entorhinal cortex to other cortical areas for long-term storage. There is also a bi-directional pathway through the fornix which provides connection to subcortical structures. Many other connections exist, which are not shown here for simplicity.

term memory network continues to operate as in the intact model, except that the new representations provided by the entorhinal network are biased only by stimulus–stimulus redundancy compression, but not by the other representational biases attributed to the hippocampal region as a whole.

A simple example of a compression-based task is latent inhibition, in which unreinforced pre-exposure to a cue slows later acquisition of a conditioned response to that cue (Lubow, 1973). In our intact model of Fig. 2.4A, latent inhibition is caused by compression of the pre-exposed cue with co-occurring and equally nonreinforced contextual cues. The subsequent increase in learning time results because the model must first redifferentiate the cue from the context before a response can be selectively associated with the cue (Fig. 3.6). Because this effect is assumed to depend primarily on redundancy compression, the entorhinal network in the H-lesioned model is sufficient to produce latent inhibition. Consistent with this model behaviour, rats with selective hippocampal lesions but no entorhinal damage show normal or even enhanced latent inhibition (Honey & Good, 1993; Reilly, Harley & Revusky, 1993). Obviously, more experimental tests need to be performed, but this is at least initial support for the Myers et al. (1995) proposed dissociation of hippocampal and entorhinal function.

Eichenbaum and Bunsey (1995) have recently addressed this same issue and have suggested that the parahippocampal region mediates the "fusion" of co-occurring or nearly coincident stimuli; this process is essentially identical to the redundancy compression function we have proposed. It is interesting to note that whereas their fusion theory derives from behavioural observations comparing paired-associate learning in intact, hippocampal-lesioned and parahippocampal-lesioned animals, our similar compression theory arises from an integration of both physiologically based and behaviourally based computational models of hippocampal-region function. We hope the convergence of these two widely different approaches to theory development is a sign that stimulus compression is a useful and accurate description of parahippocampal-region function.

Modelling Cholinergic Modulation in Septohippocampal Pathways

In other, more recent work, we have also shown that a simple extension of the model can successfully account for the retarded classical conditioning that occurs after septohippocampal disruption via anticholinergic drugs (Myers et al., 1996). This last is important because septohippocampal pathways may be damaged in a variety of ways. Basal forebrain damage may occur in cases of Alzheimer's Dementia, but more commonly occurs in cases of aneurysm rupture of the anterior communicating artery (ACoA). The ACoA aneurysm survivors are an especially interesting group because they often manifest an anterograde amnesia syndrome which is superficially very similar to that shown by hippocampal amnesics (DeLuca & Diamond, 1995)—although the ACoA amnesics have no direct lesion to the hippocampus. The problem in these patients may result from basal forebrain damage, indirectly interfering with proper hippocampal functioning. Neuroimaging to directly assess basal forebrain lesion extent is difficult because ACoA aneurysm is often treated by surgical placement of ferromagnetic clips on the ruptured artery. MRI is therefore contraindicated in these cases as it may result in displacement and heating of the metallic clip which could kill the patient (Klucznik, Carrier, Pyka, & Haid, 1993). Alternate neuroimaging techniques such as angiography and computerised tomography (CT scan) may be used in these amnesic patients recovering from stroke; however, the placement of the metallic clip often obscures precise imaging of the basal forebrain region. Therefore, an interesting potential application of this work is to develop behavioural tests that are sensitive to the damage of particular neural structures—thus aiding in the assessment of lesion extent in these patients.

Summary

Our long-term goal is to use computational models to develop a comprehensive view of hippocampal-region function that illuminates common behavioural functions, and underlying neural mechanisms, in both animal and human memory. Our work to date illustrates some initial progress to this end, and may help provide predictions and directions to guide further empirical and theoretical research in human memory and amnesia. Our hope is that the insights gained from these initial analyses of a simple learning behaviour will lead to a deeper understanding of the hippocampal region in more complex forms of learning and memory, in both animals and humans.

REFERENCES

Akase, E., Alkon, D.L., & Disterhoft, J.F. (1989). Hippocampal lesions impair memory of short-delay conditioned eyeblink in rabbits. *Behavioral Neuroscience, 103*(5), 935–943.

Alvarez, P., & Squire, L. (1994). Memory consolidation and the medial temporal lobe: A simple network model. *Proceedings of the National Academy of Sciences, 91,* 7041–7045.

Anderson, J. (1977). Neural models with cognitive implications. In D. LaBerge & S. Samuels (Eds.), *Basic processes in reading: Perception and comprehension* (pp.27–90). Hillsdale, NJ: Lawrence Erlbaum Associates Inc.

Barto, A., & Sutton, R. (1982). Simulation of anticipatory responses in classical conditioning by a neuron-like adaptive element. *Behavioral Brain Research, 4,* 221–235.

Berger, T., & Orr, W. (1983). Hippocampectomy selectively disrupts discrimination reversal learning of the rabbit nictitating membrane response. *Behavioral Brain Research, 8,* 49–68.

Berger, T.W., Rinaldi, P., Weisz, D.J., & Thompson, R.F. (1983). Single-unit analysis of different hippocampal cell types during classical conditioning of the rabbit nictitating membrane response. *Journal of Neurophysiology, 50*(5), 1197–1219.

Blaxton, T.A., Zeffiro, T.A.,Gabrieli, J.D.E., Bookheimer, S.Y., Carrillo, M.C., Theodore, W.H., & Disterhoft, J.F. (1995). Mapping the neuroanatomical correlates of human learning: A PET activation study of eyeblink conditioning. Manuscript submitted for publication.

Bliss, T., & Lomo, T. (1983). Long-lasting potentiation of synaptic transmission in the dentate area of anaesthetized rabbit following stimulation of the perforant path. *Journal of Physiology, 232,* 331–356.

Buzsaki, G. (1989). Two-stage model of memory-trace formation: A role for "noisy" brain states. *Neuroscience, 31*(3), 551–570.

Carlson, N.R. (1991). *Physiology of behavior* (4th edn.). Needham Heights, MA: Allyn & Bacon.

Clark, G.A., McCormick, D.A., Lavond, D.G., & Thompson, R.F. (1984). Effects of lesions of cerebellar nuclei on conditioned behavioral and hippocampal neuronal responses. *Brain Research, 291,* 125–136.

Cohen, N. (1984). Preserved learning capacity in amnesia: Evidence for multiple learning systems. In L. Squire & N. Butters (Eds.), *Neuropsychology of memory* (pp.83–103). New York: Guilford Press.

Daum, I., Channon, S., & Canavan, A. (1989). Classical conditioning in patients with severe memory problems. *Journals of Neurology, Neurosurgery and Psychiatry, 52,* 47–51.

Daum, I., Schugens, M.M., Ackermann, H., Lutzenberger, W., Dichgans, J., & Birbaumer, N. (1993). Classical conditioning after cerebellar lesions in humans. *Behavioral Neuroscience, 107*(5), 748–756.

DeLuca, J., & Diamond, B. (1995). Aneurysm of the anterior communicating artery: A review of neuroanatomical and neurophysiological sequelae. *Journal of Clinical and Experimental Neuropsychology, 17*(1), 100–121.

Disterhoft, J.F., Coulter, D.A., & Alkon, D.L. (1988). Conditioning-specific biophysical alterations in rabbit hippocampus. In C.D. Woody, D.L. Alkon, & J.L. McGaugh (Eds.), *Cellular mechanisms of conditioning and behavioral plasticity* (pp.89–104). New York: Plenum Publishing Corporation.

Douglas, R., & Pribam, K. (1966). Learning and limbic lesions. *Neuropsychologia, 4,* 192–222.

Eichenbaum, H., & Buckingham, J. (1990). Studies on hippocampal processing: Experiment, theory and model. In M. Gabriel & J. Moore (Eds.), *Learning and computational neuroscience: Foundations of adaptive networks* (pp.171–231). Cambridge, MA: MIT Press.

Eichenbaum, H., & Bunsey, M. (1995). On the binding of associations in memory: Clues from studies on the role of the hippocampal region in paired associated learning. *Current Directions in Psychological Science, 4.*

Eichenbaum, H., Cohen, N.J., Otto, T., & Wible C. (1992). Memory representation in the hippocampus: Functional domain and functional organization. In L.R. Squire, G. Lynch, N.M. Weinberger, & J.L. McGaugh (Eds.), *Memory organization and locus of change* (pp.163–204). Oxford: Oxford University Press.

Eichenbaum, H., Fagan, A., & Cohen, N.J. (1986). Normal olfactory discrimination learning set and facilitation of reversal learning after medial-temporal damage in rats: Implication for an account of preserved learning abilities in amnesia. *Journal of Neuroscience, 6*(7), 1876–1884.

Eichenbaum, H., Fagan, A., Mathews, P., & Cohen, N.J. (1988). Hippocampal system dysfunction and odor discrimination learning in rats: Impairment or facilitation depending on representational demands. *Behavioral Neuroscience, 102*(3), 331–339.

Eichenbaum, H., Otto, T., & Cohen, N. (1994). Two functional components of the hippocampal memory system. *Behavioral and Brain Sciences, 17*(3), 449–518.

Eichenbaum, H., Otto, T., Wible, C., & Piper, J. (1991). Building a model of the hippocampus in olfaction and memory. In J. Davis & H. Eichenbaum (Eds.), *Olfaction as a model for computational neuroscience* (pp.167–210). Cambridge, MA: MIT Press.

Estes, W.K. (1993). Models of categorization and category learning. *The Psychology of Learning and Motivation, 29*, 15–56.

Gabrieli, J., McGlinchey-Berroth, R., Carrillo, M., Gluck, M., Cermak, L., & Disterhoft, J. (1995). Intact delay-eyeblink classical conditioning in amnesia. *Behavioral Neuroscience, 109*(5), 819–827.

Glickstein, M., Hardiman, M.J., & Yeo, C.H. (1983). The effects of cerebellar lesions on the conditioned nictitating membrane response of the rabbit. *Journal of Physiology, 341*, 30–31.

Gluck, M., & Bower, G. (1988a). From conditioning to category learning: An adaptive network model. *Journal of Experimental Psychology: General, 117*(3), 225–244.

Gluck, M., & Myers, C. (1993). Adaptive stimulus representations: A computational theory of hippocampal-region function. In S. Hanson, J. Cowen, & C. Giles (Eds.), *Advances in neural information processing systems 5* (pp.937–944). San Mateo, CA: Morgan Kaufmann.

Gluck, M., & Myers, C. (1995). Representation and association in memory: A neurocomputational view of hippocampal function. *Current Directions in Psychological Science, 4*(1), 23–29.

Gluck, M.A., & Bower, G.H. (1988b). Evaluating an adaptive network model of human learning. *Journal of Memory and Language, 27*, 166–195.

Gluck, M.A., Bower, G.H., & Hee, M.R. (1989). A configural-cue network model of animal and human associative learning. In *Proceedings of 11th Annual Conference of Cognitive Science Society, Ann Arbor: MI* (pp.323–332).

Gluck, M.A., & Oliver, L.M. (1995). Early vs. late performance in normal and hippocampal-impaired learning: A neurocomputational perspective on Knowlton, Squire and Gluck (1994). Manuscript in preparation.

Gluck, M.A., Oliver, L.M., & Myers, C.E. (in press). Late-training amnesic deficits in probabilistic category learning: A neurocomputational analysis. *Learning and Memory.*

Good, M., & Honey, R.C. (1991). Conditioning and contextual retrieval in hippocampal rats. *Behavioral Neuroscience, 105*(4), 499–509.

Gormezano, I., Kehoe, E.J., & Marshall, B.S. (1983). Twenty years of classical conditioning research with the rabbit. *Progress in Psychobiology and Physiological Psychology, 10*, 197–275.

Hall, G., & Honey, R. (1989). Contextual effects in conditioning, latent inhibition, and habituation: Associative and retrieval functions of contextual cues. *Journal of Experimental Psychology: Animal Behavior Processes, 15*(3), 232–241.

Hall, G., & Honey, R. (1990). Context-specific conditioning in the conditioned-emotional-response procedure. *Journal of Experimental Psychology: Animal Behavior Processes, 16*(3), 271–278.

Hanson, S.J., & Burr, D.J. (1990). What connectionist models learn: Learning and representation in connectionist networks. *Behavioral and Brain Sciences, 13*, 471–518.

Hayes-Roth, B., & Hayes-Roth, F. (1977). Concept learning and the recognition and classification of exemplars. *Journal of Verbal Learning and Verbal Behavior, 16*, 321–338.

Hinton, G. (1989). Connectionist learning procedures. *Artificial Intelligence, 40*, 185–234.

Hirsh, R. (1974). The hippocampus and contextual retrieval of information from memory: A theory. *Behavioral Biology, 12*, 421–444.

Honey, R., & Good, M. (1993). Selective hippocampal lesions abolish the contextual specificity of latent inhibition and conditioning. *Behavioral Neuroscience, 107*(1), 23–33.

Hulstijn, W. (1978). The orienting reaction during human eyelid conditioning following preconditioning exposures to the CS. *Psychological Research, 40*, 77–88.

James, W. (1896). *The principles of psychology.* New York: Henry Holt & Co.

Jarrard, L. (1993). On the role of the hippocampus in learning and memory in the rat. *Behavioral and Neural Biology, 60*, 9–26.

Jones, B., & Mishkin, M. (1972). Limbic lesions and the problem of stimulus-reinforcement association. *Experimental Neurology, 36*, 362–377.

Kaye, H., & Pearce, J. (1987). Hippocampal lesions attenuate latent inhibition and the decline of the orienting response in rats. *Quarterly Journal of Experimental Psychology, 39B*, 107–125.

Kehoe, E.J. (1988). A layered network model of associative learning. *Psychological Review, 95*(4), 411–433.

Klucznick, R.P., Carrier, D.A., Pyka, R., & Haid, R.W. (1993). Placement of ferromagnetic intracerebral aneurysm clip in a magnetic field with a fatal outcome. *Radiology, 187*, 855–856.

Knowlton, B., Squire, L., & Gluck, M. (1994). Probabilistic classification learning in amnesia. *Learning and Memory, 1*, 106–120.

Krushke, J.K. (1992). ALCOVE: An exemplar-based connectionist model of category learning. *Psychological Review, 99*(1), 22–44.

Lawrence, D.H. (1952). The transfer of a discrimination along a continuum. *Journal of Comparative and Physiological Psychology, 45*, 511–516.

Levy, W.B., Brassel, S.E., & Moore, S.D. (1983). Partial quantification of the associative synaptic learning rule of the dentate gyrus. *Neuroscience, 8*(4), 799–808.

Lubow, R. (1973). Latent inhibition. *Psychological Bulletin, 79*, 398–407.

Lubow, R.E., Rifkin, B., & Alek, M. (1976). The context effect: The relationship between stimulus pre-exposure and environmental pre-exposure determines subsequent learning. *Journal of Experimental Psychology: Animal Behavior Processes, 2*(1), 38–47.

Lye, R.H., O'Boyle, D.J., Ramsden, R.T., & Schady, W. (1988). Effects of a unilateral cerebellar lesion on the acquisition of eye-blink conditioning in man. *Journal of Physiology (London), 403*, 58P.

Mackintosh, N. (1983). *Conditioning and associative learning.* Oxford: Oxford University Press.

McClelland, J., McNaughton, B., & O'Reilly, R. (1994). *Why we have complementary learning systems in the hippocampus and neocortex: Insights from the successes and failures of connectionist models of learning and memory.* Technical Report No. PDP.CNS.94.1. Carnegie Mellon University, Pittsburgh.

Medin, D.L., Altom, M.W., Edelson, S.M., & Freko, D. (1982). Correlated symptoms and simulated medical classification. *Journal of Experimental Psychology: Learning, Memory, & Cognition, 8*, 37–50.

Medin, D.L., & Schwanenflugel, P.J. (1981). Linear separability in classification learning. *Journal of Experimental Psychology: Human Learning and Memory, 7*, 355–368.

Molchan, S.E., Sunderland, T., McIntosh, A.R., Hersovitch, P., & Schreus, B.G. (1994). A functional anatomical study of associative learning in humans. *Proceedings of the National Academy of Sciences of the United States of America, 91*, 8122–8126.

Moyer, J., Deyo, R., & Disterhoft, J. (1990). Hippocampectomy disrupts trace eye-blink conditioning in rabbits. *Behavioral Neuroscience, 104*(2), 243–252.

Murre, J. (1994). *A model for amnesia.* Unpublished manuscript.

Myers, C., & Gluck, M. (1994). Context, conditioning and hippocampal re-representation. *Behavioral Neuroscience, 108*(5), 835–847.

Myers, C., & Gluck, M. (1996). Cortico-hippocampal representations in simultaneous odor discrimination learning: A computational interpretation of Eichenbaum, Mathews & Cohen (1989). *Behavioral Neuroscience, 110*(4), 1–22.

Myers, C., Gluck, M., & Granger, R. (1995). Dissociation of hippocampal and entorhinal function in associative learning: A computational approach *Psychobiology, 23*(2), 116–138.

Myers, C.E., Ermita, B., Harris, K., Hasselmo, M., Solomon, P., & Gluck, M.A. (1996). A computational model of the effects of septohippocampal disruption on classical eyeblink conditioning. *Neurobiology of Learning and Memory, 66*, 51–66.

Nadel, L., & Willner, J. (1980). Context and conditioning: A place for space. *Physiological Psychology, 8*(2), 218–228.

O'Keefe, J., & Nadel, L. (1978). *The hippocampus as a cognitive map.* Oxford: Clarendon University Press.

Oliver, L.M., & Gluck, M.A. (1995). A hippocampal-based model of human learning: implications for the distinction between integral and separable dimensions. Manuscript in preparation.

Olton, D. (1983). Memory functions and the hippocampus. In W. Seifert (Ed.), *Neurobiology of the Hippocampus* (pp.335–373). London: Academic Press.

Parker, D. (1985). *Learning logic,* Technical Report, Center for Computational Research in Economics and Management Science, MIT.

Pearce, J., & Hall, G. (1980). A model for pavlovian learning: Variations in the effectiveness of conditioned but not of unconditioned stimuli. *Psychological Review, 87*, 532–552.

Penick, S., & Solomon, R. (1991). Hippocampus, context and conditioning. *Behavioral Neuroscience, 105*(5), 611–617.

Phillips, R. & LeDoux, J. (1994). Lesions of the dorsal hippocampal formation interfere with background but not foreground contextual fear conditioning. *Learning & Memory, 1*, 34–44.

Port, R., Mikhail, A., & Patterson, M. (1985). Differential effects of hippocampectomy on classically conditioned rabbit nictitating membrane response related to interstimulus interval. *Behavioral Neuroscience, 99*(2), 200–208.

Port, R., Romano, A., & Patterson, M. (1986). Stimulus duration discrimination in the rabbit: Effects of hippocampectomy on discrimination and reversal learning. *Physiological Psychology, 4*, 124–129.

Port, R., & Patterson, M. (1984). Fimbrial lesions and sensory preconditioning. *Behavioral Neuroscience, 98*, 584–589.

Port, R., Romano, A., & Patterson, M. (1986). Stimulus duration discrimination in the rabbit: Effects of hippocampectomy on discrimination and reversal learning. *Physiological Psychology, 4*(3&4), 124–129.

Rawlins, J. (1985). Associations across time: The hippocampus as a temporary memory store. *Behavioral and Brain Sciences, 8*, 479–496.

Reilly, S., Harley, C., & Revusky, S. (1993). Ibotenate lesions of the hippocampus enhance latent inhibition in conditioned taste aversion and increase resistance to extinction in conditioned taste preference. *Behavioural Neuroscience, 107*(6), 996–1004.

Rescorla, R., & Wagner, A. (1972). A theory of Pavlovian conditioning: Variations in the effectiveness of reinforcement and non-reinforcement. In A. Black & W. Prokasy (Eds.), *Classical conditioning II: Current research and theory* (pp.64–99). New York: Appleton-Century-Crofts.

Ribot, T. (1882). *The diseases of memory.* New York: Appleton.

Riley, D. (1968). *Discrimination learning.* Boston: Allyn & Bacon.

Ross, R., Orr, W., Holland, P., & Berger, T. (1984). Hippocampectomy disrupts acquisition and retention of learned conditional responding. *Behavioral Neuroscience, 98*(2), 211–225.

Rumelhart, D., Hinton, G., & Williams, R. (1986). Learning internal representations by error propagation. In D. Rumelhart & J. McClelland (Eds.), *Parallel distributed processing: Explorations in the microstructure of cognition* (pp.318–362). Cambridge, MA: MIT Press.

Schmajuk, N. (1994). Stimulus configuration, classical conditioning, and spatial learning: Role of the hippocampus. In *World Congress on Neural Networks*, 2 (pp.II723–II728). San Diego: INNS Press.

Schmajuk, N., & DiCarlo, J. (1990). *Backpropagation, classical conditioning and hippocampal function* (Technical Report, Northwestern University).

Schmajuk, N., & Moore, J. (1985). Real-time attentional models for classical conditioning. *Physiological Psychology, 13*(4), 278–290.

Schmalz, L., & Theios, J. (1972). Acquisition and extinction of a classically conditioned response in hippocampectomized rabbits (*Oryctolagus cuniculus*). *Journal of Comparative and Physiological Psychology, 79*, 328–333.

Shanks, D.R. (1991). Categorization by a connectionist network. *Journal of Experimental Psychology: Learning, Memory, & Cognition, 17*(3), 1–11.

Shanks, D.R., & Gluck, M.A. (1994). Tests of an adaptive network model for the identification, categorization and recognition of continuous-dimension stimuli. *Connection Science, 6*(1), 59–89.

Shepard, R. (1958). Stimulus and response generalization: Deduction of the generalization gradient from a trace model. *Psychological Review, 65*, 242–256.

Silveira, J., & Kimble, D. (1968). Brightness discrimination and reversal in hippocampally-lesioned rats. *Physiology and Behavior, 3*, 625–630.

Solomon, P. (1977). Role of the hippocampus in blocking and conditioned inhibition of the rabbit's nictitating membrane. *Journal of Comparative and Physiological Psychology, 91*(2), 407–417.

Solomon, P., & Moore, J. (1975). Latent inhibition and stimulus generalization of the classically conditioned nictitating membrane response in rabbits (*Oryctolagus cuniculus*) following dorsal hippocampal ablation. *Journal of Comparative and Physiological Psychology, 89*, 1192–1203.

Solomon, P.R., Stowe, G.T., & Pendlebury, W.W. (1989). Disrupted eyelid conditioning in a patient with damage to cerebellar afferents. *Behavioral Neuroscience, 103*(4), 898–902.

Squire, L. (1987). *Memory and brain.* New York: Oxford University Press.

Squire, L., & Frambach, M. (1990). Cognitive skill learning in amnesia. *Psychobiology, 18*(1), 109–117.

Stanton, P., & Sejnowski, T. (1989). Associative long-term depression in the hippocampus induced by Hebbian covariance. *Nature, 339*, 215–218.

Sutherland, N., & Mackintosh, N. (1971). *Mechanisms of animal discrimination learning.* New York: Academic Press.

Sutherland, R., & Rudy, J. (1989). Configural association theory: The role of the hippocampal formation in learning, memory and amnesia. *Psychobiology, 17*(2), 129–144.

Sutton, R., & Barto, A. (1981). Toward a modern theory of adaptive networks: Expectation and prediction. *Psychological Review, 88*, 135–170.

Terrace, H. (1963). Discrimination learning with and without "errors". *Journal of Experimental Analysis of Behavior, 6*(1), 1–27.

Thompson, R. (1971). Sensory preconditioning. In R. Thompson & J. Voss (Eds.), *Topics in learning and performance* (pp.105–129). New York: Academic Press.

Thompson, R. (1986). The neurobiology of learning and memory. *Science, 233*, 941–947.

Thompson, R. (1990). Neural mechanisms of classical conditioning. *Philosophical Transactions of the Royal Society, London [Biology], 329* 161–170.

Topka, H., Valls-Sole, J., Massaquoi, S.G., & Hallett, M. (1993). Deficit in classical conditioning in patients with cerebellar degeneration. *Brain, 116*, 961–969.

Weiskrantz, L., & Warrington, E.K. (1979). Conditioning in amnesic patients. *Neuropsychologia, 17*, 187–194.

Werbos, P. (1974). *Beyond regression: New tools for prediction and analysis in the behavioral sciences.* PhD dissertation, Harvard University.

Widrow, B., & Hoff, M. (1960). Adaptive switching circuits. *Institute of Radio Engineers, Western Electronic Show and Convention Record, 4*, 96–104.

Winocur, G. (1990). Anterograde and retrograde amnesia in rats with dorsal hippocampal or dorsomedial thalamic lesions. *Behavioral Brain Research, 38*, 145–154.

Winocur, G., Rawlins, J., & Gray, J. (1987). The hippocampus and conditioning to contextual cues. *Behavioral Neuroscience, 101*(5), 617–625.

Woodruff-Pak, D. (1993). Eyeblink classical conditioning in HM: Delay and trace paradigms. *Behavioral Neuroscience, 107*(6), 911–925.

Zola-Morgan, S., & Squire, L. (1986). Memory impairment in monkeys following lesions limited to the hippocampus. *Behavioral Neuroscience, 100*(2), 155–160.

Zola-Morgan, S., & Squire, L. (1992). Components of the medial temporal lobe memory system. In L. Squire & N. Butters (Eds.), *Neuropsychology of memory* (2nd edn.) (pp.325–335). New York: Guilford Press.

Zola-Morgan, S., Squire, L., & Amaral, D. (1989). Lesions of the amygdala that spare adjacent cortical regions do not impair memory or exacerbate the impairment following lesions of the hippocampal formation. *Journal of Neuroscience, 9*(6), 1922–1936.

Zola-Morgan, S., Squire, L., Rempel, N., Clower, R., & Amaral, D. (1992). Enduring memory impairment in monkeys after ischemic damage to the hippocampus. *Journal of Neuroscience, 12*(7), 2582–2596.

MEMORY, 1997, 5 (1/2), 213–232

Implicit and Explicit Memory in Amnesia: Some Explanations and Predictions by the TraceLink Model

Jacob M.J. Murre

University of Amsterdam, The Netherlands

After a brief overview of some of the characteristics and neuroanatomy of amnesia, a new model of amnesia is described: the TraceLink model. One novel aspect of the model is that it makes specific and testable predictions regarding semantic dementia, a recently described disorder that is viewed here as being related to amnesia. The TraceLink model consists of: a trace system (roughly the neocortix), a link system (hippocampus and adjacent areas), and a modulatory system (certain basal forebrain nuclei). Different forms of learning in the TraceLink model are explained, followed by a discussion of implicit and explicit memory, prominence (ease of recall) and persistence (resistance to brain damage), consolidation, and Ribot gradients in retrograde amnesia. Patterns of recovery from retrograde amnesia are also discussed, and novel predictions are derived regarding implicit memory and various forms of amnesia.

INTRODUCTION

In this paper we describe a model of amnesia, the TraceLink model, which aims to integrate data from several related sources in neuropsychology, neuroanatomy, neurophysiology, and connectionism. The model is certainly incomplete; we have focused on the most important aspects of the disorder, leaving many details aside for the moment. But, as we shall show, even a simple and global model such as this can yield clear and testable predictions. We shall mainly focus on implicit and explicit learning in amnesia and some related disorders. A more detailed account of the model with simulations of some of the effects is presented in Murre (submitted). In the latter paper, we also discuss in detail how the TraceLink model compares to existing models of memory and amnesia (e.g.

Requests for reprints should be sent to Jacob Murre, Department of Psychonomics, University of Amsterdam, Roetersstraat 15, 1018 WB Amsterdam, The Netherlands. Email: murre@psy.uva.nl

Part of this work was carried out while the author was at the MRC Applied Psychology Unit in Cambridge, UK.

This work was supported by the Medical Research Council and by a fellowship of the Royal Netherlands Academy of Arts and Sciences.

Alvarez & Squire, 1994; McClelland, McNaughton, & O'Reilly, 1995; Milner, 1989; Teyler & DiScenna, 1986; Treves & Rolls, 1994). Most of these models share an overall architecture and approach. They often differ more in the justification of the structure and function than in their general properties. Other differences stem from the type of data modelled, the detail of the assumptions and derivations, and the formalism used.

Since the work of Ribot in 1881 we know that recent episodic memories are more vulnerable to brain damage than more remote memories. The loss of existing memories is called *retrograde amnesia*, the inability to form new episodic memories is called *anterograde amnesia*. Because every human being builds up a different reservoir of memories during a lifetime, it has proved to be very difficult to study retrograde amnesia. Even though first reported in the last century, for a long time the existence of the "Ribot gradient" was disputed and even today it is not completely clear with what types of pathologies we find the characteristic disproportionate loss of recent memories (i.e. "flat gradients" are sometimes observed as well). We are not able to describe in detail here the neuropsychology of amnesia but must instead refer to recent reviews on the subject (see for example Kopelman, in press; Mayes & Downes, this issue; and Squire, 1992).

One important difference of the TraceLink model from existing models of amnesia is that it also covers aspects of *semantic dementia*, a newly discovered memory disorder. In fact, we will treat semantic dementia as a form of amnesia, partially because it fits in very well with the structure of the model. Under the current definition, with semantic dementia the patient has a selective impairment of semantic memory (Hodges, Patterson, Oxbury, & Funnell, 1992; Snowden, Goulding, & Neary, 1989; Snowden, Griffiths, & Neary, 1994). Category information is lost with better preservation of superordinate categories initially. It can be argued that the term "semantic dementia" is not completely correct because it appears that the memory loss is not limited to semantic memories; early autobiographical and other episodic types of memory cannot be accessed either (Graham, & Hodges, in press). A possible alternative term might be "*reverse retrograde amnesia*" because, as predicted by the TraceLink model, *reverse* Ribot gradients will be observed, with largely spared episodic learning. Very recently this prediction has indeed been verified reliably by six patients with semantic dementia (Graham, & Hodges, in press).

In the following, we will sketch the essence of the empirical data we want to address, of the neuroanatomical structures involved, and of the structure of the model. Concentration on this essence has the advantage that the logic of the decisions is more exposed, but it has the disadvantage that some of the richness and subtlety of the data and possible arguments is lost. A more elaborate account of the data and the model, including an analysis and simulations, is given in Murre (submitted).

SOME IMPORTANT EMPIRICAL FACTS
REGARDING AMNESIA

Ribot Gradients

1. Both short-range and persistent long-range retrograde amnesia (RA) does occur, and temporal "Ribot gradients" have been found under a large variety of circumstances, including with animal experiments (Squire, 1992) and with several short-lasting forms of RA (see point 5). A "Ribot gradient" (Ribot 1882/1881) refers to the finding that recent memories are lost whereas older memories are preserved, a phenomenon that runs exactly opposite to that observed in most connectionist models (Murre, 1992b).

Dissociation of RA and AA

2. Persistent, dense anterograde amnesia (AA) can occur in isolation, with minimal RA.

3. Isolated (focal) RA can occur in isolation, that is, with only weak AA (Kapur, 1993). Although this occurs rarely, it is an important finding because it suggests a dissociation of AA and RA. In general, especially with diffuse lesions such as in closed-head injury, RA and AA show an (imperfect) correlation with each other, with the severity of the injury, and with completeness of final recovery (Whitty & Zangwill, 1977).

4. Even though the dissociation of RA and AA in (2) and (3) suggests that both forms of amnesia may have different causes, the finding that RA is always accompanied by AA *initially* suggests that there is also a common factor involved.

Reversibility of RA and AA

5. RA is often reversible, for example with closed-head injury. This is called "shrinkage" because the period of memory loss shrinks. In the case of transient global amnesia (sudden RA and AA that last for up to 24 hours only, see Hodges & Ward, 1989) or amnesia induced by electroconvulsive therapy (Cahill & Frith, 1995; Squire, Slater, & Chace, 1975), near-complete shrinkage is usually observed, although full recovery may take many weeks.

Shrinkage of RA follows a broadly chronological order but in some cases memory is restored abruptly. Isolated "islands" of preserved memories may occur before full shrinkage has been completed (Whitty & Zangwill, 1977).

6. AA is often reversible as well, but specific experiences during the AA period will not be remembered, even if normal episodic learning capacity has returned.

Implicit Memory

7. Implicit memory is preserved in AA. It is still an open issue, empirically, to what extent it is affected in RA and semantic dementia.

Forgetting Rates

8. Long-term forgetting rates in AA are largely normal, provided that the patients' recognition is brought to the same level as the control group, which may take many more trials (Huppert & Piercy, 1978; Kopelman, 1985).

Some Implications for Models of Amnesia

Ribot gradients run counter to normal forgetting gradients and also counter to all forgetting gradients observed in neural networks (e.g. forgetting due to interference, see Murre, 1995). Moreover, very strong recent memories are not better preserved, with the exception of isolated islands of vivid memories that are observed occasionally (Whitty & Zangwill, 1977). To resolve this paradox we need at least two different processes or structures (also see Wickelgren, 1974); (i) a process that makes memories resistant to brain damage (i.e. causing "persistence"), and (ii) another that causes memories to be recalled easily (causing "prominence"). We need two such processes because resistance to brain damage cannot be predicted from ease of recall, although it may be argued that those early memories that are preserved in RA could most probably also be recalled before the lesion occurred. In the latter case, prominence does predict persistence.

AA and RA *can* occur in isolation but tend to co-occur. RA is always accompanied by AA initially. This suggest that there are at least two underlying major structures involved: (i) a structure that with dysfunctioning may—but may not–cause AA exclusively (called *modulatory system* in the TraceLink model), and (ii) a structure that with severe dysfunctioning (e.g. directly after injury) causes both AA and RA but that allows for considerable *recovery* of AA, usually—but not necessarily—accompanied by comparable recovery in RA. In some cases, however, no recovery in RA is observed (Kapur, 1993), as will be discussed in the last section. This structure is called the *link system* in the model.

NEUROANATOMY OF AMNESIA

The neuroanatomy underlying amnesia is patched together on the basis of diverse sources such as single-case studies of patients with brain lesions and memory disorders, where MRI, SPECT scans, and post-mortem research can reveal many lesion sites. Occasionally, the lesions are made deliberately as a form of treatment of, for example, severe epilepsy. Additional information is gleaned from experiments during such brain surgery (e.g. stimulating certain brain areas may induce amnesia), and also from electroconvulsive therapy, from the working and study of certain drugs, and from a large number of animal experiments, in particular with rats and monkeys. A review of these sources and their implications for the TraceLink model can be found in Murre (submitted). Here, we merely present a summary of the key aspects.

Anterograde Amnesia

Since the work of Bekhterev (1900) we know that the lesions in the medial temporal lobes can cause anterograde amnesia. In 1957, Scoville and Milner reported that lesions of the "hippocampal zone" are sufficient to cause profound AA. In addition, lesions in the basal forebrain, in particular the septum, may cause AA, as well as in the fornix, which among others connects the basal forebrain to the hippocampus.

Retrograde Amnesia

Retrograde amnesia can be caused by lesions in the hippocampus proper (a two-year, mild RA was observed in the patient reported in Zola-Morgan, Squire, & Amaral, 1986). In addition, it can be caused by bilateral lesions to the temporal cortex not necessarily involving the hippocampus (e.g. Kapur et al., 1992). Unilateral ablation of the left-anterior and lateral temporal cortices causes mild RA (Barr, Goldberg, Wasserstein & Novelly, 1990).

Semantic Dementia

This disorder is caused by focal atrophy of the neocortex. The few studies that have appeared to date point towards lesions in the left infero-lateral temporal lobe (Graham, Hodges, in press; Hodges et al., 1992) with sparing of the hippocampal areas.

Three Principal Neuroanatomical Systems

The aforementioned neuroanatomical data can be summarised as three neuroanatomical systems that can be implicated separately in amnesia. *System 1* involves the basal forebrain nuclei, the hippocampus (as a "controller"), and the structures that connect these two brain areas such as the fornix. From other sources we know that the basal forebrain structures are involved in modulating plasticity in the brain (Hasselmo, 1995; McGaugh, 1990; Singer, 1990). In the TraceLink model, therefore, we call this system the modulatory system. *System 2* also involves the hippocampus, as well as areas adjacent to the hippocampus, such as the entorhinal cortex. For reasons explained later, we call this the link system. *System 3*, finally, includes the rest of the neocortex, although we expect to be able to refine this section of the model and include more details about the localisation of different types of memory (Kopelman & Murre, in prep.). We assume that ultimately a memory becomes stored in system 3 (Abeles, 1991; Braitenberg & Schüz, 1991), which is why we call it the trace system.

THE TRACELINK MODEL

Following our summary of the neuroanatomy, the TraceLink model consists of three systems: (i) the trace system, (ii) the link system, and (iii) the modulatory system (as a controller). A schematised drawing is given in Fig. 1.

The trace system roughly corresponds to the neocortex. In the model its function is the bulk storage of all memories. The optimal, inferred connectivity of the neocortex (Murre & Sturdy, 1995) is mimicked in the model by a large number of modules (Mountcastle, 1978; Szentágothai, 1975) with dense internal connections but with only sparse connections on a global or long-range scale (also see Murre, 1992a). In addition, neighbouring nodes are densely connected. In accordance with Braitenberg and Schüz's (1991) model of the cortex, the majority of connections is excitatory and modifiable. In addition, short-range inhibitory connections are present. These are non-modifiable and their function is mainly to keep the average activation level in a given area at a certain target value. This target value is generally very low (cf Abeles, Vaadia, & Bergman, 1990). An implementation of such a trace system, using stochastic, binary nodes

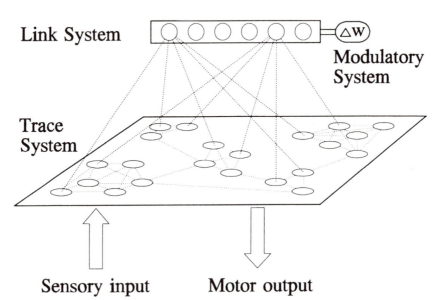

FIG. 1.   The TraceLink model, showing its three major systems: link system, trace system, and modulatory system. Within-trace connections are mostly local with very sparse long-range connections. There is extensive, random connectivity between the trace system and the link system, and vice versa. (Only a few nodes and connections have been drawn in order to prevent clutter in the drawing.)

(abstracted neurons or groups of neurons) is described in Robertson and Murre (submitted), and in Murre (submitted).

The link system is thought to include the hippocampus and surrounding structures, and possibly other structures that appear high in the Felleman and Van Essen (1991) hierarchy (e.g. certain frontal areas are likely candidates although this is extremely speculative at the moment). The function of the link system is to form (temporary) links between the elements of young episodic memories. These links ensure that rehearsal can take place in a sufficiently specific manner, so that cortico-cortical connections can be formed (i.e. within the trace system). The nodes in the link system are similar to those in the trace system, but their connections are more easily modified. A node in the link system receives connections from a random subset of nodes in the trace system. This corresponds to the fact that as far as is known no corticotopical organisation can be discerned in the representations of the neurons in the hippocampus (e.g. in contrast to the organisation of the basal forebrain nuclei, where we do find such an organisation, Mesulam, Murson, Levely, & Wainer, 1983).

Thus, whereas the connectivity within the trace system is sparse, the connectivity between the trace and link system is relatively dense. This is possible because the link system itself is hypothesised to be relatively small. The hierarchical organisation of connectivity between trace system (cortex) and link system (hippocampus) resembles that of a telephone network with local, national, and international exchange stations. A similar, hierarchical architecture can also be shown to be effective when constructing extremely large computers (Heemskerk & Murre, submitted).

Because its storage capacity is also more limited, link nodes will frequently be re-used for new episodic memories. The link system is, therefore, sensitive to interference from additional learning.

One way to counteract such interference is by only making weight changes that are "useful". This was argued earlier for the entire brain, but it is especially true for the link system. The hippocampus plays a pivotal role in this system and its high plasticity and limited capacity make it especially prone to interference. Frugal use of the available resources is thus of the highest importance. Interference is often caused by overlap of (distributed) representations in neural networks and reduction of this overlap reduces "catastrophic interference" in such networks (French, 1992; Murre, 1992a,b). Marr (1971) has already proposed that one of the functions of the hippocampus is to expand the representation space so that overlap becomes less probable, although it is not completely clear to what extent this function can be identified in the neuroanatomy of the hippocampus (McNaughton, 1990).

In addition to a reduction in overlap of representations, an effective way of reducing such interference is control of plasticity (Murre, 1992a; Murre, Phaf, & Wolters, 1989, 1992). In our view, the hippocampus also plays an important role in the control of plasticity. Evidence for this can be gleaned from the connectivity structure of the hippocampus: it sends many connections to the basal forebrain, which is an important executive centre for inducing or preventing plasticity in the brain (e.g. through the working of acetylcholine in the septum, see review by Hasselmo, 1995). The hippocampus is also highly innervated with connections from the basal forebrain, which are probably contributing towards the hippocampus's high plasticity. In short, the hippocampus is in a very good position, anatomically speaking, to control its own plasticity via mediation by the basal forebrain nuclei. In addition, sitting at the top of the neuroanatomical hierarchy the hippocampus and surrounding structures have a bird's eye view of the activity in the cortex, which also puts them in an excellent position to judge the "usefulness" of potential episodic memories, for example, the overall novelty of a new memory.

The modulatory system, finally, is thought to involve the basal forebrain nuclei and to be associated closely with the hippocampus, although a range of "central states"—not all mediated by the hippocampus—may affect its operation. Its function is to increase or decrease plasticity in the link system and possibly also in the trace system (symbolised by the hatched ΔW often used to indicate weight changes). In the absence of the modulatory system only very slow, baserate learning takes place. When the modulatory system is behaving erratically (i.e. as opposed to simple dysfunctioning), all systems under its plasticity control will show strongly impaired learning behaviour, worse than baserate (Myers, Ermita, Harris, Hasselmo, Solomon, & Gluck, 1996). This may also lead to increased forgetting because it is effectively learning noise which has the effect of "wiping clean" the weights, although the weights themselves may be "re-used" as soon as the modulatory system becomes functional again.

LEARNING IN THE TRACELINK MODEL

In the present framework learning can take place in at least three different ways. The first one is similar to what is often called "explicit learning" the latter two are forms of "implicit memory":

Type I.   Normal, episodic learning followed by consolidation.

Type II.   Learning by strengthening of existing connections formed by prior learning.

Type III.   Learning by "sheer repetition". This may work particularly well with connections that are already present because of the neuroanatomy of the brain (e.g. connections between nearby nodes or neurons on the cortex, and simple stimulus–response contiguities mediated by the cerebellum, Murre & Sturdy, 1995).

These types of learning are not mutually exclusive. On the contrary, during any given learning task several of these types may take place.

Episodic Learning

In the TraceLink system, episodic learning takes place in four stages. This process is sketched in Fig. 2. In Stage 1, the representation has just entered the system. All memory representations in the trace system enter either through hypothetical sensory systems or they may result from internal, sequential processing (voluntary attention).

In Stage 2, the representation has activated a number of link nodes. The combination of link nodes must be novel and sufficiently distinct from other combinations, but individual link nodes may participate in several distinct representations. In Stage 2, the modulatory system is highly activated, reflecting the fact that the system has determined that this is a "useful" memory to remember. The resulting increase in plasticity causes the connection weights between the trace and link system to be increased. In this stage, the long-range connections within the trace system have not yet had time to emerge.

This occurs in Stage 3 as the result of some rehearsal or consolidation process, possibly also accompanied by an activated modulatory system. The result is the slow growth of long-range, trace–trace connections.

In Stage 4, the latter process is complete. There is now a strong trace basis of connections for the representation. The trace–link connections are no longer

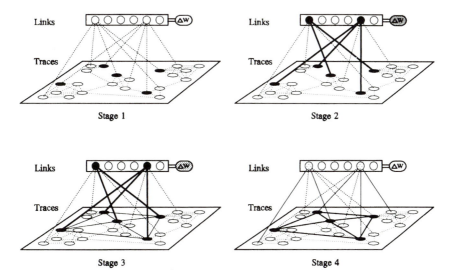

FIG. 2. Four stages in normal episodic learning and consolidation. *Stage 1:* A new memory representation activates a number of trace elements (shown as filled, black circles). *Stage 2:* Several link elements are activated and the relevant trace–link connections are strengthened (shown as thicker connections). Also, the modulatory system has been activated. *Stage 3:* Weak trace–trace connections are developing. The modulatory system is weakly activated. *Stage 4:* Strong trace–trace connections have been formed. Trace–link connections have decayed and the modulatory system no longer responds noticeably to the stimulus.

necessary for the reliable activation of the entire memory from fragments and they may now be erased safely.

Explicit and Implicit Memory

What distinguishes explicit learning from implicit learning in the TraceLink model? In other words, what causes the formation of episodic as opposed to implicit memories? The two distinguishing factors of episodic learning in the TraceLink model are that the memory representation in the trace system must both (i) activate a sufficient number of novel nodes in the link system, and (ii) cause their connections to be modified rapidly in order to assign these link nodes to the memory representation in the trace system. Thus, at least the link system and the modulatory system must function properly while the trace system must at least be able to hold a representation.

Under normal, non-pathological circumstances the trace system will always fulfil this requirement, even during sleep. For the modulatory system to be activated the memory representation must be properly focused and sufficiently stable. It must also be perceived as novel, "useful", and "interesting" (e.g. in the sense of biologically relevant). Furthermore, the organism itself must be awake and vigilant, but perhaps not too aroused (cf Yerkes & Dodson, 1908). The link system's nodes will be activated according to elaboration (Graf & Mandler, 1984), interest, and "level of processing" (Craik & Lockhart, 1972). Thus, a pattern that has little meaning such as a random dot pattern or an image of a rock will cause some but not many activated link nodes. A more meaningful pattern will cause many more activated nodes. For example, when a geologist views a rock this will automatically activate many associated representations in his or her brain and these will cause the activation of many link nodes. For a layperson, such associated representations may be called up by conscious interpretation and elaboration ("This structure looks like a seahorse...") and they are hypothesised to also activate additional link nodes in the TraceLink model.

If a memory representation (or aspect thereof) does not succeed in activating link nodes, it cannot take part in an episodic memory representation. If any of the learning conditions of type II or III are fulfilled, the activated representation can still be learned, but this learning will be of an implicit nature. In particular, this means that any such strengthened representations are not integrated into a global whole and this in turn implies that no "context" or time-space references are attached to it. The latter can be consciously remembered time markers such as the state of the weather, daylight, dates or time of day, etc., or some position in a narrative or other higher-order structure. The consequence of the failure to activate enough link nodes is that implicitly learned representations cannot be accessed by reference to any situational context (e.g. involving time or space). Two examples of this are learning of categories of novel random dot patterns and implicit learning of weakly attended items that already have memory representations.

Learning of Novel Representations in Implicit Memory. Categories of random dot patterns will generally fail to activate a sufficient number of link nodes, because they are largely meaningless. They are thus not well remembered consciously (explicitly). They can be learned in an implicit manner, however, both by amnesic patients and normal subjects with an approximately equal learning rate (Kolodny, 1994; Knowlton & Squire, 1993). The learning task takes many repetitions and eventually leads to a correct classification of random dot patterns into the correct category.

In the TraceLink model we explain this as type III learning because of the prolonged repetition and because of the low-level nature of the patterns. By the latter we mean that they show great resemblance at a near-perceptual or image level. This makes it likely that connections already exist at a cortical level because the representation of pattern elements (i.e. the ''dots'') will be located closely together at the visual cortex. Many, overlaid ''dot-to-dot'' connections can lead to the formation of category representations (Knapp & Anderson, 1984). The process of low-level category formation can be contrasted with artistic stimuli, such as the paintings of Van Gogh. These show a clear resemblance in style and can easily be grouped into one category when compared with any other painter, but they will be completely distinct at an image level. There is thus much less provision for ''dot-to-dot'' connections to be formed.

Because dot patterns are largely meaningless, the link system will only be weakly involved. In particular, it will be involved to the extent that the patterns evoke higher-level meanings (e.g. ''This pattern looks like chair''). We thus expect that the learned categories are not easily accessed explicitly because only a few time-space markers will be attached to them. Artistic stimuli on the other hand, will be meaningful and they will therefore strongly activate the link system so that they can form episodic memories. This allows comparison across different paintings, for example, by explicitly remembering paintings so that categories or artistic styles can be assessed at a higher level. Amnesic subjects will not have this option at their disposal and they are thus expected to do poorly when learning to recognise artistic styles, as has recently been found by Kolodny (1994).

The experiments with dot patterns demonstrate that novel patterns of information and skills *can* be learned by amnesic patients (in an implicit manner). The TraceLink model postulates that this is possible because two conditions are fulfilled that underlie this type of learning in general: (i) The pattern or skill elements are not distant on a neuro-anatomical level. This postulate favours pattern elements that are similar at a perceptual or motor level (e.g. simple skills). (ii) The patterns are repeated many times. The reason for this is the absence of a precise, internal rehearsal mechanism (i.e. non-involvement of the link-system) and this must be compensated by an equally precise, external rehearsal mechanism.

Implicit Learning of Existing Representations.   In all cases where existing memory representations are weakly activated we have at least learning of type II and we can thus expect some form of implicit memory as a result of this. A well-studied example of this is implicit memory for weakly attended stimuli ("distractors") in some identification task or other incidental learning task. Such weakly attended stimuli do not cause activation of a sufficient number of link nodes to ensure integration into the entire episode and thus they cannot be accessed explicitly, but they may still show priming (see Phaf, 1994, for experiments and a model). For such priming to occur it is necessary that the pattern is well represented in the brain. Although the pattern elements will generally not be proximal at a neuro-anatomical level, connections will have developed between them in a process of rehearsal and consolidation. The TraceLink model postulates that implicit memory is the result of slight increases of these existing connections.

Prominence and Persistence

When a memory representation progresses well into Stage 3 and especially when it enters Stage 4 it will become less and less dependent on the link system. This progression is accompanied by an increase in persistence: damage to the link system will have less and less influence on the memory representation. Persistence, meaning "resistance to brain damage", refers only to lesions that involve the link system. Extensive damage to the trace system would cause the opposite syndrome: progression towards Stage 4 and especially the associated loss of trace–link connections (no longer necessary in Stage 4) would lead to increased vulnerability to brain damage (this is simulated in Robertson & Murre, submitted). Because the hippocampus itself is a very sensitive structure, possibly because of a much smaller extracellular space (McBain, Traynelis, & Dingledine, 1990), this situation is relatively rare: in closed-head injury, hypoxia, and with Alzheimer's disease the link system is much more easily damaged than the trace system.

With semantic dementia, however, there is evidence that the neocortex's white matter is damaged extensively, especially the infero-lateral temporal neocortex (Damasio, Damasio, Tranel, & Brandt, 1990; Graham, & Hodges, in press; Hodges et al., 1992) but with sparing of the hippocampus. It has recently been reported that in a controlled study with six subjects, recent memories (i.e. at Stage 2) are spared relative to more remote (Stage 3 and 4) memories (Graham, & Hodges, in press), an effect that was specifically predicted by the TraceLink model (Murre, submitted). As far as is known to us, such reverse

Ribot gradients have not been observed in patients with acute brain lesions but we predict the possibility of this: extensive damage to the white matter of the neocortex, but with complete sparing of the hippocampal area and the areas associated with the modulatory system may show reverse Ribot gradients. For reasons set forth earlier this syndrome will be rare, but it may be observed in experimental animals.

Consolidation

A crucial aspect of the TraceLink model is the constant activity of all memory representations: there is a continuous movement from Stage 1 to Stage 4. Even at Stage 4, we may expect further activity directed towards maintaining the cortical representation of a memory. The reason for this is that synaptic couplings are volatile and may need constant updating. There is abundant neuroanatomical evidence that the brain remains plastic throughout life (Kolb, in press).

It is presently an open issue how the consolidation of memories takes place. Several current connectionist models of amnesia (Alvarez & Squire, 1994; McClelland et al., 1995) favour dream sleep as the process, building on earlier suggestions that sleep may be involved in aspects of consolidation, for example, by Crick and Mitchison (1986), and citing recent data about reactivation of hippocampal cells during sleep in rats by Wilson and McNaughton (1994). These data are certainly very exciting but this should not distract from the fact that we have not even scratched the surface of this crucial research problem (for an analysis and simulations, see Murre, in press).

Ribot Gradients and Shrinkage of RA

As will be clear from the preceding discussion, Stage 2 memories are fully dependent on the link system, and hence any damage to this structure will cause recent memories to suffer. More remote memories, however, need not be affected. This prediction of the model can be stated more precisely by refining the structure of the TraceLink model. For reasons of simplicity the model in Figs. 1 and 2 have been drawn with two main "layers" (i.e. link and trace system). Especially in the light of such anatomical hierarchies as that of Felleman and Van Essen (1991), a more complicated and detailed model would have intermediate layers as well, yielding a more modular architecture. The intermediate modules combine functions of the link and trace system: the higher a module in the hierarchy, the more of a link function it has. In this view, we follow the ideas of Damasio and co-workers (e.g. Damasio, 1989; Damasio & Damasio, 1994), who call such intermediate structures "convergence zones". Damasio also stresses that the backprojections to the lower areas are crucial for recall. It is in these lower areas that the details of an explicitly recalled memory are generated and filled in.

We thus propose a continuum from pure "vertical linkage" to pure "horizontal storage of a trace". This implies a roughly chronotopic mapping of memories onto the brain. Some evidence for this has been reported (Doty, 1990; Penfield & Mathieson, 1974), but as it stands this is still mainly a prediction that needs to be verified more thoroughly. In addition to the hypothesis of chronotopic mapping we must add that in the initial stages (early Stage 2) the memory is much more vulnerable to disruption by brain damage than in the later stages. In addition to this, the mere sparsity of connectivity in the initial stages (the principle of "frugal assignment of resources") will cause increased sensitivity to brain damage. In this way, we can explain how relatively uniform lesions such as in closed-head injuries can nevertheless cause Ribot gradients in which the time period of recent memories lost correlates broadly with the severity of the injury (Whitty & Zangwill, 1977): younger memories reside in more vulnerable areas and have also formed fewer connections than older memories.

Other explanations for this effect are possible, such as a pure trace strength hypothesis (e.g. Weiskrantz, 1966), but the latter has difficulties coping with the fact that even very prominent recent memories (i.e. that are very easily recalled) can nevertheless be lost, whereas relatively weak but more remote memories are preserved. A more elaborate form of trace strength hypothesis is the "knitting hypothesis" (Baddeley, personal communication; described in more detail in Murre, submitted), which postulates that recent memories are "knitted" into a general memory fabric (cf the changing time-index discussed earlier). Disruption of that fabric causes access problems with the most recently "knit" memories.

In the TraceLink model, trace strength is defined in terms of strength and number of connections in the trace and link system. It plays a role in partially counteracting the effects of loss of link nodes. This enables isolated island of strong and related Stage 2 memories to survive where others perish (Whitty & Zangwill, 1977).

The TraceLink model is able to explain the different patterns of shrinkage of RA observed, including the variability in recovery from AA, as follows. Suppose that in all cases link nodes are unavailable at first. This causes both severe RA and severe AA. Now, the links may become available again but the original connection weights may have been lost. If the modulatory system recovers as well, then we will observe that AA recovers nearly completely, but that there is no shrinkage of RA. Such a course of events could explain the rare cases of focal or isolated retrograde amnesia that have recently been reported (Kapur, 1993). A more common situation is that in which most link nodes become available again and whereby only part of the weights has eroded. In this case we expect significant but not complete shrinkage of RA. Finally, all link nodes may commence functioning again with intact weights, causing near-complete shrinkage of RA as is, for example, frequently observed in transient global amnesia (Hodges & Ward, 1989).

Furthermore, on the basis of our general analyses of recovery from brain damage (Robertson & Murre, submitted) we postulate that a very gradual process of self-repair continues after initial and rapid shrinkage has occurred. This slow process is based on actual repair of some of the connections lost.

Implicit Memory in Semantic Dementia and in Retrograde Amnesia

Even when both the link system and the modulatory system are lesioned, implicit learning can still take place. Thus, in general with AA and RA we expect unimpaired implicit memory in the TraceLink model. The only situation where we would expect impaired implicit learning is in the case of extensive damage to the trace system, especially to the connections (i.e. white matter of the cortex). In that case the learning conditions of type II and III will not be fulfilled as easily, because even nearby neurons may have far fewer connections, and connections formed by prior learning will have degraded notably. Hence, if a significant percentage of the connections in the trace system is lesioned, but not in the link system, we expect a selective impairment in implicit memory performance. Enough information must still reach the link system to allow Stage 2 memories to be formed. If too many pathways are severed in the trace system, no learning can take place at all. In that case, it is also extremely unlikely that identification can take place. Gabrieli et al. (1995) have recently described a subject with a large, isolated lesion in the right occipital lobe that was carried out at age 14 (unilateral, all of Brodmann's area 17 and 18, and part of area 19). This has left him with a left homonomous hemianopsia, but does not impair his day-to-day functioning. This case fulfils the condition of a severe lesion of the trace system with an intact link system and sufficient remaining connectivity to allow identification. As would be predicted by the TraceLink model, this patient is selectively impaired in implicit memory, namely in visual priming. Another condition where there is relatively isolated, extensive damage to the trace system (i.e. part of the neocortex) is semantic dementia. It is, therefore, a prediction of the model that with this disorder there will be an impairment in implicit memory in semantic dementia. This prediction has not been tested, so far.

As explained earlier, in retrograde amnesia we expect Stage 2 memories to suffer most. When the link nodes are no longer available, a memory representation fractionates into separate components and in particular it becomes dislodged from the space-time markers, making it impossible to access it in an explicit manner (i.e. by reference to a specific episode located in time and space, or in a comparable structure). We predict that in many cases the fragments of the fractionated memory can still be activated (see also Mayes & Downes, this issue) and although they are not amenable to conscious or explicit access their existence can be shown in implicit memory tests. This will be more likely with memory representations that are not solely dependent on the link system (i.e. Stage 3 and 4). Thus, the more "Stage 2" a memory in RA is, the less likely it is that its fragments can be primed, and the more "Stage 3 and 4" the more likely it is that various tests of implicit memory can reveal its existence. In other words, we predict a Ribot-like curve for implicit memory in retrograde amnesia. So far, there has been very little investigation of implicit memory in RA, but a few studies suggest that priming of lost memory fragments is possible in some cases (e.g. McCarthy & Warrington, 1992; Warrington & McCarthy, 1988).

CONCLUDING REMARKS

Several predictions of the TraceLink model have been mentioned. Some of these have not been tested in detail, such as the prediction that there will be implicit memory in retrograde amnesia and that this will follow a Ribot gradient, but for many other predictions empirical support has been cited throughout the text. Unfortunately, for many important cases the data are still lacking in necessary detail. In these cases, however models of amnesia are often able to suggest specific mechanisms from which specific predictions can be derived and tested.

For focal RA (i.e. RA without AA, Kapur, 1993), for example, we suggest that in the case where we have a clear Ribot gradient (as opposed to a flat gradient), the synaptic "weights" in the link system have been wiped, but both the link system and the modulatory system are still functional. In Robertson and Murre (submitted) we discuss several mechanisms of neural repair that may have such an effect (also see Kolb, in press). Given that such a "wiping process" will take time, we can derive from this that no acute focal RA can occur; there will always be a period of dense AA during which the link system is recovering. If we observe a case of focal RA where episodic memory is unimpaired immediately following the trauma, the link system cannot be involved. In such a case we favour the explanation of Squire and Alvarez (1995) that the "knowledge base" is affected. They locate this base in the anterior and lateral temporal neocortex, in what we would call the trace system. As a corollary to the latter explanation we can derive the prediction that in such a case no Ribot gradient will be observed (or even a reverse gradient), because there has not been a preferential erasure of recent memories (except for some trace strength effects). Also, as the "wiping process" will be largely irreversible, we predict that there will be no shrinkage from focal RA under the "wiping hypothesis", whereas under the "lost knowledge base hypothesis" such shrinkage may well occur.

Another area where empirical data are still scarce is semantic dementia. For this disorder we predicted reverse Ribot gradients (see earlier discussion) and these have indeed been found recently (Graham, & Hodges, in press). We count this as a successful empirical test of the TraceLink model. Further predictions about semantic dementia have not yet been tested, such as impaired implicit memory and increased long-term forgetting gradients (which are largely normal in both amnesic and normal subjects, see earlier), but such work is currently being planned.

The most important unresolved issue at this point in time is the precise nature of the consolidation process. Future modelling attempts and additional neurophysiological and psychological experimentation will help to uncover the working of this process.

REFERENCES

Abeles, M. (1991). *Corticonics: Neural circuits of the cerebral cortex.* Cambridge: Cambridge University Press.

Abeles, M., Vaadia, E., & Bergman, H. (1990). Firing patterns of single units in the prefrontal cortex and neural network models. *Network, 1,* 13–25.

Alvarez, R., & Squire, L.R. (1994). Memory consolidation and the medial temporal lobe: A simple network model. *Proceedings of National Academy of Sciences (USA), 91,* 7041–7045.

Barr, W.B., Goldbert, E., Wasserstein, J., & Novelly, R.A. (1990). Retrograde amnesia following unilateral temporal lobectomy. *Neuropsychologica, 28,* 243–255.

Bekhterev, V.M. (1990). Demonstration eines Gehirns mit Zerstörung der vorderen und inneren Theile der Hirninde bei Schläferlappens. *Zeitschrift für Neurologie, 19.*

Braitenberg, V., & Schüz, A. (1991). *Anatomy of the cortex.* Berlin: Springer-Verlag.

Cahill, C., & Frith, C. (1995). Memory following electroconvulsive therapy. In A.D. Baddeley, B.A. Wilson, & F.N. Watts (Eds.), *Handbook of memory disorders* (pp.319–335). Chichester, UK: Wiley.

Craik, F.I.M., & Lockhart, R.S. (1972). Levels of processing: A framework for memory research. *Journal of Verbal Learning and Verbal Behavior, 11,* 671–684.

Crick, F., & Mitchison, G. (1986). REM sleep and neural nets. *Journal of Mind and Behavior, 7,* 229–249.

Damasio, A.R. (1989). The brain binds entities and events by multiregional activation from convergence zones. *Neural Computation, 1,* 123–132.

Damasio, A.R., & Damasio, H. (1994). Cortical systems and the retrieval of concrete knowledge: The convergence zone framework. In C. Koch & J.L. Davis (Eds.), *Large-scale neuronal theories of the brain.* Cambridge, MA: MIT Press.

Damasio, A.R., Damasio, H., Tranel, D., & Brandt, J.P. (1990). The neural regionalization of knowledge access: Preliminary evidence. *Quantitative Biology, 55,* 1039–1047. Cold Spring Harbor, NY: Cold Spring Harbor Laboratory Press.

Doty, R.W. (1990). Time and memory. In J.L. McGaugh, N.M. Weinberger, & G. Lynch (Eds.), *Brain organization and memory: Cells, systems, and circuits* (pp.145–158). Oxford: Oxford University Press.

Felleman, D.J., & Van Essen, D.C. (1991). Distributed hierarchical processing in the primate cerebral cortex. *Cerebral Cortex, 1,* 1–47.

French, R.M. (1992). Semi-distributed representations and catastrophic forgetting in connectionist networks. *Connection Science, 4,* 365–377.

Gabrieli, J.D.E., Fleischman, D.A., Keane, M.M., Reminger, S.L., & Morrell, F. (1995). Double dissociation between memory systems underlying explicit and implicit memory in the human brain. *Psychological Science, 6,* 76–82.

Graf, P., & Mandler, G. (1984). Activation makes words more accessible, but not necessarily more retrievable. *Journal of Verbal Learning and Verbal Behavior, 23,* 553–568.

Graham, K.S., & Hodges, J.R. (submitted). *Distinguishing the roles played by the hippocampal system and the neocortex in long-term memory storage.*

Hasselmo, M.E. (1995). Neuromodulation and cortical function: Modeling the physiological basis of behavior. *Behavioral and Brain Research, 67,* 1–27.

Heemskerk, J.N.H., & Murre, J.M.J. (submitted). Brain-size neurocomputers: analyzes and simulations of fractal architectures.

Hodges, J.R., Patterson, K., Oxbury, S., & Funnell, E. (1992). Semantic dementia: Progressive fluent aphasia with temporal lobe atrophy. *Brain, 115,* 1783–1806.

Hodges, J.R., & Ward, C.D. (1989). Observations during transient global amnesia. *Brain, 112,* 595–620.

Huppert, F.A., & Piercy, M. (1978). Dissociation between learning and remembering in organic amnesia. *Nature, 275,* 317–318.

Kapur, N. (1993). Focal retrograde amnesia in neurological disease: A critical review. *Cortex, 29,* 217–234.

Kapur, N., Ellison, D., Smith, M.P., McLellan, D.L., & Burrows, E.H. (1992). Focal retrograde amnesia following bilateral temporal lobe pathology. *Brain, 115,* 73–85.

Knapp, A.G., & Anderson, J.A. (1984). Theory of categorization based on distributed memory storage. *Journal of Experimental Psychology: Learning, Memory, and Cognition, 10,* 616–637.

Knowlton, B.J., & Squire, L.R. (1993). The learning of categories: Parallel brain systems for item memory and category knowledge. *Science, 262,* 1747–1749.

Kolb, B. (in press). *Brain plasticity and behavior.* Hillsdale, NJ: Lawrence Erlbaum Associates Inc.

Kolodny, J. (1994). Memory processes in classification learning: An investigation of amnesic performance in categorization of dot patterns and artistic style. *Psychological Science, 5,* 164–169.

Kopelman, M.D. (1985). Rates of forgetting in Alzheimer-type dementia and Korsakoff's Syndrome. *Neuropsychologia, 15,* 527–541.

Kopelman, M.D. (1993). The neuropsychology of remote memory. In F. Boller & H. Spinnler (Eds.), *The handbook of neuropsychology,* (Vol. 8, pp.215–238). Amsterdam: Elsevier Science.

Marr, D. (1971). Simple memory: A theory for archicortex. *Philosophical Transactions of the Royal Society B, 262,* 23–81.

Mayes, A.R., & Downes, J.J. (this issue). What do theories of the functional deficit(s) underlying amnesia have to explain? *Memory, 5*(1/2).

McBain, C.J., Traynelis, S.F., & Dingledine, R. (1990). Regional variations of extracellular space in the hippocampus. *Science, 249,* 674–677.

McCarthy, R.A., & Warrington, E.K. (1992). Actors but not scripts: The dissociation of people and events in retrograde amnesia. *Neuropsychologia, 30,* 633–644.

McClelland, J.L., McNaughton, B.L., & O'Reilly, R.C. (1995). Why there are complementary learning systems in the hippocampus and neocortex: Insights from the successes and failures of connectionist models of learning and memory. *Psychological Review, 102,* 419–457.

McGaugh, J.L. (1990). Significance and remembrance: The role of neuromodulatory systems. *Psychological Science, 1,* 15–25.

McNaughton, B.L. (1990). Neuronal mechanisms for spatial computation and information storage. In L. Nadel, L.A. Cooper, P. Culicover, & M. Harnish (Eds.), *Neural connections, mental computation.* Cambridge, MA: MIT Press.

Mesulam, M.M., Murson, E.J., Levely, A., & Wainer, B.H. (1983). Cholinergic innervation of cortex by the basal forebrain: Cytochemistry and cortical connections of the septal area, diagonal band nuclei, nucleus basalis (substantial innominata), and bypothalamus in the rhesus monkey. *Journal of Comparative Neurology, 214,* 170–197.

Milner, P.M. (1989). A cell assembly theory of hippocampal amnesia. *Neuropsychologia, 6,* 215–234.

Mountcastle, V.B. (1978). An organizing principle for cerebral function: The unit module and the distributed system. In G.M. Edelman & V.B. Mountcastle (Eds.), *The mindful brain.* Cambridge, MA: MIT Press.

Murre, J.M.J. (1992a). *Categorization and learning in modular neural networks.* Hemel Hempstead, UK: Harvester Wheatsheaf; Hillsdale, NJ: Lawrence Erlbaum Associates Inc.

Murre, J.M.J. (1992b). The effects of pattern presentation on interference in backpropagation networks. In *Proceedings of the Fourteenth Annual Conference of the Cognitive Science Society* (pp.54–59). Hillsdale, NJ: Lawrence Erlbaum Associates Inc.

Murre, J.M.J. (submitted). A model of amnesia.

Murre, J.M.J. (1995). Transfer of learning in backpropagation networks and in related neural network models. In J. Levy, D. Bairaktaris, J. Bullinaria, & P. Cairns (Eds.), *Connectionist models of memory and language* (pp.73–93). London: UCL Press.

Murre, J.M.J. (in press). consolidation of memories in the brain: Analysis and simulations. *Hippocampus*, Special Issue (M.A. Gluck, Ed.).

Murre, J.M.J., Phaf, R.H., & Wolters, G. (1989). CALM networks: A modular approach to supervised and unsupervised learning. *Proceedings of the International Joint Conference on Neural Networks, Washington DC, 1*, 649–656.

Murre, J.M.J., Phaf, R.H., & Wolters, G. (1992). CALM: Categorizing And Learning Module. *Neural Networks, 5*, 55–82.

Murre, J.M.J., & Sturdy, D.P.F. (1995). The connectivity of the brain: Multi-level quantitative analysis. *Biological Cybernetics, 73*, 529–545.

Myers, C.E., Ermita, B., Harris, K., Hasselmo, M., Solomon, P., & Gluck, M.A. (1996). A computational model of the effects of septohippocampal disruption on classical eyeblink conditioning. *Neurobiology of Learning and Memory, 66*, 2034–2043.

Penfield, W., & Mathieson, G. (1974). Memory; Autopsy findings and comments on the role of hippocampus in experiential recall. *Archives of Neurology, 31*, 145–154.

Phaf, R.H. (1994). *Learning in natural and connectionist systems: Experiments and a model.* Dordrecht: Kluwer Academic Publishers.

Ribot, T. (1882/1881). *The diseases of memory.* New York: Appleton. [Published in French in 1881: *Les maladies de la memoire.*]

Robertson, I.H., & Murre, J.M.J. (submitted). Recovery and rehabilitation following acquired brain damage in adults: A neuropsychological analysis in a connectionist framework.

Scoville, W.B., & Milner, B. (1957). Loss of recent memories after bilateral hippocampal lesions. *Journal of Neurology, Neurosurgery and Psychiatry, 20*, 11–21.

Singer, W. (1990). Ontogenetic self-organization and learning. In J.L. McGaugh, N.M. Weinberger, & G. Lynch (Eds.), *Brain organization and memory: Cells, systems, and circuits* (pp.211–233). Oxford: Oxford University Press.

Snowden, J.S., Goulding, P.J., & Neary, D. (1989). Semantic dementia: A form of circumscribed cerebral atrophy. *Behavioral Neurology, 2*, 167–182.

Snowden, J.S., Griffiths, H., & Neary, D. (1994). Semantic dementia: Autobiographical contribution to preservation of meaning. *Cognitive Neuropsychology, 11*, 265–288.

Squire, L.R. (1992). Memory and the hippocampus: A synthesis from findings with rats, monkeys, and humans. *Psychological Review, 99*, 195–231.

Squire, L.R., & Alvarez, P. (in press). Retrograde amnesia and memory consolidation: A neurobiological perspective. *Current Opinion in Neurobiology, 5*.

Squire, L.R., Slater, P.C., & Chace, P.M. (1975). Retrograde amnesia: Temporal gradient in very long-term memory following electroconvulsive therapy. *Science, 187*, 77–79.

Szentágothai, J. (1975). The 'module-concept' in the cerebral cortex architecture. *Brain Research, 95*, 475–496.

Teyler, T.J., & DiScenna, P. (1986). The hippocampal memory indexing theory. *Behavioral Neuroscience, 100*, 147–154.

Treves, A., & Rolls, E.T. (1994). Computational analysis of the role of the hippocampus in memory. *Hippocampus, 4*, 374–391.

Warrington, E.K., & McCarthy, R.A. (1988). the fractionation of retrograde amnesia. *Brain and Cognition, 7*, 184–200.

Weiskrantz, J. (1966). Experimental studies of amnesia. In C.W.M. Whitty & O.L.Zangwill (Eds.), *Amnesia* (pp.1–35). London: Butterworth.

Whitty, C.W.M., & Zangwill, O.L. (1977). Traumatic amnesia. In C.W.M. Whitty & O.L. Zangwill (Eds.), *Amnesia* (pp.118–135). London: Butterworth.

Wickelgren, W.A. (1974). Single-trace fragility theory of memory dynamics. *Memory and Cognition, 2,* 775–780.

Wilson, M.A., & McNaughton, B.L. (1994). Reactivation of hippocampal ensemble memories during sleep. *Science, 255,* 676–679.

Yerkes, R.M., & Dodson, J.D. (1908). The relation of strength of stimulus to rapidity of habit formation. *Journal of Comparative Neurological Psychology, 18,* 459–482.

Zola-Morgan, S., Squire, L.R., & Amaral, D.G. (1986). Human amnesia and the medial temporal region: Enduring memory impairment following a bilateral lesion limited to field CA1 of the hippocampus. *Journal of Neuroscience, 6,* 2950–2967.

MEMORY, 1997, 5 (1/2), 233–253

Predicting Syndromes of Amnesia from a Composite Holographic Associative Recall/ Recognition Model (CHARM)

Janet Metcalfe

Columbia University, USA

The composite holographic associative recall/recognition model (CHARM) is used to predict the amnesia syndromes that are expected under conditions of discrete lesions to different components of the model. The components that are needed to allow recognition, recall, and rehearsal are: (1) perceptual/lexical processing and pattern identification, (2) consciousness or working memory, (3) association formation, (4) composite storage, (5) novelty monitoring and control, and (6) retrieval. Deficits in each of these components will have specific effects on memory, generating characteristic profiles of performance. Comparison of the profiles exhibited by patients to the component-based profiles predicted by the model identify the component impaired in a given patient, and connect the memory impairments to the underlying infarcted brain structures. The model, thus, relates the memory tasks to the particular memory components that allow enactment of those tasks, and shows how the dysfunction of particular components produces specific impairments.

INTRODUCTION

Mayes and Downes (this issue) point out that: "Most hypotheses about the functional deficits in amnesia have tended to assume that the syndrome is unitary and has a single underlying functional deficit" (p.4). This article challenges that view, and proposes, instead, that different syndromes of amnesia can be produced as a result of the breakdown of any one of several components of memory, each of which will produce a characteristic profile indicative of the locus of dysfunction. The many different unitary factors that have been proposed as the locus of amnesia include encoding, retrieval, interference, storage, forgetting, type of information, failure of attention, and failure of deep

Requests for reprints should be sent to Professor Janet Metcalfe, Department of Psychology, 401 Schermerhorn Hall, Columbia University, New York, N.Y. 10027, USA.

Preparation of this article was facilitated by National Institute of Mental Health grant MH48066 and a grant from the James S. McDonnell Foundation to the author. I thank Walter Mischel, Margaret Funnell, and John Downey for their helpful comments.

processing, to give a few. The unitary cause position is undermined first of all by a striking lack of agreement over which factor is critical. It is further questioned by the fact that (a) different memory tasks differentially show impairments or the lack of impairments, (b) results from one lab often fail to replicate those of other labs, (c) amnesics with different lesions show different patterns of impairments, and (d) there appears to be general agreement that normal memory itself is not unitary but instead requires different components to function. It thus seems reasonable to explore the alternative view of human amnesia as a multifaceted phenomenon whose analysis must take account of the component operations and their interaction.

To enable a more detailed understanding of the necessary components and their function, I turn, here, to a formal model of human memory—CHARM (composite holographic associative recall model)—which has been shown to account for a broad sweep of human memory data (Metcalfe, 1990, 1991, 1993a,b, 1994; Metcalfe Eich, 1982, 1985). My working assumption is that each of the components needed in the formal model, to allow it to enact the tasks that normal humans can perform, is anatomically discrete (though connected to other components and interactive) and could break down separately. In this paper, I outline the implications of dysfunction in each of the components in terms of which tasks are expected to show impairment, and also in terms of the reasons for those impairments. To the extent that diseases and infarcts in humans affect components in a correlated manner, rather than individually, the analysis given here will be oversimplified. Although the localisation of components is a topic of great interest and importance, the formal model itself does not stand or fall on the assignment of components to anatomical locations.

AN OUTLINE OF CHARM

The basic components of the CHARM model are shown in Fig. 1. The model assumes that *sensory, perceptual, lexical processing, and identification* of events have already occurred before events are at the level of processing necessary for encoding, storage, and retrieval in the episodic memory system which is deeply embedded in the cognitive system. Formally, the events in the model are represented as multidimensional vectors of features that may vary in their similarity to one another, and over which attentional focusing may highlight some features and not others. Two such items, at the *level of consciousness (or, in working memory)*, may be *associated with one another by the operation of convolution*, which weaves all of the features into a complex new associative vector. Multiple associations are stored by being superimposed or added into a *composite memory trace*, which is itself a vector. The weighting on the association being entered into the composite trace is determined by a *monitoring and control circuit* that calculates novelty or familiarity and adjusts the weighting of the incoming event as an inverse function of its similarity to the

CHARM

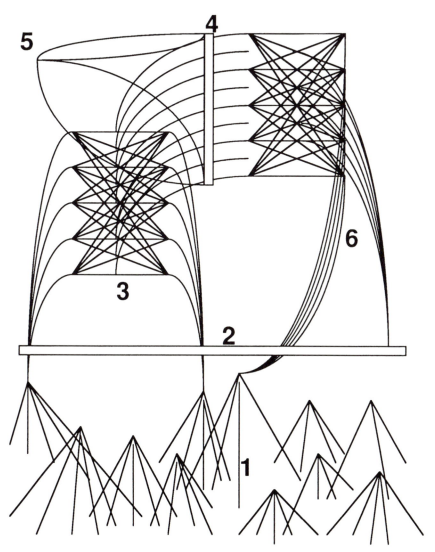

FIG. 1. An overview of CHARM. The components are (1) the perceptual system and lexicon, (2) working memory or consciousness, (3) association formation by convolution, (4) the composite memory trace, (5) novelty monitoring and control, and (6) retrieval by correlation.

composite trace. At time of test the retrieval cue, itself a vector of features that is available to consciousness, is *correlated* with the composite memory trace resulting in a retrieved vector, which is also at the level of consciousness. This retrieved item may be systematically distorted and is always noisy. Therefore the retrieved item must be *identified* (again in the lexicon or perceptual processor) if a discrete word is to be the response, or some other decision, such as a recognition judgement, must be made. The implications of selective impairment in each of these components is given in summary form in Table 1 and discussed in the sections that follow.

TABLE 1
CHARM Model Predictions

Component Damaged	Impaired	Spared
Perceptual and Lexical processing	deficit not labelled amnesia	
Working Memory Mild to Moderate Impairment	span	cued recall
		free recall
		rehearsal (elaborative and rote)
		priming
		categorisation
		recognition
		normal forgetting
		novelty response (Von Restorff)
		release from PI
		primacy
		spacing effects
		feeling of knowing judgements
Severe Impairment	span	recognition
	cued recall	priming
	free recall	
	elaborative rehearsal	
	forgetting rate	
Association formation (convolution) Mild to Moderate	graceful degradation of everything given under severe impairment	
Severe Impairment	cued recall	span
	free recall	priming
	elaborative rehearsal	categorisation
	binding tasks, within items	familiarity-based recognition
	forgetting rate	novelty response
	new association "priming"	release from PI
		primacy
		spacing effects
		feeling of knowing judgements
	anterograde amnesia	retrograde amnesia

Composite Memory Trace

	degraded performance on all episodic memory functions	span
		priming
	both retrograde and anterograde amnesia	categorisation
		familiarity-based recognition
		novelty response
		release from PI
		primacy
		spacing effects
		feeling of knowing judgements

Novelty Monitoring and Control

	feeling of knowing judgements	span
	release from PI	priming
	novelty response:	
	Von Restorff effect & P300	recognition
	spacing effects	cued recall
	exacerbated interference	
	primacy	
	habituation	
	memory tasks enhanced by clustering and categorisation	

Retrieval

	impaired performance on all episodic memory functions	span
		priming
		fluency-based recognition
	both retrograde and anterograde amnesia	

Perceptual Identification, Lexical and Response Processing

Normal Functioning

It is assumed that events that impinge upon the senses are perceptually analysed prior to entry into the episodic memory system. Such events may be characterised as patterns of features, or as vectors, and if these events are words they activate a representation in a pre-episodic mental lexicon. Further processing in the episodic memory system, then, is predicted upon perceptual analysis. Plasticity may occur in this pre-episodic system—it is not assumed that only the episodic memory system exhibits plasticity. Hence, people can learn skills, concepts, categorisations, and show adaptive responding or learning and conditioning to a variety of stimuli that may never enter into the episodic memory system. This model, then, is consistent with the views of other theorists (Mishkin & Petri, 1984; Moscovitch, 1982, 1992; O'Keefe & Nadel, 1978,

Schacter, 1987; Squire, 1992; Tulving, 1985) who distinguish among a core episodic system and other more peripheral systems that underlie skill effects, priming effects, comprehension, motor and linguistic competence, and learning.

Mayes and Downes (this issue) note that amnesics show sparing of intelligence as measured by the Wechsler Adult Intelligence Scale. Presumably the tasks on this test (aside from those on the memory scale) can be enacted by the perceptual/motor/lexical system that exists outside the episodic memory system proper. A well-established phenomenon in the amnesia literature is that repetition and associative priming measured by lexical decision, fragment completion, homophone spelling, free association, and word identification tasks are spared even though recognition and recall—episodic memory tasks—are impaired (Buschke, 1965, 1968, 1984; Gardner, Boller, Morienes, & Butters, 1973; Graf, Shimamura, & Squire, 1985; Graf, Squire, & Mandler, 1984; Jacoby & Witherspoon, 1982; Moscovitch, 1982; Schacter, 1987; Shimamura, 1986). This result is consistent with the structure of the model in which it is necessary to go through the perceptual system to get to the episodic system. Even if the episodic system were damaged, the perceptual system and the lexicon feeding into it could support the priming effects and the effects of skill learning.

Memorial Consequences of Impairment of Functioning

If the perceptual system, the lexicon, or the output system were damaged in isolation, the syndrome would not be labelled amnesia, but rather aphasia, agnosia, anomia, prosopagnosia, dyslexia, cortical blindness or deafness, and so on, depending on the nature and location of the deficit. Impairments in these systems will have consequences for later remembrances of the events that occurred, of course.

Consciousness/Working Memory

Normal Functioning

If items are to be associated with one another (allowing later retrieval) then they must be capable of existing in a working memory buffer—available to consciousness—such that they can participate in the associative operation. Without a temporal store, holding *at least two* mental items, the episodic memory system could not function. In fact, it appears that human working memory can hold more than the minimal two items. Furthermore, retrieval, in the model, brings back into consciousness or working memory representations of past events.

It is assumed that a particular level of representation, which I have called the "item" level (Metcalfe & Murdock, 1981), is needed for phenomenological awareness. If representations are not yet transformed to this form, or if they are further transformed beyond this form, they are not consciously interpretable. An analogy may be useful. We can only hear sounds within a certain bandwidth. But, if it serves our purposes, sounds can be transformed so that we can no longer hear them, by operations such as frequency modulation. Radio waves are hearable sounds that have been so transformed for transmission through the air. With the help of a radio receiver these signals can be reconverted into a form that is again available to our hearing sense. Similarly, it is proposed that there are forms of active neural representations that are not available to our conscious sense (e.g. the patterns that exist on the retina or at the level of the cochlea, or in memory proper), and a form of representation that is available to consciousness. This level of representation exists after lexical and perceptual representation and processing, and before association formation and storage in episodic memory. Items at this level of representation can exist in working memory, and focal attention may be directed to them. This level of representation is a necessary but not sufficient condition for entry into the episodic memory system.

The anatomical location of working memory is under investigation. Goldman-Rakic (1987) has demonstrated that particular neurons in the frontal cortex of monkeys fired selectively when the stimulus was not present but was being "held in mind". Other researchers have implicated the occipital and parietal lobes in related functions, so working memory may or may not be restricted to frontal cortex. Baddeley (1986, 1994), Shallice (1993), and others (McGlynn & Schacter, 1989; Stuss & Benson, 1986) have suggested that the frontal lobes may be implicated in the central executive and control functions of working memory, as well as in the function of holding items in mind.

Memorial Consequences of Impairment of Functioning

Attentional Disorder.   An impairment in working memory, as is sometimes seen in Alzheimer's, Korsakoff, and frontal lobe patients, might not always be labelled amnesia, but could rather be diagnosed as an attentional or a motivational deficit.

Impaired Span With Normal Long-term Memory.   Measurement of a patient's memory span provides a method of assessing the integrity of the working memory component. The CHARM model is resilient to very restricted working-memory capacity limitations—an impairment in this system will only show up as an impairment in the remainder of the episodic system if the deficit is so severe that the person cannot hold two items in working memory. If span sinks below two, the model predicts that the person will be unable to form inter-item associations. In the absence of inter-item associations, rehearsal will be impaired, although the system may be able to enact rote repetition of one item. Note, however, that a patient could show considerable deviation from normal working memory span and still be well above the level necessary for adequate associative processing, rehearsal, and retrieval from the core episodic memory system, accounting for the sometimes-observed finding of a working or short-term memory impairment in the absence of a long-term memory deficit (Shallice & Warrington, 1970). An alternate explanation given by Baddeley and Hitch (1974) is that working memory has three components, and could rely on alternative components given impairments. Although it is likely that working memory is complex and may have separable components, we may also have overestimated the requirements for entry of associations into long-term episodic memory, as suggested by CHARM.

The deficits that follow refer to implications of severe restriction of working memory, below the minimum requirement of two items. As long as the capacity is not restricted below two items, all of these functions may be normal, even in the presence of abnormally low span measures.

Impaired Associative Recall but Unimpaired Recognition. If a person cannot maintain two items in consciousness he or she will be unable to enact inter-item associations. Under such conditions, retrieval-based recognition memory, which depends only on the association of one item with itself, may be intact, but cued recall, which depends on inter-item association, will be impaired. Hirst et al. (1986) and Hirst, Johnson, Phelps, and Volpe (1988) found this result with amnesic patients (cf. Squire et al., 1990).

Impaired Elaborative Rehearsal. Rehearsal is a process requiring explanation because the to-be-rehearsed items are not themselves available to consciousness. Therefore, in the model, rehearsal, like recall, entails retrieval. Rehearsal depends on the two items in consciousness first being associated. Then one of the items that is available to consciousness is used as a retrieval cue (see Metcalfe & Murdock, 1981). This conscious item is correlated with the composite memory trace to retrieve a representation (of the associated item) that is itself in a form available to consciousness and which can be identified by the lexicon and used as a retrieval cue to bring a different item (with which it was associated) into consciousness. One item retrieves the other until a new item enters consciousness from the senses rather than from memory. That new item is associated with whatever is being rehearsed, and is then itself used as a retrieval cue, to continue the process of rehearsal.

This simple rehearsal loop produces patterns of data like those found in studies of overt rehearsal (e.g. Rundus & Atkinson, 1970; Murdock & Metcalfe, 1978). People rehearse items in a backward graded function in which, in any given rehearsal interval, they say the last item most frequently, the next to last item next most frequently, and so on. The rehearsal loop in the model predicts that one would mostly think about or rehearse events from the close past, but occasionally rehearse events from the distant past (depending on their connections or associations to the present). Once people are rehearsing events from the more distant past, they would tend to rehearse events that were associated with them for a period of time before once again being pulled into more ongoing present thoughts.

If working memory is so severely limited that only a single item can be maintained, then elaborative rehearsal, which is based on associative recall, cannot occur and only a single item will be repeated. Cermak, Naus, and Reale (1976) studied the overt rehearsal patterns of Korsakoff patients. They found the patterns of data produced by these patients to be abnormal—the Korsakoff patients tended only to rehearse the last word that was presented, whereas normals rehearsed a number of different words together, during any particular rehearsal interval.

Rate of Forgetting.   If rehearsal causes the rehearsed events to be stored in the composite trace (see Bjork, 1988; Rundus & Atkinson, 1970, for evidence bearing on the idea that retrieval of an event, and not just its initial study presentation, is causal in that event's later memorability) then the psychological process of rehearsal may correspond to the construct of consolidation used in the neuroscience literature. Furthermore, if elaborative rehearsal allows events from the non-immediate past to be re-entered into the composite trace, then the rate of forgetting will be related to the extent to which the person is able to enact this kind of rehearsal. If rehearsal is prevented or impaired, the forgetting curve will be steeper than if rehearsal is normal. One would, therefore, expect that patients who have a severe impairment in working memory (to the extent that they cannot hold two items and consequently cannot associate and rehearse normally) will secondarily exhibit abnormally precipitous forgetting.

Free Recall.   When normals are asked to free recall, their recall protocols are reminiscent of their rehearsal protocols—they recall a variety of items from the end of the list immediately—apparently chaining from one item to another through an associative network (see Metcalfe & Murdock, 1981), and then shift to the start of the list, chaining again through associated items. According to Cermak et al. (1976), Korsakoff patients' free recall is severely limited, consisting primarily of the last item presented—much as would be expected if they were unable to form the inter-item associations necessary for such chaining (either because the associative operation is impaired or because of severe restrictions of working memory). Indeed, all tasks that require memory for more than one item will be impaired if there is such a severe deficit in working memory.

Association Formation or Binding

Normal Functioning

In the model, two items, represented as vectors (at the level of consciousness), may be associated by the operation of convolution, whereby all of the features within the two items are bound to one another. The association is a complex interactive combination of all the features of one item with all the features of the other. This transformation renders the association consciously uninterpretable, and retrieval is needed to return either item to a conscious form. Inter-item associations are needed to allow one item to provide a retrieval cue for another item; autoassociations underlie recognition memory, allowing an item to retrieve a representation of itself.

Memorial Consequences of Impairment of Functioning

Because all of the elements within and across items are interwoven by the operation of convolution, this model is a distributed-memory model, and will exhibit graceful degradation of information with impairment or lesion to this component. Only if the entire association component is completely lesioned will the association or binding function fail entirely.

Anterograde But Little Retrograde Amnesia.   By some views of human memory, particularly those asserting that remembering consists of redoing the same operations enacted in encoding, the fact that amnesics frequently show anterograde but not retrograde amnesia is puzzling. The dissociation is, however, consistent with the componential model in which associative encoding is one kind of operation (convolution) and is assumed to take place in a different brain location from storage and from retrieval, which is a different kind of operation (correlation). By this view, once events have been associated and stored in the composite memory trace, damage to the area in which the association formation is conducted (presumably the hippocampus) will largely spare the memory for the events that have already been associated and stored, although new associations may not be laid down. Thus, as in the case of HM (Scoville & Milner, 1957) or RB (Zola-Morgan, Squire, & Amaral, 1986), in which the hippocampal damage occurred with an acute onset, new associations and explicit memories tended no longer to be formed after the damage— resulting in anterograde amnesia in the absence of notable retrograde amnesia.

There is one caveat to the claim that with damage to the association formation component, there will be little if any retrograde amnesia. Rehearsal may mediate the storage process of events after the time of nominal acquisition. In so far as rehearsal is needed to allow memories to be consolidated, and rehearsal is impaired when the convolution or association formation component is damaged, it follows that there should be *some* retrograde amnesia for events that were shown prior to the amnesia-inducing trauma because they will receive less rehearsal than they normally would.

Relational Memory.   If association formation were selectively impaired, then memory tasks that require the establishment of new relations should be impaired, as is frequently seen in the data. Thus, the tasks of cued recall, retrieval-based recognition, free recall, and rehearsal should all show impairment. Indeed, all tasks that require the generation of more than one item (at a delay that allows that working memory is not impacting on performance), or that depend on having bound the elements within an event together (as in retrieval-based recognition), should show impairment if the association operation were impaired.

Spared Item But Not New-association Priming.   The model predicts that complete obliteration of the association formation operation should still allow spared item priming, via the lexicon and perceptual systems, but, because association formation between events represented beyond the level of consciousness (although not the simple associations underlying classically or operantly conditioned responses) is thought to occur only in the convolution component, patients with complete inability to form new associations should show impaired priming of new associations. Graf and Schacter (1985) presented subjects with unrelated pairs, such as WINDOW–REASON, either embedded in a meaningful sentence or simply as pairs. Subjects were then given a stem completion task, either with the same context (WINDOW–REA____) or a different context (OFFICER–REA____). Both normals and amnesics benefited from the list context, in contradiction to what the model would, at first blush, predict. However, this priming may have resulted because of feedback from a *partially* intact associative component. As the association formation operation in the model is distributed, partial damage is possible and the result would be ''graceful degradation'' of new association ''priming''. Schacter and Graf (1986) reported that the associative effect only occurred for *mildly* amnesic patients, and was not found with severely amnesic subjects. Similarly, Shimamura and Squire (1989) found *no* associative priming effect with patients who showed severe amnesia. Graf and Schacter's (1985) original results do point to feedback from the episodic system onto the lexical system in normals and mildly amnesic patients, as do other results such as subtle differences in the temporal course of priming effects in normals and severe amnesics.

Recognition Memory.   Recognition memory responses, in the model, can stem from two sources. First, the normal recognition procedure in the model involves retrieval from the composite memory trace. The recognition probe is correlated with the composite trace, and then the item that is retrieved is matched to the probe. If it matches, above a certain criterion, then the model calls that item old. However, recognition could, under some circumstances, also be enacted by assessing the fluency of primed items in the lexicon or perceptual system (see Jacoby, Kelley, & Dywan, 1989, and also see Mandler, 1980). The former kind of recognition should suffer from impairment to the associative operation; the later kind should be unaffected.

Mishkin and Murray (1994) have reported that monkeys with surgically induced bilateral hippocampal lesions were able to enact an object-recognition task. Assuming that the hippocampus is the site of association formation or binding, it would appear that one would have to account for this result by recourse to the possibility that recognition in their task was based on feature fluency rather than on event retrieval. Indeed, nothing in their task forced the use of associative coding or binding information. The mere familiarity with or fluency of the parts of the objects would have been sufficient to allow the monkeys to distinguish the old probes from the new probes. In contrast, Kroll et al. (1996) used recognition tasks in which all of the elements or features within a probe, in the critical condition, were old, having occurred in different events at time of study. For example, subjects saw a list of faces at time of study. At test some of the probe faces consisted of the eyes and nose of one face inserted into the background of another face (see Reinitz, Lammers, & Cochran, 1992). On the basis only of familiarity or fluency of the parts, these faces (and other similarly constructed stimuli) should have been called old, as all of the parts had been seen in the previously studied list. To determine that these conjunction events were new, the subject needed to be able to access what information had co-occurred in the previous list—a kind of knowledge that is derivable, in CHARM, only as a result of the associative operation of convolution. Normal subjects were more able to correctly reject these conjunctions than were patients with hippocampal damage, who tended incorrectly to accept them as old. Interestingly, on the items that were actually old as compared to items that were entirely new, the patients performed normally—a result consistent with those of Mishkin and Murray (1994).

Finally, it has been shown (Metcalfe Eich, 1985) that similarity effects due to the study context in recognition memory, and levels of processing effects in recognition memory, are attributable, in CHARM, to the associative operation. Thus, these should fail to show up with extreme damage to the associative operation (even though noncontextual recognition might be spared).

Spared Classification. To the extent that classification performance does not depend on within-event binding, the model predicts that classification performance may be spared despite damage to the system underlying association formation. I have conducted extensive computer simulations of the model on this paradigm, and in general they show that the binding operation in the model results in hyperspecificity. Thus, with impairment to the associative operation, the model predicts not a failure of classification, but rather good generalisation to categorically similar events. Knowlton and Squire (1994) have shown effects of spared classification in amnesic patients.

Composite Memory Trace

Normal Functioning

Multiple associations are stored, in CHARM, by being superimposed or added into a composite memory trace. Because of the use of the operations of convolution and correlation, the CHARM model is said to be "holographic". In physical holograms, if some part of the film is destroyed the stored images may still be reconstructed, but the reconstruction will be less clear than it would have been had the entire film been used in the reconstruction. Similarly, in the model, if part of the composite memory trace were ablated, the remaining part of the composite memory trace would allow reconstruction (albeit degraded) of entire memories.

Memorial Consequences of Impairment of Functioning

If brain damage resulted in partial trace loss and nothing else, then, according to CHARM, the trace would still support at least some recall, recognition, cued recall, and so on, although memory would be degraded. It is extremely rare that a patient is unable to remember anything from his or her past. To my knowledge, there is only one patient who may be an exception to this general rule. That patient, KC, is reported to be unable to retrieve any episodic information about any events that occurred in his life, either before or after the motorcycle accident that was the cause of his amnesia (Tulving, Hayman, & MacDonald, 1991; Tulving, Schacter, McLaughlin, & Moscovitch, 1988), such as might occur with total trace loss. However, KC's lesion is both extremely extensive and diffuse, suggesting that caution needs to be exercised in interpreting his deficit.

Novelty Monitoring and Control

Normal Functioning

A novelty monitoring and control circuit is needed and employed in CHARM (Metcalfe, 1993b). This circuit assesses the novelty of the incoming association with respect to the pre-existing composite trace, and computes a global familiarity value. The value is assumed to provide the informational basis for feeding-of-knowing judgements. To stabilise the composite memory trace, the monitoring/control circuit damps down the input into the trace as an inverse function of the computed novelty/familiarity value. Novel events are given high weightings in memory; familiar events are given low weightings. This circuit solves an inherent problem in the basic memory system. By so doing, it produces an adaptive memory system that is responsive to novelty and relatively unresponsive to already learned events. Impairment of this circuit should give rise to a characteristic novelty-based deficit syndrome outlined later. The thumbprint of this amnesic syndrome shows up with Korsakoff and sometimes frontal lobe patients.

Memorial Consequences of Impairment of Functioning

Feeling of Knowing.   It has been argued that familiarity-based feeling of knowing judgements are based on the computation given by the novelty or familiarity of the cue (Metcalfe, 1993a,b, 1994). A number of experiments have shown that the feeling-of-knowing judgement is affected by manipulations that alter the cue familiarity, as predicted by the model (Metcalfe, Schwartz, & Joaquim, 1993; Reder & Ritter, 1992; Schwartz & Metcalfe, 1992) but not by manipulations that alter the retrievability of the target itself. Converging evidence for this proposal has been given by Metcalfe (1993b). Shimamura and Squire (1986) have shown that Korsakoff patients show abnormal patterns on the feeling-of-knowing task. Other amnesic patients do not show impairment on this task. Janowsky, Shimamura, and Squire (1989) have shown that frontal patients (who may have novelty-circuit impairment without damage to other parts of the memory system) also show selective impairment (although not as severe as the Korsakoff patients) on the feeling-of-knowing task.

Release From PI.   In the release from proactive inhibition paradigm, subjects are presented with several trials of to-be-remembered triads from a single category. Performance decreases with each successive triad. This is expected as an offshoot of the familiarity monitor because the trace is becoming more and more like the triads with each successive presentation, and so familiarity of the incoming item to the trace is increasing, and the weighting on successive triads will decrease. When the materials are shifted to a new category, subjects' performance increases. In the model this occurs because the different-category triad is novel with respect to the already encoded events in the trace, and hence is assigned a high weighting. Several studies have shown that Korsakoff amnesics have abnormal release from proactive inhibition (Cermak, Butters, & Moreines, 1974; Squire, 1982; Winocur, Kinsbourne, & Moscovitch, 1981). Squire's study is of particular interest because other amnesics do not show this impairment. Some studies suggest frontal involvement (see Moscovitch, 1982; cf. Petrides, 1995), although studies with frontal patients have sometimes been equivocal (perhaps because the precise locale of this circuit within the frontal lobes is unknown).

Von Restorff Effects and P300s.   Von Restorff effects provide another straightforward example of a memory effect attributable to the novelty monitoring system. A list of words from one category is presented to the subject. One of the words, however, is from a different category. That different word is remembered better than would have been the case had the item in its serial position been from the background category. In the model, the von Restorff effect occurs because the novelty monitor assigns the novel word a high weighting. An event related potential deflection called the P300 (or sometimes the "late positivity", Picton, 1993; Sutton, Braren, Zubin, & John, 1965) is related to von Restorff effects (Fabiani, Gratton, Chiarenza, & Donchin, 1990; Fabiani, Karis, & Donchin, 1986). It is plausible to suppose that it, too, is ascribable to the novelty monitoring circuit (Metcalfe, 1993a). In particular, the circuit must match the incoming event to the trace (presumably in the hippocampus), assess its novelty (presumably a frontal function), and feed back a signal to modulate the weighting of the association in the trace. This latter step may relate to the synchronous firing in the hippocampus that is responsible for the P300 deflection. Disturbance anywhere in this circuit should impact on the P300 (see Metcalfe, 1993a). Knight (1984) showed that frontal lobe patients exhibit an impairment on the P3A (and early component related to the P300)—indicating that this event related potential may rely on the adequate functioning of a circuit that monitors the state of the hippocampus, computes this state, and then feeds back a signal to control the amplification of what is currently being registered in the hippocampus.

Spacing Effects.   Some spacing effects (Metcalfe, 1993a) have been attributed to the novelty monitoring circuit. If a word is repeated immediately, the second repetition is highly similar to the trace at that moment (by virtue of the strong presence from the first repetition of the critical item in the trace) and so its weighting will be less than if it is repeated after some spacing (when its similarity to the trace will be decreased because the trace has changed with the intervening items). After some time has passed, a function of the sum of the initial weightings (which favours the spaced condition) will be apparent in memory performance. However, if the test is immediate, the first presentation of the word will still be heavily weighted in the trace (because of its recency) and will have a considerable impact on memory performance. With immediate test the recency of the first presentation will dominate, and so massed rather than spaced items will seem to be stronger. The differential weighting as a function of trace similarity is needed, in the model, to account for these effects. Impairment of the novelty monitoring circuit, selectively, should therefore impact on spacing effects: they should be less apparent for Korsakoff patients than for other amnesic patients. I know of no studies investigating spacing effects with amnesics.

Interference Effects.   In CHARM simulations of the release from proactive interference paradigm (Metcalfe, 1993b), a difference in the pattern of intrusions from previous lists, which depends on whether or not the novelty monitor was used, can be observed. When the novelty monitor was used in the simulations, the responses tended to issue primarily from the last-presented list, whereas when the novelty monitor was disengaged, there were more intrusions from previous lists. The idea that frontal damage results in an increase in interference, or an inability to gate information, is often proposed as an explanation of memory impairments in these patients (Knight, Scabini, & Woods, 1989; Shimamura, 1994). Shimamura et al. (1995) found selective disruption in frontal lobe patients in an AB–AC test and in an AB–ABr test, both of which were designed to measure interference.

Primacy.   The primacy effect is probably due, at least in part, to the fact that people rehearse the first words in a list more than they do other words in a list (Murdock & Metcalfe, 1978; Rundus & Atkinson, 1970). However, primacy shows up even when the presentation rate is so fast that people are unable to rehearse at all. It is postulated that this second factor in the primacy effect may be attributable to the novelty monitor. The first item in a list is always different from the mental activity that preceded it, by virtue of being the first to-be-remembered item. We would expect it, then, to receive a novelty boost. Abnormal primacy effects, with frontal damage, have been reported by Petrides (1995).

Habituation.   The novelty monitor not only provides a boost in weighting for novel items, but it also decreases the weighting on items that are similar to or identical with those that have come before—that is, it is responsible for habituation effects. The failure to habituate appropriately may be responsible for many of the abnormalities seen in Korsakoff and frontal patients. Hypervigi-lance is characteristic of some of these patients—everything seems novel. The reverse syndrome of apathy is also commonly observed—nothing seems novel. Both of these may be attributable to a failure to appreciate that a stimulus is either novel, and should be attended, or not novel, and hence may be safely ignored.

Retrieval

Normal Functioning

When a retrieval cue is given, it is perceptually analysed and used to retrieve a representation from the composite trace. The retrieval operation of correlation is the inverse operation to convolution. The item that is retrieved from memory is in a form available to phenomenological awareness. Interestingly, these retrieved items are noisy, distorted, and degraded. Retrieval has the characteristic, in this model, of being redintegrative: a part of an event is sufficient to retrieve the whole. Similarity effects fall out automatically. Furthermore, everything that was associated with a particular retrieval cue will be retrieved by that cue—resulting in the superimposed retrieval of multiple events that allows the model to account for such diverse phenomena as episodic classification learning and generalisation (Metcalfe Eich, 1982), interference in the A–B A–C paradigm (Metcalfe Eich, 1982), and the effects of misleading suggestions on eyewitness testimony (Metcalfe, 1991).

Memorial Consequences of Impairment of Functioning

If there were a retrieval deficit, all episodic memories would be affected. The patient would experience both retrograde and anterograde amnesia, and all episodic function would be lost. Squire, Knowlton, and Musen (1993) report a number of examples of patients who exhibit the combined syndrome of both retrograde and anterograde amnesia. As mentioned earlier, KC is the only patient for whom the claim is made that he can recollect no episodic events from his past, and, as with the interpretation that this implies that he has complete trace loss, the interpretation that this means he has a complete retrieval failure needs to be viewed with extreme caution because of the extent and complexity of his brain damage. All non-episodic functions could be spared, as could working memory functions, in the face of severe retrieval deficits.

CONCLUSION

If this analysis is correct in the assumption that different amnesic syndromes result from a complex interaction of the requirements of particular tasks with the memory components that are needed to perform them, then we search in vain for a unitary cause of amnesia. The analysis of the memory tasks by models that can actually perform those tasks, and the isolation of the processes that are needed in their performance, appears to be necessary to further our understanding of human amnesia. Computational models, such as CHARM, allow the specific delineation of profiles of impairments that can be expected when particular components are impaired. The CHARM model, itself, was not initially designed to address the causes of human amnesia, but rather, was intended more simply to be a model of how normal people represent mental items or events, associate those items in episodic memory, store the associations, and then later, how they retrieve an item from memory when given a cue. Its use, in designating the patterns of impairments that are expected with breakdown of each of the major components of memory, provides a means to begin to disentangle and reconcile the perplexing results found in the amnesia literature, and, in particular, the seeming lack of replicability and stability. Such apparent variability is expected if multiple syndromes—each different in its underlying cause and in its manifestations—have been inappropriately conceptualised as if they comprised a unitary entity.

At a theoretical level CHARM permits a fine-grain differentiation of specific syndromes of human amnesia that allows us to articulate in considerable detail the various deficits that could occur under "ideal" conditions in which the underlying components were lesioned clearly and selectively. Empirically, of course, in many if not most patients, such discrete effects are unlikely. Thus, even the somewhat complex pure syndromes predicted by discrete failure of selective memory components, as given in this article, may be found only rarely, and the prospect remains that further empirical investigation may more frequently reveal mixed and partial cases.

REFERENCES

Baddeley, A.D. (1986). *Working memory.* Oxford: Oxford University Press.

Baddeley, A.D. (1994). Working memory: The interface between memory and cognition. In D.L. Schacter & E. Tulving (Eds.), *Memory systems 1994.* Cambridge, MA: Bradford Book, MIT Press.

Baddeley, A.D., & Hitch, G.J. (1974). Working memory. In G.H. Bower (Ed.), *The psychology of learning and motivation* (Vol.8, pp.47–89). New York: Academic Press.

Bjork, R.A.(1988).Retrieval practice and the maintenance of knowledge. In M.M. Gruneberg, P.E. Morris, & R.N. Sykes (Eds.), *Practical aspects of Memory: Current research and issues* (Vol. 1, pp.396–401). Chichester, UK: Wiley.

Buschke, H. (1965). Impairment of short-term memory, *Neurology, 15,* 913–918.

Buschke, H. (1968). Interaction of long term and short term memory. *Journal of Nervous and Mental Disease, 147,* 580–586.

Buschke, H. (1984). Cued recall in amnesia. *Journal of Clinical Neuropsychology, 6,* 433–440.

Cermak, L.S., Butters, N., & Moreines, J. (1974). Some analyses of the verbal encoding deficits of alcoholic Korsakoff patients. *Brain and Language, 1,* 141–150.

Cermak, L.S., Naus, M.J., & Reale, L. (1976). Rehearsal and organizational strategies of alcoholic Korsakoff patients. *Brain and Language, 3,* 375–385.

Fabiani, M., Gratton, G., Chiarenza, G.A., & Donchin, E. (1990). A psychophysiological investigation of the Von Restorff paradigm in children. *Journal of Psychophysiology, 4,* 15–24.

Fabiani, M., Karis, D., & Donchin, E. (1986). Effects of mnemonic strategy manipulation in a Von Restorff paradigm. *Electroencephalography and Clinical Neurophysiology, 75,* 22–35.

Gardner, H., Boller, F., Moreines, J., & Butters, N. (1973). Retrieving information from Korsakoff patients: Effects of categorical cues and reference to the task. *Cortex, 9,* 165–175.

Goldman-Rakic, P.S. (1987). Circuitry of primate prefrontal cortex and regulation of behavior by representational memory. In F. Plum (Ed.), *Handbook of physiology—The nervous system (Vol. 5)* (pp.373–417). Bethesda MD: American Psychological Society.

Graf, P., & Schacter, D.L. (1985). Implicit and explicit memory for new associations in normal and amnesic subjects. *Journal of Experimental Psychology: Learning, Memory, and Cognition, 11,* 501–518.

Graf, P., Shimamura, A.P., & Squire, L.R. (1985). Priming across modalities and priming across category levels: Extending the domain of preserved function in amnesia. *Journal of Experimental Psychology: Learning, Memory, and Cognition, 11,* 385–395.

Graf, P., Squire, L.R., & Mandler, G. (1984). The information that amnesic patients do not forget. *Journal of Experimental Psychology: Learning, Memory, and Cognition, 10,* 164–178.

Hirst, W., Johnson, M.K., Kim, J.K., Phelps, E.A., Risse, G., & Volpe, B.T. (1986). Recognition and recall in amnesics. *Journal of Experimental Psychology: Learning, Memory, and Cognition, 12,* 445–451.

Hirst, W., Johnson, M.K., Phelps, E.A., & Volpe, B.T. (1988). More on recall and recognition in amnesia. *Journal of Experimental Psychology: Learning, Memory, and Cognition, 14,* 758–762.

Jacoby, L.L., Kelley, C.M., & Dywan, J. (1989). Memory attributions. In H.L. Roediger & F.I.M. Craik (Eds.), *Varieties of memory and consciousness: Essays in honor of Endel Tulving* (pp.391–422), Hillsdale, NJ: Lawrence Erlbaum Associates Inc.

Jacoby, L.L., & Witherspoon, D. (1982). Remembering without awareness. *Canadian Journal of Psychology, 38,* 631–668.

Janowsky, J.S., Shimamura, A.P., & Squire, L.R. (1989). Memory and metamemory: Comparisons between frontal lobe lesions and amnesic patients. *Psychobiology, 17* 3–11.

Knight, R.T. (1984). Decreased response to novel stimuli after prefrontal lesion in man. *Electroencephalography and Clinical Neurophysiology, 59,* 9–20.

Knight, R.T., Scabini, D., & Woods, D.L. (1989). Prefrontal gating of auditory transmissions in humans. *Brain Research, 504,* 338–342.

Knowlton, B., & Squire, L. (1994). The information acquired during artificial grammar learning, *Journal of Experimental Psychology: Learning, Memory, and Cognition, 20,* 79–91.

Kroll, N.E.A., Knight, R., Metcalfe, J., Wolf, E., & Tulving, E. (1996). Cohesion failure as a source of memory illusions. *Journal of Memory and Language, 2,* 176–196.

Mayes, A.R., & Downes, J.J. (this issue). What do theories of the functional deficit(s) underlying amnesia have to explain? *Memory, 5*(1/2).

Mandler, G. (1980). Recognizing: The judgment of previous occurrence. *Psychological Review, 87,* 252–271.

McGlynn, S.M., & Schacter, D.L. (1989). Unawareness of deficits in neuropsychological syndromes, *Journal of Clinical and Experimental Neuropsychology, 11,* 143–205.

Metcalfe, J. (1990). A composite holographic associative recall model (CHARM) and blended memories in eyewitness testimony. *Journal of Experimental Psychology: General, 119,* 145–160.

Metcalfe, J. (1991). Recognition failure and the composite memory trace in CHARM. *Psychological Review, 98,* 529–553.

Metcalfe, J. (1993a). Monitoring and gain control in an episodic memory model: Relation to P300 event-related potentials. In A.F. Collins, S.E. Gathercole, M.A. Conway, & P.E. Morris (Eds.), *Theories of memory* (pp.327–354). Hillsdale, NJ: Lawrence Erlbaum Associates Inc.

Metcalfe, J. (1993b). Novelty monitoring, metacognition, and control in a composite holographic associative recall model: Implications for Korsakoff amnesia. *Psychological Review, 100,* 3–22.

Metcalfe, J. (1994). Novelty monitoring, metacognition, and frontal lobe dysfunction: Implications of a computational model of memory. In J. Metcalfe & A.P. Shimamura (Eds.), *Metacognition: Knowing about knowing,* Cambridge, MA: MIT Press.

Metcalfe, J., & Murdock, B.B. Jr. (1981). An encoding and retrieval model of single-trial free recall. *Journal of Verbal Learning and Verbal Behavior, 20,* 161–189.

Metcalfe, J., Schwartz, B.L., & Joaquim, S.G. (1993). The cue-familiarity heuristic in metacognition. *Journal of Experimental Psychology: Learning, Memory, and Cognition, 19,* 851–861.

Metcalfe Eich, J. (1982). A composite holographic associative recall model. *Psychological Review, 89,* 627–661.

Metcalfe Eich, J. (1985). Levels of processing, encoding specificity, elaboration, and CHARM, *Psychological Review, 91,* 1–38.

Mishkin, M., & Murray, E.A. (1994). Stimulus recognition. *Current Opinion in Neurobiology, 4,* 200–206.

Mishkin, M., & Petri, H.L. (1984). Memories and habits: Some implications for the analysis of learning and retention. In L.R. Squire & N. Butters (Eds.), *Neuropsychology of memory.* New York: Guilford Press.

Moscovitch, M. (1982). Multiple dissociations of function in amnesia. In L.S. Cermak (Ed.), *Human memory and amnesia* (pp.337–370). Hillsdale, NJ: Lawrence Erlbaum Associates Inc.

Moscovitch, M. (1992). Memory and working with memory: A component process model based on modules and central systems. *Journal of Cognitive Neuroscience, 4,* 257–267.

Murdock, B.B. Jr., & Metcalfe, J. (1978). Controlled rehearsal in single-trial free recall. *Journal of Verbal Learning and Verbal Behavior, 17,* 309–324.

O'Keefe, J., & Nadel, L. (1978). *The hippocampus as a cognitive map.* Oxford: Clarendon Press.

Petrides, M. (1995). *The frontal lobes and memory.* Presentation at the Annual Meeting of the Mc-Donnell-Pew Foundation on Cognitive Neuroscience, April, Tucson, AZ.

Picton, T.W. (1993). The P300 wave of the human event-related potential. *Journal of Clinical Neurophysiology, 9,* 456–479.

Reder, L.M., & Ritter, F.E. (1992). What determines initial feeling of knowing? Familiarity with question terms, not with the answer. *Journal of Experimental Psychology: Learning, Memory, and Cognition, 18,* 435–452.

Reinitz, M.T., Lammers, W.J., & Cochran, B.P. (1992). Memory-conjunction errors: Miscombination of stored stimulus features can produce illusions of memory. *Memory & Cognition, 20,* 1–11.

Rundus, D., & Atkinson, R.C. (1970). Rehearsal processes in free recall: A procedure for direct observation. *Journal of Verbal Learning and Verbal Behavior, 9,* 99–105.

Schacter, D.L. (1987). Implicit memory: History and current status. *Journal of Experimental Psychology: Learning, Memory, and Cognition, 13,* 501–518.

Schacter, D.L., & Graf, P. (1986). Preserved learning in amnesic patients: Perspectives on research from directed priming. *Journal of Clinical Experimental Neuropsychology, 8,* 727–743.

Schwartz, B.L., & Metcalfe, J. (1992). Cue familiarity but not target retrievability enhances feeling-of-knowing judgments. *Journal of Experimental Psychology: Leaning, Memory, and Cognition, 18,* 1074–1083.

Scoville, W.B., & Milner, B. (1957). Loss of recent memory after bilateral hippocampal lesions. *Journal of Neurology, Neurosurgery and Psychiatry, 20,* 11–21.

Shallice, T. (1993). Neuropsychological investigation of supervisory processes. In A.D. Baddeley & L. Weiskrantz (Eds.), *Attention: Selection, awareness, and control. A tribute to Donald Broadbent.* Oxford: Oxford University Press.

Shallice, T., & Warrington, E.K. (1970). Independent functioning of verbal memory stores: A neuropsychological study. *Quarterly Journal of Experimental Psychology, 22,* 261–273.

Shimamura, A.P. (1986). Priming effects in amnesia: Evidence for a dissociable memory function. *Quarterly Journal of Experimental Psychology, 38A,* 619–644.

Shimamura, A.P. (1994). Frontal lobes and memory. In M.S. Gazzaniga (Ed.), *The cognitive neurosciences.* Cambridge, MA: MIT Press.

Shimamura, A.P., Jurica, P.J., Mangels, J.A. Gershberg, F.B., & Knight, R.T. (1995). Susceptibility to memory interference effects following frontal lobe damage: Findings from tests of paired-associate learning. *Journal of Cognitive Neuroscience, 7,* 144–152.

Shimamura, A.P., & Squire, L.R. (1986). Memory and metamemory: A study of the feeling-of-knowing phenomenon in amnesic patients. *Journal of Experimental Psychology: Learning, Memory, and Cognition, 12,* 452–460.

Shimamura, A.P., & Squire, L.R. (1989). Impaired priming of new associations in amnesia. *Journal of Experimental Psychology: Learning, Memory, and Cognition, 15,* 721–728.

Squire, L.R. (1982). Comparisons between forms of amnesia: Some deficits are unique to Korsakoff's syndrome. *Journal of Experimental Psychology: Learning, Memory, and Cognition, 8,* 560–571.

Squire, L.R. (1992). Declarative and nondeclarative memory: Multiple brain systems supporting learning and memory. *Journal of Cognitive Neuroscience, 4,* 232–243.

Squire, L.R., Knowlton, B., & Musen, G. (1993). The structure and organization of memory. *Annual Review of Psychology, 44,* 453–495.

Squire, L.R., Zola-Morgan, S., Cave, C.B., Haist, F., Musen, G., & Suzuki, W.A. (1990). Memory: Organization of brain systems and cognition. *Cold Spring Harbor Symposia on Quantitative Biology, VL,* 1007–1023.

Stuss, D.T., & Benson, D.F. (1986). *The frontal lobes.* New York: Raven Press.

Sutton, S., Braren, M., Zubin, J., & John, E.R. (1965). Evoked potential correlates of stimulus uncertainty. *Science, 150,* 1187–1188.

Tulving, E. (1985). How many memory systems are there? *American Psychologist, 40*, 385–398.

Tulving, E., Hayman, C.A., & MacDonald, C.A. (1991. Long-lasting perceptual priming and semantic learning in amnesia: A case experiment. *Journal of Experimental Psychology: Learning, Memory and Cognition, 17*, 595–617.

Tulving, E., Schacter, D.L., McLaughlin, D.R., & Moscovitch, M. (1988). Priming of semantic autobiographical knowledge: A case study of retrograde amnesia. *Brain and Cognition, 8*, 3–20.

Winocur, G., Kinsbourne, M., & Moscovitch, M. (1981). The effect of cueing on release from proactive interference in Korsakoff amnesic patients. *Journal of Experimental Psychology: Human Learning and Memory, 7*, 56–65.

Zola-Morgan, S., Squire, L., & Amaral, D.G. (1986). Human amnesia and the medial temporal region: Enduring memory impairment following a bilateral lesion limited to field CA1 of the hippocampus. *The Journal of Neuroscience, 6*, 2950–2967.

MEMORY, 1997, 5 (1/2), 255–300

New Approaches to the Study of Amnesic Patients: What Can a Neurofunctional Philosophy and Neural Network Methods Offer?

Alan D. Pickering

St. George's Hospital Medical School, University of London, UK

In this paper I first consider a *neurofunctional* approach to the study of amnesic patients. This approach stresses the need for theorising about the processing operations of brain regions and circuits rather than for theorising about neuropsychological syndromes. A syndrome—such as amnesia—may not exist, in any meaningful sense, if there is marked heterogeneity within the patients grouped together in this way. Powerful neuroimaging techniques may now allow a more useful basis for grouping patients in terms of lesion location rather than aetiology. In turn this will allow an evaluation of the information processing functions subserved by the lesioned structures. The second strand to the present paper stresses the weakness in the specification of current theories. This has made it difficult to select experimental tasks that decisively measure the key components of those theories. The paper makes the case that explicit neural network models are a useful way to try to overcome this problem.

In line with these ideas, the paper begins to build a model of how the brain may achieve useful kinds of stimulus representations. Considerations of human behaviour in category learning tasks have emphasised parallel and interacting roles for both exemplar- and element-based stimulus representations. It is suggested that the hippocampus itself may encode exemplar representations, and these may provide a basis for episodic memory as well as some types of category learning. It is further suggested that the ventral striatum may encode the element-based representations. The model allows some new and detailed predictions for the performance of amnesic subjects related to lesion location.

Requests for reprints should be sent to Dr. Alan D. Pickering, Department of Psychology, St George's Hospital Medical School, University of London, London SW17 0RE, UK. Email: a.pickering@sghms.ac.uk

There are a great number of individuals who have contributed to the development of the ideas discussed in this paper and the related work mentioned. Mike Page, Jane Powell, Neil McNaughton, Jeffrey Gray, and Andrew Mayes have made helpful comments on earlier, long and impenetrable drafts of this and related papers. Mike Joseph has been an invaluable discussant on neurochemical issues; Jeffrey Gray's published work has shown me the value of neurofunctional thinking in other contexts. I am also indebted to Mike Page, Albert Nigrin, and Nestor Schmajuk for reorienting my explorations of the neural network literature in more profitable directions; these directions have directly shaped my approach to the model developed in this paper.

INTRODUCTION

The remit of articles for this special issue of *Memory* was to describe a theoretical account of amnesia with emphasis on generating novel predictions. It was further suggested that, where possible, the predictions made should be as specific as possible to the theoretical framework being developed; that is, the most interesting predictions would be those that other possible frameworks would not generate. Obviously, such requirements are the essence of good theory building, but were they unrealistic goals to set the contributors?

The phrase "theory of amnesia" may suggest that one is attempting to explain a single homogeneous entity. A broad class of memory abilities (such as those that appear impaired in amnesia) may well be dependent on several key processing operations, each of which may be localised in partially separate neural circuitry. This suggests that a large number of partially distinct amnesic states could exist, each resulting from the particular combination of structures that are damaged. I shall refer to this alternative view as the *amnesic heterogeneity hypothesis*, for short.

Although many researchers believe that amnesic heterogeneity is likely, it is arguable that no distinction between different types of amnesia can claim the support of any firm behavioural evidence. Indeed, some theorists have apparently abandoned some distinctions they once favoured (see, for example, Squire, Knowlton, & Musen, 1993, for an acknowledgement of this kind in connection with rate-of-forgetting data). There may be good reasons why reliable differences between *groups* of amnesics are hard to find: until recently there have been few ways, other than aetiology, by which to differentiate the groups. If aetiology does not respect information-processing boundaries in the brain, then members of an aetiological group may represent different amnesic states, increasing within-groups variance and reducing the power of between-groups comparisons. A new era in amnesia research may be approaching, however, in which powerful neuroimaging techniques make it possible to group amnesic patients together in terms of the brain regions structurally damaged, or functionally compromised.

These concerns about the possibility of amnesic heterogeneity are consistent with a different approach to the study of amnesia. I shall refer to this as the *neurofunctional approach* because it starts by trying to identify some of the information processing functions that may be necessary, but not sufficient, for normal memory functioning. A distinctive aspect to this approach is the recognition that some of the critical processing functions may well be involved in mental activity outside the purely mnemonic sphere. This argument goes directly against the near-universal view that "pure" amnesic states must result from a deficit specific to the domain of memory processing. An example of a more general processing function, which could be compromised in some amnesic states, is *response selection*. I contend that it is hard to conceive of a memory system without a response selection mechanism (e.g. to choose between a group of competitor responses that are strongly specified by a retrieval cue). It is possible, in fact plausible, that the brain may use a general-purpose response selection device across a range of mental activities (e.g. memory retrieval, selective attention, goal-directed planning etc.). If this device were damaged in an amnesic patient then the patient would be markedly deficient in the whole range of behaviours for which response selection is important. While these behaviours might include certain memory activities, other information processing, without a memory load, could also be compromised.

Furthermore, a deficit in a function such as response selection may not be sufficient, on its own, to produce what would be currently recognised as an amnesic state; this might arise only when response selection failure is combined with other deficits. In fact, this analysis raises the further possibility that a response selection failure, in combination with yet another type of processing deficit, might give rise to a different type of neurological or neuropsychiatric condition altogether. A neurofunctional perspective is naturally conducive to the integration of diverse sets of ideas: the present paper hopes to encourage the exploration and modelling of the similarities between amnesia and other conditions (such as schizophrenia) which share pathology in similar brain regions (see Grey et al., 1991, for references) and which have an overlapping neuropsychological profile (McKenna et al., 1990; Saykin et al., 1991).

The next step in the neurofunctional approach is to try to map each function being considered onto a particular neural substrate. Clearly, any amnesic patients with demonstrable damage to the proposed neural substrate would be impaired at the processing function while other amnesics (or controls), lacking damage to the region concerned, would be able to execute the key processing function normally. Testing this kind of prediction constitutes the central step in refuting/confirming the proposed neurofunctional mapping, and hinges on the successful selection of two sets of tasks, one set strongly dependent on the processing function concerned and another set largely independent of it. If tasks with these properties cannot be convincingly selected, the empirical evidence for or against the neurofunctional mapping cannot be acquired.

Weaknesses in the mapping of processes onto experimental tasks could be regarded as the main obstacle to the progress of neuropsychology in general. I shall suggest later (in the second major theme of this paper) that the recent emphasis on neural network (NN) models in cognitive psychology offers hope that soon we shall have models of task performance that are powerful enough to begin to overcome the difficulties of unequivocal task selection.

The ultimate goal of the neurofunctional approach converges with that of the more traditional mode of studying amnesia; both approaches aim to lead to an understanding of the functioning of the brain regions concerned with human memory. The main differences stem from the different view of the modular organisation of the brain inherent in each approach. The traditional approach implies the existence of "memory modules" which can either be viewed as systems or collections of memory-dedicated processes. This implies that the knowledge gained from the study of amnesia would be of little direct use in understanding complex human mental activities other than memory. The neurofunctional approach, by contrast, strives to build up an understanding of "modular" processing functions which can combine (with other functions) to discharge a wider range of human cognition than memory alone.

I would predict two reactions to this introduction: one will be to argue that the amnesic heterogeneity hypothesis is fundamentally wrong and so endorse the concept of a small number of core amnesic syndromes; the second will be to argue that amnesia research already broadly follows the neurofunctional approach. Although I accept that the first argument may well be correct, I disagree with the second. There are only a few accounts of amnesia with a neurofunctional flavour and they emphasise only some elements of the neurofunctional approach. However, I suspect there may be a trend towards such theorising. I shall consider one prominent recent account shortly to illustrate the use of neurofunctional thinking. The present article does not assume the neurofunctional approach is necessarily the best, or only, way to study amnesia. The article is presented as an attempt to see the directions in which the neurofunctional philosophy might lead.

RELATIONAL PROCESSING BY THE HIPPOCAMPAL REGION: A PARTIALLY NEUROFUNCTIONAL ACCOUNT

I shall argue that the recent model by Eichenbaum, Otto, and Cohen (1994) can be considered *partially* neurofunctional. Indeed, in the title of their article the authors stress "two functional components of the hippocampal memory system", although this also shows that such theories are usually presented as an attempt to account for the functioning of a particular brain region rather than amnesia *per se*. The essence of the neurofunctional approach is to stress the need for theorising about the processing operations of brain regions and circuits rather than for theorising about neuropsychological syndromes. I shall concentrate on Eichenbaum et al.'s model because I think it is a useful view of hippocampal processing (similar to several others) and it can serve to show how a neurofunctional approach might profitably reorient our approach to amnesia research. Research addressing relational processing also illustrates the need for precise models of the behaviours in question—the other theme addressed in this article.

The two functions proposed by Eichenbaum et al. were the intermediate-duration storage of information in the parahippocampal region (comprising perirhinal, parahippocampal, and entorhinal cortices) and *relational processing* in the hippocampal formation (comprising the dentate gyrus, hippocampal subfields, subiculum, and fornix), with the latter dependent on the former but not *vice versa*. The argument that relational processing depends on intermediate-term memory follows from logical considerations. If (as Eichenbaum et al. argue) a currently processed item of information is to be relationally processed with another item in memory, then some kind of memory buffer must output the retrieved information upon which such processing is to be carried out.

Relational processing is used for the extraction of higher-order relations between single items. For example, a stimulus comprising two spatially organised components (AB), and another stimulus with the same components in a different spatial organisation (BA), can be treated as two separate stimuli. Alternatively, they may be seen as related exemplars of a common stimulus (A) in different arrangements with an irrelevant contextual component (B). If both stimuli are interpreted as versions of the component A, then a kind of higher-order relationship between AB and BA may have been established.

Eichenbaum and his colleagues (Eichenbaum, Fagan, Mathews, & Cohen, 1988; Eichenbaum, Mathews, & Cohen, 1989) used an odour-discrimination procedure with the structure of the AB/BA pairings just described. In this task rats were reinforced for a response that was spatially compatible with the position of component A when either of the odour pairs AB or BA were presented. Detailed probe testing revealed that the control rats behaved as if they were extracting a relational structure across AB and BA pairs (although other interpretations are possible; see Pickering, 1994). Fornix-sectioned rats were also able to learn some of these discrimination problems quite well, but their detailed behaviour under probe testing suggested that they learned the discriminations in a qualitatively distinct way. The lesioned animals did not appear to have extracted the relationship between the AB and BA odour pairings; rather, they treated each odour pair as a separate stimulus. As a result the lesioned animals did not appreciate the significance of the A component, and thus were unable to respond to novel probes AD and DA (where A once again indicated the appropriate spatial position for the response) at above chance levels.

In summary, relational processing allows different single items to be treated as exemplars of the same class of related items and thus receive the same response. This process allows categorical clustering of stimuli, leads to a reduction in memory and attentional load, and enables the efficient and flexible generalisation of existing responses to novel items.

Eichenbaum et al.'s ideas stop short of the strong neurofunctional perspective described in this paper. Before considering where these differences lie, we must address the critical stage in which (sets of) tasks are designed to measure specific processes. I have shown (Pickering, 1994) that two severe medial temporal lobe amnesics performed a visual-discrimination analogue of the Eichenbaum odour-discrimination tasks in much the same way as normal controls or Eichenbaum's control rats, dealing very flexibly with the novel probe stimuli. It can plausibly be argued, however, that the tasks were being accomplished via non-relational means in these cases (see Pickering, 1994). If one makes such an argument one enters a circular logic in which relational processing is invoked only on the occasions when the hippocampal subjects are showing impairments on the tasks, thus inoculating the hypothesis from refutation. In the absence of knowing when (or even if) relational processing will be employed on a particular task, the original evidence in favour of the relational processing model must also be seriously devalued. Eichenbaum et al.'s observations of qualitative differences between normal and fornix-sectioned rats are not in question (and remain to be explained), but the suggestion that the differential use of relational processing underpins the behavioural observations is seriously weakened. It should also be reiterated that Eichenbaum et al.'s model is far from unique in experiencing these difficulties. In my view, amnesia research must look for the theoretical tools that can reduce such quibbles concerning the means by which a task can be accomplished. The present paper will try to illustrate that neural network modelling may be one such tool.

Eichenbaum et al.'s model departs from the neurofunctional approach in at least two ways. They appear to see the relational processing executed by the hippocampal formation as specific to memory. Their argument that relational processing of information depends on the intermediate-term storage of the information concerned makes this clear. At no point do they consider whether tasks without a memory load might depend on relational processing. As they have described it, however, it appears that relational processing should be critically involved in a range of mental activities (e.g. reasoning from currently available, rather than retrieved, information) outside the memory domain. The framing of their model would thus seem to imply that other brain structures (not usually damaged in amnesics) execute relational processing in these non-mnemonic cases, but when relational processing is applied to information retrieved over an intermediate-term period, the hippocampus takes on this responsibility. This may well be correct. The neurofunctional approach, as described earlier, would be concerned in addition to explore the more parsimonious view that all forms of relational processing may be discharged via a common neural substrate. If this substrate is the hippocampal formation then amnesics with damage restricted to that region should fail to achieve relational processing in test situations without a memory load.

The neurofunctional viewpoint would therefore encourage the use of a wider range of methods for testing the theory than the more traditional, memory-specific, view. One well-known test which might depend on relational processing (under conditions of relatively low memory load) is the Wisconsin Card-Sorting Test (WCST). Subjects have to relate the stimulus features of the to-be-sorted card to those of the "key cards" with which a match must be made. The cards have to be seen as exemplars of a common category (e.g. green cards) by ignoring other stimulus features (the numbers of elements and their shape) in much the same way that Eichenbaum et al.'s animals appear to have interpreted the AB and BA odour-pairs as exemplars of the significant odour (e.g. A) in the presence of an irrelevant feature (odour B). It is therefore interesting to note that, although some medial temporal lobe amnesics can perform the WCST normally, patients with complex partial seizures of temporal lobe origin show significantly increased perseveration on this task (Hermann, Wyler, & Richey, 1988).

Another divergence from the neurofunctional view is apparent in Eichenbaum et al.'s (1994, p.450) treatment of the widely-acknowledged "effects of hippocampal system damage on behaviours that are only indirectly related to learning and memory, including studies on orientation, distraction, exploration, motor patterns, operant schedules, [and] emotion". They ignore these effects by making the usual assumption (1994, p.450) "that changes in these behaviours after hippocampal system damage are either a consequence of amnesia or an indirect result of disconnections of the limbic system that have non-mnemonic *as well as* mnemonic effects' [emphasis added]. On grounds of parsimony again, one might prefer a neurofunctional account in which some of the mnemonic and non-mnemonic effects of the lesions could be understood in terms of disturbances to a common set of processing elements. As has already been noted, one might then profit from a theoretical integration between the study of amnesia, clinical anxiety states, and schizophrenia, in which disturbances to similar brain regions are clearly implicated (Gray, 1982; Gray et al., 1991). McNaughton (1994) makes a similar criticism of Eichenbaum et al.'s theory.

I hope that the background issues, exemplified through the preceding discussion of the work of Eichenbaum et al., are clearly established. If so, the exploration of the neurofunctional approach can begin in earnest. The remainder of this paper applies a neurofunctional approach to the issue of stimulus representation. This issue is naturally approached in a neurofunctional way, because stimulus representations, although necessary but not sufficient for memory functioning, are used in a wide range of tasks outside the mnemonic domain.

It is likely to be adaptive for humans, and indeed other mammals, to be able to respond to the information conveyed by the elements of the current stimulus array both when considered separately and when combined as a whole unit. We shall see later that formal studies of human category learning reinforce this commonsense viewpoint, and recent work by Nosofsky and Kruschke in particular has emphasised the importance of representations of whole stimulus exemplars. Clearly, exemplar representations have strong links with the kinds of episodic memory function typically impaired in amnesic patients. In this paper I shall try to combine the ideas emerging from the study of category learning, with some suggestions about stimulus representation that emerge from a consideration of the functioning of mesolimbic dopamine system. As this part of the basal ganglia interacts intimately with the hippocampus, implications for the behaviour of human amnesic patients may again follow naturally. I shall start with category learning.

EXEMPLAR-BASED ACCOUNTS OF CATEGORY LEARNING: THE ALEX MODEL

Two opposing ideas have dominated theories of human category learning in recent decades: one idea (e.g. Rosch, 1975) argues that categories are built up by abstracting and storing a representation of a category *prototype* from the experiences with individual members of the category; the other idea (e.g. Medin & Shaffer, 1978) suggests that a representation of each individual category *exemplar* is stored and argues that the statistical properties of this ensemble of stored exemplars is responsible for the features of human category learning. Exemplar (or instance) models are currently very popular, and have been extended to other bodies of data in cognitive psychology (see Logan, 1988, for an instance-based account of the development of skilled performance).

Some authors, however, have challenged the value of the prototype/exemplar distinction (e.g. Barsalou, 1990), while others have stressed the unavoidable contribution of abstraction processes in exemplar models (Medin & Florian, 1992). Despite these cautionary voices one exemplar-based account has, as noted earlier, proved remarkably successful in explaining human category learning: Nosofsky's (1986, 1987) generalisation of Medin and Shaffer's (1978) *context model*. This formal psychological theory has been implemented as the ALCOVE/ALEX neural network by Kruschke (1992, 1993; Kruschke & Erickson, 1994; Nosofsky & Kruschke, 1992). Much of the rest of this paper will be concerned with suggestions for a biologically plausible and neurally mapped implementation of some of the features of this network. By rendering the ideas in an explicit biological context I hope to be able to make predictions for the performance of amnesic subjects on category learning and related tasks.

A number of key principles have been argued (see Kruschke, 1993) to underlie the success of the ALEX model, particularly relative to other models (such as standard backpropagation networks; Rumelhart, Hinton, & Williams, 1986) in which some of these features are absent or critically different. First, the network has a discrete neural unit representing each of the exemplars encountered during learning, with each exemplar representation encoding the position of the exemplar in a multidimensional psychological space (see later for details). Second, each active exemplar representation is gradually associated with a category node, via a delta (error-correcting) rule ensuring competition between weights connecting activated units. Third, the network architecture is a typical feedforward network (a layer coding the incoming stimulus connected to a layer of ''hidden'' exemplar representation nodes connected in turn to a layer of category nodes), with the weights of the network being adjusted via the familiar backpropagation of error from the category nodes towards the input layer. However, a fourth more unusual aspect of this model is the attentional weighting of the input pathways from the stimulus coding to the exemplar representations. These attentional weights, also learned by a backpropagated delta rule, reflect the relative importance of each of the stimulus dimensions for the learning task concerned. A fifth feature, a subsequent modification to the model (Kruschke & Erickson, 1994), involved the addition of a rule-encoding (prototype) pathway linking the same stimulus input to the same category nodes in parallel to the standard exemplar-based feedforward route. The interaction between these two routes was controlled by a competitive gating node.

We shall consider the way in which some of these features enable the ALEX model to capture human performance so well. I shall begin by filling in considerable detail about the role of exemplar representations. The level of detail is needed so that the importance and remarkable predictive accuracy of the ALEX model can be fully appreciated. However, the possible relevance of powerful exemplar models to amnesia is summarised first in the following simple argument: exemplar representations for encountered items, e.g. within a category learning task, would naturally be formed within any episodic memory system that stored each distinct item as a separate memory event. If the brain is equipped with an episodic memory storage system, then it would be parsimonious for the brain to recruit this memory store in tasks requiring the use of exemplar representations (examples of such tasks will be given later). It is quite commonly claimed (e.g. Rolls, 1989) that the hippocampus may be the site of an episodic memory store. These converging arguments would therefore suggest that exemplar representations may be encoded within the hippocampus, and exemplar representations may therefore be unavailable to patients with amnesia resulting from damage to the hippocampus or related structures. If models using exemplar representations can give precise accounts of performance on certain tasks, then the behaviour of some amnesic patients may be quite precisely predicted. I hope that this promise of rich theoretical pickings may sustain the reader, who may be impatient to see the implications for amnesia, through the unavoidable detail in the following sections.

THE SIGNIFICANCE OF EXEMPLAR REPRESENTATIONS: SPEED OF LEARNING AND PATTERN SEPARATION

The first advantage of an exemplar memory system may be speed of learning. A system that stores memories for individual learning episodes must have the capability to learn fast, often in a single trial, in order to represent each learning experience before the occurrence of the next related (but episodically distinct) experience. Other learning mechanisms, elsewhere in the brain, may acquire new information more gradually. In many learning situations, a mixture of fast and slow learning mechanisms may cooperate to optimise performance.

Hippocampal amnesics, in these situations, may lack a contribution from exemplar memory and would therefore be forced to rely on slow learning exclusively. This suggestion appears consistent with the very slow, yet robust, new learning demonstrated by amnesics in some situations (e.g. Glisky, Schacter, & Tulving, 1986).

In order to develop a proper set of exemplar representations the system has to achieve *pattern separation.* This term refers to the ability of the system to map very similar input patterns onto different output neurons (or, more generally, onto orthogonal patterns of output firing). Rolls (1989) has built an eloquent case that the internal architecture of the hippocampus is ideally suited for pattern separation and hence for episodic storage, and he offered an outline of a neural network implementation.

Pattern separation leads directly to a major advantage during new learning: the use of exemplar representations can substantially reduce interference. Imagine one has already formed a representation of stimulus exemplar A and associated this with a particular response. Then a new stimulus exemplar (B) is presented; this has many overlapping features with A but requires a different response. Consider two things that would happen if the stimulus representation for A were to be activated by B. First, the response associated with stimulus A would be activated and this could proactively interfere with acquisition of a different response for stimulus B. Second, the representation for A would be overwritten so that it would now code the properties of stimulus B (or a composite of B and A) instead of those of stimulus A. This would be a retroactive interference effect. These sources of interference would be avoided by a pattern separation mechanism that prevented stimulus B from activating of the representation for stimulus A.

Many types of neural networks, including the widely used backpropagation (BP) models, suffer from catastrophic levels of interference—unlike human subjects—due to a lack of pattern separation (McCloskey & Cohen, 1989; Ratcliff, 1990). Exemplar representations improve a network's pattern separation capabilities and so reduce interference. This is one of the key advantages of the ALEX model relative to BP models. The loss of an episodic exemplar representation system, as I have suggested might be occurring in hippocampal amnesia, would naturally lead to an increase in interference. Mayes, Pickering, and Fairbairn (1987) argued similarly that a loss of the modulatory influence of episodic memory might explain amnesic patients' increased susceptibility to interference under certain conditions. Subsequently, and independently, Baddeley and Wilson (1994; Wilson, Baddeley, Evans, & Shiel, 1994) have also stressed the value of episodic memory for interference reduction and they have proposed a rehabilitation strategy for amnesic patients based on these arguments.

Total pattern separation is neither easy to achieve nor desirable. It would imply no generalisation across closely related exemplars. The success of the

ALEX model in explaining aspects of human category learning critically depends on a *limited* degree of cross-exemplar generalisation. The limits on generalisation can be seen in the activation of a stored exemplar representation by a test stimulus. Activation in ALEX is a sharply decreasing (typically exponential) function of the *psychological distance* between the test item and the exemplar coded in the representation. The psychological distance between two stimuli is simply a metric inversely expressing the degree to which a subject would rate the two stimuli as similar. The exponential generalisation function means that a test stimulus will significantly activate the representations of only those stored exemplars that are close (similar) to it.

ALEX relies on these generalisation gradients to classify novel stimulus exemplars. In training, each exemplar representation becomes associated with a specific category. Categorisation decisions for a test item reflect the resulting activations of stored exemplar representations. The total of the activations of the exemplar representations from one category (e.g. category "X"), relative to the overall activation of the stored exemplars from all categories, determines the probability of making a "category X" response.

An exemplar-based representation system with a limited degree of cross-exemplar generalisation may represent an effective trade-off between the benefits of generalisation against the costs of interference effects. In such a system the activation of the representation for stimulus A by stimulus B would only occur if B were very similar to A. Of course, when A and B are very similar it is unlikely that the two stimuli would require different responses. The interference costs in this case are thus likely to be incurred only infrequently.

THE IMPORTANCE OF EXEMPLAR MAPS IN THE ALEX MODEL

The similarity (psychological distance) relations between stored exemplars can be described as constituting an *exemplar map*. The emphasis on exemplar maps in the ALEX model highlights the awkward questions concerning the psychological similarity between two stimuli; such questions are implicit in the stimulus coding schemes of all neural net models. In such models, one must decide how to code stimuli in the input layer of the neural net. One can do this only by assuming how any similarity in the physical stimuli being processed will be reflected in the similarity of their input neural activity patterns. The ALEX model finesses the uncertainties that surround such assumptions by empirically estimating the psychological distances between stimuli directly. As described earlier, the distances then specify the patterns of hidden node (exemplar representation) activation produced by similar stimuli.

How can the exemplar map be empirically estimated for the stimuli to be used in, say, a category learning experiment? The simplest method is to carry out separate studies (using similar subject samples) of the similarity ratings for each pairwise combination among the stimuli to be used in the learning experiment. Shin and Nosofsky (1992) and Kruschke (1993) provide examples of this approach. The similarity data are fitted statistically by multidimensional scaling (MDS) techniques to reveal the psychological distances—the exemplar map—between the stimuli. These parameters are then fixed for the application of the ALEX model (or one of its earlier variants) to the categorisation data using the generalisation gradient and category decision rules discussed earlier. The fits to the category data are very good (see Shin & Nosofsky, 1992; Kruschke, 1993). It is impressive that the same scaling solution that was estimated for similarity ratings can provide an excellent fit to the category learning performance.

Another approach to the estimation of the exemplar map has been to record the confusion matrix produced while subjects learn to identify each exemplar uniquely. An example of a stimulus identification study is provided by Nosofsky's (1987) work with Munsell colours. He used 12 Munsell variants on a single (reddish) hue; Munsell colours within a single hue are designed to vary along two other measured psychophysical parameters: brightness and saturation. Nosofsky tested one group of undergraduate subjects for their ability to learn to identify the 12 colours (via arbitrary number labels). Across the trials of this task, he recorded the confusion matrix of identification errors. Nosofsky incorporated MDS techniques within a larger model of the identification learning processes, and fitted the model against the confusion matrix. The scaling solution suggested that the colours varied on two dimensions: after appropriate rotation one dimension was akin to the physical brightness dimension, and one was akin to the physical saturation dimension. Confirming the classic Munsell results obtained with different methods (Nickerson, 1936), Nosofsky showed that, in determining psychological distances, two units on the scale of physical saturation were equivalent to one unit on the scale of physical brightness. The psychological maps for the classic Munsell solution and that obtained by Nosofsky are shown in Fig. 1, upper panel.

The full model explained between 97.5 and 99.7% of the variance across the twelve stimulus items over the three blocks of colour identification learning. The other important data from Nosofsky's study were obtained from further subjects who learned to categorise some, or all, of the same 12 colour items into pairs of categories. He used six different types of category structures, including NLS problems. Two of the category structures he used are illustrated in the lower panels of Fig. 1. Using the same scaling solution as emerged from stimulus identification learning, a version of ALEX accounted for the subjects' performance extremely well (see Nosofsky & Kruschke, 1992, Fig. 6). In fact, it was possible, even with a simpler precursor of ALEX, to explain between 97.1% and 99.7% of variance in categorisation performance across items depending on the type of category structure (Nosofsky, 1987; Table 5). Clearly, ALEX and related exemplar models do an excellent job in capturing category

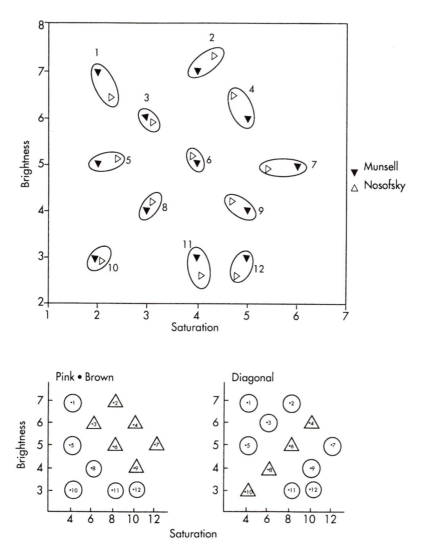

FIG. 1. *Upper panel:* The psychological map of the twelve Munsell colour stimuli used by Nosofsky (1987). The map was derived by fitting a multidimensional scaling solution to the confusion matrix of errors obtained from subjects attempting to learn to identify each colour by an arbitrary numerical label. Note the close correspondence between Nosofsky's scaling solution and the classic Munsell solution (Nickerson, 1936). Note also the fact that the psychological map has involved a rescaling from the psychophysical colour parameters; stimuli that differ by two saturation units are as discriminable as stimuli that differ by one brightness unit. *Lower panels:* The same stimuli (plotted now in terms of the psychophysical colour parameters) are shown as they were used for category learning experiments by Nosofsky (1987). Circles denote stimuli in one category; triangles denote stimuli in the other category. Two different category assignments are depicted with the names assigned by Nosofsky (1987).

learning. It is important, however, to consider whether other kinds of model might fare as well.

Learning tasks that can be solved only by the simultaneous use of more than one stimulus dimension are referred to as *condensation* tasks. Such tasks may be contrasted with *filtration* tasks for which a single stimulus dimension is sufficient for perfect categorisation (see Kruschke, 1993). The ability of human subjects to learn condensation tasks implies the use of representations that also condense across several stimulus elements. ALEX employs exemplar representations for this condensation function, but other neural net models suggest alternative types of representation.

COMPARING ALEX WITH OTHER MODELS OF CATEGORISATION

A major impetus to the recent explosion of neural network models was the development of a learning mechanism (backpropagation) which could provide the hidden representations needed to solve certain classes of condensation category learning tasks (Rumelhart et al., 1986). Technically, these problems are referred to as *non-linearly separable* (NLS). Although the hidden representations of standard backpropagation (BP) networks allow NLS problems to be learned, they always lead to slower learning relative to linearly separable (LS) problems. Human subjects, by contrast, can sometimes learn NLS problems faster than LS problems (Medin & Schwanenflugel, 1981). ALEX depends specifically on its use of exemplar nodes as hidden units to capture this effect (Kruschke, 1993).

The comparison with other models is most easily made for the extended version of ALEX considered by Kruschke and Erickson (1994). I have already noted that, in the extended model, the exemplar representation pathway is supplemented by an element-based pathway with which it is in competition. Learning based on individual elements within a stimulus array can be thought of as conducive to rule-based learning ("if the stimuli are blue then they are in category A"). Moreover, element-based learning allows the system to retain some category learning abilities in the absence of exemplar representations; it clearly may also be more relevant to filtration-type, rather than condensation-type problems. Several other contemporary models of categorisation emphasise dual pathways for stimulus–response linkage. A generalised representation of various "dual-route" categorisation models is depicted in Fig. 2, and this figure may be a useful starting point for comparisons between ALEX and other contemporary models. If the figure were used to depict the extended ALEX model, then pathway Y_1 would be the standard ALEX pathway using hidden exemplar representations and Y_2 would be the additional element-based pathway.

The comparison of models is also facilitated by considering further evidence which may support the earlier contention that ALEX's exemplar representation

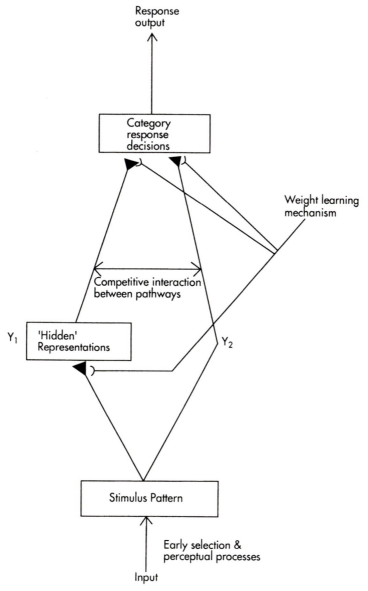

FIG. 2.   A generalised representation of category learning in which there are two pathways Y_1 and Y_2 between the pre-processed stimulus code and the category response nodes. Y_1 is an indirect pathway involving the participation of hidden representations; Y_2 is a direct pathway. There may be some kind of explicit competitive mechanism between the pathways, or it may arise indirectly through the nature of the weight-learning mechanism. Filled triangles represent modifiable synapses. In the text, various theoretical accounts are mapped onto this Figure at the levels of both proposed mechanisms and brain structures involved.

system may be localised in the hippocampus. Rudy and Sutherland (1989) have studied the learning of a NLS problem (negative patterning) in the rat, and claimed that the ability to acquire negative patterning was abolished by hippocampal system damage while the ability to acquire simple discriminations was left unimpaired. Rudy and Sutherland's finding is consistent with the role of exemplar representations in the (sometimes relatively rapid) acquisition of NLS learning problems, particularly when this result is taken in conjunction with the plausible involvement of the hippocampus in the development of exemplar representations. In Fig 2, therefore, we might tentatively map pathway Y_1 as involving the hippocampus. The result of Rudy and Sutherland also suggests the first prediction of the current paper: *(i) amnesic patients with damage localised to the hippocampus proper should fail on category learning (and related) tasks that depend on exemplar representations.* Put another way, such patients should be able to achieve only those kinds of learning that can be achieved via the non-exemplar pathway (Y_2 in Fig. 2). Later I shall suggest some ways to try to test this general prediction.

Although the replicability of Rudy and Sutherland's findings has been questioned (Davidson, McKernan, & Jarrard, 1993), another neural network (Schmajuk & DiCarlo, 1992) has been developed to account for the negative patterning data, and is also able to account for a number of other classical conditioning phenomena reasonably well. In this model, the authors try to develop a biologically plausible version of backpropagation in which a separate circuit is dedicated to computing the error-signal to be used in weight learning. Schmajuk and DiCarlo's model also fits closely to the framework of Fig. 2, involving two pathways, one direct and one via a set of units coding hidden representations. In essence, their model is like a standard BP network with the input and output layers connected directly, as well as via the hidden units. Schmajuk & DiCarlo also proposed a neural mapping for their model, in which the hidden units on pathway Y_1 are cortically localised. The hippocampus is also given a pivotal role; it is the proposed site of the error computation. Despite the different localisation of the hidden units, Schmajuk and DiCarlo's model is similar to the present account because it is suggested that stimulus-to-hidden-unit learning requires the involvement of the hippocampus. Thus hippocampal lesions are predicted to impair tasks (such as NLS learning problems) that depend on the hidden units.

The differences from the present model once again derive from the nature of the hidden unit representations. Schmajuk and DiCarlo refer to these units as coding *configural associations* between elements of the input stimuli. Sutherland and Rudy (1989) regard the hippocampus as critical for the formation of these kinds of association. Several other authors (e.g. Gluck, 1991; Pearce, 1994) have also stressed the importance of configural representations in a variety of human and animal learning phenomena. What are configural representations? As an example, when one sees a red circle one can consider it as a stimulus with a particular feature-value (red), or as a combination (i.e. a configuration) of specific colour and shape attributes which are processed and represented indivisibly. Clearly, if one has a representation of a whole stimulus exemplar one also has a type of configural representation for that stimulus. It is therefore suggested, in this paper, that an episodic memory system provides exemplar representations for stimuli and these representations are (one of) the principal means by which stimuli are treated as configurations of their constituent elements.

Although configural stimuli and exemplar representations obviously have a lot in common, there are clear differences in the operation of the hidden units subserving them. In the Schmajuk and DiCarlo BP model the hidden units, as a complete set, serve the role of coding for configural associations, although there are a large number of possible ways (reflecting different random starting weights and training orders) in which particular stimulus combinations may become mapped onto a particular hidden unit. In fact, it is unlikely that a particular unit will code for the particular configuration of stimulus elements present in a specific exemplar. I have already noted that BP networks suffer from inadequate pattern separation (leading to catastrophically high levels of retroactive interference; McCloskey & Cohen, 1989; Ratcliff, 1990) and relative slowness of learning of some NLS problems. These problems stem from the nature of the hidden units that are developed (Kruschke, 1992, 1993). Because it is a BP model, these problems are thus likely to be inherent in the Schmajuk and DiCarlo model too.

One can also fit another major model (the *configural cue* model; Gluck, 1991; Gluck & Bower, 1988) within the framework of Fig. 2. In a typical coding scheme (see Gluck, 1991) a neural unit that encoded the configuration of red colour and circular shape would fire in an all-or-none fashion only if both features were present. There would also be single-feature units which would fire for any red stimulus or any circular stimulus respectively. Therefore, we might localise the configural units as hidden representations at Y_1 firing in response to combinations of features present in the single-feature coding at X. This scheme can learn some NLS problems faster than some LS problems but the detailed fit to the human data is not very close (Gluck, 1991). A detailed comparison of the fits of ALEX and the configural cue model across a variety of tasks (Kruschke, 1992) favoured ALEX. Comparisons with other models (see Kruschke, 1993) were also favourable.

The exemplar map in the ALEX model seems to confer considerable advantages over rival models. However, a major problem for the ALEX model is that it has no learning mechanism by which the exemplar representations are acquired. Rather, the representations are assumed *a priori* and then learning of the associations between activated representations and correct category responses is explicitly modelled. This criticism also applies to the configural units used in the configural cue model. We must therefore consider whether a biologically plausible neural network could lead to the learning of such an exemplar map.

LEARNING A MAP OF EXEMPLAR REPRESENTATIONS

A major advantage of the Schmajuk and DiCarlo model is that it has an actual learning mechanism by which the hidden representations may be developed. Unfortunately, this model may lack the required pattern separation properties. The model proposed by Rolls (1989), noted earlier, both has a learning mechanism and achieves good pattern separation. However, it appears that this model does not produce the pattern of limited cross-exemplar generalisation that is the basis of an exemplar map.

A remarkable type of neural network—the Kohønen map (Kohønen, 1984; Ritter & Kohønen, 1989)—may be able, however, to provide a learning mechanism, pattern separation, and the relevant mapping properties. In essence a Kohønen network takes a series of stimulus inputs and maps them onto a set of hidden units, often arranged in a two-dimensional lattice. Each stimulus pattern maximally activates a single unit in the lattice while activating the surrounding units more weakly (as a decreasing function of distance across the lattice). The present paper proposes that each of the "maximal activation" nodes may be taken as equivalent to the exemplar nodes of the ALEX model. The analogy seems plausible given that the main property of the Kohønen network is that similar stimulus patterns, after a phase of lattice stabilisation, eventually activate units that are close to one another in the lattice. The lattice of a Kohønen network is thus a map of the psychological distances between the inputs learned. For example, Ritter and Kohønen (1989) showed how a stimulus coding for a series of animals (in terms of binary input nodes for size, along with various physical attributes and behaviours) led to a Kohønen map in which the lattice unit maximally responsive to the input pattern for horse, was close to that for zebra, and both these units were far from those for owl and eagle, which were in turn quite close to one another.

A test of the Kohønen network would be afforded by seeing what kind of exemplar map such a network would create for the 12 Munsell colours used by Nosofsky (1987). To do this it was first necessary to consider what inputs to the Kohønen net would be used. Before entering a central system that can form representations of incoming stimuli, primary perceptual processes will "transduce" the incoming physical stimulation into a pattern of neural activity at the entry point to the central representation system. Neuroscientists have little idea of this process in higher organisms and so one does not know the type of neural pattern for which a representation is to be developed. This is the basic difficulty that ALEX avoids by estimating empirically, for each stimulus studied, the relative activations of the representations themselves. One goal of the simulation presented here is to try to fill the step being avoided in the ALEX model. Hence, the incoming neural signal was coded in as simple a fashion as possible. Each stimulus was represented by the activations of just two neurons, one coding for brightness and the other coding for saturation. Moreover, the activation of each neuron was taken to be a linear function of the actual psychophysical value of the stimulus on the relevant dimension. The use of such a strongly localised network model is a gross simplification but it is assumed that the behaviour of a single neuron will be qualitatively similar to that of a population of neurons each obeying the same network equations; this is a common assumption (Anderson & Bjork, 1994, p.313). The assumptions about the coding of the stimulus dimensions were also made for theoretical neutrality, in the sense that they imply that the "perceptual transduction" of physical stimulus inputs into neural code is *independent and equally efficient* for both stimulus brightness and saturation.

A Kohønen network is an *unsupervised* learning system: it finds the psychological distances between stimuli without using reinforcing or tutoring signals to drive the learning. It would be possible to bolt on an associative mechanism to the lattice nodes, so that not only would the map form but stimulus identification (or categorisation) responses could be acquired. Direct fitting to Nosofsky's data would then be possible. However, I have suggested that the topography of the Kohønen map represents the exemplar map that underlies both identification and category learning. The distance relations inherent in the stable Kohønen lattices should therefore be comparable to those inherent in the underlying scaling solution that Nosofsky fitted to his data. This provides an easy way to test the mapping properties of the Kohønen net.

I therefore simulated unsupervised Kohønen map formation for Nosofsky's Munsell colour stimuli (coded as described earlier). Further details of the simulation are presented in Appendix 1, and a resultant stable lattice for a single "network subject" is shown in Fig. 3, upper panel. (One network subject is a single run of the simulation with random starting weights.) Figure 3 shows that, as is required for an exemplar map, each of the 12 stimuli produces its maximal activation as a distinct locus in the lattice. In order to maximise correspondence with ALEX, the activation of lattice node N by a particular familiar stimulus (which produces its maximum activation at lattice node M) was modelled as an exponentially decreasing function of the Euclidean distance between nodes N and M. Apart from this, no other features of the simulation were chosen to help the Kohønen map resemble the map underlying the performance of Nosofsky's subjects. The map formed by the Kohønen net simply reflects the way that its activation and learning rules extract the (statistical) relationships present in the stimulus input codes encountered. It is an empirical question as to whether the network will extract the same relationships as those extracted by human subjects.

By visual inspection one can compare the lattice of each network subject (e.g. Fig. 3, upper panel) with Nosofsky's scaling solution (Fig. 1). It can be easily

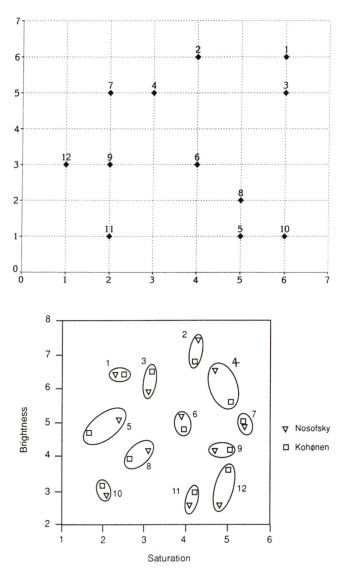

FIG. 3. *Upper panel:* A stable Kohønen lattice produced for one artificial subject in the simulation detailed in Appendix 1. The numbered diamonds highlight the nodes in the lattice that respond maximally to each of the Munsell colour stimuli depicted in Fig. 1. In the text it is suggested that Kohønen maps may represent a means by which the brain could develop a psychological exemplar map for a set of similar stimuli. *Lower panel:* A multidimensional scaling solution based on inter-stimulus distances present in the Kohønen lattices obtained for five artificial subjects such as the one shown in the upper panel of this Figure. Note the scaling solution inherent in the Kohønen lattices is, without any parameter fitting, close to the scaling solution that characterises the colour identification performance of Nosofsky's (1987) subjects.

274

seen that, although the lattice is rotated with respect to the scaling solution, each stimulus colour has similar "neighbourhood relations" in each figure. The nearest neighbours of Stimulus 1, for example, are Stimuli 2 and 3 in both figures, and Stimuli 11 and 12 are furthest away in the opposite corner of the graph space.

However, we need a more formal method to show that the psychological distances inherent in the Kohønen lattices are closely related to the distances of Nosofsky's scaling solution, and we need to show that the correspondence is true, not just for an individual resulting lattice, but for a composite lattice averaged across all network subjects. It is natural to do this using multi-dimensional scaling techniques very close to those used by Nosofsky to generate his original scaling solution. Using the Euclidean distances between the "maximal activation" nodes in the Kohønen lattices of five network subjects, I produced a multidimensional scaling solution (using INDSCAL; Kruskal & Wish, 1978).

How close are the two psychological maps? In Fig. 1, Nosofsky's solution has been rotated to show the close correspondence with the earlier Munsell solution. A similar rotation procedure for the Kohønen scaling solution was undertaken to show the correspondence with that obtained by Nosofsky. The result is depicted in the lower panel of Fig. 3. The correspondence between the Kohønen scaling solution and Nosofsky's solution is very close, the fit being as good as that between the Nosofsky and Munsell solutions. The fit of the Kohønen model is particularly compelling, as there was no attempt to find the parameters of the model sketched in Appendix 1 that would best fit Nosofsky's data; the values were genuinely the first that were tried. The very simple input coding scheme, discussed earlier, must also be remembered, and it remains to be seen whether the network is highly sensitive to the coding scheme used. (Very similar results were obtained with a Kohønen net in which the brightness of the stimulus was coded as a binary sequence in one set of nodes and saturation was similarly coded in a separate set of nodes. In both cases the number of bits set for each stimulus dimension was the same linear function of the psychophysical stimulus values.)

It is clear, then, that the Kohønen network is able to map the psychophysical stimulus "coordinates" of the Munsell colours onto a set of psychological coordinates that match the psychological coordinates underlying human stimulus identification and category learning. Both the exemplar maps reflect the fact that stimuli that differ by one unit of brightness are as discriminable as stimuli that differ by two units of saturation. In this light, the neutral input coding assumptions used with the Kohønen net become important: the map produced by the Kohønen net was achieved without any differences in the nature and/or efficiency of the perceptual processes transducing the physical stimulus parameters into a neural code. Work is underway to understand the Kohønen mapping process more fully but, in part, it reflects the properties of the whole cohort of stimuli being studied. Psychological studies measuring, and then modelling, the effects of changing the properties of the stimulus cohort will offer an even stronger test of the model's mapping capabilities.

In the context of the current paper we briefly consider the biological plausibility of Kohønen nets. Of course, most neural nets contain many implausible features within a framework loosely grounded in biology. It is therefore only the most highly implausible models that may be rejected on these grounds. Furthermore, given the suggested localisation of the exemplar representation system in the hippocampus proper, we should also note whether the architecture of this structure is at all suitable for developing a Kohønen map. The original formulation (Kohønen, 1984) was biologically based, arising from the typical lateral excitatory and inhibitory interactions between (cortical) neurons, often described by a "Mexican hat" function. The Mexican hat is so-named because there is a strong narrow excitatory activation zone, centred on the active neuron, surrounded by a weaker, but broader, inhibitory zone. Clearly, the abundance of collateral fibres in parts of the hippocampus (noted by Rolls in his model), may be well suited to this aspect of the Kohønen mapping process. At a more abstract level there is also some appeal to the idea that the hippocampus can form a psychological ("cognitive") map of a set of inputs to which it is exposed, given the strong historical precedents for viewing the hippocampus in this way (O'Keefe & Nadel, 1978). Most simulations of a Kohønen net adopt a "short-cut" algorithm to simplify implementation, and there are some serious questions about the extent to which the mapping properties are a product of the short-cut algorithm rather than the full, biologically inspired, lateral interaction model (Acker & Kurz, 1990). Nonetheless, the potential of the Kohønen model, demonstrated here, suggests that work concerned directly with its biological plausibility would be worthwhile.

The model schematised in Fig. 2 has three principal components: an exemplar representation system; an element-based representation system; and mechanisms for the interaction of the two. In the present paper, I have begun to develop the first third of the model in considerable depth. The storage of exemplar representations has been localised in the hippocampus, by which I mean the dentate gyrus, the hippocampal subfields, and the subiculum. Amnesia, resulting from damage to these structures, will be characterised by the inability to utilise exemplar representations in task performance. In the rest of the paper I will have space only to make some outline suggestions concerning the neural substrate and operation of element-based representations; detailed considerations of this system and its modes of interaction with the exemplar representation system will be presented elsewhere. However, in order to begin thinking about element-based representations, and to make detailed predictions for amnesic patients, further aspects of the exemplar system and its relationship to task performance must be considered first. I shall start with the inputs to, and outputs from, the proposed exemplar system; next the existing data on amnesic categorisation will be considered; and then finally the relationship between categorisation and recognition memory will be noted.

INPUTS TO THE HIPPOCAMPUS

In the primate brain, the perirhinal and parahippocampal cortices (PRPH) represent a major point of multimodal convergence in the stream of information processing that starts at primary sensory cortex. These multimodal neural codes are then passed to entorhinal cortex (and this constitutes the majority of entorhinal cortex input), which in turn provides the major source of hippocampal input. In terms of the model described earlier, the entorhinal cortex is taken to be the locus of the multimodal stimulus inputs to the hippocampal exemplar memory system. It is clear, then, that destruction of a large part of the entorhinal cortex should produce a set of memory deficits which include those that are found after damage restricted to the hippocampus proper. Entorhinal cortex, of course, projects to structures other than the hippocampus and so damage to this structure should produce a more extensive memory deficit than that resulting from hippocampal damage alone. It will be suggested later that other projections from entorhinal cortex will form from the inputs to the element-based representation pathway in Fig. 2.

In the current model, the large amount of processing that leads to neural codes in the entorhinal cortex is being taken for granted. Given the prior passage of the neural signals through sensory, unimodal, and then polymodal association cortices, this processing seems certain to encompass many perceptual and selective attentional processes. As with many other neural net models it is assumed (Houghton & Tipper, 1994, p.65) that the perceptual systems are "delivering up multiple object-based representations of the external world in parallel [and the] informational content of each object representation is bound together to form a unity distinct from other entities [taking] for granted that the [perceptual] system automatically attempts to organise spatio-temporally distributed features into objects on the basis of grouping (gestalt) principles". The current model assumes that the entorhinal cortex is in receipt of information pre-processed in this way.

When input derived from a single stimulus is processed in the current model, the input represents one of the object-based representations discussed earlier, and the unity of the perceptual object is achieved simply through the treatment of the input neurons (entorhinal cortex cells) as a coordinated assembly. All the neurons project to the same target neurons and all parts of this assembly are processed simultaneously under identical parameters. It is also assumed that the features of the stimulus object, although bound together in this way, can exert independent influences on target neurons. This is ensured by local feature coding within the input assembly: for the Munsell colours I used separate neurons to code for brightness and for saturation. Such an assumption is a gross simplification, but is one way of instantiating the idea that higher-order stimulus codes in the brain must at least partially preserve the independent content of their lower-order components.

OUTPUTS FROM THE HIPPOCAMPUS

The present paper has specified some computational goals and mechanisms for the hippocampal memory/representation system; it is clearly important to consider the output signals that result. The output from the hippocampus is predominantly via the subiculum from where the major bundle of efferent fibres—the fornix—arise. This output system projects to a wide range of cortical and subcortical structures, including feedback to the entorhinal cortex (which provides the major source of input to the hippocampal system) and the well-known pathways through anteroventral thalamus and hypothalamus (mammillary bodies) to cingulate cortex and on to motor and sensorimotor cortex.

The feedback route to the entorhinal cortex (which itself has feedback pathways to its input structures and so on) is widely presumed to offer a means whereby hippocampal processing may influence the neocortical regions from which the hippocampal inputs arise and where very long term memory storage is presumed to take place. In the current model, it is assumed (in line with the thinking of many other authors) that the hippocampal memory store is of intermediate duration, determined by the finite number of synapses available (see Rolls, 1989). Thus, the feedback output pathways would allow the hippocampal system to participate in the early stages of the development of more permanent memory stores. After this initial phase it is widely suggested that the ongoing modifications of older memories becomes progressively more independent of hippocampal involvement (e.g. see Squire, 1992). Recently, McClelland, McNaughton and O'Reilly (1995) have discussed possible mechanisms for this long-term disengagement of the exemplar memory system.

Another possible role for the feedback pathways could be to confer pattern completion properties on the relevant exemplar representational neurons in the hippocampus. From the way that exemplar representations were described earlier, it follows that a partial input cue, derived from a familiar past exemplar, could successfully activate the appropriate exemplar representation, but there is no mechanism for pattern completion of the missing parts of the input. Synaptic modifications (via standard pseudo-Hebbian learning mechanisms; see Appendix 1) in the feedback pathways might operate to ensure that each representation neuron stores a record of the input patterns that have previously led to its activation. Therefore, when activated by an incomplete pattern of ''bottom-up'' input firing, the activated representation provides ''top-down'' signals which can complete the input pattern. This kind of mechanism has been emphasised for many years by Grossberg (e.g. Carpenter & Grossberg, 1987). If this ''input completion effect'' were fed back to sensory cortex, then it might provide the basis for the experiential qualities of episodic memory (e.g. a feeling that one is almost re-perceiving the sensory aspects of the event concerned, even those parts not present in the retrieval cue).

Next, consider fornical outputs from the hippocampus via the mammillary bodies, mammillothalamic tract, and the anteroventral thalamus. One might simply suggest that active exemplar representation cells in the hippocampus itself may become associated, via these pathways, with response representations in prefrontal and motor cortices. In category learning, therefore, any associations between the exemplar representation and the category naming response might be mediated via these pathways. Damage to these pathways has been shown to be the most consistent component of diencephalic amnesia (Graff-Radford, Tranel, Van Hoesen, & Brandt, 1990; see also Mayes & Downes, this issue), and is consistent with the pathology of Korsakoff amnesics. Patients who are amnesic as a result of diencephalic (mammillothalamic) damage may therefore be unable to associate exemplar representations with responses, in contrast to patients with amnesia arising from damage to the hippocampus itself, who would be unable to form exemplar representations in the first place. In category learning tasks, for example, the fate of the two types of patient would be the same: they would be unable to perform normally in condensation category learning tasks in which control subjects typically employ exemplar representations. Amnesics' performance on such tasks would reflect the properties of the alternative element-based route depicted in Fig. 2. This might be a useful point at which to consider how amnesics actually perform in category learning tasks.

EXISTING DATA ON CATEGORY LEARNING BY AMNESICS

Knowlton and Squire (1993) studied the ability of a group of amnesic patients of mixed aetiology (including hippocampal and diencephalic amnesics) to learn new arbitrary category labels for sets of dot patterns. (Members of a category are formed by statistical perturbations applied to the prototype dot pattern on which that category is based.) The amnesics' performance was statistically unimpaired relative to controls. Knowlton and Squire concluded that category learning may be a form of habit learning subserved by a memory system that is independent of the explicit memory system compromised in amnesia. This general conclusion is at odds with the central argument of the current paper, namely that some category learning tasks are normally strongly dependent on the hippocampal memory system compromised in amnesia. How might this conflict be resolved?

Kolodny (1994) confirmed and extended Knowlton and Squire's findings for dot patterns in a further group of amnesics, but showed also that the same patients could not acquire the correct categorisations for the paintings of Italian Renaissance artists. Although these data are important in showing that amnesic patients cannot acquire all types of new category knowledge normally, they are of little additional value. Kolodny did not have a clear model of the processes at work in the two category learning tasks that he used and so he was forced to make the entirely *post hoc* suggestion that the contribution of episodic memory may be far more important in the categorisation of paintings than in the categorisation of dot patterns. The emptiness of this conclusion provides a compelling illustration of the need to choose and construct experimental tasks in accordance with an explicit theory.

In fact, Kolodny's conclusion was also ignoring the evidence from normal subjects concerning dot-pattern category learning. An exemplar-based model, a simpler precursor of the ALEX model, has proved remarkably successful in this task too, accounting for between 95 and 97% of the variance in subjects' performance across items, depending on the precise version of the model used (Shin & Nosofsky, 1992). In the current paper I have suggested that amnesics do not form, and/or cannot employ, exemplar representations. Their ability at dot-pattern classification would therefore depend on other available routes (see Fig. 2) for category learning. To pre-empt later discussion somewhat, I will argue that the element-based route of Fig. 2 operates to form representations of prototypical stimuli. It is therefore interesting that Shin and Nosofsky showed that a pure prototype model, while inferior to their pure exemplar model, was able to account for 83% of variance across items in dot pattern classification. It therefore follows that, if a small group of amnesic patients were relying on prototype information, and a small group of control subjects were relying largely on exemplar information, there would be unlikely to be sufficient statistical power to detect patient vs. control differences in the level of dot-pattern category learning. In line with this speculation, amnesics' dot pattern categorisation performance was numerically inferior to that of controls in all the published experiments (Knowlton & Squire, 1993; Kolodny, 1994).

A much more revealing experiment would be afforded by employing a categorisation task for which a pure prototype model produced a much poorer account of normal category learning. Classifying paintings may be just such a task, but it would probably be impossible to carry out an experiment to establish this *a priori*. Guidance on the selection of a possible task may come from an important paper by Nosofsky (1992). In this meta-analysis, he compared the ability of models to fit data gathered in a large number of published categorisation experiments. In many cases the exemplar model (a simple precursor of the ALEX model) was markedly superior to prototype models (a variety of alternative formulations of the prototype model were considered). For example, three of the six category structures used in Nosofsky's (1987) Munsell colour experiments were much more poorly modelled by a prototype model; in the other three the exemplar model was only slightly superior. We shall consider later how we might use this information to make the powerful prediction that amnesic patients should succeed on one category learning task while failing on another task employing the same stimulus materials and test procedures.

RELATING CATEGORY LEARNING AND RECOGNITION MEMORY

One other advantage of exemplar models is that they make possible an explicit link between categorisation performance and item recognition. If each exemplar used in category learning may be discretely represented, then recognition memory for test items might logically depend on accessing the same representations as those that underlie (the exemplar route to) categorisation performance. The present paper emphasises this argument by suggesting that the exemplar memory system is localised in the hippocampus, and we would expect damage to this structure to impair recognition memory for the specific category exemplars encountered during training. Indeed, both Knowlton and Squire (1993) and Kolodny (1994) reported that their amnesics, while performing within normal limits at dot-pattern category learning, were significantly impaired at recognising the specific training items used.

The formal modelling of dot pattern category learning by Shin and Nosofsky (1992) casts a clear light on these data. They modelled recognition of a test item in terms of the sum of the similarities of that item to each of the exemplars stored during training. If the sum exceeds a threshold then the test item will be "recognised". (Recall that ALEX, and closely related models, model categorisation decisions for a test item on the item's summed similarities to exemplars in one category relative to the summed similarities to exemplars in all the categories.) This recognition model means that false recognition would be likely to occur for a novel test item that is highly similar to several of the training exemplars. If the subject were limited to representations of just the prototypical (i.e. average) stimuli for each category then one can model item recognition using the sum of the similarities of the test item to each of the category prototypes. Shin and Nosofsky (1992) found that recognition memory across a range of test items was well predicted by the exemplar model (93% of variance explained), but very poorly predicted by the prototype model (the best-fitting model explained only 45% of the variance). Imagine that, for both category learning and recognition decisions, amnesic subjects were able to use only the prototypes formed during category training, rather than individually stored exemplars. This could therefore explain why recognition memory, but not category learning, was significantly impaired in the amnesic subjects studied by either Knowlton and Squire (1993) or Kolodny (1994).

In fact a detailed look at Shin and Nosofsky's modelling data is even more illuminating. When the recognition test item was a training item, the prototype model tended to predict recognition probabilities that were lower than the observed probability obtained from studies of healthy subjects. By contrast, when the recognition test item was a new item, even the previously unseen prototypes from which the training stimuli were generated, the prototype model predicted (false) recognition probabilities that exceeded those produced by healthy subjects. From this one could predict that amnesics, relative to healthy controls, would have a lower recognition hit rate for old training items and a higher false positive rate for new (untrained) items. Kolodny reported data relevant to this prediction; the hit rates for old items (amnesics 59%, controls 67%) and the false alarm rates for new items (amnesics 68.9%, controls 51.5%) were as predicted. False recognition was even more prevalent among the more prototypical novel items, and once again the amnesics exceeded the controls (73% vs. 63%).

I believe that this analysis of dot pattern category learning is very revealing. When the work was conducted in something of a theoretical vacuum, the authors were led to an erroneous conclusion: Knowlton and Squire (1993) argued that their data strongly implied the dissociation of category learning from episodic memory and therefore that the validity of exemplar models of categorisation was challenged. If these authors had been armed with a formal model of the tasks at hand, and the idea that amnesics (lacking episodic exemplar memory) would be forced to fall back on prototype representations, they would not have used dot-pattern categorisation at all. The residual strategy, putatively available to amnesic patients, has been shown to handle dot pattern category learning, but not item recognition, almost as well as the exemplar model. With an underlying formal model, the authors would have arrived at a more profitable choice of categorisation tasks for study. I shall suggest one such choice later.

EPISODIC FAMILIARITY/NOVELTY SIGNALS

The specifics of the modelling of item recognition, discussed earlier, also suggest that a different type of output needs to be read out from the exemplar representation system. I have noted that outputs specific to each representation can serve for associations with responses, but for item recognition Shin and Nosofsky employed a non-specific signal based on the sum of the activities of all the representations activated by a test item. A signal of this kind can be thought of as constituting a unidimensional scale of episodic familiarity (or its obverse, novelty). Recent evidence from healthy subjects, again based on a formal modelling approach, suggests that such a unidimensional scale might exist (Hintzman, Curran, & Caulton, 1995). A common scale of this kind, it was suggested, underpinned subjects' ability to compare the frequency of presentation of different kinds of stimulus material (words vs. pictures).

How could such an output signal be obtained from the Kohønen net model of exemplar representations? Areas of lattice could feed the activity levels of all the representations in that region into a common output pathway. The signal strength along that pathway would reflect episodic familiarity. For reasons beyond the scope of the present article, I believe that there may be benefits if this signal were inverted so that it reflects episodic novelty. This can easily be achieved if, for example, the summed activity reflecting episodic familiarity is used to inhibit a tonically active node. The novelty output from this latter node would therefore be reduced as the familiarity signal grew in strength (e.g. across repetitions). In ongoing work, I am exploring ways to model the process by which this episodic novelty signal might be converted into recognition responses.

How could the novelty signal be fed out from the brain's hippocampal exemplar system and to where might this signal project? One might suppose that this non-specific signal would be carried in a part of the fornical output from the subiculum (hippocampus) that is topographically distinct from that carrying the specific outputs used to bind particular exemplars to responses. Gray et al. (1991), in their model of schizophrenic symptoms, placed emphasis on the excitatory glutamatergic projection from subiculum to ventral striatum (nucleus accumbens), arguing that it conveys novelty information. In the rat this projection runs from the subicular cells bordering the hippocampal CA1 field, along the septal temporal axis and reaches the accumbens via the fornix (Groenewegen, Vermeulen-Van der Zee, te Kortschot, & Witter, 1987).

I have already argued that the mammillothalamic lesions, which are putatively responsible for diencephalic amnesia, would affect the patients' use of exemplar representations by preventing the association of these representations with responses. It is possible that these mammillothalamic lesions might leave the non-specific output intact, if this output is sent from the subiculum to the ventral striatum via the pathway just described. This would open up the possibility that some diencephalic amnesics might be able to compute overall episodic novelty normally, unlike amnesics with septohippocampal damage affecting the subiculo-accumbens output. If one could find a task that depended on the use of this non-specific episodic novelty signal then one would be able to test this idea in amnesics with appropriately localised lesions (verified by quality neuroimaging data). Hintzman et al.'s (1995) frequency judgement task might be appropriate: indeed, it is already known that Korsakoff (diencephalic) amnesics appear, unlike control subjects, to perform a similar frequency judgement task using the overall familiarity of the stimuli rather than more specific sources of information (Meudell, Mayes, Ostergaard, & Pickering, 1985). This effect would have been predicted by the preceding speculations. However, a later study showed that the similar results characterised a mixed-aetiology group of amnesics, some of whom were presumed to have hippocampal tissue damage (Mayes et al., 1989). Although this would not follow from the model, without quality neuroimaging data to determine lesion location accurately one cannot evaluate these data fully.

One can also glean clues for another relevant task, in a truly neurofunctional way, from Gray et al.'s model of schizophrenic symptoms. The task around which their model revolves is the animal conditioning task of latent inhibition (LI). LI refers to the loss of conditionability that occurs when a potential conditioned stimulus (CS) is repeatedly pre-exposed without consequence to the subject prior to the conditioning phase. In simple terms, some CS novelty appears to be required for conditioning to occur. However, LI is more than simple habituation of the potential CS because LI (but not habituation) depends on the episodic context (usually the animal's cage) in which the stimulus was pre-exposed (see Gray et al., 1991, for a review). Therefore, LI may specifically reflect a lack of *episodic* novelty of the CS.

This interpretation of LI is compatible with the earlier suggestion that the episodic novelty output from the hippocampal system may be transmitted along the subiculo-accumbens pathway. There is a great deal of evidence implicating this pathway in LI (see Gray, 1995, for a review). Importantly, neurotoxic destruction of the cells of the hippocampus, leaving fibres of passage (and the subiculo-accumbens output pathway) intact, did not abolish latent inhibition (Honey & Good, 1993). Instead, the context-sensitive nature of LI was lost, strengthening the view that hippocampal processing confers episodic specificity to the novelty signal being sent to the nucleus accumbens. A model of LI is being prepared elsewhere, and its careful application to the variety of LI procedures now available for testing human subjects (Lubow & Gewirtz, 1995) is planned. This may allow a task to be developed that could test the idea that some diencephalic amnesics, unlike hippocampal amnesics, may be normally sensitive to the non-specific episodic familiarity/novelty of a stimulus, and may therefore be able to show context-sensitive LI.

We are now in a position to consider the alternative element-based representational system of Fig. 2. In the following sections, I will argue that the representations of this alternative system are stored in the nucleus accumbens. It is therefore worth noting that the pathway just described (between the subiculum and the nucleus accumbens) might also provide one of the routes for the competitive interaction (see Fig. 2) between the alternative representational systems. Speculations on the nature of this interaction will be developed elsewhere. For understanding amnesia, the importance of the competitive interactions between representational systems has been emphasised by Eichenbaum et al.'s (1994) account of hippocampal system functioning (see Gluck, Myers, & Goebel, 1994, for a brief outline of a closely related neural network view).

AN OUTLINE OF AN ELEMENT-BASED
REPRESENTATIONAL SYSTEM

I have referred to the non-exemplar representational system, throughout this paper, as being "element-based". This name is intended to distinguish the fact that the exemplar pathway represents combinations of elements (stimulus features; multiple stimuli etc.) whereas the non-exemplar system has the capacity for basing its representation on specific elements from within the combinations experienced. A variety of alternative names would have served as well, particularly—as I have already intimated—referring to the non-exemplar representations as "prototypes". The prototyping property of this pathway comes from a consideration of the learning rules for synaptic modification.

A learning rule in a neural net model is a differential (or difference) equation which describes the change in a synaptic weight (efficiency) over time. A simple pseudo-Hebbian rule, which describes the change in the weight (Δw_{ij}) connecting a presynaptic terminal (i) with a post-synaptic cell (j), is given by the equation:

$$\Delta w_{ij} = (k_1 \times a_j \times a_i) - (k_2 \times a_j \times w_{ij})$$

where a_j is the post-synaptic activity, a_i is the presynaptic activity and k_1 and k_2 are constants. This equation contains two terms, one giving an increase in synaptic weight between an active post-synaptic cell and active afferent axons, the other giving a decrease in synaptic weight between an active post-synaptic neuron and an inactive afferent axon. There is physiological evidence for both these effects in the phenomena of long-term potentiation and associative long-term depression respectively (see Anderson & Bjork, 1994; Rolls, 1989, for references). This biological basis suggests that one might prefer this weight-learning rule to the more popular delta (error-correcting) rules which have no such physiological support.

For simplicity we can assume $k_1 = k_2 = k$, and the equation becomes:

$$\Delta w_{ij} = k \times a_j \times (a_i - w_{ij})$$

The equilibrium value of this equation (when there is no further weight change) occurs when the weight has reached a value equal to the activity on the input line (a_i). It can easily be shown that, across stimuli, for each input line separately, this rule will track the average value of the inputs associated with the post-synaptic cell. This learning rule thus extracts a prototype of the inputs that activate the post-synaptic cell and in so doing allows the element-based operation of this representational system. If all the stimuli activating the post-synaptic cell for one category are red, rather than blue, then the average values on the input lines coding for "redness" will be high and those for blue will be low. This will be reflected in the weights formed to the cell, and these weights will ensure in the absence of any other counterveiling features that all red stimuli will be assigned to the category concerned. This type of representation may also be seen as instantiating certain simple rules ("if it's red, then it's in category A").

It is important to appreciate that this prototyping action of the weight-learning rule can also lead to a failure of pattern separation. Imagine only one input pattern has been learned. A cell representing the particular input pattern in the manner described might be activated by the usual scalar product rule. This rule states that the net input to the cell is the scalar product of the input activity vector and the vector of synaptic weights connecting the input lines to the cell; and the activity of the cell is a monotonic function of the net input to the cell. Under this activation scheme, inputs similar (but not identical) to the previously learned input will activate the cell very strongly. As the inputs become less similar to the learned input, the activation remains quite strong (see Pearce, 1994); in other words, the generalisation gradient for the activation of the cell is much shallower than that described earlier for the exemplar system. The cell's "receptive field" of input patterns is therefore very large. Moreover, if a new pattern succeeds in activating the cell, and it is presented a large number of times, the synaptic weights to the cell will be driven towards the new input pattern and away from the previous pattern. The old learning will be overwritten, and catastrophic levels of interference will be observed.

In neural net models, with simple, physiologically reasonable learning rules, these characteristics are the norm. Special mechanisms are required to maintain pattern separation and to limit the extent of generalisation. The Kohønen model uses one set of such mechanisms because, as is shown in Appendix 1, it uses the same learning rule as that given earlier. Exemplar representations therefore constitute a more impressive achievement for a neural net model. This is why the present paper sets store by its demonstration that the Kohønen model appears to capture accurately the topography of the exemplar representations acquired and used by human beings who are learning to identify Munsell colours.

Standard prototype models assume that the subject forms a separate prototype for a category by abstracting an averaged representation of all the exemplars in that category. If all the exemplars of a category came to activate the same representational unit in the element-based system, then the learning rule discussed earlier would extract a prototype for the category concerned. However, given the differences in input pattern that might occur between prototypical exemplars and atypical exemplars within the same category, is it reasonable to expect that they would active the same representational unit and that the unit would be activated by no members of another category? A consideration of the supervised nature of new category learning suggests a way in which this might occur.

One way in which stimulus–response (S–R, or *habit*) learning may be viewed is as the gradual transfer of the control of response production. Responses are initially derived from internally generated intentions (based on schematic knowledge) and eventually may come almost entirely under the control of external stimuli (via specific learned associations). One can alternatively describe this shift as the change from controlled to automatic processing (see Logan, 1988). In a typical category learning experiment the subject usually has no specific prior knowledge on which the initial responses might be made, but has to begin a process of strategic guesswork that is gradually refined through trial-and-error. This early stage might be neurally modelled (see Fig. 4) via top-down projections from *planning/intention* (PI) centres which have the existing connections to enable the activation of appropriation populations of *executive* neurons. We are not presently concerned with the processes by which the PI centres have learned to enact particular plans in particular contexts. Presumably these processes depend heavily on schema formation. (For example, experience shows that healthy subjects, when told by an experimenter to respond to each stimulus by calling it ''category A'' or ''category B'', can draw on an acquired schema that enables them to confine themselves to saying ''A'' or ''B''.)

The specific executive neurons, activated by the intention to make a specific guess, are also assumed to have learned associations with the *motor output* centres that carry out the response (the subject already has the ability to make the intended vocal response). A possible scheme, one of several feasible alternatives, would require that when the executive neurons reach the threshold at which they start to trigger the motor output they also trigger an inhibitory feedback signal to the PI centres. This arrangement ensures that the PI centres deactivate when the response intention is actually executed, preventing perseverative response repetition and conferring the possibility that the system will have ''knowledge'' that the planned action has been effected. Now in order to allow the gradual transfer of the responses to appropriate stimuli, there must be neural pathways along which the S–R links may be forged. I propose that the element-based representation neurons, currently under discussion, act in this *bridging* capacity between the neurons coding the input stimuli and the executive neurons discussed earlier.

If the incoming stimulus patterns are highly novel they may initially be incapable of activating a bridging neuron solely via stimulus-to-bridging neuron synapses. Assistance from an excitatory novelty signal (such as the non-specific hippocampal output discussed earlier) might therefore play a useful role in this situation. However, this would be likely to mean that the pattern of activation across the set of bridging neurons would probably be very diffuse. It could be localised if there were mechanisms for competition between partially activated bridging neurons, particularly if some bridging neurons received a further boost to their activation. I propose that the activated PI neurons send localised projection (based on random patterns of neural connection) to the set of bridging neurons. Thus, the bridging neurons most strongly activated by a novel stimulus are likely to be those that (by chance) happen to be connected to the active PI neurons. This proposal can also be of value if the incoming stimulus, or some of its elements, are strongly associated with an existing response that conflicts with the new response currently being acquired. The pre-existing response will be mediated by strong connections between the stimulus input and certain bridging neurons. However, these bridging neurons will not be in receipt of top-down signals from the currently active PI neurons (which specify a different response

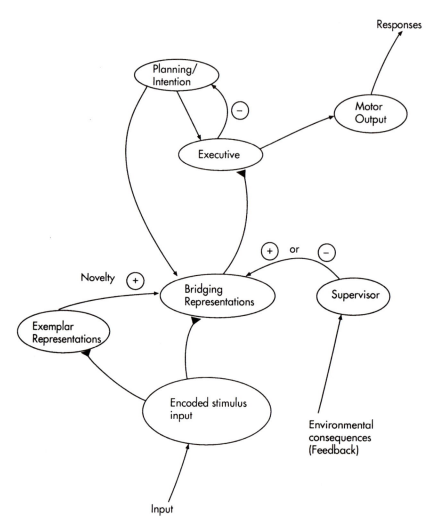

FIG. 4. A possible architecture for a feature-based representation system is shown. A speculative neural mapping for the functional units depicted in this Figure is given in the text. In the Figure, plus or minus symbols represent the excitatory or inhibitory nature of the proposed neural connections. Filled triangles represent the modifiable synapses where learning may occur. The feature-based (or prototype) representations act as bridging representations between coded stimulus input and the response structures. One possible feedforward and feedback arrangement connecting the bridging representations and response systems is depicted (for details refer to the text). The feature-based system receives a novelty input from the exemplar representation system (which itself processes the same stimulus input as the feature-based system). The novelty signal is one possible means of interaction between the representational systems. The bridging representations also receive reinforcement signals (functionally excitatory or inhibitory as appropriate) from the supervisor. The supervisor is activated by the environmental consequences (feedback) arising following particular responses.

intention), and thus the pre-existing bridging representation will not be activated by the stimulus in this context. Catastrophic levels of intrusion errors (due to proactive interference) may be avoided in this way.

The association between the (post-synaptic) activated bridging neuron, and the (pre-synaptic) neural patterns produced by the stimulus input, can be strengthened by the learning equation given earlier. The bridging neurons must, however, also be in receipt of *supervisory* signals from centres activated by success/failure feedback (usually verbal responses from the experimenter in learning tasks with human subjects; these serve a similar role to primary biological reinforcers in animal learning). The supervision must be functionally excitatory in the case of success in order to increase and prolong the activation of the bridging neuron and, with this, further strengthen the S–R association. In the case of failure (an error), the supervision must be functionally inhibitory, so that the bridging neuron is deactivated. This will prevent further association between the specific stimulus pattern and executive neurons. (Further sophistications can also be added which serve to promote the chance that one of the alternative, potentially correct, responses will be made the next time the stimulus is encountered. These need not concern us here.) In a category learning situation, for example, the system I have just sketched allows the exemplars of each category to activate the same bridging neurons and, by the properties of the learning equation discussed earlier, extract a prototype for that category.

A POSSIBLE NEURAL LOCUS FOR ELEMENT-BASED (BRIDGING) REPRESENTATIONS

I have already foreshadowed the fact that I am going to suggest that the element-based representations reside in the ventral striatum (specifically the matrix of spiny I cells in the nucleus accumbens; the inhibitory output from these cells is transmitted via gamma-amino butyric acid, GABA). The wiring requirements inherent in the system proposed here are strongly consistent with this localisation.

The nucleus accumbens is at the centre of a hub of input and output pathways, many arranged in complex feedback loops (see Gray, 1995; Gray et al., 1991 for details and further references). The accumbens receives (pre-processed) stimulus input from the entorhinal cortex. (This is particularly relevant to the schematic model of Fig. 2, as the entorhinal cortex also provides the majority of the input to the parallel hippocampal exemplar representation system.) I propose that some synaptic modification occurs here, along the lines of the equations given earlier. The accumbens also receives excitatory glutamatergic inputs from parts of the prefrontal cortex and, as has already been noted, along the subiculum-fornix pathway. This is in keeping with the proposed activation of bridging neurons by active plans/intentions and by stimulus novelty. The matrix of GABAergic accumbens neurons is in an arrangement with laterally inhibitory connections between the cells. This may provide one mechanism for the proposed competition between bridging neurons. Competition may also be assisted by the diffuse inhibitory dopaminergic inputs reaching the accumbens from the ventral tegmental area (VTA, also known as A10). These ascending dopaminergic inputs can be thought of as providing a thresholding mechanism so that only those accumbens neurons in receipt of high levels of excitatory input begin to activate, and thereby enter the competition for full activation.

Another major input to the accumbens is from the amygdala. This is in keeping with the need for an input of supervisory/reinforcement signals. The amygdala-accumbens pathway is thought to utilise the excitatory transmitter glutamate. Interestingly, there appear to be two distinct modes of action of glutamate on accumbens cells (see Gray et al., 1991; Swerdlow, 1995 for references). One effect appears to be a direct pre-synaptic excitation on the GABAergic accumbens cells. The other is via a potentiation of release in the terminals of the dopaminergic VTA-accumbens axons which synapse on the same accumbens neurons. As the action of dopamine on the accumbens cells is inhibitory, this second glutamate effect operates in the opposite direction to the simple excitatory mechanism. It is possible that these two mechanisms could support the differential effects required of supervisory signals. Success/reward requires an excitatory signal while failure/punishment requires an inhibitory signal.

A major output target of the accumbens is the ventral pallidum (VP). The VP cells themselves send inhibitory GABAergic projections to various sites, including various thalamic nuclei (Gray, 1995; Lavin & Grace, 1994). Thus, activation of accumbens cells, by inhibiting VP cells, dishabituates the projection targets of the VP. One thalamic target, the dorsomedial nucleus, has reciprocal projections with the cingulate and prefrontal cortices. These sites are widely considered to be involved in response selection and control functions (Posner & Raichle, 1994) of the kind ascribed to the executive neurons of Fig. 4. If synapses along these pathways are modifiable by learning, then these pathways could represent a means for the activated bridging neurons to become associated with the active executive neurons.

PREDICTIONS FOR CATEGORY LEARNING BY AMNESIC SUBJECTS

Armed with the aforementioned neurally-mapped model, we are in a position to suggest a powerful category learning experiment for amnesic subjects. The bottom panels of Fig. 1 show two of the six Munsell colour category structures used by Nosofsky (1987). He called one structure (bottom right, Fig. 1) ''diagonal'' for obvious reasons, and the other ''pink-brown'' as this was a reasonable description of the colours in the two categories. By inspection one can see that the category prototypes in the diagonal structure are going to be at almost the same location in the psychological space, whereas they will be at well-separated loci in the pink-brown condition. Nosofsky (1987) showed that a prototype model accounted well (95%) for the variance in performance across the items of the pink-brown categorisation and poorly (33%) for the variance in the diagonal categorisation. (This is as expected given that the pink-brown categorisation is linearly separable, whereas the diagonal categorisation is not.) The neurally implemented prototype model suggested earlier would also fail to acquire the diagonal categorisation. Separate category prototype units would be set up, but as items were tested they would be about equally likely to access either unit (given that the prototypes are so close in the psychological space). Inconsistent factors (such as the just-prior training sequence) would determine which category would be activated by a given item and therefore learning would fail to progress consistently.

Amnesic patients with a residual element-based (prototype) representation learning system would therefore be predicted to be able to learn the pink-brown categorisation as well as normal controls. The pattern of success and failure over the items would be similar as well, although acquired in different ways in the two groups (the controls could employ an intact exemplar representational system). To the extent that the controls develop and use exemplar representations, their item recognition for the trained items should be superior to that of the amnesics (who will show the characteristic recognition pattern discussed earlier in relation to Kolodny's dot-pattern task). By contrast, the same amnesics will be unable to acquire the diagonal categorisation and will perform significantly more poorly than controls. Amnesic item recognition will again be poorer than that of controls. This is a particularly powerful between-tasks comparison because the stimuli and procedures can be genuinely identical in the two tasks—all that changes is the assignment of stimuli to the categories.

It is possible to consider which amnesics, in neuroanatomical terms, would be able to learn the pink-brown categorisation while failing the diagonal categorisation. Amnesics with damage restricted to the hippocampus itself should be unable to develop exemplar representations of the task stimuli. Such patients, as long as damage was limited to the hippocampus itself, should be able to utilise the element-based representations in the nucleus accumbens and thus achieve prototype-based learning. Diencephalic amnesics with damage to anteroventral thalamus and/or mammillary bodies and/or the mammillothalamic tract should, as suggested earlier, be unable to associate the exemplar representations (formed within their intact hippocampal system) with executive and response systems. They too should therefore fail the diagonal category test. (Similar predictions would be made for patients with amnesia resulting from fornix or retrosplenial cortex damage.) If the output pathway carrying the non-specific novelty signal is intact in some diencephalic amnesics then these patients may also be able to achieve good levels of item recognition by using this signal. It was, however, also suggested that the element-based representations in the nucleus accumbens may be associated with executive and response neurons via the pathways through ventral pallium and dorsomedial thalamus. Diencephalic amnesics would therefore be expected to show preserved prototype learning only when this pallido-thalamic feedforward pathway is intact. Although large thalamic infarcts might compromise this pathway, it is becoming increasingly clear that diencephalic amnesia need not be associated with dorsomedial thalamus damage (see Mayes & Downes, this issue). On the other hand, if amnesics with clear (neuroimaging-verified) dorsomedial thalamus damage were unable to achieve prototype learning, then the model is wrong in at least some aspects. It may be, of course, that the association between element-based representations and response systems is mediated via another route.

Some amnesics might be expected to show other patterns of performance. Amnesics with extensive entorhinal cortex damage would be predicted to fail on both kinds of category learning problem, as they would be unable to deliver proper input messages to either the exemplar or element-based representation systems. Amnesia consequent on rupture and/or repair of aneurysms of the anterior communicating artery (ACoAA amnesia) is characterised by pathology that is often concentrated in the cholinergic basal forebrain, with probable consequent disruption of hippocampal functioning (see Mayes & Downes, this issue). On this basis, such patients should show deficits on category learning tasks dependent on exemplar representations. However, a post-mortem study (Phillips, Sangalang, & Sterns, 1987) has revealed that the lesion may sometimes include the nucleus accumbens and the VP (substantia innominata). This would therefore be predicted additionally to impair the use of element-based representations in prototype-based category learning. It must be emphasised that the lesions resulting from this particular aetiology vary from case to case, and are often quite large. Specific predictions, such as that just made, can therefore be safely interrogated only in cases with verified lesion locations; a simple reliance on the aetiological basis of the amnesia is likely to be unhelpful.

CAN AMNESIC PATIENTS LEARN PROTOTYPES?

In light of these predictions, it is natural to question whether there is any existing evidence to suggest that amnesics may have a preserved element-based representational system. A study by Musen and Squire (1993) may provide such evidence. They compared a mixed-aetiology group of amnesics and controls over six blocks of trials in terms of ink-naming latencies in a Stroop-like task. In each block, each of seven ink colours was used once, with each ink colour being consistently associated with a particular unrelated word (e.g. WINDOW) across each of the blocks. Musen and Squire found that both amnesics and controls showed a reduction in ink-naming latencies across the six blocks, and that this reduction was statistically equivalent for both groups. Musen and Squire interpreted this effect as a demonstration of the implicit learning of novel nonverbal (colour–word) associations; they believed it was implicit because the subjects in either group performed at chance on a forced-choice recognition test for the colour–word associations.

Musen and Squire's further experiments revealed a number of very interesting features of this learning. They confirmed that the effect was a long-term memory phenomenon as the reduction in ink-naming latencies was maintained, in both groups, over a five-minute delay between the end of the sixth block and the start of six subsequent blocks. Importantly, the effect was shown to be mediated by the specific colour–word associations and not by a general habituation process reducing the salience of all the to-be-ignored text across trials. Musen and Squire showed this by switching to a new set of fixed colour–word pairings for a subsequent set of trial blocks (blocks 7 to 12). Ink naming latencies on the seventh block significantly increased (in both groups, and to the same extent) relative to the last block before the switch.

It is very natural to interpret this effect as being mediated by the element-based learning system sketched earlier. The stimulus feature bundle for each study item will include features of both the ink colour and the text word. In terms of the present model, interference in ink-naming will be produced by the text features beginning to activate a familiar word representation in the nucleus accumbens. The word representation will then compete for full activation (and control of associated responses) with the representation of the ink colour. The ink colour representation eventually wins out perhaps with the assistance of top-down signals from PI centres responsive to task demand (see Cohen, Dunbar, & McClelland, 1990, for a similar idea in a purely computational model). The ink-naming response is therefore produced, albeit somewhat slowly. However, owing to the prototyping properties of the learning equation discussed earlier, the consistent text–colour pairings will result in the text input features becoming bound onto the fully activated ink colour representation. This learning will strengthen the initial activation of the ink colour representation on subsequent trials and thus improve the speed of resolution of the competition between ink colour and text word representations. Ink-naming latencies will therefore reduce over trials, just as Musen and Squire observed.

It was also noted earlier that the element-based system is likely to have limited potential for pattern separation and so be associated with higher levels of interference. The Musen and Squire task could be extended into a third block of trials, in which the colour–word associations from the first trial block were re-presented. If learning in the Musen and Squire task is mediated, as described earlier, by the element-based system, then it would be predicted that ink-naming latencies would increase between the last trial in the second block to the first trial of the third block. This follows because the associations formed in the second block would be predicted to overwrite the associations formed in the first block; the subject would thus perform the third block of trials with little benefit, if any, from the prior experience of the colour–word pairings in the first block. Performance on the task could be directly compared with a structurally identical associative learning task in which subjects would be asked to learn colour–word pairings explicitly. The present model would predict that such instructions, plus removal of the necessity for speeded responses in a cued recall test format, would allow healthy subjects to engage the exemplar representation system, thus dramatically reducing the level of interference observed. If this predicted qualitative difference between analogous tasks (using identical materials) were found, then it would be strongly supportive of the model and the proposed distinction between the two representational systems.

The details of the present paper are now complete. I hope that the specificity of the predictions that I have been able to make are the best advertisement for the approach I have been advocating. Moreover, I believe the predictions made, although focused on a narrow range of tasks, have quite broad implications for our understanding of amnesic patients. There is unfortunately no room to consider the use of neural nets in clarifying and modelling the possible different stages (encoding/storage/consolidation/retrieval) in which memory processing can be compromised. In the current model I have suggested that hippocampal damage prevents the formation of exemplar representations; this is most simply construed as an item storage deficit. Diencephalic amnesia has been seen as an ability to associate stored exemplar representations with item-specific response information; this is most simply construed as an association storage deficit. Other stages of deficit could be proposed and directly modelled. However, one final point merits attention. The explicit relationship between the current model and that of Eichenbaum et al. (1994) should be briefly noted.

BEHAVIOURAL FLEXIBILITY AND COMPRESSED REPRESENTATIONS

I have noted that memory based on prototype representations alone will be more prone to interference than memory based on episodic exemplar memory representations. Paradoxically, this property derives because exemplar representations are less flexible (generalisable) than prototype representations based on stimulus elements. This is in direct contrast to the proposal (Eichenbaum et al., 1994) that the hippocampal memory system confers flexibility (generalisability) to learning, and contrasts with the inflexible, non-generalisation of learning displayed by Eichenbaum et al.'s fornix-lesioned rats.

The conflict arises because the hippocampal exemplar representations, proposed in the current model, reflect a further *compression* of stimulus information beyond the level inherent in the entorhinal cortex inputs to the exemplar system. The result of the model's exemplar mapping process is neurons that code for the whole multidimensional stimulus input. By contrast, Eichenbaum and colleagues assume that the highest level of stimulus compression occurs at the entorhinal cortex, and argue that either this compressed representation may control behaviour or further hippocampal relational processing may operate to pick out stimulus components (across items) that are more optimal cues for behaviour. In the current model, rather than have a stage of compression followed by hippocampal decompression, the partially compressed entorhinal cortex code will be taken as the input to both the exemplar and feature-based pathways of Fig. 2. As noted, the representation is further compressed in the exemplar pathway (hippocampus). The processing that has been proposed for the element-based pathway has emphasised, under some circumstances, the selecting out of relevant stimuli or stimulus dimensions. This general description reveals that the functions of the element-based pathway are rather close to the functions ascribed by Eichenbaum et al. to the hippocampal system. Therefore, the two models are, in their neuroanatomical aspects, mirror images of one another, although both accounts try to capture the processes by which behaviour can come under the control of representations with the appropriate level of compression. Several kinds of experiment using amnesic patients, which could differentiate between these alternative views, can be made but suggestions will have to be deferred to a subsequent paper. For now, one might note that Eichenbaum et al.'s model would appear to suggest that hippocampal amnesics, with spared entorhinal cortex, should not be able to perform filtration tasks normally (e.g. category learning tasks with a single stimulus dimension determining category membership) but should be unimpaired at habit-learning tasks involving condensation across stimulus dimensions (e.g. non-linearly separable category learning tasks such as Nosofsky's diagonal problem). These predictions are the direct converse of those that flow from the current model.

SUMMARY OF THE MODEL AND ITS PREDICTIONS
FOR AMNESIC PATIENTS

A model has been presented which proposes that multimodal feature bundles encoded within the entorhinal cortex activate parallel but interacting pathways for exemplar- or element-based (prototype) representations. It is suggested that the exemplar representations are encoded within the hippocampus itself, while the element representations are encoded within the ventral striatum (n. accumbens). It is suggested that both these representations are computed from inputs from a common structure (entorhinal cortex). Although the exemplar system may be capable of unsupervised learning, supervised learning is made possible in the element-based system by the inputs from the amygdala to the nucleus accumbens. Some emphasis was placed on the subiculo-accumbens pathway as a means of interaction between the two representational systems. It was further suggested that this pathway may reflect the non-specific episodic novelty of an item, computed from (the inverse of) the sum of the activations the item produces in the exemplar system. This signal may be useful in certain item recognition situations.

The model proposed that Kohønen nets may provide a viable model for the acquisition, and resulting psychological map, of exemplar representations. A simple, biologically plausible learning equation for the element-based pathway was also proposed. The model stressed that behaviour must depend on activated stimulus representations (in various combinations of either kind) being associated, via separate thalamic/mammillothalamic feedforward pathways, with response and executive representations in anterior brain structures.

Amnesic subjects with damage limited to the exemplar system (the hippocampus itself), or the thalamic/mammillothalamic feedforward pathways used for exemplar–response associations, were therefore predicted to be impaired at habit-learning tasks that require the participation of exemplar representations (e.g. non-linearly solvable category learning problems). These deficits should be accompanied by normal levels of performance on closely related learning tasks (category learning or certain speeded reaction time tasks), in which successful performance is possible based solely on prototype representations averaged across specific exemplars. When learning is success-fully achieved using prototype representations, it is predicted that excessive levels of interference will be observed. Amnesics with widespread damage to the input structure common to both systems (the entorhinal cortex) should show deficits on both exemplar-dependent and prototype-dependent learning tasks; this may also be true for those amnesics with basal ganglia damage. Finally, the non-specific episodic novelty signal may be intact in some diencephalic amnesics, leading to differences in some item recognition or frequency judgement tasks relative to amnesics with hippocampal damage. For the same reason, it was suggested that diencephalic amnesics may be able to demonstrate context-sensitive latent inhibition, unlike amnesics with hippocampal damage.

REFERENCES

Acker, R., & Kurz, A. (1990). On the biologically motivated derivation of Kohønen's self-organising feature maps. In R. Eckmiller, G. Hartmann, & G. Houske (Eds.), *Parallel processing in neural systems and computers* (pp.229–232). North Holland: Elsevier Science Publishing.

Anderson, M.C., & Bjork, R.A. (1994). Mechanisms of inhibition in long-term memory. In D. Dagenbach, & T.H. Carr (Eds.), *Inhibitory processes in attention, memory, and language* (pp.265–325). London: Academic Press.

Baddeley, A.D., & Wilson, B.A. (1994). When implicit learning fails: Amnesia and the problem of error elimination. *Neuropsychologia, 32*, 53–67.

Barsalou, L.W. (1990). On the indistinguishability of exemplar memory and abstraction in category representation. In T.K. Srull & R.S. Wyer (Eds.), *Advances in social cognition (Vol. 3): Content and process specificity in the effects of prior experiences.* Hillsdale, NJ: Lawrence Erlbaum Associates Inc.

Carpenter, G.A., & Grossberg, S. (1987). ART 2: Self-organization of stable category recognition codes for analog input patterns. *Applied Optics, 26,* 4919–4930.

Cohen, J.D., Dunbar, K., & McClelland, J.L. (1990). On the control of automatic processes: A parallel distributed processing account of the Stroop effect. *Psychological Review, 97,* 332–361.

Davidson, T.L., McKernan, M.G., & Jarrard, L.E. (1993). Hippocampal lesions do not impair negative patterning: A challenge to configural association theory. *Behavioral Neuroscience, 107,* 227–234.

Eichenbaum, H., Fagan, A., Mathews, P., & Cohen, N.J. (1988). Hippocampal system dysfunction and odor discrimination rats: Impairment of facilitation depending on representational demands. *Behavioral Neuroscience, 102,* 331–339.

Eichenbaum, H., Mathews, P., & Cohen, N.J. (1989). Further studies of hippocampal representation during odour discrimination learning. *Behavioral Neuroscience, 103,* 1207–1216.

Eichenbaum, H., Otto, T., & Cohen, N.J. (1994). Two functional components of the hippocampal memory system. *Behavioral and Brain Sciences, 17,* 449–518.

Glisky, E.L., Schacter, D., & Tulving, E. (1986). Computer learning by memory impaired patients: Acquisition and retention of complex knowledge. *Neuropsychologia, 24,* 313–328.

Gluck, M. (1991). Stimulus generalization and representation in adaptive network models of category learning. *Psychological Science, 2,* 50–55.

Gluck, M.A., & Bower, G.H. (1988). From conditioning to category learning: An adaptive network model. *Journal of Experimental Psychology: General, 117,* 227–247.

Gluck, M.A., Myers, C.E., & Goebel, J.K. (1994). A computational perspective on dissociating hippocampal and entorhinal function. *Behavioral and Brain Sciences, 17,* 476–477.

Graff-Radford, N.R., Tramel, N., Van Hoesen, G.W., & Brandt, J.P. (1990). Diencephalic amnesia. *Brain, 113,* 1–25.

Gray, J.A. (1982). *The neuropsychology of anxiety: An enquiry into the functions of the septo-hippocampal system.* Oxford: Oxford University Press.

Gray, J.A. (1995). The contents of consciousness: A neuropsychological conjecture. *Behavioral and Brain Sciences, 18,* 659–722.

Gray, J.A., Feldon, J., Rawlins, J.N.P., Hemsley, D.R., & Smith, A.D. (1991). The neuropsychology of schizophrenia. *Behavioral and Brain Sciences, 14,* 1–84.

Groenewegen, H.J., Vermeulen-Van der Zee, E., te Kortschot, A., & Witter, M.P. (1987). Organization of the projections from the subiculum to the ventral stritum in the rat. A study using anterograde transport of *Phaseolus vulgaris* leucoagglutinin. *Neuroscience, 23,* 103–120.

Hermann, B.P., Wyler, A.R., & Richey, E.T. (1988). Wisconsin Card Sorting test performance in patients with complex partial seizures of temporal lobe origin. *Journal of Clinical and Experimental Neuropsychology, 10,* 467–476.

Hintzman, D.L., Curran, T., & Caulton, D.A. (1995). Scaling the episodic familiarities of pictures and words. *Psychological Science, 6,* 308–313.

Honey, R.C., & Good, M. (1993). Selective hippocampal lesions abolish the contextual specificity of latent inhibition and conditioning. *Behavioral Neuroscience, 107,* 23–33.

Houghton, G., & Tipper, S.P. (1994). A model of inhibitory mechanisms in selective attention. In D. Dagenbach, & T.H. Carr (Eds.), *Inhibitory processes in attention, memory, and language* (pp.53–112). London: Academic Press.

Knowlton, B.J., & Squire, L.R. (1993). The learning of categories: Parallel brain systems for item memory and category knowledge. *Science, 262,* 1747–1749.

Kohønen, T. (1984). *Self-organization and associative memory.* Berlin: Springer-Verlag.

Kolodny, J.A. (1994). Memory processes in classification learning: An investigation of amnesic performance in categorisation of dot patterns and artistic styles. *Psychological Science, 5,* 164–169.

Kruschke, J.K. (1992). ALCOVE: An exemplar-based connectionist model of category learning. *Psychological Review*, *99*, 22–44.

Kruschke, J.K. (1993). Human category learning: Implications for backpropagation models. *Connection Science*, *5*, 3–36.

Kruschke, J.K., & Erickson, M.A. (1994). Learning of rules that have high-frequency exceptions: New empirical data and a hybrid connectionist model. *Proceedings of the Sixteenth Annual Conference of the Cognitive Science Society* (pp.514–519). Hillsdale, NJ: Lawrence Erlbaum Associates, Inc.

Kruskal, J.B., & Wish, M. (1978). *Multidimensional scaling* (Sage University paper series on Quantitative Applications in the Social Sciences, No.07-001). Beverly Hills, CA: Sage.

Lavin, A., & Grace, A. (1994). Modulation of dorsal thalamic cell activity by the ventral pallidum: Its role in the regulation of thalamocortical activity by the basal ganglia. *Synapse*, *18*, 104–127.

Logan, G.D. (1988). Toward an instance theory of automatization. *Psychological Review*, *95*, 492–527.

Lubow, R.E., & Gewirtz, J.C. (1995). Latent inhibition in humans: Data, theory, and implications for schizophrenia. *Psychological Bulletin*, *117*, 87–103.

Mayes, A.R., Baddeley, A.D., Cockburn, J., Meudell, P.R., Pickering, A., & Wilson, B. (1989). Why are amnesic judgments of recency and frequency made in a qualitatively different way from those of normal people? *Cortex*, *25*, 479–488.

Mayes, A.R., & Downes, J.J. (this issue). What do theories of the functional deficit(s) underlying amnesia have to explain? *Memory*, *5*(1/2).

Mayes, A.R., Pickering, A., & Fairbairn, A. (1987). Amnesic sensitivity to practice interference: Its relationship to priming and the causes of amnesia. *Neuropsychologia*, *25*, 211–220.

McClelland, J.L., NcNaughton, B.L., & O'Reilly, R.C. (1995). Why there are complementary learning systems in the hippocampus and neocortex: Insights from the successes and failures of connectionist models of learning and memory. *Psychological Review*, *102*, 419–457.

McCloskey, M., & Cohen, N.J. (1989). Catastrophic interference in connectionist networks: The sequential learning problem. In G.H. Bower (Ed.), *The psychology of learning and motivation*. New York: Academic Press.

McKenna, P.J., Tamblyn D., Lund, C.E., Mortimer, A.M., Hammond, S., & Baddeley, A.D. (1990). Amnesic syndrome in schizophrenia. *Psychological Medicine*, *20*, 967–972.

McNaughton, N. (1994). The hippocampus: Relational processor or antiprocessor? *Behavioral and Brain Sciences*, *17*, 487–488.

Medin, D.L., & Florian, J.E. (1992). Abstraction and selective coding in exemplar-based models of categorization. In A. Healy, S. Kosslyn, & R. Shiffrin (Eds.), *From learning processes to cognitive processes: Essays in honor of William K. Estes. Vol. 2* (pp.207–234). Hillsdale, NJ: Lawrence Erlbaum Associations Inc.

Medin, D.L., & Schwanenflugel, P.J. (1981). Linear separability in classification learning. *Journal of Experimental Psychology: Human Learning and Memory*, *7*, 355–368.

Medin, D.L., & Shaffer, M.M. (1978). Context theory of classification. *Psychological Review*, *85*, 207–238.

Meudell, P.R., Mayes, A.R., Ostergaard, A., & Pickering, A. (1985). Recency and frequency judgments in alcoholic amnesics and normal people with poor memory. *Cortex*, *21*, 485–513.

Musen, G., & Squire, L.R. (1993). Implicit learning of color–word associations using a Stroop paradigm. *Journal of Experimental Psychology: Learning, Memory, and Cognition*, *7*, 789–798.

Nickerson, D. (1936). The specification of color tolerances. *Textile Research*, *6*, 505–514.

Nosofsky, R.M. (1986). Attention, similarity, and the identification–categorisation relationship. *Journal of Experimental Psychology: General*, *115*, 39–57.

Nosofsky, R.M. (1987). Attention and learning processes in the identification and categorisation of integral stimuli. *Journal of Experimental Psychology: Learning, Memory, and Cognition*, *13*, 87–108.

Nosofsky, R.M. (1992). Exemplars, prototypes and similarity rules. In A. Healy, S. Kosslyn, & R. Shiffrin (Eds.), *From learning processes to cognitive processes: Essays in honor of William K. Estes. Vol. 1* (pp.149–167). Hillsdale, NJ: Lawrence Erlbaum Associates Inc.

Nosofsky, R.M., & Kruschke, J.K. (1992). Investigations of an exemplar-based connectionist model of category learning. In D.L. Medin (Ed.), *The psychology of learning and motivation* (pp. 207–251). New York: Academic Press.

O'Keefe, J., & Nadel, L. (1978). *The hippocampus as a cognitive map.* Oxford: Oxford University Press.

Pearce, J.M. (1994). Similarity and discrimination: A selective review and a connectionist model. *Psychological Review, 101,* 587–607.

Phillips, S., Sangalang, V., & Sterns, G. (1987). Basal forebrain infarction. *Archives of Neurology, 44,* 1134–1138.

Pickering, A.D. (1994). The flexibility of implicit memory: An exploration using discrimination learning. In G. Humphreys & J. Riddoch (Eds.), *Cognitive neuropsychology and cognitive rehabilitation* (pp.549–569). Hove, UK: Lawrence Erlbaum Associates Ltd.

Posner, M.I., & Raichle, M.E. (1994). *Images of mind.* New York: Scientific American Library.

Ratcliff, R. (1990). Connectionist models of recognition memory: Constraints imposed by learning and forgetting functions. *Psychological Review, 97,* 285–308.

Ritter, H., & Kohønen, T. (1989). Self-organizing semantic maps. *Biological Cybernetics, 61,* 241–254.

Rolls, E.T. (1989). Functions of neuronal networks in the hippocampus and neocortex in memory. In J.H. Byrne & W.O. Berry (Eds.), *Neural models of plasticity: Experimental and theoretical approaches* (pp.240–265). New York: Academic Press.

Rosch, E.H. (1975). Cognitive representations of semantic categories. *Journal of Experimental Psychology, 104,* 192–233.

Rudy, J.W., & Sutherland, R.J. (1989). The hippocampal formation is necessary for rats to learn and remember configural discriminations. *Behavioral Brain Research, 34,* 97–109.

Rumelhart, D.E., Hinton, G.E., & Williams, R.J. (1986). Learning internal representations by error propagation. In D.E. Rumelhart & J.L. McClelland (Eds.), *Parallel distributed processing: Explorations in the microstructure of cognition. Vol. I: Foundations* (pp.318–362). Cambridge, MA: MIT Press.

Saykin, A.J., Gur, R.C., Gur, R.E., Mozley, D., Mozley, L.H., Resnick, S.M., Kester, B., & Stafniak, P. (1991). Neuropsychological function in schizophrenia: Selective impairment in memory and learning. *Archives of General Psychiatry, 48,* 618–624.

Schmajuk, N.A., & DiCarlo, J.J. (1992). Stimulus configuration, classical conditioning, and hippocampal function. *Psychological Review, 99,* 268–305.

Shin, H.J., & Nosofsky, R.M. (1992). Similarity scaling studies of dot-pattern classification and recognition. *Journal of Experimental Psychology: General, 121,* 278–304.

Squire, L.R. (1992). Memory and the hippocampus: A synthesis from findings with rats, monkeys, and humans. *Psychological Review, 99,* 195–231.

Squire, L.R., Knowlton, B., & Musen, G. (1993). The structure and organization of memory. *Annual Review of Psychology, 44,* 453–495.

Sutherland, R.J., & Rudy, J.W. (1989). Configural association theory: The role of the hippocampal formation in learning, memory and amnesia. *Psychobiology, 17,* 129–144.

Swerdlow, N.R. (1995). Don't leave the "un" off "consciousness". *Behavioral and Brain Sciences, 18,* 699–700.

Wilson, B.A., Baddeley, A.D., Evans, J., & Shiel, A. (1994). Errorless learning in the rehabilitation of memory impaired people. *Neuropsychological Rehabilitation, 4,* 307–326.

APPENDIX 1

This Appendix gives details of the simulation of the psychological map of the 12 Munsell colours, used by Nosofsky (1987). The colours were represented by activities in two input nodes. One node represented brightness and the other represented saturation. The inputs representing the colours were coded by the psychophysical brightness and saturation values, each divided by 20 to keep them in the 0 to 1 range. The inputs were not normalised. A 6×6 Kohønen lattice was used and the weights from the input layer to the lattice nodes were initially drawn from a uniform random distribution between 0 and 0.2. The activity centre (most active node) for each input colour was determined by the standard Kohønen short-cut of finding the node for which the Euclidean distance between the input vector and the vector of weights projecting to that node was smallest. The node at the activity centre was given a post-synaptic activation of 1.0. An adjacent node in the lattice, denoted r, was activated in relation to its Euclidean distance (D_r), across the lattice, from the activity centre. The post-synaptic activation of lattice node r (h_r) was determined by an exponential function of D_r, rather than the more usual Gaussian:

$$h_r = \exp(-C \times D_r)$$

where C is a parameter that determines the steepness of the decrease in activation with distance across the lattice. C was set at 1.0 at the start of learning for each simulated subject. The weight vector to lattice node r (W_r) was adjusted according to the following difference equation:

$$\Delta W_r = g \times h_r \times (I - W_r)$$

where g is a learning rate parameter and I is the input vector.

Each of the five simulated subjects was created by a different random weight initialisation. For each subject there were 20 cycles through the 12 colour stimuli, with each subject and cycle having a different random order of stimuli. Across each cycle the C parameter was increased by 0.05. Across trials, this change in C steepens the decrease in activation of nodes with distance from the activity centre. This therefore reduces the zone of lattice nodes, around the activity centre, which receive weight adjustment. This feature has been found to stabilise the resulting stimulus maps (Kohønen, 1984). For a single trial with each stimulus, the weight learning equation was iterated 50 times with the learning rate decreasing from 0.1 to 0 linearly over the 50 iterations, again to produce a more stable mapping. The learning rate parameter was reset to 0.1 for the next stimulus. The stability of the maps produced by this simulation was checked by iterating the procedure beyond the 20 cycles chosen, although no attempt was made to find the point at which the maps had stabilised during the 20 cycles.

MEMORY, 1997, 5 (1/2), 301–311

Concluding Comments: Common Themes, Disagreements, and Future Directions

John Joseph Downes
University of Liverpool, UK

Andrew R. Mayes
University of Sheffield, UK

In this final article in the special issue of *Memory* on Theories of Organic Amnesia, we select just three linked topics for further discussion: neuroanatomy, computational considerations, and tasks and procedures. Advances in each of these areas are reviewed and some recommendations for future directions are given.

INTRODUCTION

This special issue of *Memory* on Theories of Organic Amnesia has succeeded in attracting a variety of different contributions: computational models derived strictly from processing considerations (Metcalfe); models that are closely tied to neuroanatomy (Aggleton & Saunders); models that are both neuroanatomically based and rely on functional analyses of either animal learning/memory tasks (Gluck et al.), or human learning/memory tasks (Murre; Paller), or both (Cohen et al.; Pickering). Other contributors have taken the opportunity to address specific issues raised: implicit memory (Curran & Schacter); retrograde amnesia (Kapur); or to comment more generally on the target article (Kopelman; Parkin & Hunkin). It would not be possible to do justice to the full range of theoretical ideas expressed in these papers, and in this final contribution we restrict ourselves to a discussion of just a few of the topics covered.

TO GROUP OR NOT TO GROUP

Many contributors raised the important issue of whether it is sensible, or indeed defensible now, to attempt to develop a theory about "the" amnesic syndrome. We agree that this particular approach is in a moribund state. The syndrome

---

Requests for reprints should be sent to John Joseph Downes, Department of Psychology, University of Liverpool, P.O. Box 147, Liverpool L69 3BX, UK.

We thank Dimitris Tsivilis for commenting on an earlier version of this paper.

Undated citations refer to papers in this special issue.

almost certainly comprises several functional deficits with their own distinctive neuroanatomies. Given the crudity of some clinical memory measures currently used to provide primary evidence for the amnesic syndrome, it would be foolishly optimistic to expect any theoretically useful or interpretable outcome if grouping of subjects was based on behavioural/functional considerations alone. However, it would be a non sequitur to argue that all group studies of memory impairment should, therefore, be abandoned. Nor does it follow from this that a commitment to group studies necessarily rules out the single-case-study approach (see also Parkin & Hunkin). In fact, we believe that most progress can be achieved by a combined approach.

There are several reasons why a watershed has been reached. One of the most important of these is that we now have technology sophisticated enough to map out with acceptable accuracy, and at an affordable cost, the extent of the structural lesion(s) underlying human subjects' memory impairments. Post-mortem studies have, of course, always offered this facility (and certain detailed histological analyses are obtainable only via this procedure), but the time-lags are unacceptable. Linked with this has been a growth in knowledge about the detailed architecture of brain structures, systems and/or networks underlying memory performance, which comes from animal studies, and a development of clearer ideas about the functions and representations necessary for normal episodic memory formation, which comes from various modelling exercises. Another area of progress has been the development of new experimental paradigms such as the process dissociation procedure of Jacoby (controversial though this may be), which tap specific memory processes. As our knowledge of the architecture of significant memory-related structures becomes more detailed, and the experimental paradigms and theoretical "grammar" available for describing functional deficits become more sophisticated, so it becomes imperative to link both. Given that some lesions are likely to be rare, it does not matter whether this aim is achieved by detailed single-case studies, or group studies in which the grouping factor is based on more common forms of structural damage. Either way, clearer insights into the structure–function relationships underlying normal and abnormal memory performance, and more precise theories of the functional (or probably more precisely, "neurofunctional"; cf. Pickering) deficits underlying amnesia will result.

Irrespective of the arguments about whether or how amnesic subjects should be grouped, the "desiderata" for theory development in amnesia research, as outlined in our target article, stand. Thus, amongst other things, it becomes even more necessary to clearly articulate exactly what kinds of functional deficit are predicted by particular theories, identify areas of overlap or disagreement with other competing theories, and begin the process of developing paradigms that can unambiguously test hypotheses derived from those theories.

NEUROANATOMICAL CONSIDERATIONS

Past attempts to relate precisely memory function to discrete neuroanatomical sites using both human and animal subjects have been hampered by a lack of precision. Studies of human subjects have tended to group amnesics by behavioural criteria or by aetiology in which case there is no guarantee that a particular aetiology leaves all victims with the same underlying structural damage, or that different aetiologies lead to completely independent patterns of structural damage (Paller; Parkin & Hunkin). Animal lesion studies, having potentially greater control over the structural damage caused, may nevertheless suffer a similar imprecision, because, as pointed out by Aggleton and Saunders, surgical techniques such as aspiration often lead to incidental damage to adjacent memory-related structures. Thus, many earlier animal studies which examined the effects of lesions to the hippocampal system and/or diencephalic sites are in need of re-evaluation because damage would have also been caused to parahippocampal and/or perirhinal regions or their thalamic projections, which are now known to be involved in certain memory functions.

Fortunately, problems of this type are less likely to affect future studies because, as noted earlier and by most of the contributors, sophisticated neuroimaging techniques (morphometric and functional) now allow finer-grained specifications of human lesions, and the more widespread use of stereotactic surgical techniques combined with neurotoxic lesions in animals means that surgery can achieve considerably greater levels of accuracy.

There is broad agreement about the neuroanatomical circuitry underlying memory functions, but the details still remain unresolved. Thus, the most important structures have been identified, and associated major afferent and efferent fibre tracts have been mapped onto these. Similarly, a considerable amount of detail is known about the internal architecture of structures like the hippocampus—knowledge that has been of use to those interested in modelling the function of structures using neural network techniques. Nevertheless, the precise location of all the thalamic and basal forebrain lesions that cause amnesic symptoms remains uncertain.

Recent work attests to the importance of the medial temporal lobe cortical structures that underlie the hippocampal formation. A number of animal studies have shown that lesions in the region of entorhinal, perirhinal, and parahippocampal (EPP) cortices can lead to severe and long-lasting deficits on delayed non-matching to sample (DNMS) tasks, while damage to the hippocampus, fornix, mammillary bodies, or anterior thalamic nuclei (the so-called *extended hippocampal system*, EHS; Aggleton & Saunders) produce only mild deficits (at most) on the same task. However, damage to another diencephalic site, the dorso-medial thalamic nucleus (DMN), does produce DNMS deficits, and these are exacerbated by sectioning the fornix. Explanation of this particular pattern of deficits has been advanced through a number of studies by Aggleton's group, reviewed in their contribution. This is important because it is known that selective damage to the DMN does not lead to memory problems in humans.

The work reviewed by Aggleton and Saunders shows that the degree of interconnectedness between hippocampal system and diencephalic structures is considerably more complex than was previously thought. Although projections from the hippocampus, via the subicular complex, are conveyed to the major diencephalic targets (anterior thalamus and mammillary bodies) exclusively by the fornix, regions of the EPP neocortex send additional independent projections to a range of diencephalic targets, both via the fornical and via amygdalofugal pathways. The DMN receives projections both from perirhinal cortex and, to a lesser extent, from entorhinal cortex, which may explain its involvement in the aforementioned set of memory tasks. Future animal studies will need to examine, using a range of memory tasks, the interaction between the EHS and diencephalic sites, including the latero-dorsal thalamic nuclei, which receive fornical projections from the hippocampus, a lighter projection directly from the subicular complex, in addition to a further heavy projection, via the pulvinar, from the entorhinal cortex.

In contrast to the lack of severe impairment on DNMS following lesions to regions of the EHS, the same lesions can lead to severe deficits on a different set of tasks. Although studies looking at the effects of EPP lesions on this latter set of tasks have yet to be carried out, there is recent evidence that the two sets of tasks doubly dissociate in groups of animals with lesions either to the fornix or the perirhinal cortex (Gaffan, 1994a). This suggests that, although there are serial connections between EPP and EHS regions, these regions may be involved in separate and independent computational functions, an issue explored in more detail in the next section.

COMPUTATIONAL CONSIDERATIONS

There was consensus in this special issue of *Memory* about the basic types of computation necessary for the formation of new episodic memories. Detailed descriptions of the architecture and the dynamic aspects of such systems can be found in the contributions by Cohen et al., Gluck et al., Metcalfe, Murre, Paller, and Pickering. For most contributors, the major computational requirement for the formation of new episodic memories is the ability of the "system" to relate or associate units of information: either from the "outcomes" (cf. Cohen et al.) of a number of different processing streams, simultaneously, or from the outcomes of the same processing stream, sequentially. It is worth noting that for most, the type of information involved is unimportant (but see Mayes & Downes; Parkin & Hunkin). Most contributors would probably agree that amnesics can encode associations successfully in the sense that they can consciously represent them, but that they fail to put these representations into long-term storage. This is the sense in which we use the term "encoding" (but see Cermak). It remains to be demonstrated convincingly that amnesics with hippocampal system damage fail to perform the storage operation normally (see Concluding Comments for a way of doing this).

That the neural substrate for this relational or associative computation is the hippocampus is now incontrovertible. This follows, in part, from some of the animal studies reviewed in this special issue. However, as has recently become evident from a small number of animal studies, the nature of the association(s) that is/are an intrinsic part of the computed representation has important implications for the types of human amnesic deficit that might emerge following damage to the hippocampus and/or related structures.

The pattern of results from animal studies, showing that lesions to EPP neocortex and the EHS produce impairments on DNMS and spatial (and other) memory tasks respectively, led Aggleton and Saunders to predict that human subjects with lesions restricted to the EHS would show normal recognition memory with impaired recall. This followed because it was assumed that the DNMS task is an analogue of the human recognition memory task, and that both types of task could be "solved" by the computation of a familiarity index, which, in turn, was dependent on neural activity in EPP neocortex. Furthermore, consideration of the type of task on which EHS-lesioned animals are impaired, led Aggleton and Saunders (p.55–56), following Gaffan (1994b), to suggest that the EHS serves to "... distinguish or re-create the unique scene associated with the to-be-remembered item ... a process that will reduce interference from other similar events." This class of animal tasks, therefore, was assumed to have much more in common with human memory tasks involving the active retrieval of associations, such as free recall.

Evidence in support of their prediction comes from the finding that patients with MRI-confirmed lesions restricted to the EHS show normal recognition memory performance (at least on the Warrington Recognition Memory Test) together with free recall deficits as severe as those observed in patients with more extensive lesions believed to encroach EPP neocortex, who also have recognition memory impairments (Aggelton & Shaw, 1996). One of us (Mayes) has been studying a patient with relatively selective bilateral hippocampal damage who exactly fits the prediction, in that she shows completely normal recognition performance on a wide range of tests, but severely impaired verbal and nonverbal free recall. Interestingly, patients with lesions that primarily affect the head of the caudate nucleus (Hanley, Davies, Downes, & Mayes, 1994) or the frontal lobes (Parkin, Yeimans, & Bindschaedler, 1994) have also been reported to show selective free recall deficits. It remains to be determined whether the functional impairment underlying these selective free recall deficits differs depending on whether the lesion is to the EHS or to a frontal-basal ganglia circuit that may mediate executive functions. One possibility is that whereas EHS lesions disrupt storage of associations, frontal-basal ganglia lesions disrupt elaborative encoding and retrieval operations so that associations are inadequately encoded and retrieved.

The conclusion that follows from these considerations is that the EPP system is more than just a relay station for pre-processed information from unimodal and polymodal association cortices, and has intrinsic computational properties of its own. Eichenbaum, Otto, and Cohen (1994) have previously suggested that one function of this region of neocortex might be the maintenance of intermediate-term representations prior to hippocampal processing. This hypothesis is consistent with features of Gluck et al.'s, Metcalfe's, and Pickering's models. Metcalfe, for example, has proposed that items that are to be associated with one another must be available in a temporary store or working memory buffer, if they are to participate in the associative operation. The idea that EPP neocortex is a temporary memory buffer would explain how it can support normal recognition memory, although the capacity of such a buffer would have to exceed that which has previously been attributed to working or short-term memory.

Assuming this is correct, what remains unclear is how correct recognition decisions, if they are based on familiarity, are achieved, and what the characteristics of the representations maintained by the EPP system, are. Concerning the former, a number of the contributors (Metcalfe, Murre, Pickering) have included a "novelty monitoring" component in their models which would allow, amongst other things, familiarity indices for maintained representations to be computed. It has to be said, however, that one would not expect recognition to be completely normal if it is based solely on familiarity, because recollection is probably a more important contributor to normal recognition memory. With respect to the second point, one obvious implication of the findings reviewed earlier is that EPP representations lack relational or associative qualities—exactly those qualities about which there is consensus concerning the role of the hippocampus. Some contributors (Cohen et al., Gluck et al., Pickering), however, have reached the opposite conclusion, that the EPP system is involved in computations that *are* associative, but differ in one important respect from representations created by the hippocampus.

Evidence for two types of associative representation comes from a series of studies by Eichenbaum and colleagues (cited in Cohen et al.). The task used was an odour paired-associate task in which animals have to learn to discriminate target (rewarded) odour pairings from unrewarded stimuli, which are formed either by recombining single odours from different target pairs (mispairings), or pairing single target odours with new ones (nonrelational pairs). Rats with lesions to the EPP region were just as likely to respond to mispairings as to target pairs, unlike the control animals which gradually learned to discriminate between the two stimulus types. However, discrimination of target and nonrelational pairs was equally efficient in both groups of animals (Bunsey & Eichenbaum, 1993). The EPP lesion was assumed to eliminate the contributions of both that area and the hippocampus. When selective neurotoxic lesions were made to the hippocampus alone, both groups of animals learned about the nonrelational pairs, but the hippocampal-lesioned animals actually showed a *facilitation* effect, relative to control animals, in their ability to discriminate target pairs from mispairings (Eichenbaum & Bunsey, 1995). This is an intriguing result, suggesting that with a normally functioning hippocampus the EPP associative representations are somehow suppressed (although this would surely cause normal performance, not an enhancement following hippocampal damage), possibly as a result of the feedback loop from the hippocampus to the EPP system, or alternatively, because the link with behavioural responses is usually made via hippocampal connections with other midline structures (Pickering). The effect was believed to result from the specific qualities of the associative representation formed by the EPP system.

According to Cohen et al. (p.171) the two types of association differ in that those formed by the hippocampus "... maintain the compositionality of the elemental representations and organise them according to the relevant relationships among the items." The second type of representation, computed by the EPP, they refer to as a "fused representation", and the computation performed to create such representations has been referred to as "redundancy compression" by Gluck et al. (see also, Murre; Pickering for related ideas). These representations are noncompositional which means that the elements are bound together in a rigid, inflexible structure.

It is possible to see how the fused associative representations (that might mediate a kind of recollection) computed by the EPP could lead to normal performance levels on single item recognition memory tasks in patients with EHS lesions, as shown by Aggleton and Saunders. Of greater theoretical interest, though, is whether such representations can support recognition memory for item associations in human subjects. As yet, there is no available evidence for subjects with confirmed selective hippocampal damage on this type of task. A recent study by Kroll et al. (1996; cited in Metcalfe) suggests, however, that patients with more extensive (hippocampal plus associated neocortex) damage, like Bunsey and Eichenbaum's EPP-lesioned rats, were more likely than healthy control subjects to make false alarms to mispairings (or conjunction errors).

This highly selective overview gives some indication of the number and complexity of computational stages likely to be involved in normal memory functioning. One encouraging feature is that models developed purely from computational considerations sometimes yield counter-intuitive predictions which are confirmed by animal studies (see Cohen et al.; Gluck et al.).

MEMORY TASKS AND PROCEDURES

Studies of implicit memory performance in amnesia have dominated publications for the last 10 years, so it was surprising to find so few references to this work in the special issue contributions. However, a number of important points do emerge. Studies that have looked at perceptual specificity effects in implicit memory have sometimes found that subjects benefit from maintaining the same perceptual features between study and test. Work described in Curran and Schacter's contribution show that amnesics also show this effect, but not consistently (Schacter & Church, 1995; Schacter, Church, & Bolton, 1995). Whether or not amnesics benefit from a reinstatement of the particular combination of target item and perceptual feature encountered during study, seems to depend on the other combinations of target items and perceptual features which are used at test. If the test combinations include "new" perceptual features, then amnesics appear normal. If, however, the perceptual features used at test are the same as those used during study, combined in different ways with target items, then amnesics fail to benefit from the reinstatement of study combinations. This work is important for two reasons. First, it forces a re-evaluation of tasks, like the auditory priming studies described by Curran and Schacter, which typically have not been taken to involve an associative component. Second, because we have argued that such studies have the potential for informing us about the types of information that can be stored normally in amnesia, test conditions that promote interactive cue use (cf Curran & Schacter), which may only be possible if representations are associatively structured, need to be delineated. Further studies are needed, because it is unclear why subjects sometimes use available information (cues) in an additive fashion, and sometimes use the same information interactively.

Implicit memory tasks about which there seemed to be little doubt concerning their associative nature, are scrutinised in Cohen et al.'s contribution. Although a number of studies have failed to find evidence of novel information (or new association) lexical priming in amnesia (e.g. Mayes & Gooding, 1989; Paller & Mayes, 1994), there are a few that have. Moscovitch, Winocur, and McLachlin (1986), for example, report data from speeded reading experiments, which appear to show that amnesics of mixed aetiologies benefit to the same extent as normal subjects when studied word-pairs remain unchanged at test compared with re-combined pairs. In a series of unpublished experiments, however, Cohen et al. convincingly demonstrate that this "novel association" effect is due to the procedural tuning of output phonological processes particularly involving the inter-word sound transitions. Again, the value of this work, like Curran and Schacter's, lies in the fact that it forces a re-evaluation of what was a straightforward interpretation of an uncomplicated finding. Both these contributions, in addition to the research on category learning described by Pickering, suggest that we now need to exercise considerable caution when working with paradigms designed to measure implicit memory processes (a similar conclusion to one arrived at, for different reasons, in our target article).

Of course, as in any research endeavour, progress inevitably means that the paradigms used, and the way in which data are interpreted, increase in sophistication. This is evident, for example, in studies that are attempting to measure the separate contributions of implicit and explicit memory using variants of Jacoby's (1991) process dissociation procedure. It should be apparent from the previous paragraph that the main area in which paradigms are likely to go through similar stages of development is associative memory. For explicit memory at least, there are currently only a small number of paradigms available for probing the associative structure of memory representations (see Kroll et al., 1996). One avenue that has yet to be fully exploited is animal learning which has a well-established track record in elucidating the processes involved in associative learning. Although many of these tasks will turn out to be too transparent in their cognitive demands, at least some are likely to be imported into the human domain. Both Gluck et al. and Pickering, for example, make a strong case for latent inhibition as one such task.

CONCLUDING COMMENTS

What is immediately apparent from the contributions to this special issue of *Memory* is that for those who presented fully developed theories, there was considerable overlap in terms of their general structure, and in terms of the specific computations that have been postulated as necessary stages in the formation of new episodic memories. As noted earlier, it was particularly encouraging that models deriving from very different theoretical backgrounds showed a similar convergence of ideas.

We conclude with two points. The first is to re-emphasise one of the main points of the target article, which was that theories of the functional deficits that underlie amnesia should focus on the predictions that distinguish them from other accounts of the deficit. If a theorist does not wish to account for a particular memory phenomenon related to amnesia, it needs to be argued convincingly why this is justified. Otherwise, such phenomena should be predicted by the theory. Beware theories that ignore memory phenomena related to amnesia!

The second is that since the target article was written, nearly three years ago, there has been considerable development of work using memory challenge studies with neuroimaging procedures such as positron emission tomography (PET) and, more recently, functional magnetic resonance imaging (fMRI). Some of this work has been reviewed by Ungerleider (1995). These studies provide another method of testing hypotheses about the amnesia syndrome, which can be used in conjunction with examining the effects of focal lesions on animals and human patients. Thus, if the hippocampus and the EHS are concerned with storing certain kinds of association, then not only should selective lesions to parts of this system disrupt memory for such associations, but the structures in the system should become activated in a correlated fashion when an individual encodes and also probably retrieves associations. Furthermore, patients with intact medial temporal lobe structures who have lesions downstream in the EHS should fail to show normal hippocampal activation in PET and fMRI studies despite evidence that they have represented the associations normally at input if the hippocampus is involved in storing these associations. The better spatial resolution of fMRI makes it ideal for testing this hypothesis. Finally, fMRI would also be ideal for testing whether the hippocampus is only required for retrieving associative memories until they have been reorganised, at which point presumably only neocortical structures will be involved in retrieving the memories.

REFERENCES

Aggleton, J.P., & Saunders, R.C. (this issue). The relationships between temporal lobe and diencephalic structures implicated in anterograde amnesia. *Memory, 5*(1/2).

Aggleton, J.P., & Shaw, C. (1996). Amnesia and recognition memory: A re-analysis of psychometric data. *Neuropsychologia, 34,* (51–62).

Bunsey, M., & Eichenbaum, H. (1993). Paired associate learning in rats: Critical involvement of the parahippocampal region. *Behavioural Neuroscience, 107,* 740–747.

Cohen, N.J., Poldrack, R.A., & Eichenbaum, H. (this issue). Memory for items and memory for relations in the procedural/declarative memory framework. *Memory, 5*(1/2).

Curran, T., & Schacter, D.L. (this issue). Implicit memory: What must theories of amnesia explain? *Memory, 5*(1/2).

Eichenbaum, H., & Bunsey, M. (1995). On the binding of associations in memory: Clues from studies on the role of the hippocampal region in paired associate learning. *Current Directions in Psychological Science, 4,* 19–23.

Eichenbaum, H., Otto, T., & Cohen, N.J. (1994). Two component functions of the hippocampal memory system. *Behavioural and Brain Sciences, 17,* 449–517.

Gaffan, D. (1994a). Dissociated effects of perirhinal cortex ablation, fornix transection and amygdalectomy: Evidence for multiple memory systems in the primate temporal lobe. *Experimental Brain Research, 99,* 411–422.

Gaffan, D. (1994b). Scene-specific memory for objects: A model of episodic memory impairment in monkeys with fornix transection. *Journal of Cognitive Neuroscience, 6,* 305–320.

Gluck, M.A., Ermita, B.R., Oliver, L.M., & Myers, C.E. (this issue). Extending models of hippocampal function in animal conditioning to human amnesia. *Memory, 5*(1/2).

Hanley, J.R., Davies, A.D.M., Downes, J.J., & Mayes, A.R. (1994). Impaired recall of verbal material following rupture and repair of an anterior communicating artery aneurysm. *Cognitive Neuropsychology, 11,* 543–578.

Jacoby, L.L. (1991). A process dissociation framework: separating automatic and intentional uses of memory. *Journal of Memory and Language, 30,* 513–541.

Kapur, N. (this issue). How can we best explain retrograde amnesia in human memory disorder? *Memory, 5*(1/2).

Kopelman, M.D. (this issue). Comments on Mayes and Downes (1997): What do theories of the functional deficit(s) underlying amnesia have to explain? *Memory, 5*(1/2).

Kroll, N.E.A., Knight, R.T., Metcalfe, J., Wolf, E.S., & Tulving, E. (1996). Cohesion failure as a source of memory illusions. *Journal of Memory and Language, 35,* 176–196.

Mayes, A.R., & Downes, J.J. (this issue). What do theories of the functional deficit(s) underlying amnesia have to explain? *Memory, 5*(1/2).

Mayes, A.R., & Gooding, P. (1989). Enhancement of word-completion priming in amnesics by cueing with previously novel associates. *Neuropsychologia, 27,* 1057–1072.

Metcalfe, J. (this issue). Predicting syndromes of amnesia from a composite holographic associate recall/recognition model (CHARM). *Memory, 5*(1/2).

Moscovitch, M., Winocur, G., & McLachlan, D. (1986). Memory as assessed by recognition and reading time in normal and memory-impaired people with Alzheimer's disease and other neurological disorders. *Journal of Experimental Psychology: General, 115*, 331–347.

Murre, M.J.M. (this issue). Implicit and explicit memory in amnesia. Some explanations and predictions by the TraceLink model. *Memory, 5*(1/2).

Paller, K.A. (this issue). Consolidating dispersed neocortical memories: The missing link in amnesia. *Memory, 5*(1/2).

Paller, K., & Mayes, A.R. (1994). New-association priming of word identification in normal and amnesic subjects. *Cortex, 30*, 53–73.

Parkin, A.J., & Hunkin, N.M. (this issue). How should a database on human amnesia evolve? Comments on Mayes and Downes "What do theories of the functional deficit(s) underlying amnesia have to explain?". *Memory, 5*(1/2).

Parkin, A.J., Yeomans, J., & Bindschaedler, C. (1994). Further characterisation of the executive memory impairment following frontal lobe lesions. *Brain and Cognition, 26*, 23–42.

Pickering, A.D. (this issue). New approaches to the study of amnesic patients: What can a neurofunctional philosophy and neural network methods offer? *Memory, 5*(1/2).

Schacter, D.L., & Church, B.A. (1995). Implicit memory in amnesic patients: When is auditory priming spared? *Journal of the International Neuropsychological Society, 1*, 434–442.

Schacter, D.L., Church, B.A., & Bolton, E. (1995). Implicit memory in amnesic patients: Impairments of voice-specific priming. *Psychological Science, 6*, 20–25.

Ungerleider, L.G. (1995). Functional brain imaging studies of cortical mechanisms for memory. *Science, 270*, 769–775.

Subject Index

Notes to Authors

MANUSCRIPT SUBMISSION

Authors should submit **FOUR** copies of their paper, typed throughout in double space with wide margins.

Submission of a paper is taken as acceptance by the author that it contains nothing libellous or infringes copyright. When a paper is accepted for publication, the copyright will belong to the publisher.

Manuscripts should be sent to Susan E. Gathercole or Martin A. Conway, Editors of *Memory*, at the Centre for the Study of Memory and Learning, Department of Psychology, University of Bristol, 8 Woodland Road, Bristol, BS8 1TN, UK.

FORMAT

Papers should be prepared in the format prescribed by the *American Psychological Association*. For full details of this format, please see the Publication Manual of the *APA* (4th Edition).

Title   This should be as concise as possible, and typed on a separate sheet, together with the name(s) of the author(s) and the full postal address(es) of their institution(s). Proofs and requests for reprints will be sent to the first author unless otherwise indicated. A short running title of not more than 40 characters (including spaces) should also be indicated if the title is longer than this.

Abstract   An abstract of 100–150 words should follow the title page on a separate sheet.

Headings   Indicate headings and subheadings for different sections of the paper clearly. Do not number headings.

Acknowledgements   These should be as brief as possible and typed on a separate sheet at the beginning of the text.

Permission to quote   Any direct quotation, regardless of length, must be accompanied by a reference citation that includes a page number. Any quote over six manuscript lines should have formal written permission to quote from the copyright owner. It is the author's responsibility to determine whether permission is required from the copyright owner, and if so, to obtain it.

Footnotes   These should be avoided unless absolutely necessary. Essential footnotes should be indicated by superscript figures in the text and collected on a separate sheet at the end of the manuscript.

Reference citations within the text   Use authors' last names, with the year of publication in parentheses after the last author's name, for example: Jones and Smith (1987); alternatively: (Brown, 1982; Jones & Smith, 1987; White, Johnson, & Thomas, 1990). On first citation of references with three or more authors, give all names in full, thereafter use first author "et al." If more than one article by the same author(s) in the same year is cited, the letters a, b, c etc. should follow the year.

Reference list   A full list of references quoted in the text should be given at the end of the paper in alphabetical order of authors' surnames (or chronologically for a group of references by the same authors), commencing as a new sheet, typed double spaced. Titles of journals and books should be given in full, as in the following examples:

Books:

Cronbach, L.J., & Gleser, G.C. (1965). *Psychological tests and personnel decisions* (2nd ed.). Urbana, IL: Glencoe Press.

Chapter in edited book:

Jones, R.R., Reid, J.B., & Patterson, G.R. (1975). Naturalistic observation in clinical assessment. In P. McReynolds (Ed.), *Advances in psychological assessment* (Vol.3, pp. 234–297). San Francisco, CA: Jossey-Bass.

Journal article:

McReynolds, P. (1979). Interactional assessment. *Behavioural Assessment, 1*, 237–247.

Tables   These should be kept to the minimum. Each table should be typed double spaced on a separate sheet, giving the heading, for example, Table 2, in Arabic numerals, followed by the legend, followed by the table. Make sure that appropriate units are given. Instructions for placing the table should be given in parentheses in the text, for example (Table 2 about here).

Figures   Figures should only be used when essential. Where possible, related diagrams should be grouped together to form a single figure. Figures should be drawn to professional standards, and it is recommended that the linear dimensions of figures be approximately twice those intended for the final printed version. (Maximum printed figure size 181 mm x 114 mm, including caption.) Make sure that axes of graphs are properly labelled, and that appropriate units are given. The figure captions should be typed in a separate section, headed, For example, Figure 2, in Arabic numerals. Instructions for placing the figure should be given in parentheses in the text, for example (Figure 2 about here). More detailed *Guidelines for the Preparation of Figure Artwork* are available from the publisher: Psychology Press Ltd, 27 Church Road, Hove, East Sussex BN3 2FA, UK (*Email:* paul@psypress.co.uk).

Statistics   Results of statistical tests should be given in the following form:

$F=25.35$, $df=1,9$, $P<.001$ or $F(1,9)=25.35$, $P<.001$

similarly for t, χ^2 and other tests.

Abbreviations   Abbreviations should be avoided except in the most standard of cases. Experimental conditions should be named in full, except in tables and figures.

AFTER SUBMISSION

Offprints   Contributors receive 50 copies of their printed article free. Additional offprints may be ordered on a form provided by the publishers at a time the proofs are sent to the authors.

New...

MEMORY IN THE REAL WORLD
Second Edition

GILLIAN COHEN (The Open University)

*"The 1st edition of Memory in the Real World was a very good book. This thoroughly
revised and expanded 2nd edition is outstanding and will, in my view, become the standard
text in this area for some years to come. It is clearly written to a high level of scholarship
and brings together a very wide range of everyday memory research that is simply not
accessible to the non-expert. The clarity of the presentation and comprehensiveness of the
coverage is such that students of everyday memory will find whole areas of research, which
previously were only available in journal articles, made coherent and highly
accessible...This really is an excellent book which will be very widely read and I will
certainly use it in my own teaching and recommend students to buy it."* **Martin Conway
(University of Bristol)**

This new edition of *Memory in the Real World* has been extensively updated and
extended to include the latest research in all areas of everyday memory. The
controversy about the value of naturalistic research, as opposed to traditional
laboratory methods is outlined and the views of both critics and defenders put
forward. The current trend toward convergence of the two approaches is evaluated.
This book provides a comprehensive state-of-the-art review, bringing together
studies on many different topics such as memory for plans and actions; for names
and faces; for routes and maps; conversations and stories; autobiographical
experiences, and childhood events. Further chapters focus on memory for general
knowledge and for specialist domains such as music, chess, and computer
programming. Emphasis is also given to memory for internal mental events such as
thoughts and dreams. Topics that have recently attracted attention, such as false
memory syndrome, memory for health events, and social remembering are included.
This new edition spells out the links between naturalistic and applied studies and the
models, and theories that support them. It shows how theoretical frameworks such as
schemas, scripts, mental models and production systems, and concepts such as
encoding specificity, implicit memory and rule-based and case-based reasoning, are
needed to explain and interpret the findings and observations derived from the study
of memory in the real world.

Contents: The Study of Everyday Memory. Memory for Intentions, Actions and
Plans. Memory for Places: Routes, Maps and Object Locations. Memory for Events:
Eyewitness Testimony and Flashbulb Memory. Memory for People: Faces, Voices and
Names. Memory for Personal Experiences: Autobiographical Memory. Memory for
Knowledge and Metaknowledge. Memory for Expertise. Memory for Discourse:
Conversation, Texts and Stories. Memory for Thoughts and Dreams. Overview:
Conclusions and Speculations.

0-86377-728-7 1996 368pp. £29.95 hbk
0-86377-729-5 1996 368pp. £12.95 pbk

Published by Psychology Press

Revised Edition...

HUMAN MEMORY
Theory and Practice

A.D. BADDELEY (University of Bristol)

Review of first edition

> *"It is written in an unusually lucid and entertaining way, while nevertheless managing to grapple with important theoretical issues. Secondly, Baddeley appears to have fewer theoretical axes to grind than many writers of academic books. As a consequence, he succeeds in presenting balanced evaluations of the theories and experiments he discusses."* **M.W. Eysenck** (*Royal Holloway and Bedford New College, University of London) in **British Journal of Psychology**.

Review of the revised edition

> *"It will make a significant contribution to the field."* **Stephan Lewandowsky** (*University of Western Australia*).

This new edition of *Human Memory: Theory and Practice* contains all the chapters of the previous edition, unchanged in content but reformatted to a more generous page size, plus three new chapters. The first edition was published at a time when there was intense interest in the role of consciousness in learning and memory, leading to considerable research and theoretical discussion, but comparatively little agreement. For that reason, the topic was regretfully omitted. Since that time the field has crystallised, making it possible to incorporate three additional chapters concerning this, the most active area of memory research over the last decade. While other areas of research have of course progressed, theoretical views have not changed dramatically, and the existing book has therefore not been rewritten. The revision comprises three additional chapters, one concerned with the philosophical and empirical factors influencing the study of consciousness, a second concerned with implicit knowledge and learning, while the third is concerned with the evidence for implicit memory and its relationship to the phenomenal experience of "remembering" and "knowing".

The book is aimed at a university or college student taking a course in human memory, but assumes that memory lies at the centre of cognition. Consequently the links between memory and attention, perception, action and emotion are stressed, making it a core text for a more general course on cognitive psychology.

Contents: Why do We Need Memory? Perceiving and Remembering. How Many Kinds of Memory? The Evidence for STM. The Role of Memory in Cognition: Working Memory. Visual Memory and the Visuo-spatial Sketchpad. Attention and the Control of Memory. When Practice Makes Perfect. Organizing and Learning. Acquiring Habits. When Memory Fails. Retrieval. Recollection and Autobiographical Memory. Where Next? Connectionism Rides Again. Knowledge. Memory, Emotion and Cognition. Understanding Amnesia. Treating Memory Problems. Consciousness. Implicit Knowledge and Learning. Implicit Memory and Recollection.

0-86377-431-8 1997 432pp. £14.95 pbk

Published by Psychology Press